A History of American Life

A HISTORY OF AMERICAN LIFE

IN

TWELVE VOLUMES

ARTHUR M. SCHLESINGER
DIXON RYAN FOX

Editors

CARL BECKER

Consulting Editor

A HISTORY OF AMERICAN LIFE

A HISTORY OF AMERICAN LIFE
Volume IV

THE REVOLUTIONARY GENERATION

1763 - 1790

BY

EVARTS BOUTELL GREENE

DEWITT CLINTON PROFESSOR OF AMERICAN HISTORY, EMERITUS,
COLUMBIA UNIVERSITY

New York
THE MACMILLAN COMPANY

This Country Can not be long subject to great Britain, nor Indeed to any Distant power, its Extent is so great the Daily Encrase of its Inhabitants So Considerable, and haveing every thing necessary within themselves for (more than) their own Defence, that no Nation whatsoever seems beter Calculated for independency . . . .

"Journal of a French Traveller in the Colonies, 1765," *American Historical Review,* XXVII, 84.

It seemed as if the war not only required, but created talents. Men whose minds were warmed with the love of liberty, and whose abilities were improved by daily exercise, and sharpened with a laudable ambition to serve their distressed country, spoke, wrote, and acted, with an energy far surpassing all expectations which could be reasonably founded on their previous acquirements.

DAVID RAMSAY, *The History of the American Revolution* (Philadelphia, 1789), II, 316.

CONTENTS

ILLUSTRATIONS

(By the Editors)

ment (British) and assistant engineer. His view, as of 1766-1767, was engraved on copper by T. Kitchin and issued January 12, 1776. The "Bowry Lane," near the center of the map, was the road to both Boston and Albany. From I. N. P. Stokes, *Iconography of Manhattan Island* (N. Y., 1915), I, plate 42.

IV. THE DEVELOPMENT OF THE NEW ENGLAND MEETINGHOUSE

This drawing is from J. F. Kelly, *Architectural Guide for Connecticut* (New Haven, 1935), 32. The first type had long disappeared and the second type showed but rare survivals when the Revolutionary period began. The Congregational Church of Farmington (illustrated for the third type, but with ends reversed for convenience in arranging the page) was built in 1771 and still stands—broadside to the road. Captain Judah Woodruff was the architect and master builder. End-entrance churches (fourth type) date in Connecticut from that in Abington in 1751, but did not become common until after the Revolution.

V. POHICK CHURCH

In Fairfax County, Va., near Lorton. This church, still standing, was built in 1769-1773 to replace an older wooden structure. The building committee included George Washington, George Mason (1725-1792) and George William Fairfax (1724-1787). Like other churches of colonial Virginia it stands due east and west. Its brick is laid in Flemish bond; the high hip roof runs over a denticulated cornice to an unusually long overhang. Local sandstone was used for the prominent quoining and the framing of the three portals. Each portal has Ionic pilasters, full entablature and a severe pediment. The building has been carefully restored. Illustration from photograph by Bastrup, reproduced in Helen Hill, *George Mason, Constitutionalist* (Cambridge, Mass., 1938), 66.

VI. HARVARD COLLEGE IN 1767

From an engraving by Paul Revere, in the Harvard College Library, based on a drawing by Joshua Chadwick, in the Museum of the Essex Institute, Salem, Massachusetts.

Proceeding from right to left: Massachusetts Hall was built in 1718 as a dormitory, and is now used partly for administrative offices. Next to it, Stoughton College, erected in 1699 and named after its donor, the "witchcraft judge" (see portrait in *A History of American Life*, II), was torn down in 1781 and a new building called Stoughton Hall was put up near by. Harvard Hall (1766), in the center, long held the Chapel, the Library, the Commons (scene of the famous butter rebellion in 1766) and the Philosophical Chamber with its scientific apparatus. Hollis Hall was built by the Colony in 1763 because the Corporation found that the students who lived with private families were "less orderly and well regulated than those within the walls." At the extreme left is Holden Chapel, constructed in 1744 and named for the English benefactress who made it possible. For a time it housed the medical school. All these buildings except the original Stoughton are still standing, though somewhat remodeled. The three dormitories were used as barracks by the Continental soldiers in the siege of Boston and were sadly injured by this occupation.

VII. TRYON'S PALACE

Built by Governor William Tryon (1725-1788) between 1766 and 1770 at New Bern, N. C., to serve both as a state house and as a residence. It was planned by John Hawks, an English architect who came to America with Governor Tryon in 1764, and was modeled after an English country house. After the Revolution the building deteriorated and was largely destroyed by fire in 1798. The drawing here reproduced was probably the final plan used in construction; it is now in the British Record Office. The reproduction is from A. T. Dill, jr., "Tryon's Palace: a Neglected Niche of North Carolina History," *North Carolina Historical Review*, XIX, 144.

VIII. THE WEST

From the map opposite page 1 in James Adair (ᶜ1709-ᶜ1783), *A History of the American Indians* (London, 1775). Adair, an Irish trader and government agent, left the best account of "the West" of his time, based on many years' personal observation. He traded with the Catawba, Cherokee and Choctaw Indians, and lived six years with the Chickasaw, always working for their adherence to the British rather than the French. He described the pre-Revolutionary West and his book has enduring value, though he failed to convince posterity that the American Indians were descended from the tribes of Israel.

IX. A COLONIAL ALMANAC

Edes & Gill's North-American Almanack, for the Year of our Lord, 1769. From copy in New York Historical Society library. Benjamin Edes (1732-1803) and John Gill (1732-1785) founded the *Boston Gazette and Country Journal* in 1755, making it a strong Whig organ as Revolutionary thought developed. In 1773 the Tea Party patriots disguised themselves in Edes and Gill's printing office and set forth for Boston Harbor. The partnership was dissolved in 1775, but Edes continued the paper until 1798, and Gill published his own *Continental Journal and Weekly Advertiser* from 1776 to 1785. One hundred and fifty individual imprints are listed as coming from their

PLATE

portrait (30 x 24 in.) in 1795. His list of sitters is almost a roll of the rich and famous Americans of his time; see Lawrence Park, comp., *Gilbert Stuart: an Illustrated Descriptive List of His Works* (4 vols., N. Y., 1926). The illustration is taken from vol. iv, 338.

XIV. AN IRONMASTER'S HOME

The John Jacob Faesch house. From C. S. Boyer, *Early Forges & Furnaces in New Jersey* (Phila., 1931), 136. Faesch, a Swiss who had been a superintendent with Peter Hasenclever, built his Mount Hope Furnace near Dover, N. J., in 1773. During the Revolution he made shot and, probably, cannon; his 50 workmen were exempted from military draft, and he had the use of 30 Hessian prisoners.

XV. A TORY PRINTER

James Rivington (1724-1802), bookseller, editor, publisher and printer, came from London, where he had already achieved success in his business, to America in 1760, soon settling in New York. On April 22, 1773, he began *Rivington's New-York Gazetteer; or the Connecticut, New Jersey, Hudson's River, and Quebec Weekly Advertiser*, which eventually became the *Royal Gazette*, devoted to the Loyalist cause. After the Revolution Rivington suffered ostracism in New York and died poor. The illustration is from a portrait (36¼ x 28¼ in.) by Gilbert Stuart (1755-1828) after an unidentified artist; the painting now hangs in the gallery of the New York Historical Society.

XVI. A WOMAN PATRIOT

Catherine Van Rensselaer Schuyler (1734-1803) was the daughter of Johannes Van Rensselaer and his wife Engeltje (Livingston), and married Philip Schuyler in 1755. The portrait (30 x 25 in.), by an unidentified artist, is owned by the New York Historical Society. On learning of Burgoyne's approach Mrs. Schuyler ordered and supervised the burning of the extensive fields belonging to her husband, General Schuyler—an early instance of "scorched-earth" procedure. She was a charming and influential hostess during the Revolutionary years and later in 1789-1791 when her husband was one of the first United States senators from New York.

XVII. JOHN BEALE BORDLEY, AGRICULTURAL REFORMER

Bordley (1727-1804), of Wye Island, Md., was a "gentleman farmer," widely influential agricultural writer and founder of the Philadelphia Society for the Promotion of Agriculture (1785). The painter of this portrait, which is in the collection of the New York Historical Society, was Charles Willson Peale (1741-1827) who,

PLATE

like other American artists, studied with his compatriot Benjamin West in London and returned to paint Washington (fourteen times) and many other notables. With his brother James and three of his sons, Raphael, Titian and Rembrandt, he was a major force in developing American art. His museum in Philadelphia did as much for natural history.

XVIII. AN AMERICAN ARTIST SHOWS HIS WORK

William Dunlap (1766-1839), having studied with Benjamin West, tries to persuade his puzzled parents that art is his career; apparently he succeeds more readily with his father, on the basis of this painting of Hamlet. The group portrait (42 x 49 in.) here reproduced was done in 1788, and hangs in the collection of the New York Historical Society. Dunlap became a prolific playwright and adapter, the leading American theater manager and the historian of our early theater and art.

XIX. JEFFERSON'S "NOTES ON VIRGINIA"

The table of contents, first edition. Reproduced from the facsimile in Thomas Jefferson, *Writings* (P. L. Ford, ed., 10 vols., N. Y., 1894), III, 85. Note the ninety-three pages given to "Productions, mineral, vegetable and animal." This unpretentious volume, in its careful observations and its cogent argument against Buffon's and Raynal's thesis as to the degeneracy of Nature in America, is the primary basis of Jefferson's standing as a pioneer in American science. Jefferson later circulated it in France to correct misconceptions of American social and political life.

XX. WILLIAM COOPER, A DEVELOPER OF CENTRAL NEW YORK

William Cooper (1754-1809), born in Pennsylvania and married in New Jersey, in 1789 founded the town that bears his name on Otsego Lake, New York. In his latter days he was able to say: "I have settled more lands than any other man in America. There are forty thousand souls holding directly or indirectly under me." But he was more than a mere landlord or land-merchant; into his region he introduced the Episcopal Church, the newspaper press and academy education, along with roads and bridges, and tried to increase Federalist political influence. His portrait, painted by Gilbert Stuart, is now owned by Dr. Henry S. F. Cooper, by whose permission it is here reproduced.

EDITORS' FOREWORD

John Adams once remarked that the American Revolution ended before the first shots were fired on Lexington Common. It had taken place, he said, "in the minds and hearts of the people." In contrast, Benjamin Rush wrote in 1783, "The American war is over, but this is far from being the case with the American Revolution." Both men saw clearly that the revolution and the war were not the same thing. Adams recognized that the people fought for something they had already determined upon: not only to be independent of Europe but also to be different from Europe. Dr. Rush, at the end of the armed conflict, reminded his countrymen that only opportunity had been won and that a large part of their task of shaping a new social and political order still lay before them.

The rapid rise of an American consciousness after the French menace had been removed in 1763, the long and bloody struggle with opposition at home no less than with imperial might, and the first great steps toward organizing a new national life make up the author's central theme. Following the grand pattern which destiny imposed upon the years from 1763 to 1790, he divides his drama into three great acts—before, during, and after the War of Independence. Innumerable monographs have traced the changes in one or another phase of American thought, attitude or social action in special place or time within this epoch; but no one before Professor Greene, we believe, has attempted so fully to synthesize the whole experience of the people. The volume impresses upon the reader a sense of constant growth in many human concerns, parallel and intertwined, as might a symphony in successive movements wherein each of many themes encounters new variations as if driven by new circumstances.

Just as the author endeavors to balance his consideration of the varied aspects of American life in accordance with their respective importance and impartially penetrates the interest of every social class, so, too, it will be seen that he avoids a sectional standpoint. Depicting human enterprise scattered sparsely over a million square miles, he does not take up his headquarters, as it were, in any one region and view phenomena as near or far away. Few have treated the total scene with such sympathy and understanding. Detached in temper and harvesting the fruits of a lifetime of study, he has to a rare degree given us the story of all America as the nation awakened to a new rôle in the world.

The main interest of the era has been supposed to lie in politics, and so it does, if the word is properly understood. Never before—and possibly never since—was so much so soundly done in so short a time toward the organization of self-governing institutions. The reader is reminded of the essential character of the British imperial system, the new state constitutions and the construction of the federal system. At the same time he is shown the relationship of governmental development to the emerging life of the times, and gains as well a knowledge of numerous other matters, not less important because they never registered themselves in laws or official policies. Many will be surprised to learn the extent to which the so-called Critical Period after the war was a seed bed of new growths and creative undertakings.

Crossroads store and Indian trading post, Nantucket whaling harbor and Councilor Carter's library beside the Potomac River, village cooper and New Jersey iron-master, Irish immigrant and Quaker philanthropist, New York manor lords and the mob beginning "to think and to reason," lawyers who had read at the London Inns of Court and indomitable doctors setting up their Philadelphia medical school, political handbills and Mathew Carey's dignified *American Museum*, college graduates, itinerant artists and Douglass's American Company of actors, six-week militiamen and George Washington, families split between Whigs and Loyalists, slave traders and constitution makers—miscellaneous as these seem in chance collocation, they are shown in Professor Greene's account to be but parts of a moving picture of American life in one of its greatest epochs.

A. M. S.
D. R. F.

THE
REVOLUTIONARY
GENERATION
1763-1790

THE REVOLUTIONARY GENERATION

CHAPTER I

THE OLD WORLD IN THE NEW

IN July, 1763, the province and city of New York, then the seat of the British high command on the continent, marked with due ceremony the victorious close of the long struggle with France for predominance in North America. The militia companies formed in line from Fort George on the water front to the City Hall. The peace proclamation of His Britannic Majesty was read first at the Fort. Thence the lieutenant governor, councilors and the "principal gentlemen of the Place" proceeded to the City Hall where the royal proclamation was again read. Twenty-six years later another civic and military procession moved up Broad Street to the old City Hall, now "elegantly improved" and rechristened "Federal Hall." There George Washington, the provincial colonel of thirty years before, was installed as chief magistrate of a union of self-governing American states.[1] Between these two scenes lay an interval of less than a single generation, whose story cannot be told wholly in terms of revolutionary activities; nor was the revolution neatly confined within this period. For a century and a half, British colonials had been slowly tending toward an American type; but the

---

[1] I. N. P. Stokes, *Iconography of Manhattan Island* (N. Y., 1915-1928), IV, 729-736; V, 1235 ff.; Cadwallader Colden, *Letter Books* (N. Y. Hist. Soc., *Colls.*, IX-X), I, 220.

interaction between ancient tradition and the new outlook born of American experience did not end when
Washington took the oath of office. That dualism remained, though the balance had been altered in favor of
the new.

A European traveler visiting, for instance, the New
York of 1763 found much to remind him that men were
still living in an Atlantic rather than a strictly Western
world. If such a visitor interpreted pre-Revolutionary
America in terms merely of the provincial capitals, his
picture would have been distorted, for hardly one man
in twenty lived in urban or semiurban communities.
Nevertheless the position of these towns, as gateways for
oversea trade and as political centers, gave them a peculiar
importance. In politics they enjoyed a marked advantage over the comparatively unorganized country people; in matters also of social opinion and practice the
townsmen set standards which influenced their rural
neighbors. In any case, it was in the major provincial
capitals—Boston in New England, New York and Philadelphia in the Hudson-Delaware region, Annapolis and
Williamsburg in the Chesapeake country, and Charleston
in the Lower South—that the European factors in
colonial civilization were most conspicuous.

One way in which Old World influences reached provincial life was through the British imperial system, for
the individual officials, though appointed from without,
were variously related to the inner structure of colonial
society. How far did this political order affect the ordinary citizen? Essential to an urban and mercantile community was the post office. Regulated by Parliament,
it was administered under the direction of the postmaster-
general in London by American deputies, of whom the
ablest and best known was Benjamin Franklin. Subject
to these officials were the local postmasters. Though
the service on both sides of the Atlantic was rudimentary,

judged by twentieth-century standards, it had lately been reorganized. One substantial improvement was the establishment of a monthly transatlantic mail service for New York and Charleston. As a result, the Northern city became an important distributing point from which postriders took mail as far as southern Virginia, where letters were exchanged with carriers from the Carolinas and Georgia.[1]

On the eve of the Revolution two notable inspection tours were made by postal officials, one by Franklin in 1763 and the other in 1773-1774 by Hugh Finlay. The latter, a young Scot, kept a journal of his trip. Inspecting offices from Maine to Georgia, he found much to criticize, partly because of political disturbances, partly also because of incompetence, carelessness or dishonesty. One Yankee postrider delivered letters on his personal account to the disadvantage of the revenue, and included among his private commissions the care of a drove of oxen. On the other hand, Finlay commended the New York and Philadelphia offices for their orderly records and punctual service. Comparatively few towns had post offices, and off the main lines the service was slow and uncertain; but routes were gradually being extended. In 1764 a new one was announced between Philadelphia and Shippensburg on the eastern slopes of the mountains.[2]

Another familiar feature of a colonial port was the customs system, of which there were two kinds. Provincial officials collected duties levied by the assemblies for their respective governments, while imperial agents were responsible for duties imposed by Parliament. It was the business of the latter to see that transatlantic

[1] William Smith, *The History of the Post Office in British North America* (Cambridge, Eng., 1920), chaps. ii-iii.

[2] Hugh Finlay, *Journal* (Brooklyn, 1867), *passim*; Stokes, *Iconography*, IV, 739, citing *N.-Y. Mercury*, Jan. 2, 1764; *Pa. Gazette*, Jan. 5, Aug. 23, 1764; Oct. 24, 1765.

shipments of "enumerated articles" went only to British ports, to make certain that European goods, with few exceptions, were imported only by way of Britain, and to insure that all trade was carried in ships built and owned there or in the British colonies. Until 1764 the enforcement of these regulations was more important than revenue collection; but the sugar act of 1764 and the Townshend duty act of 1767 saddled additional responsibilities upon the customs service. The Northern merchants were most disturbed by the duties imposed to protect the sugar planters of the British West Indies against competitors in the foreign islands.

New commercial regulations, new taxes and the demand of the home government for stricter enforcement required enlarged personnel and administrative organization. Before 1767 local customs officers worked under the direction of two surveyors-general, for the Northern and Southern colonies respectively, who were in turn subject to the commissioners of customs in England. After 1767 a general American board of commissioners sat in Boston with a considerable staff. By 1774 the New York office had nine officials sufficiently important to be individually named in the governor's report to the board of trade.[1] Other royal functionaries with whom the merchants came into frequent and often unwelcome contact were the naval commanders assigned to the revenue service and the officers of the vice-admiralty courts. Still other imperial services concerned that part of the urban population which speculated in land, invested money in Indian trade or sought to exploit the forest resources of the country. These interests were administered by the surveyor-general of quitrents, the Northern and Southern superintendents of Indian affairs,

[1] Edward Channing, "American Commissioners of Customs," Mass. Hist. Soc., *Proceeds.*, XLIII, 479-490; E. B. O'Callaghan, ed., *The Documentary History of the State of New York* (Albany, 1849-1851), IV, 770.

and the surveyors of the king's woods, who were directed by another surveyor-general.

Besides the civil officials there were the fighting services. Until recently the royal military establishments in the colonies had been unimportant, but during the last French war several thousand regulars had been sent to America, some of whom remained after the peace. Presently colonial disturbances, beginning with the stamp act, furnished an additional reason for British garrisons. On the other hand, naval protection of colonial commerce had always been an essential element of British policy, and vessels of the royal navy continued to be frequent visitors in American ports.

The presence of officers and men from the fighting services was not wholly unwelcome to the townsmen. Merchants valued their trade, while the officers contributed color to local festivities, even in Puritan Boston. A "very Genteel Entertainment," given by the Boston merchants to the captain of H.M.S. *Jamaica,* was attended by James Otis and John Hancock.[1] In New York, to which the presence of the commander in chief gave somewhat the aspect of a Continental capital, such functions were frequent. On royal birthdays salutes were fired by warships and there were elaborate entertainments. On one occasion the "Gentlemen Officers of the Army" gave a ball which was marked by "the most numerous and brilliant appearance of both Sexes" ever known in the town. But other relations were less agreeable. The young Philadelphian, Alexander Graydon, complained of arrogance on the part of British military officers. There were difficulties also with the navy. In 1764 the impressing of four fishermen in New York led to mob violence and the destruction of a navy tender.[2]

[1] John Rowe, *Letters and Diary* (Annie R. Cunningham, ed., Boston, 1903), 81-82, 88, 116, 211, 216-217.

[2] E. B. Greene, "New York and the Old Empire," N. Y. State Hist. Assoc., *Quar. Journ.*, VIII, 121-132; Alexander Graydon, *Memoirs of*

Besides the imperial services—corresponding roughly with present-day federal offices—an important element of imperial control resided in the provincial governments. This was obvious in the royal provinces, which embraced a large majority of the colonial population. It was more limited in the proprietary colonies, and was least felt in Connecticut and Rhode Island, where all departments of the government were chosen directly or indirectly by the qualified voters. In the proprietary provinces of Maryland and Pennsylvania the king had parted with certain prerogatives, retaining, however, the right to approve or disapprove the choice of governors and, in Pennsylvania, that of disallowing provincial legislation. But all the colonies were subject to increasing parliamentary control. In the royal governments any exercise of authority by the governor was deemed an exercise of the royal prerogative, and in America, as in England, a crime was an offense against the king's peace.

The provincial governor was the most conspicuous embodiment of a sovereignty which reached across the sea from the king and Parliament at Westminster. Bound by royal instructions, he held office during the king's pleasure. Though he could not legislate without the consent of a representative assembly, all bills had to have his assent. If the provincials, speaking through their assembly, called for an expansion of the currency, for discriminating duties, or modifications of the criminal law, their wishes might be blocked by the governor's veto. Even if he approved, such measures might later be disallowed by the crown. As the governor's authority came from the king, so most provincial officers, executive or judicial, derived their powers directly or indirectly from the governor.

In social relations, as in politics, the governor played

His Own Time (J. S. Littell, ed., Phila., 1846), 51-54; Stokes, Iconography, IV, 742, 749.

a conspicuous part and his arrival was marked by formal ceremonies. When Lord Botetourt landed in Virginia in 1768 he was received with an artillery salute followed by other exercises at Williamsburg. The councilors escorted him to their chamber where he published his commission and took the oath of office. Then the dignitaries dined at the Raleigh Tavern and in the evening the town was brilliantly illuminated. The occasion was also celebrated by a poetical effusion in the *Virginia Gazette:*

> Sound the shrill trumpets, beat the rattling drums;
> From Great Britannia's isle, his Lordship comes.[1]

A prominent architectural feature of a provincial capital was the governor's residence. In Williamsburg his "palace" was a dignified building with ample gardens. In New York the governor's house stood conspicuously within the confines of Fort George. In such mansions the governors held levees in viceregal state for the principal personages of the town and province. Though the courtly tradition was weaker in Boston, even there it exerted an influence on manners, not wholly ended by the Revolution.

The official class varied in background and social outlook. Some, including most of the royal governors, were outsiders without previous local attachments. The four fully commissioned New York governors between 1763 and 1775 were in succession: General Robert Monckton, who had fought with Wolfe at Quebec; Sir Henry Moore, a native and former governor of Jamaica; the Earl of Dunmore, a Scotch peer; and finally William Tryon, an army officer and former governor of North Carolina. During five years of this period Virginia had two absentee governors, thus leaving the province to be

[1] L. G. Tyler, *Williamsburg, the Old Colonial Capital* (Richmond, 1907), 45.

administered by Lieutenant Governor Francis Fauquier, a liberal-minded gentleman who belonged to the Royal Society. Lord Botetourt, who followed Fauquier, had sat both in the House of Commons and in the House of Lords. Notwithstanding the stormy politics of the time he was personally popular, and his statue, voted by the Virginia assembly, still stands in the grounds of William and Mary College. Less happily remembered was Lord Dunmore, who went to his province from New York. Taken as a whole, these proconsular personages probably compared not unfavorably with contemporary office-holders in England, and their presence helped to broaden the provincial horizon.[1]

More numerous were the royal officials chosen from the American population. Conspicuous among them was Governor Thomas Hutchinson. Born and bred in Massachusetts, he had been a prosperous merchant and also an officeholder of long standing, first by election and later by royal appointment. Conservative by temperament and because of his property interests, official prefer-ment increasingly separated him from his more demo-cratic neighbors. Lieutenant Governor Cadwallader Colden of New York, though not a native of the prov-ince, had lived there most of his life, forming connec-tions with important New York families and becoming a large landowner. A man of varied intellectual inter-ests, he too was a habitual officeholder, and for about half the critical years between 1763 and 1775 was act-ing governor. In Colden's case also conservatism was to be expected. Other royal governors belonging to influ-ential provincial families were the Wentworths in New

---

[1] L. W. Labaree, "The Early Careers of the Royal Governors," *Essays in Colonial History Presented to Charles McLean Andrews by His Students* (New Haven, 1931), 145-168; Louise B. Dunbar, "The Royal Gover-nors in the Middle and Southern Colonies on the Eve of the Revolution," R. B. Morris, ed., *The Era of the American Revolution* (N. Y., 1939), 214-265.

Hampshire and Lieutenant Governor William Bull of South Carolina. Such families as these, allied by marriage with other well-to-do personages, were generally interested in maintaining the existing order, and often used official power to build their private fortunes.

The provincial councilors formed another conservative group. An interesting example is that of the New York merchant, John Watts. The son of a Scotch-born father, he was related on his mother's side to the great landowning families of Van Rensselaer and Van Cortlandt. He himself married a De Lancey and through his wife's family was connected with the Coldens, Commodore Warren of the British navy and Sir William Johnson. Three of his daughters married, respectively, William Alexander, better known as the Revolutionary general, "Lord Stirling"; a son of Sir William Johnson; and Captain Archibald Kennedy of the royal navy. Kennedy inherited an earldom and his son—the grandson of a New York merchant—became a marquis. During this period two De Lancey brothers sat together in the council with three others of the same connection. Similar conditions existed elsewhere, notably in Virginia.[1]

Old World traditions had their influence even in the assemblies. It was not only because of royal instructions that most colonial leaders favored a restricted suffrage. Though property qualifications were more easily acquired in America than in England, yet only a minority, often a small minority, of the adult males could vote for members of the legislature. The representation of certain manors in the New York assembly and the influence of the Virginia gentry in viva-voce elections resembled somewhat the parliamentary influence of the English squirearchy. Moreover, British procedure affected the

[1] Watts, *Letter Book* (N. Y. Hist. Soc., *Colls.*, LXI), introduction.

colonial assemblies to a considerable extent. In Virginia, representatives of rural constituencies somewhat oddly called themselves "burgesses," and South Carolina had its "Commons House of Assembly." The Virginia burgesses met at Williamsburg in quarters suggestive of the House of Commons at Westminster, and on opening a new assembly they were "commanded" by the governor to attend him in the council chamber. Returning to their own room, they chose a speaker, who was presented to the governor for formal approval. Messages were duly exchanged between the lower house and the legislative council, and both houses claimed privileges based on British precedents.[1] Though assemblies frequently clashed with the governors, these conflicts may be overemphasized. The legislatures generally met in centers of population, where oversea contacts were closest, and where social pressure as well as public patronage helped to impress the official point of view. Some officeholders sat in the lower house, and others had family connections there.

The pressure of transatlantic influence was somewhat less felt in the local governments. Among the major provincial capitals Boston maintained most successfully its local autonomy, through town meetings and popularly elected officials. In Charleston, however, provincial and municipal business were hardly distinguishable. Philadelphia was governed by a close corporation. Filling its own vacancies as in an English borough, its members annually chose one of their number as mayor. In New York, municipal councilors were elected by the freeholders and freemen, but three of the principal officers were appointed by the governor. Even in rural areas the prerogative element entered into the local gov-

[1] S. M. Pargellis, "The Procedure of the Virginia House of Burgesses," *William and Mary College Quar.*, ser. 2, VII, 73-86, 143-157; Mary P Clarke, "Parliamentary Privilege in the American Colonies," *Essays in Colonial History*, 124-144.

ernments through the governor's appointment of sheriffs and justices of the peace.[1]

Not only politics but other phases of town life gave evidence of important oversea contacts. A striking feature of the port towns was their comparatively large concern with maritime trade. A business man in Philadelphia, reading the marine news on a summer day in 1765, would find notices of Philadelphia vessels at three English and Irish ports, and of Boston ships at four English ports and one Irish. An interesting list of eleven South Carolina entries in British harbors included six at Cowes, with one each at five other places. There were arrivals also at six Continental European ports—three German, two Dutch and one Portuguese. Through advertising columns merchants were offered cargo space for exports, or an assortment of goods brought in the latest vessels from London, Bristol and Liverpool. In John Rowe's diary shipping items are numerous. On going to his wharf one July Sunday he noted the departure of three captains—two to England and one to Oporto; on a single day in August three others sailed for London.[2] Today most residents of Boston, New York or Philadelphia live so far from the sea that maritime activities pass almost unnoticed; but nearly all their colonial inhabitants dwelt within easy walking distance of the docks, where vessels were loaded and unloaded for oversea trade.

Provincial churchmen also had transatlantic connections. In the capital towns the Anglican communion was strongly represented, even in Puritan Boston and Quaker Philadelphia. In the South it was supported by

[1] E. S. Griffith, *History of American City Government; the Colonial Period* (N. Y., 1938), *passim*; A. E. Peterson and G. W. Edwards, *New York as an Eighteenth Century Municipality* (N. Y., 1917), pt. i, chap. i; pt. ii, chap. i.

[2] *Pa. Gazette*, Aug. 1, 1765; Rowe, *Letters and Diary*, 65, 82, 88, 104.

a legal establishment, and in the two Chesapeake capitals
it possessed a practical monopoly. In New York, Trinity Church was a conspicuous landmark. No other
religious body enjoyed equal prestige among the "best
people," and it was closely associated with the governing
class. The congregations which assembled at King's
Chapel in Boston or Bruton Church in Williamsburg
used the English liturgy authorized by act of Parliament, with its prescribed prayers for the royal family.
The officiating clergyman in the South was often an
English university graduate; if educated in a New England college, as many of the Northern clergy were, he
had at least crossed the water for ordination, and his
orthodoxy was certified by the bishop of London.

Similarly, other communions had organic relations
with churches abroad. The Dutch Reformed congregations, though moving toward greater autonomy, still
relied upon the Classis of Amsterdam for ministerial supplies and guidance; the American Friends corresponded
with the London yearly meeting; the Moravian clergy
were subject to a governing board in Germany; and the
small Methodist groups acknowledged the authority of
John Wesley. So, too, the Catholic congregation in
Philadelphia looked to Rome and to more immediate
superiors in England. Though the Scotch and Irish
Presbyterians had no such official connections, there was
a less formal relationship of real importance; and the
German Lutherans depended on the fatherland for their
clergy. Even the New England Congregational ministers kept in touch with British dissenters.

Transatlantic influences likewise affected education.
In 1765 the colleges of New York, Philadelphia and
Williamsburg were headed by ordained clergy of the
Church of England, two of whom were English uni-
versity graduates and the third a master of arts from
the University of Aberdeen. Not only the New York

and Philadelphia colleges but also Harvard and Yale conducted money-raising campaigns in England. Harvard received substantial contributions, especially for its library. Other intellectual contacts, which will be dealt with later, included the training of provincial lawyers at the English Inns of Court; the education of medical practitioners and teachers at Edinburgh, London and Leyden; the liberal borrowing by American periodicals from their British contemporaries; and the proportionately large newspaper space given to European news.

In superficial matters as well, colonial townsmen looked across the sea. Hairdressers and tailors liked to advertise either British experience or expert knowledge of London modes. It was hard for a young woman, even during patriotic boycotts of British goods, to "let a horrid homespun (which can become none but a country wench)" take the place of imported fabrics.[1] So it was with popular entertainments. Theatergoers in New York, Philadelphia, Williamsburg and Charleston saw almost exclusively plays performed by English actors.

[1] *N.-Y. Post-Boy,* quoted in Stokes, *Iconography,* IV, 755.

CHAPTER II

THE OLDER COUNTRYSIDE

OLD World contacts and Old World patterns were most apparent on the seaboard. The country districts exhibited marked variations. In Virginia and Massachusetts social and political standards were largely maintained by men three, four or sometimes five generations removed from pioneering ancestors. In rural New England the introduction of later strains, though not negligible, had been comparatively slight. In the Chesapeake provinces eighteenth-century immigration introduced important new elements; but in the tidewater and the eastern piedmont these later arrivals had not radically changed the social structure. Conditions differed somewhat in the Carolinas; but in South Carolina a large proportion of the influential personages belonged to families well acclimated on this side of the water. The society of the Middle colonies was more largely molded by later stocks, though some rural communities were already over a century old.

In so far as the older rural population had rooted itself in the New World, it had been partially Americanized and the force of the European tradition correspondingly weakened. There were, however, opposing factors. One was the natural effect of the overcoming of pioneer conditions. With greater social maturity folkways and mental attitudes characteristic of an older society tended to reappear. The other factor, which varied in different regions, was the persistence of economic and social requirements that could be met only by maintaining contact with a more advanced civilization.

14

This latter influence was artificially reënforced by British commercial policies and the political machinery through which they were applied.

The extent to which such generalizations are valid can only be seen by conditions in different areas. The Chesapeake tidewater, the oldest settled region in the thirteen colonies, contained market towns at or near the falls of the rivers: Petersburg on the Appomattox, Richmond on the James, Fredericksburg on the Rappahannock, Alexandria and Georgetown on the Potomac. The line between tidewater and piedmont did not, however, correspond precisely with political subdivisions or significant social differences. In the James Valley, Patrick Henry's Hanover County had come to have a preponderance of black over white inhabitants, though much of it lay within the piedmont and its best-known spokesman was a vigorous opponent of the planter aristocracy. In the Northern Neck between the Rappahannock and the Potomac, tidewater families like the Carters had moved from the lower country into "Old Prince William" to meet newcomers from the North: Pennsylvania Quakers, Irish Presbyterians, French and German Protestants; but this mixed population was dominated by families from the tidewater. Several piedmont counties now had more Negroes than whites and were obviously allied in interest with their lowland neighbors.[1]

In this Chesapeake region Old World practices had left their mark. Quitrents payable in perpetuity were due to king or proprietor, though they were moderate in amount, loosely administered and disappointing as sources of revenue. The provincials themselves followed English precedents in encouraging the perpetuation of large landed estates through entail and primogeniture.

[1] E. B. Greene and Virginia D. Harrington, comps., *American Population before the Federal Census of 1790* (N. Y., 1932), 152, 154; Fairfax Harrison, *Landmarks of Old Prince William* (Richmond, 1924), 1, preface.

Though, in the absence of a will, the real estate went to the eldest son, not all lands were so entailed as to prevent distribution among heirs by gift or bequest. There were also legal processes by which entails might be, and were, broken. Nevertheless, as Jefferson declared, entail and primogeniture had "raised up a distinct set of families who, being privileged by law in the perpetuation of their wealth were thus formed into a Patrician order." [1]

Meantime it had become increasingly difficult for the yeoman farmer to compete with well-to-do neighbors who worked their plantations with numerous Negro hands. Those of the yeoman class who were not content with this situation moved southward or westward to new or sparsely settled areas. In the eighteenth-century development of slaveholding certain facts stand out: the growth of the number of slaveholders; the substantial majority of this group who had only moderate holdings; and the large proportion of the servile blacks held by a few owners. [2]

The situation in two Virginia counties—Gloucester on Chesapeake Bay and Washington's county of Fairfax in the Northern Neck—as shown by the census figures of 1782 and 1783 was fairly typical. In Gloucester a total of about three hundred whites owned over three thousand slaves, an average of around ten to each master. But fifty-seven individuals—less than one fifth—owned more than half the whole number. In Fairfax County eight slaveholdings included nearly a fifth of the Negroes, with Washington possessing the largest group. In the older Maryland counties similar conditions existed. In eight counties the percentage of slave population varied from forty to slightly over fifty. Of somewhat

[1] Thomas Jefferson, *Works* (P. L. Ford, ed., N. Y., 1904-1905), I, 58.
[2] J. T. Adams, *Provincial Society, 1690-1763* (*A History of American Life*, III), 197-202.

over ten thousand Negroes in Anne Arundel County, about ten per cent belonged to eight heads of families.[1]

Important as were the great planters as economic, social and political figures, the "middling class" cannot be ignored. They comprised, in fact, a majority of the slaveholders. Owning from four or five to a dozen Negroes each, they did not reside in impressive Georgian houses, and their living standards ranged between those of the planter aristocracy and those of the "poor whites." This middle group has left fewer records, but we know about them from contemporary travelers. One observer credited them with natural vigor, hospitable if crude manners, and intellectual capacity, "though in a great measure unimproved." He noted, however, less agreeable characteristics: rudeness, ferocity and haughtiness—due partly to intercourse with slaves over whom they exercised "an harsh and absolute command"—and an excessive addiction to sports, including "that most barbarous of all diversions—cock-fighting."[2]

In Washington's day planters large and small had some common problems. For eastern Virginia and Maryland, tobacco was still of prime importance. Landon Carter observed in 1776, "Tobacco seems to be our only proper staple." It was still the chief measure of value in public and private business and the main item of export. Prices depended largely on the market abroad.[3]

Under the acts of trade, now fairly well enforced in this respect, all tobacco must first go to British ports. Much of it went to Scotch merchants, thus contributing

[1] T. J. Wertenbaker, *The Planters of Colonial Virginia* (Princeton, 1922), chaps. vii-viii; U. S. Bureau of the Census, *Heads of Families at the First Census of the United States Taken in the Year 1790* (Wash., 1907-1908), *Virginia*, 16-18, 53-54; *ibid.*, *Maryland*, 9-16; Greene and Harrington, *American Population*, 133.

[2] J. F. D. Smyth, *A Tour in the United States of America* (London, 1784), I, chap. ix.

[3] Landon Carter, "Diary," *William and Mary College Quar.*, XX, 174.

largely to the British customs revenue in spite of some smuggling. How much of this burden was carried by the planter and how much by the European consumer is a moot question. Certainly the planter's part was important, though a recent student of Southern agriculture emphasizes that of the consumer. By 1774 most of the "ultimate consumers" were in Continental Europe, and in case of such reëxportation certain British duties were refunded. Though these parliamentary restraints proved troublesome, other annoyances bulk more largely in contemporary correspondence. Prices fluctuated widely according to the size of the crop and economic conditions abroad. In 1765 and 1766 Virginia tobacco brought good prices, but in 1773 prices fell off by nearly half, with consequent hard times. Sometimes the planter complained of poor marketing service. Washington declared that his London correspondent was not selling his tobacco at prices equal to those obtained by others. There was dissatisfaction also with the return cargoes on which the planters depended for luxuries and many essentials of comfortable living.[1]

Especially irritating was the debtor-creditor relation between the colonial growers and the British merchants. Against tobacco sales were charged advances for freight and duties. The planters suffered also from unfavorable rates of exchange. Nor was it easy in long-range trading to keep a nice balance between income and expenditure. Jefferson estimated that in 1775 Virginians owed British merchants at least two million pounds sterling, and he believed that these unfavorable balances resulted partly from unfair dealing by the merchants; the planters thus became "a species of property annexed to certain

[1] L. C. Gray, *History of Agriculture in the Southern United States to 1860* (Carnegie Inst., *Publs.*, no. 430), I, chaps. xi-xii; U. B. Phillips, ed., *Plantation and Frontier* (J. R. Commons and others, eds., *A Documentary History of American Industrial Society*, Cleveland, 1910-1911, I-II), I, 301-304.

mercantile houses in London." No more popular than the oversea merchants were their agents in the province. The latter, often Scotch, frequently maintained something like "chain stores" on Chesapeake Bay and its tributaries, selling European goods and buying tobacco. A large part of the tobacco sent to England was handled by such factors. In spite of competition among them, they were also accused of combining to the planter's disadvantage; "they confederate," wrote Charles Carroll, "to oppress us." [1]

Though tobacco continued to be the chief staple, wheat was gaining. Josiah Quincy, passing through this region, noted the decline of tobacco culture while that of grain was "rising fast." The diaries of Landon Carter and Washington tell a similar story. A plantation in the Northern Neck was advertised as particularly suited to wheat, for which there was "a constant demand"; near by was a flour mill "equal to any in America." Landon Carter practised crop rotation, supplied neighbors with turnip seed, raised hemp and flax and experimented with cotton. [2]

The management of a large plantation required executive ability. The planter had many troubles. Work might be held up by illness among the slaves or by slack management; more rarely there was serious disorder. The *Virginia Gazette* (Rind's) of January 25, 1770, reported a plantation rising in which the Negroes temporarily overpowered the steward; some blood was shed before it ended. The treatment of slaves depended on the individual owner or his overseer. In 1765 the

---

[1] Gray, *Agriculture*, I, chap. xv; Charles Carroll, *Unpublished Letters* (T. M. Field, ed., U. S. Catholic Hist. Soc., *Monograph Ser.*, I), 91; Jefferson, *Works*, V, 28.

[2] Josiah Quincy, "Journal," Mass. Hist. Soc., *Proceeds.*, XLIX, 469; *Pa. Gazette*, Jan. 18, 1775; Carter, "Diary," *William and Mary College Quar.*, XIV, 39.

Scotch traveler, Lord Adam Gordon, found Virginia Negroes better clothed than those to the southward; and the author of *American Husbandry* thought the Virginia overseers less exacting than those of Jamaica. In their own interest, intelligent masters urged their agents to feed the slaves properly and to give special consideration to "breeding wenches." The English clergyman Andrew Burnaby noted, however, the failure of the law to protect the Negro against his master's violence. Another British observer, who spoke of the "brutal authority" of the overseer, nevertheless found most of the blacks carefree and cheerful.[1]

The plantation country, especially in Maryland, had also its white workers, including indentured servants and wage-earners such as carpenters, smiths and masons. In 1763 the elder Carroll proposed importing a workman to stucco his house. After serving two years for his passage such a man might develop an independent business. Washington was a considerable employer of white labor. The most responsible white service was that of the overseer, foreman or manager, on whom the effective handling of the slaves largely depended. Within this group, however, there were marked differences. On a lower level was the slave driver, so conspicuous later in antislavery literature. Brutal to his Negro hands, he was often a sore trial to his employer. One planter complained of a "dog of a foreman," "a lazy villain," failing to care for his slaves properly. Sometimes, as manager for an absentee owner, a young man of the

---

[1] [Lord Adam Gordon], "Journal of an Officer's Travels in America and the West Indies, 1764-1765," N. D. Mereness, ed., *Travels in the American Colonies* (N. Y., 1916), 406; anon., *American Husbandry* (London, 1775), II, 139; Andrew Burnaby, *Travels through the Middle Settlements in North-America* (London, 1775), 18; Phillips, *Plantation and Frontier*, I, 109; Thomas Anburey, *Travels through the Interior Parts of America* (Boston, 1923), II, 192-194.

planter class learned "the stewardship and management of a Virginia estate." [1]

The typical tidewater economy was on the decline. Soil exhaustion, due to erosion and incessant tobacco cropping, was one factor. Though the burden of indebtedness resulted partly from an oppressive commercial system, another cause was, in the words of a friendly critic, "the cult of magnificence." In Virginia, as elsewhere, there was adverse criticism of colonial agriculture because of careless cropping, neglect of stock and failure to use proper implements; but Washington and some of his neighbors were trying to keep up with progress in England through fertilizers, better plowing and crop rotation.[2]

Though men of more modest position were beginning to assert themselves, the great landowners still mainly determined social standards, and the leaders of the Revolution were largely drawn from this class. One outstanding Virginian was Councilor Robert Carter, an extensive landowner and the master of several hundred slaves. Though he had an "elegant and spacious" home at Williamsburg, his principal residence was Nomini Hall in the lower Potomac Valley. This establishment included a two-story brick house of generous proportions approached by a broad avenue. Standing on high ground with its pillared portico, it was a striking feature of the landscape for miles around. Social amenities were served by a ballroom, but there was also a study with a library of over a thousand volumes. About the mansion were grouped the schoolhouse, stable, coach house, washhouse, slave quarters and other outbuildings.

[1] Carroll, *Unpublished Letters*, 78; Carter, "Diary," *William and Mary College Quar.*, XIII, 48; XIV, 40.

[2] A. O. Craven, *Soil Exhaustion as a Factor in the Agricultural History of Virginia and Maryland, 1606-1860* (Univ. of Ill., *Studies*, XIII, no. 1), chaps. i-ii; U. B. Phillips, *Life and Labor in the Old South* (Boston, 1929), 40.

The young Princeton graduate engaged as tutor for the Carter children regarded the master and mistress as persons of dignity, cultivation and charm. Farther up the Northern Neck was Landon Carter's Sabine Hall, where he dwelt in patriarchal style with his children and grandchildren about him. His hospitalities were on a lavish scale. One "three days festival" brought together some sixty relatives and friends.[1]

Of the Virginia planters who became leaders in the Revolution, George Mason of Gunston Hall and Washington of Mount Vernon are excellent examples. Both were large landowners with numerous slaves, raising tobacco and wheat besides conducting various domestic industries. Active in both church and state, they were members of the same parish vestry, justices of the peace and burgesses. Compared with Nomini Hall, their homes were modest, though Gunston Hall was an admirable specimen of Georgian architecture. Charles Carroll of Carrollton had a more cosmopolitan background. Heir to his father's extensive properties, he was educated in Jesuit schools on the Continent and also visited England, where he possessed important social connections. Though his Catholic faith barred him from colonial offices and subjected him to other disabilities, he was an outstanding citizen. The Carrolls were good examples of the planter-business man, with money at interest and investments in iron manufacturing.[2]

Coastal North Carolina had a rural society in some respects like that of Virginia. Here, too, well-to-do planters raised tobacco and employed numerous slaves,

[1] P. V. Fithian, *Journal and Letters, 1767-74* (J. R. Williams, ed., Princeton, 1900), 115, 128-132, 278-279; Louis Morton, *Robert Carter of Nomini Hall* (H. D. Farish, ed., *Williamsburg Restoration Historical Studies*, II), 39-40, 205-209; Carter, "Diary," *William and Mary College Quar.*, XIII, 45-47, 53, 162.

[2] Kate M. Rowland, *Life and Correspondence of Charles Carroll of Carrollton* (N. Y., 1898), *passim*; Carroll, *Unpublished Letters*, introduction and chap. ii.

but they also exported naval stores and provisions. In the province as a whole this class was less important than in Virginia and its influence was diminishing. In the Cape Fear River Valley recent arrivals, including many Scots, formed communities of planters and merchants somewhat detached from the older northern settlements. Meantime newcomers were swelling the population of the backcountry to a point where it exceeded that of the tidewater.

In South Carolina the characteristics of the Southern tidewater appeared in extreme form. In two of the three coastal districts the ratio of blacks to whites was approximately three to one. The rural part of the Charleston district contained nearly eighty holdings of a hundred or more Negroes. Four fifths of the heads of families owned thirty or more each.[1] While in Virginia the slave population was for the most part stabilized, South Carolina was now importing Negroes in considerable numbers. The total brought in during the year 1773 has been estimated at over eleven thousand. Such representative citizens as Henry Laurens were disturbed by this development and there were temporary checks on importation. But notwithstanding Laurens's misgivings, large importations continued until stopped by the Continental Association of 1774. Observers found the planters making money fast. Visitors to Charleston were impressed by its prosperity and the refinements of living which wealth made possible.[2]

Charleston was unique in colonial America as the focal point of a rural-urban society. Laurens was a leading merchant, but he was also an extensive planter. His contemporary, Gabriel Manigault—merchant, money

[1] U. S. Bureau of the Census, *Heads of Families: South Carolina*, *passim*; U. B. Phillips, *American Negro Slavery* (N. Y., 1928), 95-96.

[2] Elizabeth Donnan, "The Slave Trade into South Carolina before the Revolution," *Am. Hist. Rev.*, XXXIII, 804-828; anon., *American Husbandry*, I, 424-426.

lender and conspicuous citizen—left an estate of over forty-seven thousand acres with nearly five hundred slaves. This semiurbanized planter class, the distinguishing feature of South Carolina society, dominated provincial politics, with both authority and administration largely centered in the capital city. Between the tidewater and the piedmont settlements the line was more sharply drawn. The city-state system did not readily adapt itself to the needs of the backcountry, thereby resulting in serious friction, as in North Carolina.[1]

Some planter families were built on foundations laid by seventeenth-century ancestors. So it was with Manigault and Laurens of the Huguenot stock, and the English Middletons, Bulls and Lynches. Yet South Carolina also had its "new men." Thomas Ferguson, son-in-law of Christopher Gadsden, beginning as sawyer and plantation overseer, ultimately acquired nine plantations. Joseph Alston is said to have started his career with only five Negroes but later owned five plantations with a hundred slaves on each.[2]

Advertisements in the *South-Carolina Gazette* for 1772 offer interesting pictures of great plantations and their varied activities. Properties advertised for sale by the heirs of Richard Beresford aggregated seventeen thousand acres, chiefly in the Charleston district, including one with a tanyard and another boasting a yearly output of seven hundred thousand bricks. The estate also contained many acres of "exceeding fine Rice Land." Another plantation advertised "an exceeding good Brick Dwelling House," an overseer's house, barn, corn house, kitchen, dairy, coach house and stables.[3] But even in South Carolina the poorer planters and farmers with few

[1] D. D. Wallace, *Henry Laurens* (N. Y., 1915), *passim;* A. H. Hirsch, *The Huguenots of Colonial South Carolina* (Durham, 1928), 230-231.
[2] Phillips, *Life and Labor in the Old South*, 307-308; Quincy, "Journal," 453.
[3] *S.-C. Gazette*, Sept. 24, 1772.

slaves or none cannot be ignored. Inspector Finlay, who experienced the lavish hospitality of planters ready to "kill you with kindness," noted also the primitive living in the poorer houses. In general, however, this part of rural America contained a relatively large proportion of whites who were at least moderately well-to-do.[1]

The older rural communities of New England preserved to a considerable extent their seventeenth-century patterns. The "embattled farmers" of Concord and Bunker Hill came largely from small holdings of from one to two hundred acres. Some were renters, but freehold tenure was general without quitrents payable to an overlord. This wide diffusion of land ownership owed something to legislation under which sons and daughters shared in the distribution of the father's estate, but even more to physical conditions. "In some countries," wrote Samuel Deane in his *New-England Farmer; or, Georgical Dictionary,* "men choose to hold large farms. But in places where labor is dear, as in this country, small farms are to be preferred. One hundred acres of good land may be enough for a man, whose work is mostly done by himself and family." Such conditions encouraged the so-called "levelling spirit." "Everybody," wrote a British traveler, "has property and every body knows it."[2] Though there were social distinctions and other limitations on democracy, these were not what most impressed European observers or persons in other colonies. Generally speaking, New England society had no large servile class, black or white. Slaves were comparatively few and white servitude much less common than elsewhere. The farmer's hired man and the housewife's helper were on quite a different footing from the

---

[1] Hugh Finlay, *Journal* (Brooklyn, 1867), 62-67.
[2] P. W. Bidwell and J. I. Falconer, *History of Agriculture in the Northern United States, 1620-1860* (Carnegie Inst., *Publs.,* no. 358), chaps. v, ix; Samuel Deane, *The New-England Farmer; or, Georgical Dictionary* (2nd edn., Worcester, 1797), 104; [Gordon], "Journal," 451.

Negro slave or the indentured servant who could be bought and sold.

What Charles Francis Adams said of the people in Braintree—that they "lived on themselves and each other"—was true of many country towns. Nevertheless, while most of the farmer's product was consumed at home or reached only a local market, this was not always the case. In 1774 John Adams heard of the "stream of provisions continually running from Connecticut," whose flaxseed went to New York in exchange for salt, while provisions, cattle and horses were sent to the West Indies in exchange for rum, sugar and molasses.[1]

Interest in agricultural improvement was slight. New England's most serious student of the subject, Jared Eliot, died in 1763 and no equally important writer appeared before the Revolution. The author of *American Husbandry* (1775) was sharply critical of Yankee farming, with no proper rotation of crops, ill-made farm implements and neglected livestock. John Adams, after seeing rural Pennsylvania, confessed to his wife, "I am ashamed of our farmers. They are a lazy, ignorant set." Some British visitors, however, took a more favorable view. Lord Adam Gordon predicted that the region between Hartford and Springfield would in thirty years rival "the most beautiful part of England." Even the author of *American Husbandry* admitted that the small farmers here were better off than the corresponding class in England. "In New England," he wrote, "the little freeholders and farmers live in the midst of a plenty of all the necessaries of life; they do not acquire wealth, but they have comforts in abundance."[2]

[1] C. F. Adams, *Three Episodes of Massachusetts History* (Boston, 1892), II, 696; John Adams, *Works* (C. F. Adams, ed., Boston, 1856), II, 341-342.

[2] Anon., *American Husbandry*, I, 80, 90; John and Abigail Adams, *Familiar Letters* (C. F. Adams, ed., Boston, 1875), 278; [Gordon], "Journal," 448.

Though comparatively democratic, the New England rural community nevertheless maintained social distinctions. In Braintree the Quincy family inherited a well-recognized leadership. Colonel John Quincy, the head of the clan during this period, possessed a substantial fortune. His position was not wholly unlike that of an English country gentleman. An active participant in local affairs, he served year after year as moderator of the town meeting and was at various times colonel of the county militia, speaker of the house of representatives and provincial councilor. Between his family and that of John Adams, whose ancestors were yeoman farmers, there was a real difference though no impassable gulf. Young John was a fellow student of Edmund Quincy at Harvard and married a granddaughter of the old colonel. The Connecticut Valley also had its rural magnates—the "River gods," including the future Loyalist, Israel Williams. Conspicuous in this comparatively small group of New England "country gentlemen" were the Tory brigadier, Timothy Ruggles, and General William Heath of the Continental army. Among other agricultural elements account must be taken of the skilled workman who farmed on a small scale but might also be a mason, carpenter or house painter, besides taking a modest part in public affairs as constable or surveyor of highways. On a still lower economic level were the poorer laborers and the paupers whose support formed a relatively important item in the town budget.[1]

The country store was at best a small affair. Gathering up produce from the neighboring farms for Boston and other market towns, it offered in exchange "West India goods"—sugar, molasses, liquor, spices and salt—besides European dress goods and hardware. An occasional country merchant broadened his horizon, as when Connecticut's future war governor, Jonathan Trumbull

[1] Adams, *Three Episodes*, II. chaps. vi-vii.

of Lebanon, traded with the West Indies and even European ports. As a social center, the country store had a competitor in the tavern, where the farmers imbibed rum, smoked their pipes and discussed politics. John Adams thought there were too many taverns, with unfortunate consequences for politics, health and morals. Their patrons, he said, could be "induced by rum and flip to vote for any man whatever." The better sort of tavern keeper, however, was often a substantial citizen.[1]

The Congregational meetinghouse kept its central position in the typical country town. Its minister was supported by public taxation, with some concessions to dissenters who maintained their own services. Though only a minority of the adult inhabitants were usually full members, many others were willing adherents. Rationalistic tendencies appeared here and there; but the rural churches were relatively conservative, and though the clergy had lost some of their prestige, this also was less evident in the country, where the minister was usually still the best-educated person in the community. He influenced the political philosophy of his parishioners and was sometimes, like Jared Eliot, a comparatively intelligent medical adviser. He was commonly also a farmer. The diary of one New Hampshire pastor tells not only of baptisms and funerals, but also of hog killing, fencing, sowing flaxseed and oats and trading cider for rum.[2]

Town dockets reflected rural interests. The voters chose not only the selectmen and constables but also fence viewers, haywards and hogreeves. A Brookline (Muddy River) town meeting had to decide "whether the hoggs run at large the ensuing year." Other normal agenda dealt with the church, the schools and poor relief. Largely occupied with tax rates, Yankee countrymen

[1] Adams, *Three Episodes*, II, chap. xii; Adams, *Works*, II, 84.
[2] Timothy Walker, "Diaries," N. H. Hist. Soc., *Colls.*, IX, 143-152.

naturally took an interest in that phase of British legislation. The town meeting was not strictly democratic. In Massachusetts the local suffrage was limited to freeholders and other male inhabitants owning property valued at twenty pounds. From a contemporary standpoint, however, this rural assembly embodied what Charles Francis Adams has called a "rude and almost stern equality." Though the moderator was commonly a well-to-do citizen, the meeting was not always easily led and social prestige did not always prevail. "Each individual," wrote the historian William Gordon, "has an equal liberty of delivering his opinion, and is not liable to be silenced or browbeaten by a richer or greater townsman than himself; and each vote weighs equally whether that of the highest or lowest inhabitant." Gordon's statement had a substantial element of truth.[1]

In the Middle provinces landholding was generally subject in theory to quitrents, though nowhere was this obligation thoroughly enforced. The New Jersey farmers were conspicuously successful in resisting proprietary claims. Quitrents in Pennsylvania and New York yielded some revenue, but the actual collections were comparatively small. In New York primogeniture and entail favored the maintenance of great landed domains; but in the other Middle colonies law and custom encouraged wider distribution. The most nearly feudal and aristocratic society of the Northern countryside centered in the New York manors, notably those along the Hudson. The "Manor and Lordship of Livingston" extended several miles from north to south and eastward

---

[1] J. F. Sly, *Town Government in Massachusetts, 1620-1930* (Cambridge, 1930), chap. iv; Inhabitants of Brookline, *Muddy River and Brookline Records, 1634-1838* (Boston, 1875), 117-196, *passim*; S. A. Bates, ed., *Records of the Town of Braintree, 1640-1793* (Randolph, Mass., 1886), entries 1763, 1764; Adams, *Three Episodes*, II, chap. xiv; William Gordon, *The History of the Rise, Progress, and Establishment, of the Independence of the United States of America* (London, 1788), I, 263.

to Massachusetts. Such an estate was partly worked by the owner with his black and white servants and partly leased to tenants. Even in New York, however, several counties were occupied principally by small free-holders.[1]

Pennsylvania and New Jersey possessed some large estates on which a kind of landed gentry had developed; but in northern New Jersey, emigrants from New England had introduced communities similar to those they had left behind, and in Pennsylvania the typical farm comprised between one and two hundred acres. Generally speaking, rural settlements in this section were less compact than in New England, and less likely to develop a vigorous communal life. The country town commonly included a small hamlet with its church, tavern and smithy; but homesteads were scattered and even churches were often built in isolated situations. Among the more compact communities were certain French and Dutch villages in the Hudson Valley, the Jersey townships already mentioned, some Pennsylvania market towns and the Moravian settlements at Bethlehem and Nazareth.[2]

Notwithstanding such diversities the Middle colonies resembled each other, and differed from New England, in that their commerce rested mainly on agriculture. On the eve of the Revolution, breadstuffs accounted for two thirds of the value of Pennsylvania's exports. A natural result was the remarkable development of the milling industry. Newspaper advertisements stressed the availability of mills on or near farm property. There were some transatlantic shipments, but breadstuffs from

[1] B. W. Bond, "Quit Rent System in the American Colonies," *Am. Hist. Rev.*, XVII, 510; Theodore Sedgwick, *A Memoir of the Life of William Livingston* (N. Y., 1833), 39.
[2] Bidwell and Falconer, *Agriculture*, 64-66, 115; J. D. Schoepf, *Travels in the Confederation, 1783-1784* (A. J. Morrison, ed., Phila., 1911), I, 46, 55.

New York and Philadelphia went mainly to other colonies, especially to the West Indies, which took also beef and pork. Sheep raising proved less important, providing barely enough for the local woolen manufacture. Horses were more generally used than in New England and had a better reputation. In Pennsylvania they enjoyed the advantage of fairly good roads.[1]

In general, the agriculture of this region, particularly that of Pennsylvania, fared comparatively well at the hands of critics. More wheat was said to be raised per acre than on English farms, though this was attributed to the virtue of the soil rather than the intelligence of the farmers. According to Schoepf, the "goodness of his soil gradually puts the farmer's industry to sleep . . . many of them had rather move on to take up fresh land than to be at the trouble of improving the old." Other comments were more favorable. During the Revolution the British Lieutenant Thomas Anburey described the Hudson Valley as "well-cultivated" with grain and an abundance of livestock, and a Yankee army surgeon noted the gardenlike aspect of New Jersey.[2]

About Philadelphia the city market encouraged intensive cultivation. Some well-to-do landowners, versed in agricultural literature, introduced "the English way of sowing wheat on clover lays" and used fertilizers. Contemporary notices of the German farmers were particularly favorable. At Lancaster a Church of England clergyman noted the "great and deserved reputation" of the Conestoga lands through "the excellent Management of the High Dutch." They were especially commended for their choice of limestone tracts, their excep-

---

[1] Robert Proud, *The History of Pennsylvania* (Phila., 1797-1798), II, 264-265, 269; *Pa. Gazette*, Oct. 24, 1765; Jan. 4, 1770; Schoepf, *Travels*, I, 213; II, 21-22.

[2] Anon., *American Husbandry*, I, chaps. ix, xii; Schoepf, *Travels*, I, 211-212; Anburey, *Travels*, II, 270; James Thacher, *Military Journal during the American Revolutionary War* (Boston, 1823), 157.

tional industry and their thrift; their market wagons were the "strongest and best in America." Another item to the credit of the Pennsylvania farmers was the Philadelphia market, which was noted for its cleanliness and good order.[1]

Agriculture in this section relied more on unfree labor than in New England, and in New York and Delaware much of this was supplied by Negro slaves. One Hudson River estate employed eight slaves, seven indentured white servants and two wage-earners. In 1764 a Delaware estate of two thousand acres was offered for rent with "as many Negroes of either sex and of any age" as might be desired. Even in these two provinces, however, Negroes were comparatively few, about one in seven of the population in Delaware and somewhat less in New York. In Pennsylvania slave labor was almost negligible. Far more important here was the indentured servant or redemptioner. For some immigrants servile labor proved a kind of initiation into colonial life and land ownership.[2]

Advertisements of property near Philadelphia, taken at random from the *Pennsylvania Gazette* in 1765 and 1770, are suggestive. Three of these farms contained from seventy-five to a hundred and thirty-six acres, with from forty to sixty per cent of cleared land. The largest, on the "Great Road" between Philadelphia and Lancaster, was said to have half its acreage "cleared and in good order, either for grain or pasture," with "a constant stream and plenty of water." Another farm was limed and "in very good heart." All the advertisements mention the orchards, one of them said to yield forty barrels of cider a year. Some farm buildings were of log, others of stone or brick. Delaware Valley farms also carried

[1] Anon., *American Husbandry*, I, chap. xii; T. Barton to Sir William Johnson, July 8, 1771 (supplied by Mr. C. H. Vance from the Johnson Papers, Library of Congress) ; Schoepf, *Travels*, I, 112-113, 204.

[2] Anon., *American Husbandry*, I, 110; *Pa. Gazette*, Jan. 5, 1764.

on various industrial activities. One had a limestone quarry and a kiln; another, a smith's shop, a gristmill and a sawmill; still another, enough water power for a fulling mill. One large estate possessed two river landings for shipping produce to Philadelphia.[1]

Though no Middle province had a uniformly established church or a clear majority of any one denomination, many rural churches formed natural centers of community life. On Long Island such a church might be Congregational or Presbyterian; in the Hudson Valley it might be Dutch, French or German Reformed. In Pennsylvania were meetinghouses of Quakers, Presbyterians and various German sects. The best examples of a community directed by a particular religious society were the Moravian settlements. In spiritual matters the prevailing note was religious diversity. One farm advertisement offered as a special attraction neighboring churches or meetinghouses of various denominations.[2]

A few prosperous farmers could enjoy the amenities of life. Like the manor lords of New York, the gentleman farmers of Pennsylvania seemed to a contemporary British observer much like the English gentry, living well with tables served "quite in the English taste." Such men could do much better on a given income in Pennsylvania than in England; "gentlemen of education and ideas" might here pass their time "not only in plenty, but agreeably." Of the numerous hard-working farmers, whose interests were necessarily circumscribed, we naturally know less.[3]

In this picture of pre-Revolutionary rural America regional differences are conspicuous. The plantation economy of the Southern tidewater—its comparative concentration of land ownership, its slave labor and its

[1] *Pa. Gazette*, Jan. 3, Oct. 24, 1765; Jan. 4, 1770.
[2] *Pa. Gazette*, Oct. 24, 1765.
[3] Anon., *American Husbandry*, I, chap. xiii.

special concern with export staples—stands in marked contrast with rural New England, a region of more compact settlements, widely distributed land ownership, with production mainly for near-by markets. Even within the traditional three sections there were significant local variations. Nevertheless, these rural societies were alike in one respect—in departing more or less radically from Old World patterns to meet particular regional needs.

CHAPTER III

AMERICAN BUSINESS BETWEEN TWO WARS

THE Revolutionary era witnessed significant advances in American business from comparatively simple organizations and methods toward a more complex order. In the prewar period a striking characteristic of provincial business, as compared with later times, was the almost entire absence of certain instrumentalities now thought indispensable: banks, stock exchanges, business corporations. The "big-business" man of that day collected and exported the products of plantations, forests and fisheries, and imported European and West Indian goods for local consumption or reëxportation. All this he did with extremely limited facilities for the movement of goods or the exchange of intelligence.

In the transatlantic trade the merchant employed mainly ships of from one hundred to four hundred tons and often used even smaller craft. Under favorable conditions goods might be received from four to six weeks after shipment from British ports, with longer voyages not uncommon. Some merchants had their own boats while others depended on vessels which carried miscellaneous cargoes. The *Pennsylvania Gazette* of January 5, 1764, announced that the ship *Success*, "a prime sailor" bound for Belfast and Glasgow, had its cargo space largely taken. New arrivals were advertised by city merchants, as when Samuel Purviance of Philadelphia announced a "General assortment of merchandize" just imported in the last vessels from England. In the West Indian and coasting trades small craft were often jointly owned by merchants and masters. Freight rates proved a serious matter. For exports to the West Indies they were said to amount to forty-five per cent of the prime cost; for lumber and corn the charge might run to a hundred per cent. The hazards of the sea, especially in war time, made insurance expensive. Water transportation was important even in local trade. Country produce for New York City was carried in sloops down the Hudson, by ferry from Long Island or the New Jersey shore, or by the Connecticut River and Long Island Sound from New England. Land transportation was difficult and costly.[1]

In acquiring information about markets the contrast between pre-Revolutionary conditions and our own is even more striking. Today correspondence may be exchanged across the Atlantic within a fortnight and messages by cable or telephone within a single business day. The provincial merchant, however, needed at best two months to interchange communications with a London correspondent, and a much longer interval was ordinarily required. It was hard, therefore, to deal adequately with market conditions abroad. But in one respect the situation was growing better. Though letters were mainly carried by merchant vessels sailing at irregular times, a monthly mail service to England now existed from New York and Charleston. Even on the American continent personal intercourse was slow and subject to vexatious delays. Intercolonial travel by water was, however, gradually improving. By 1771 there was a fortnightly service between New York and Providence. But a sea voyage from Boston to Charleston was still an arduous undertaking.[2]

[1] John Rowe, *Letters and Diary* (Annie R. Cunningham, ed., Boston, 1903), 73, 82, 90, 114; *Pa. Gazette*, Jan. 5, 1764; H. C. Bell, "The West India Trade before the American Revolution," *Am. Hist. Rev.*, XXII, 272-287.

[2] W. E. Rich, *The History of the United States Post Office to the Year 1829* (*Harvard Econ. Studies*, XXVII), chap. i, p. 36; James Schouler, *Americans of 1776* (N. Y., 1906), 82.

Land communication continued to be largely by horse-back, often requiring several days for what is now a matter of hours.   In bad weather the ferries were often delayed and the bridging of the larger streams had not yet been seriously undertaken.   Better roads, especially in the North, were, however, making possible swifter stage service among the principal towns.   By 1773 stagecoaches were running from Boston to Providence and New York, and from New York to Philadelphia. The through stage between New York and Philadelphia, instituted in 1764, presently offered its New York patrons a five-day round-trip rate of twenty shillings, giving them a day in Philadelphia for their business. A postrider on horseback, traveling day and night, could take New York letters to Philadelphia in twenty-four hours, and was expected to make three trips a week. Between New York and Boston there were now two mails a week.[1]

Business suffered also from the want of a uniform, reasonably stable and generally available medium of exchange.   The prime monetary standard was English sterling.   Commercial accounts were kept in pounds, shillings and pence until some years after the Revolution. Little of this money, however, circulated in the colonies, which depended largely on foreign coins—Spanish, Portuguese and French—secured through trade with southern Europe and the West Indies.   Of these the most familiar were the Spanish silver dollars, or "pieces of eight."   There are only rough estimates of the specie —British and foreign—in circulation; but according to one contemporary it amounted in 1775 to between two and three million pounds.   Whatever the total, careful merchants as well as agrarian radicals believed there was

[1] William Smith, *History of the Post Office in British North America* (Cambridge, Eng., 1920), 43-44; Michael Kraus, *Intercolonial Aspects of American Culture on the Eve of the Revolution* (Columbia Univ., Studies, no. 302), chap. i.

not enough for business requirements. In 1766 Charles Carroll of Carrollton attributed the difficulty of getting even small payments from people "in very good circumstances" to "the scarcity of circulating money." The usual remedy for this situation was a recourse to paper currency in varying quantities. Pennsylvania limited its issues sufficiently to prevent serious inflation, while Rhode Island was notorious for excessive issues and consequent depreciation.[1]

The variety and fluctuating values of paper money created serious problems. The Ames almanac for 1762 printed an interesting "Table of the Weight and Value of Coins," including the English guinea of twenty-one shillings along with Spanish and Portuguese coins, indicating the differing rates at which they passed in terms of provincial currencies. In Massachusetts six shillings of "lawful money" would then buy a Spanish dollar, but in New York eight shillings were required. According to a similar table in 1773, the pound sterling was worth in provincial paper approximately twenty-two shillings in Halifax, thirty-three in Philadelphia and thirty-five in New York. At one time during this period the rate of exchange in South Carolina was nearly eight to one. When the New York Chamber of Commerce was organized in 1768, one of its chief problems was the fixing of ratios between New York bills and those of New Jersey and Pennsylvania. The situation was further complicated by counterfeiting. In 1773 the *Virginia Gazette* reported "several very ingenious and therefore the more dangerous Forgeries" of provincial notes.[2] Moderate men tried to prevent inflation by safe-

---

[1] Lord Sheffield, *Observations on the Commerce of the American States* (6th edn., London, 1784), 170-171; Charles Carroll, *Unpublished Letters* (T. M. Field, ed., U. S. Catholic Hist. Soc., *Monograph Ser.*, I), 119.

[2] *Bickerstaff's Boston Almanack for 1773*; D. D. Wallace, *Henry Laurens* (N. Y., 1915), 52-54; New York Chamber of Commerce,

guards in the currency acts or, as in Massachusetts, by appropriating funds to reduce the paper circulation.

Meantime, English merchants, seeking with some support from American conservatives to protect their colonial investments, favored parliamentary action. In 1751 the New England legislatures had been forbidden to issue legal-tender paper; and in 1764, as will be seen, the prohibition was made general. With a limited money supply, business exchanges were carried on in other ways. Virginia used warehouse receipts for inspected tobacco while elsewhere goods and labor were largely paid for in kind. Labor and country produce were credited against merchandise, and produce might be accepted even in payment of taxes. Bills of exchange also served as money in larger transactions.[1]

An important difference between pre-Revolutionary business and that of our own times was in the securing of funds for industrial or commercial purposes. Since the first real American bank was not founded until 1781, business capital in this earlier period had to be obtained in various other ways. According to John Adams, the following groups of people commonly had money to invest: "men of fortune"; merchants whose profits exceeded what they could effectively use in their own businesses; widows and orphans with inherited estates; a moderate-income group, which included clergymen, lawyers, physicians and an occasional small tradesman or farmer; and certain institutions.

Conspicuous among the "men of fortune" were the Maryland Carrolls. In 1774 Charles Carroll, the "Signer," was perhaps the richest man in the colonies; and of his father's estate in 1764 a substantial part

Colonial Records (J. A. Stevens, jr., ed., N. Y., 1867), passim; Va. Gazette (Purdie and Dixon), Feb. 4, 1773.

[1] Edward Channing, A History of the United States (N. Y., 1905-1925), II, 496; Thomas Anburey, Travels through the Interior Parts of America (Boston 1923), II, 205.

was invested in loans at interest. Among the merchants who thus served as bankers for their fellow citizens were the Charlestonians, Henry Laurens and Gabriel Manigault. Among the lawyers William Livingston looked forward to living comfortably after retirement on the interest from his savings. There were a few professional middlemen also. In 1764 a Philadelphia conveyancer and real-estate broker offered to borrow or lend on good security "with the greatest Care, Dispatch and Secrecy." Similar advertisements appeared in Charleston.[1]

A large proportion of colonial capital was provided by British merchants in the form of goods sold on credit. Lord Sheffield estimated that four fifths of all American imports from Europe came in this way. He declared that on the outbreak of the Revolutionary War these long-term credits "made bankrupts of almost all the London merchants, trading to America." The New Yorker, Henry Cruger, who became a Bristol merchant, was distressed by the "vast debts" due from his American correspondents.[2]

As compared with modern practice, eighteenth-century business was highly individualistic. The few colonial corporations were generally organized for educational, religious, charitable or mutual-benefit purposes. An example of the last type was the Philadelphia Contributionship for the Insuring of Houses from Loss by Fire, chartered in 1768. Other corporations formed during this period were marine societies, wharf companies and the New York Chamber of Commerce. There were,

[1] E. C. Burnett, ed., *Letters of Members of the Continental Congress* (Wash., 1921-1936), II, 248; Kate M. Rowland, *Life and Correspondence of Charles Carroll of Carrollton* (N. Y., 1898), I, 60; John Adams, *Works* (C. F. Adams, ed., Boston, 1856), II, 380; Wallace, *Henry Laurens*, 50; Theodore Sedgwick, *A Memoir of the Life of William Livingston* (N. Y., 1833), 156-158; *Pa. Gazette*, Oct. 4, 1770; Aug. 23, 1764; *S.-C. Gazette*, Feb. 21, 1774.

[2] Sheffield, *Observations*, 200-203; *The Commerce of Rhode Island* (Mass. Hist. Soc., *Colls.*, LXIX-LXX), I, 119.

besides, unincorporated companies, organized more or less on a partnership basis.[1]

Thus pre-Revolutionary business was mainly conducted by merchants who acted either independently or with one or more partners. Some partnerships were only temporary, formed perhaps to finance a trading voyage or to insure a ship with its cargo. Among the more permanent ones were those founded by such Massachusetts mercantile families as the Jacksons, Lees, Higginsons and Tracys; Delancey and Watts in New York; Willing and Morris in Philadelphia; and the Browns of Providence. The leading merchants also established connections abroad in such centers as London, Lisbon, Cadiz and Amsterdam and also in the West Indies and in other colonial ports. Such an intercolonial relationship might result in an actual partnership.[2]

A coöperative spirit was gradually developing in the principal ports. Merchants' exchanges existed in some towns, and corporate feeling was further stimulated by the trade and revenue controversies of the 1760's. The Society for Encouraging Trade and Commerce within the Province of Massachusetts Bay has been called Boston's first board of trade. Organized in 1763 to oppose the threatened renewal of the British molasses act, it held annual meetings and had an *ad-interim* committee. John Rowe was its first chairman and John Hancock a prominent member. The New York Chamber of Commerce, founded in 1768 and incorporated in 1770, aimed to promote commerce and industry, settle disputes and provide necessary regulations "for the benefit of trade in general." At its meetings were discussed provincial and municipal regulations affecting commerce,

---

[1] J. S. Davis, *Essays in the Earlier History of American Corporations* (*Harvard Econ. Studies*, XVI), I, 3-107.

[2] Virginia D. Harrington, *The New York Merchant on the Eve of the Revolution* (Columbia Univ., *Studies*, no. 404), chap. ii; Bell, "West India Trade," 275.

and ways and means were proposed to regulate rates of exchange for provincial currencies. Charleston likewise had a Chamber of Commerce before the Revolution.[1]

Though Boston, New York, Philadelphia and Charleston were the chief ports, with Baltimore rising in importance, a significant part of colonial trade stemmed from such minor seaboard towns as Portsmouth, Salem, Providence, New London and New Haven. Nor should the small storekeepers of the North and of the plantation area be forgotten. Examples of the latter are James Madison, father of the Virginia statesman, who bought and sold at his country store, as well as the Scotch merchants already mentioned.[2]

New England business had a special salt-sea flavor since its chief staples came from the fisheries, the forests whose lumber went into shipbuilding, and the distilleries which made rum from West Indian molasses. Shortly before the Revolution, colonial exports of fish and whale oil, chiefly from New England, were valued at about half a million pounds sterling, ranking next to tobacco and breadstuffs. The Northern colonies in general, wrote a British author, "have nearly beaten us out of the Newfoundland fisheries . . . . the share of New England alone exceeds that of Great Britain." In 1763 the single province of Massachusetts was said to employ nearly three thousand men in the fisheries. Of prime importance was the codfishery of the North Atlantic, whose products went to the West Indies, to other colonies and to southern Europe. The mackerel and whale fisheries were also expanding. Nantucket, the chief base of the latter, had about sixty ships so engaged and the

---

[1] C. M. Andrews, "Boston Merchants and the Non-Importation Movement," Colon. Soc. of Mass., *Publs.*, XIX, 161-167; New York Chamber of Commerce, *Colonial Records*, 3-7, 89-97 and *passim;* Leila Sellers, *Charleston Business on the Eve of the American Revolution* (Chapel Hill, 1934), 73.

[2] Photostat account book, Library of Congress, Division of Manuscripts.

total number was said to have nearly doubled between 1763 and 1775. Oil, the most valuable product of this industry, went largely to Great Britain. The fisheries thus constituted a vital part of an intricate mechanism, supplying a profitable form of investment and essential material for oversea trade.[1]

Next in importance was the lumber interest, a main source of New England wealth from the beginning. Sawmills having moved up the rivers and along the coast with the recession of the forest, this industry now flourished largely in New Hampshire and Maine. The mast trade for the royal navy was handled by British contractors working with American associates, including Mark Hunking Wentworth, the brother of one New Hampshire governor and father of another. The lumber business also provided the home market with building material, furniture, fuel, timber for the shipyards and important exports to the West Indies and southern Europe. It was estimated in 1771 that New England shipyards supplied two thirds of the total output in the continental colonies. Many of their ships were sold abroad. In the seventeen-seventies these and other colonial-built vessels made up about one third of the ships in the British registry. The average size reported in 1769 was sixty tons, then considered sufficient for the coasting and West Indian trades. Some vessels, however, had a tonnage of two or three hundred. New England commerce was thus carried mainly in New England bottoms.[2]

The coasting trade formed an essential link in the

[1] Sheffield, *Observations*, tables v, vi, pp. 53-62; anon., *American Husbandry* (London, 1775), II, 241-246; C. M. Andrews, ed., "State of the Trade, 1763," Colon. Soc. of Mass., *Publs.*, XIX, 382-390; W. B. Weeden, *Economic and Social History of New England* (Boston, 1890-1891), II, chap. xix.

[2] R. G. Albion, *Forests and Sea Power* (Harvard Econ. Studies, XXIX), chap. vi, p. 246; David Macpherson, *Annals of Commerce* (London, 1805), III, 570-571; Sheffield, *Observations*, 84.

chain of colonial commerce. Arrivals at Philadelphia, reported in a single issue of the *Pennsylvania Gazette* (March 23, 1763), included eight from New England. From March, 1765, to November, 1766, one Salem sloop made seven voyages between that port and Philadelphia. On the eve of the Revolution nearly half the tonnage entered in New England ports was engaged in the coastwise traffic.[1]

In the economics and politics of New England the West Indian trade was of special importance. It was not a New England monopoly, for New York and Philadelphia played an increasing part in the business; but no other section had so vital an interest in it. Of New England's oversea traffic nearly three fifths in value was with the West Indies. Boston and Newport led, but many smaller places participated. In 1763 a committee of Boston merchants said that three hundred Massachusetts vessels were so engaged, and a year later Governor Stephen Hopkins declared that about half that number sailed from Rhode Island. Fish and lumber provided the chief cargoes along with whale oil and spermaceti candles, livestock and provisions; the latter were partly picked up from other continental colonies. The principal returns were molasses, sugar and a superior grade of spirits.[2]

Though the marine news and customs records might suggest that the Caribbean trade was carried on chiefly with the British West Indies—Jamaica, Barbados and the Leeward Islands—Governor Francis Bernard estimated that, of fifteen thousand hogsheads of molasses brought to Massachusetts, nearly all came from the foreign islands. The Americans claimed, with some official support, that British merchants at home could afford to

[1] Anon., "Early Coastwise and Foreign Shipping of Salem," Essex Institute, *Hist. Colls.*, LXII-LXIII, *passim*.

[2] Macpherson, *Annals*, III, 571; Andrews, "State of the Trade," 385.

be liberal in this respect because the colonial profits reaped from this trade made it possible to pay for British goods. Since New England exports to the West Indies generally exceeded in value the return shipments, bills of exchange on London or Holland helped to redress an unfavorable balance in the transatlantic trade.[1]

What actually happened under the molasses act and its successor, the sugar act of 1764, is shown in mercantile correspondence. In 1766 George Champlin wrote to his Newport brother from St. Eustatius, a Dutch free port much frequented by illegal traders. Sailing with provisions and slaves to a British island, where he found sugar prices were too high, he bargained with a Frenchman to meet him with a cargo near a French island. The rendezvous was kept, though some of the promised sugar had been seized. Champlin considered the prospects at Martinique and Guadeloupe unfavorable, with two hundred North American vessels waiting there for molasses, and proposed to try Danish Santa Cruz. To get his illicit cargo home, he planned to clear in ballast from British Dominica for Rhode Island. Undoubtedly illegal traders profited by official negligence, connivance and corruption.[2]

When the sugar act of 1764 threatened this irregular Caribbean trade, much was said about the use of West Indian molasses in the distilleries of Massachusetts and Rhode Island. The Rhode Islanders, who had more than thirty distilleries, regarded this business as "the main hinge" upon which their trade depended. Rum was not only consumed locally and shipped to other colonies, but it cheered the Newfoundland fishermen, supported Brit-

---

[1] Weeden, *Economic and Social History*, II, 753-755; Francis Bernard, *Letters on the Trade and Government of America* (London, 1774), 7.

[2] *Commerce of Rhode Island*, I, 143-144; A. M. Schlesinger, *The Colonial Merchants and the American Revolution, 1763-1776* (Columbia Univ., *Studies*, LXXVIII), 46.

ish competition with the French in the Indian trade and bought slaves on the African coast, thus helping to balance accounts with British merchants. The Champlins of Newport were deeply involved in the Rhode Island slave trade. In 1772 one of their captains was urged to buy Negroes as rapidly as possible before his competitors, including two from Boston, arrived on the scene.[1]

New England shipping profited by the exclusion of foreign vessels from the colonial trade. Moreover, the rule that "enumerated" articles sent to Europe had to be entered at British ports affected the New Englanders considerably less than the Virginia tobacco planters. How much they lost from having to buy European goods in England it is hard to say. Some Continental manufactures were smuggled in, but the bulk of the transatlantic trade was with the British Isles. Since comparatively few exports went to England, British hardware, drygoods and East Indian tea were paid for mainly through other commerce. In Continental Europe, Yankee skippers dealt chiefly with Spain, Portugal and the Portuguese Madeiras and Azores, carrying their own fish and lumber and also provisions from other Continental colonies. Return cargoes included salt and wines, but a favorable balance was paid partly in specie and partly in credits used for settling accounts with British merchants. Though Boston naturally led in this commerce, other ports shared in it. Salem ships sailed to Lisbon, Cadiz, Bilbao and Leghorn while Newport merchants shipped flour from Philadelphia to Lisbon. Some New England trade, legal or illegal, went on with northern Europe, including Hamburg, the Netherlands and certain French ports. Tea and various European manufactures came

---

[1] J. R. Bartlett, comp., *Records of the Colony of Rhode Island and Providence Plantations in New England* (Providence, 1856-1865), VI, 378-383; *Commerce of Rhode Island*, I, 398-399.

from this area, either directly or through the Dutch West Indies.[1]

The general currents of New England commerce may be illustrated by the activities of a few mercantile establishments. In Boston the business house built up by Thomas Hancock, and inherited by his nephew John, carried on both wholesale and retail business, imported English hardware and drygoods, West Indian sugar and rum and East Indian tea. Whale oil was one of their principal exports. Besides their intercolonial connections, they had correspondents or agencies in London, Bristol, Bilbao, Amsterdam and St. Eustatius. In their transactions with London, bills of exchange were cashed and debts collected for one or the other party. These relations did not always prove to be harmonious. John Hancock criticized his London agents for delays in correspondence and inefficient handling of orders. Like other merchants, the Hancocks were quasi bankers, selling exchange and receiving deposits subject to drafts. When the elder Hancock died, the family fortune was estimated at seventy thousand pounds, including large real-estate holdings.[2]

More representative was John Rowe. Born in England, he went to Boston as a boy and soon built up a large import and export trade, investing also in ships and wharves as well as in real estate in several towns. He was a leader in merchant meetings, an arbitrator in business disputes, a vestryman of Trinity Church and a prominent Mason, in short, a socially minded citizen. Other outstanding New England merchants were the Derbys of Salem, the Wantons and Champlins of Newport and the Browns of Providence. Rhode Island had

[1] Anon., "Early Coastwise and Foreign Shipping of Salem," *passim*; *Commerce of Rhode Island*, I, 463-465, 503; Schlesinger, *Colonial Merchants*, 41.

[2] Edward Edelman, "Thomas Hancock, Colonial Merchant," *Journ. of Econ. and Business History*, I, 87-88.

some Jewish merchants, notably Aaron Lopez of Newport, who traded with the West Indies, with Bristol, England, and with southern Europe. He too was engaged in the slave trade.[1] Besides these conspicuous traders there were small shopkeepers who bought modest stocks from the importers, a relationship not unlike that between the latter and their London correspondents. Thus a resident of Lebanon, Connecticut, asked Lopez for credit in setting up a retail business in European and West Indian goods.[2]

The Middle provinces, like New England, imported more from England than they exported to it, depending on the West Indian and southern European trades to balance the account. But there were important differences. The maritime commerce of the Hudson-Delaware country centered mainly in two ports, New York and Philadelphia, though some Pennsylvania products now went through Baltimore. Moreover, the traffic in fish and lumber was less important for New York and Pennsylvania, which built fewer ships. Fundamentally, the commerce of this region was based on agriculture. In value of exports, breadstuffs stood first, making up two thirds of the total; then came beef and pork. Flaxseed for the linen workers of Ireland was exported and also some iron.[3]

Statistics show that the Middle Atlantic ports had less tonnage than New England, with Philadelphia ahead of New York. They lagged behind New England as a whole in the coastal trade and the value of their West Indian commerce, though Philadelphia had passed Boston. If coasting traffic is left out of account, New York, and especially Philadelphia, made better show-

[1] Rowe, *Letters and Diary, passim;* B. M. Bigelow, "Aaron Lopez, Colonial Merchant of Newport," *New England Quar.,* IV, 757-776.

[2] *Commerce of Rhode Island,* I, 356.

[3] *American Museum,* IV (1788), 279; Robert Proud, *The History of Pennsylvania* (Phila., 1797-1798), II, 269.

ings, with oversea exports now exceeding in value those of New England. The Middle region also had a growing trade with Ireland. A single issue of the *Pennsylvania Gazette* listed vessels bound for Londonderry, Belfast and Dublin; three others offered to take freight and passengers for Londonderry. Irish butter and linen were imported, though a more significant Philadelphia business consisted in the traffic in servants from Ireland. In certain respects Pennsylvania and New York differed from each other. The former nearly equaled all New England in the value of British goods imported; but its exports to the mother country paid for only a fraction of these imports, leaving a balance to be made up by selling breadstuffs to the West Indies and southern Europe. New York, on the other hand, sent nearly half its exports to England, partly because of Caribbean products exported to Britain.[1]

Philadelphia was now the largest colonial city as well as the chief financial center. New York stood second in population and was gaining on Boston as a business community, profiting by war-time conditions and its position as the North American headquarters of the British army. Its commercial leaders were partly "new men" who, according to Colden, had risen "suddenly from the lowest Rank of the People to considerable Fortunes, and chiefly by illicit Trade in the last War."[2] Nevertheless, wealth and material success were closely associated with social prestige, inherited or acquired by marriage. This was true of the Dutch Van Cortlandts, Cuylers and Roosevelts, the French-Huguenot Delanceys, the Scotch Livingstons and Alexanders. Differences of origin had long since been blurred by intermarriage.

[1] Macpherson, *Annals*, III, 571-572; *Pa. Gazette*, Oct. 24, 1765; Harrington, *New York Merchant*, 165.
[2] Cadwallader Colden, *Letter Books* (N. Y. Hist. Soc., *Colls.*, IX-X), II, 68 ff.

A good representative of New York's mercantile aristocracy was John Watts. His correspondence ranged from Virginia, the West Indies and Guiana to London and Amsterdam, and through London agents he invested in British securities. Though he opposed certain forms of illicit trade, he did not favor "rigorous execution" of the sugar act. Of the enemy trade he wrote in 1762, "I never was concerned with this kind of commerce myself but I have both blamed and pitied those who were." As we have seen, he was also active politically. The Crugers, another notable trading family founded in New York about 1700 by an emigrant from Bristol, maintained business relations with English relatives. A grandson, Henry Cruger, who had settled in England to become a leading merchant, served in 1774 with Edmund Burke as parliamentary representative from Bristol. John Cruger, first president of the New York Chamber of Commerce, was for several years mayor of New York.[1]

Conspicuous among Philadelphia's older mercantile families were the Pembertons and Whartons. Israel Pemberton, one of the richest Americans of his day, was a loyal and active member of the Society of Friends, and in politics upheld the conservative point of view typical of his class. His chief philanthropic interests included the Pennsylvania Hospital. Thomas Wharton, of the firm of Stocker and Wharton, had business correspondents in London, Dublin and Lisbon, and was associated in transatlantic commerce with the Newport Champlins. Samuel Wharton, who belonged to the important house of Baynton, Wharton and Morgan, was

---

[1] John Watts, *Letter Book* (N. Y. Hist. Soc., *Colls.*, LXI), introduction and *passim*; Harrington, *New York Merchant*, 261, 267, 319 and *passim*; A. E. Peterson, "Henry Cruger," and C. W. Spencer, "John Cruger," Allen Johnson and Dumas Malone, eds., *Dictionary of American Biography* (N. Y., 1928-1937), IV, 581-582; J. A. Stevens, jr., *Colonial New York, Sketches Biographical and Historical* (N. Y., 1867), 5.

concerned in army contracts, Indian trade and Western lands. Connected with Franklin and other influential persons, British and colonial, in the Vandalia project, Samuel Wharton is an excellent example of the interrelation of business and politics. Among Philadelphia's newcomers the most notable was Robert Morris. Born in Liverpool, he became, while still in his early thirties, a leader in the local opposition to the stamp act. A vigorous member of the firm of Willing and Morris—shipowners, importers and exporters, and dealers in exchange—no one was more expert in the mysteries of commerce and speculative finance.[1]

Though the merchants held no such place in Southern society as their Northern contemporaries, they cannot be ignored. Besides the traders in the Chesapeake country, who dealt in European goods and exported tobacco on their own account or as agents of English or Scotch firms, there were cohesive business groups in Charleston, a long-established mercantile community, and in the newly developed port of Baltimore. According to Josiah Quincy, who visited Charleston in 1773, its shipping "far surpassed" that of Boston. In 1769 the total inward and outward tonnage of South Carolina, most of which went through Charleston, exceeded that of New York. It was outranked only by the much larger provinces of Massachusetts, Virginia and Pennsylvania.[2]

While Charleston's relations with the British merchants were close, with many residents serving as agents for British firms and the bulk of its staple exports going to the homeland, its trade connections were more varied

---

[1] Elizabeth M. Bacon, "Israel Pemberton," Johnson and Malone, *Dictionary of American Biography*, XIV, 412-413; W. E. Stevens, "Samuel Wharton," and J. H. Peeling, "Thomas Wharton," *ibid.*, XX, 32-34; C. W. Alvord, *The Mississippi Valley in British Politics* (Cleveland, 1917), II, 95-97.

[2] Josiah Quincy, "Journal," Mass. Hist. Soc., *Proceeds.*, XLIX, 441; Macpherson, *Annals*, III, 570-571.

than those of the Chesapeake provinces. Charleston's export business was chiefly in rice and indigo, though it included peltry, lumber, naval stores and provisions. In 1767-1768 its rice went to more than forty different ports—in Britain, Portugal, Spain, the West Indies and the continental colonies. From outside came the usual European and West Indian goods. The wealthy Charlestonians were better able than most colonials to buy Old World luxuries. Conspicuous also among the imports was human labor. While some white servants were brought in, the slave trade was far more important. Rough estimates indicate that over seven thousand Negroes were imported in 1765 and a much larger number in 1773. Though most of this traffic was in the hands of British and New England merchants, some Charlestonians were involved.[1]

Of the leading Charleston merchants, several came of French-Huguenot stock. Three of the most conspicuous were Isaac Mazyck, Henry Laurens and Gabriel Manigault. They had all inherited wealth, were planters as well as merchants and were politically influential. Mazyck sat thirty-seven years in the provincial assembly. Laurens had trade connections in Boston, New York, Philadelphia, Savannah, St. Augustine and the West Indies as well as in Europe. He was also a shipowner, money lender and dealer in exchange, and he acquired an intercolonial reputation in politics. Manigault carried on a large wholesale and retail business in slaves, liquors, sugar and other merchandise. Like Laurens, he also owned ships and was an "inveterate moneylender," investing in notes, bonds and mortgages.[2]

[1] Elizabeth Donnan, "The Slave Trade into South Carolina before the Revolution," *Am. Hist. Rev.*, XXXIII, 804 ff.; Sellers, *Charleston Business*, chap. vii; Edward McCrady, *History of South Carolina under the Royal Government, 1719-1776* (N. Y., 1899), 393-394.

[2] A. H. Hirsch, *The Huguenots of Colonial South Carolina* (Durham, 1928), 232-234; Wallace, *Henry Laurens, passim;* McCrady, *South Carolina under Royal Government*, 400-406.

Notwithstanding local variations provincial merchants faced many common problems. Among these were the difficulties of effecting the transition from war to peace. The highly hazardous business of privateering ended with the peace treaty of 1763, though privateering ships and seamen could now resume prewar activities, notably in the deep-sea fisheries, which the British conquest of Canada rendered more secure than ever before. Transatlantic traders, however, were still menaced in Atlantic and Mediterranean waters by the Barbary pirates, who could blackmail even the stronger maritime nations. To avoid this danger American vessels had to have British "Mediterranean passes." In 1764 Governor Francis Fauquier of Virginia reported that a shortage of these passes was causing "great distress." [1] Another business which fell off after the peace was that of army and navy contracts. New York, as headquarters of the commander in chief, enjoyed special advantages in this trade, though Boston and Philadelphia also shared in it. But army contracting did not altogether cease, for "Pontiac's Conspiracy" and the Western campaigns which followed kept the business alive: frontier ports had to be supplied along with presents to conciliate the Indians. Nevertheless, this business as a whole had to be adjusted to a lessened demand.

The provincial merchant, moreover, must reconsider the effect of imperial policies on his normal peace-time business. Though the essential principles of the old colonial system remained, he was now disturbed not only by additions to the list of "enumerated" articles and by certain other changes in detail, but also by a more vigorous enforcement, especially affecting West Indian commerce. Such problems were presently complicated by British efforts to secure an American revenue. From the

[1] G. L. Beer, *British Colonial Policy, 1754-1765* (N. Y., 1907), 7 n.; *Commerce of Rhode Island*, I, 453.

standpoint of the home government the need for re-
forming the administration of the acts of trade was evident.   The illicit commerce of Northern merchants with
the foreign West Indies during the war had not only interfered with the effective conduct of the war; it had also
brought into clearer light the general weakness of the
customs administration and the almost complete nulli-
fication of one statute, the molasses act of 1733, with its
prohibitive duties on sugar and molasses from the foreign
West Indies.[1]

Reputable merchants might disapprove of trading
with the enemy, but they felt differently about peace-
time interference with their West Indian commerce.
Mercantile opinion was practically unanimous in condemning the molasses act, which was to expire in 1764.
Nevertheless, despite vigorous protests from the merchants, the British government decided to renew the act
and execute it more strictly, though Parliament reduced
the unenforceable duty of sixpence a gallon to three-
pence.   Moreover, new revenue duties were added on
Portuguese wines, vice-admiralty jurisdiction in revenue
cases was strengthened, and there were other enforcement
measures.   The dissatisfaction in the colonies was inten-
sified by the currency act of 1764 and the stamp act of
the next year.   The currency act, making general the
prohibition of colonial legal-tender issues, was regarded
even by conservative merchants as particularly unwise
when restrictions on the West Indian trade tended to
reduce the supply of hard money.   The stamp act was
deemed objectionable not only because of the principle
involved, but because the tax on commercial paper was
really burdensome.   So the merchants were active in
opposing all these measures and in 1766 won substantial

[1] See J. T. Adams, *Provincial Society, 1690-1763* (*A History of
American Life*, III), 230-231, 316.

concessions, including the repeal of the stamp duties and a reduction of the molasses tax.

Nevertheless, the merchants were increasingly troubled by severer administrative regulations and closer checks on the enforcement activities of governors and customs officers. This sterner surveillance had made itself felt as early as 1763. In that year a Philadelphian noted the discouraging effect of warships in the harbor, with their officers "so very strict that the smallest things don't escape their notice."[1] In 1767 the Townshend acts still further strengthened the enforcement program, giving an American board of commissioners powers similar to those of the customs commissioners in England and enlarging the jurisdiction of colonial admiralty courts. Whatever may be said about the causes, the people in the 1760's suffered from a serious business depression marked by scarcity of cash, the slackening of trade, a mounting burden of indebtedness and the bankruptcy of important mercantile concerns.

In contrast with this general business slump one form of speculation actually profited from the successful conclusion of the intercolonial wars. Real-estate promotion had long been conspicuous in provincial life and the source of many an American fortune. One contemporary, referring particularly to Pennsylvania, noted as a familiar fact that "Every great fortune" made there during the past fifty years had "been by land." The distinguished lawyer, Andrew Hamilton, was a large owner of real estate in Lancaster, from which his heirs drew rent for many years. Charles Carroll in the neighboring province of Maryland owned twenty lots in Annapolis; and Washington, one of the founders of Alexandria, bought tickets in a lottery for this enterprise that yielded seven prizes aggregating nearly six hundred

---

[1] Quoted from Schlesinger, *Colonial Merchants*, 49. See also *ibid.*, 56-59.

acres.   Real-estate brokerage was a recognized form of business.   The intercolonial scope of land speculation may be illustrated by an advertisement in the *Pennsylvania Gazette*, August 23, 1764, of properties in New Jersey, Maryland and Virginia.[1]

Especially striking was the speculation in "wild lands" on both sides of the Alleghanies.   Vermont tracts were taken up under grants from New Hampshire, Massachusetts and New York.   One of the New Yorkers concerned was James Duane, who became an aggressive defender of New York's prior title.   Governor Cadwallader Colden reported that New Hampshire lands were advertised even in New York City, with the special inducement of freedom from New York quitrents.   Another case of land speculation involving politically prominent people was that of the Connecticut Susquehanna Company's colony in northern Pennsylvania, which led to a clash between the two governments and also disturbed the internal politics of Connecticut.[2]

Schemes for exploiting the trans-Alleghany country were numerous.   The Virginians, on the basis of their royal charter, planned to develop the Ohio Valley and the Northwest as a part of the Old Dominion.   Grants for military service were provided for in this region, though much of this land scrip was bought up by speculators.   Among the organized private groups were the Ohio Company, to which Mason and Washington belonged, and the Loyal Company, both dating from be-

---

[1] Alexander Mackraby (1768) in *Pa. Mag. of History and Biog.*, XI, 277; Rowland, *Carroll*, I, 60; George Washington, *Diaries, 1748-1799* (J. C. Fitzpatrick, ed., Boston, 1925), I, 298; J. D. Schoepf, *Travels in the Confederation, 1783-1784* (A. J. Morrison, ed., Phila., 1911), II, 10-11.

[2] E. P. Alexander, *A Revolutionary Conservative, James Duane* (D. R. Fox, ed., *N. Y. State Hist. Assoc. Ser.*, VI), chap. v; Colden, *Letter Books*, I, 236-237; L. H. Gipson, *Jared Ingersoll* (*Yale Hist. Publs. Miscellany*, VIII), chap. xi.

fore the last French war.[1] Patrick Henry was also a
speculator in this field. In conflict with the Virginia
promoters were Northern merchants and politicians,
especially the Pennsylvanians who, having no sea-to-sea
charter, were projecting new colonies. The most important scheme politically was the Grand Ohio Company, formed in 1769 to establish the Vandalia colony
in the upper Ohio Valley. Among prominent British
and American personages involved were Benjamin
Franklin, Joseph Galloway, Sir William Johnson and
Samuel Wharton. For a time the proposed new colony
seemed likely to secure royal approval; but in the end
its promoters were disappointed. An earlier and also
abortive project was that of Phineas Lyman, a general
in the French war who in 1763 organized at Hartford
a company of "Military Adventurers" to plant colonies
in the Southwest.[2]

Notwithstanding the difficulties created by the return
of peace and the unsympathetic attitude of the home
government, urban business life, in most respects, soon
resumed its normal course. An important interest in
all the leading ports was the construction and regulation
of docks. Much of the New York water front was
privately appropriated, but the city also had municipal
docks. Boston's Long Wharf belonged to an incorporated company, while others, like Rowe's Wharf,
were conducted by individuals. In Charleston the radical politician, Christopher Gadsden, was a wharf owner.
Near the docks stood the warehouses of importers and
exporters. In New York the principal merchandising
was well below Wall Street. At the present corner of
Broad and Pearl streets was Fraunces Tavern, a favorite
merchant resort; near by were the Merchants Exchange

---

[1] See Adams, *Provincial Society*, 299-300.
[2] Alvord, *Mississippi Valley in British Politics*, II (index under "Grand
Ohio Company" and "Military Adventurers").

and the customhouse. No sharp line separated wholesale and retail traders, for most business was not highly specialized. A New York firm on Cruger's Wharf sold Irish beef, Scotch bonnets and tartans, cutlery and "choice old claret." One Philadelphia concern offered drygoods, wine, tea, china, cutlery, gunpowder and stationery. The merchants had their "white-collar" workers, who, like Robert Morris, sometimes rose from clerkships to partnerships. Besides these larger dealers, there were small traders and shopkeepers, commonly allied politically with the mechanics.[1]

The public market was a conspicuous feature of urban life. New York had, among others, its Fly Market for fish, the Oswego Market for country produce, and the Bear Market, near St. Paul's Chapel. At these establishments, duly regulated by the city council, housewives bought their morning supplies, while retailers and hucksters were not expected to buy before noon. In Boston, Faneuil Hall Market, burned in 1761 and rebuilt in 1764, was a political as well as trading center. A Scotch visitor to Philadelphia in 1765 was much impressed by the "vast concourse of people" on market days.[2]

Capital investment in manufacturing was comparatively small. It was usually associated with farms or plantations, where wool and flax were worked into clothing, hides prepared for shoes and saddles, and native woods made into houses or furniture. Such products were generally for home use rather than commercial exchange. Even a large-scale Narragansett sheep raiser used his wool mainly to clothe his own household.

[1] A. E. Peterson and G. W. Edwards, *New York as an Eighteenth Century Municipality* (N. Y., 1917), 349-361; Davis, *History of American Corporations*, I, 88; *S.-C. Gazette*, Nov. 30, 1767; *N.-Y. Mercury*, Feb. 16, 1761; *Pa. Gazette*, Jan. 6, 1763.

[2] Peterson and Edwards, *New York as an Eighteenth Century Municipality*, 71-82; Justin Winsor, ed., *Memorial History of Boston, 1630-1880* (Boston, 1880-1881), II, 263-267; William Gregory, "Journal," *William and Mary College Quar.*, XIII, 228.

Some home workers, however, did dispose of surplus goods, as when New Hampshire farmers sold linen in Boston.[1]

As communities grew, home industries were supplemented by more specialized workers, such as the weaver, the neighborhood fuller, and the cobbler who visited the farms or worked in his own shop. Martin Reed, a Rhode Island weaver, was successively apprentice, an independent worker with a single loom and, finally, a cloth maker for the principal near-by families. In the bigger towns a master weaver might have several apprentices or servants. Conspicuous among the textile workers who produced for more than a local market were those of Pennsylvania.[2] The more prosperous planters and farmers employed special builders, cabinetmakers and tailors. There were neighborhood gristmills and sawmills also, and, though these crafts were not new, their specialized output was increasing.

In New England the boot and shoe industry was making substantial gains, with Lynn already the principal center. Its entrepreneurs and their wage-earning employees supplied both wholesale and retail demands. In 1768 they manufactured eighty thousand pairs of shoes. Six thousand pairs are said to have been exported from the North American colonies, mostly from eastern Massachusetts to the West Indies, though about a quarter of the total came from the Philadelphia neighborhood.[3]

In a few industries production for distant markets was important. In addition to playing a significant rôle in local shipbuilding, New England sawmills supplied

[1] Hazard, *Thomas Hazard*, xii, 9, 16-19.
[2] W. B. Weeden, *Early Rhode Island* (F. H. Hitchcock, ed., *The Grafton Historical Series;* N. Y., 1910), 283; Caroline Hazard, *Thomas Hazard* (Boston, 1893), 98-101; A. H. Cole, *The American Wool Manufacture* (Cambridge, 1926), I, 5-7.
[3] Blanche E. Hazard, *The Organization of the Boot and Shoe Industry in Massachusetts before 1875* (*Harvard Econ. Studies*, XXIII), chaps. i-ii.

boards, staves and shingles for intercolonial and oversea markets. Especially interesting was the development of flour mills in the Middle and Chesapeake colonies. Many of these "merchant mills" were to be found in the lower Delaware Valley and near the head of Chesapeake Bay. Their mechanical equipment was comparatively well advanced and improving. According to a competent authority, they were "probably the finest at that time in the world." Flour was shipped through various ports, including Philadelphia, Baltimore, Alexandria and New York. By 1770 bread and flour accounted for about a seventh of the value of all American exports to Europe and the West Indies.[1]

As has been seen, distilling flourished, especially in Massachusetts and Rhode Island, and increasingly so elsewhere. In 1771 Philadelphia exported some two hundred thousand gallons of rum. Two years later, according to the historian Proud, the total rose to two hundred and seventy-eight thousand. New York and Baltimore also had considerable distilleries.[2]

Iron manufacturing had developed sufficiently to disturb British industrialists.[3] A parliamentary statute of 1750 had tried to encourage the importation of American pig and bar iron; and in 1764 both were admitted to British ports tax-free. As an "enumerated" article, iron must be sent to British ports, while the British manufacturers, receiving raw materials free of duty, were protected against colonial competition by a prohibition of the erection of new American slitting mills, plating works or steel furnaces. Apparently, however, this legislation did not prove very effective. The Americans

[1] V. S. Clark, *History of Manufactures in the United States* (Carnegie Inst., *Contribs. to Am. Econ. History*; rev. edn., N. Y., 1929), I, 175-181; Macpherson, *Annals*, III, 572-573.

[2] Proud, *History of Pennsylvania*, II, 271; Macpherson, *Annals*, III, 572-573.

[3] See Adams, *Provincial Society*, 38-39, 233-234.

contributed only a small fraction of the bar iron imported for the British market, and governmental restrictions did not seriously check colonial iron manufactures. By 1775 the thirteen colonies possessed more forges and furnaces than England and Wales, with a greater output of pig and bar iron. Comparatively little was shipped oversea, being used instead in the colonies, much of it in the forms prohibited by law. Provincial governors appeared to overlook violations of the statute. Not only were new slitting mills and steel furnaces set up, but their products were publicly advertised. In 1770 the Pennsylvania assembly went so far as to make a grant "for encouragement in making steel." From New England to Virginia, provincial forges and furnaces supplied the people with kettles, pots and pans, cartwheels, axes, hoes and plowshares. According to Lord Sheffield, American axes acquired "a great character," causing British manufacturers to sell their own product as of New England make. Firearms formed an important branch of the industry. Among the numerous gunsmiths the outstanding figure was William Henry of Lancaster, a "principal armorer" in the French and Indian War. He maintained a kind of laboratory and devised labor-saving machinery.[1]

The Pennsylvania and New Jersey ironmasters included two later signers of the Declaration of Independence. Other politicians interested in the industry were Governor Stephen Hopkins of Rhode Island and Charles Carroll of Carrollton (two more signers) and Daniel Dulany of Maryland. In Pennsylvania some of the prominent manufacturers were German, among them the picturesque "Baron von Stiegel," the owner of works in Lancaster County, whose meteoric career ended in bankruptcy.

[1] A. C. Bining, *British Regulation of the Colonial Iron Industry* (Phila., 1933), *passim*; Sheffield, *Observations*, 14.

Another important figure, Peter Hasenclever, was a German-born British subject whose business was backed by British capital. Profiting by experience in his native country, he became the manager of the American Company for establishing manufactures in New York and New Jersey. He arrived in New York in 1764 during the postwar depression with the two hundred German workers, of whom an enthusiastic contemporary said, "There never was brought a finer or more valuable Set of people to America." Unfortunately the company soon became financially embarrassed and Hasenclever was forced into bankruptcy. Nevertheless, establishments built under his direction did excellent work and probably helped to improve the colonial technique. Two of Hasenclever's successors in the American Company were the German, J. J. Faesch, and the Scot, Robert Erskine, both capable experts who were later employed in the Continental army.[1]

Among the larger "iron plantations" was the Andover Furnace in northern New Jersey. Besides the furnace, the establishment in 1770 included an "elegant Stone Dwelling-house," a "Coal-house" for charcoal, a smithy, a sawmill, workmen's houses, water power close at hand and five thousand acres of timber for fuel, with an "inexhaustible body of ore" near by. The "iron plantation" was often a quasifeudal community, where the owner had his "big house," and the estate might include a store or even a church and a school. Both free and servile labor was used. A Maryland company was said to employ a hundred and fifty slaves, and a New Jersey

[1] A. C. Bining, *Pennsylvania Iron Manufacture in the Eighteenth Century* (Pa. Hist. Comn., *Publs.*, IV), 43, 56, 109-110, 141-142; Samuel McKee, *Labor in Colonial New York, 1664-1776* (Columbia Univ., Studies, no. 410), 54-60; I. N. P. Stokes, *Iconography of Manhattan Island* (N. Y., 1915-1928), IV, 744, quoting Weyman's *N.-Y. Gazette*, Oct. 8, 1764.

advertisement contains a reference to six Negroes as ironworkers.[1]

Less important commercially were certain other industries. Some colonial potash was exported. The New Englander, Samuel Blodget, owned several potash works, sending much of his output to a London agent. Brickmaking received considerable attention, but though bricks were sometimes shipped to the West Indies, they did not figure greatly in commerce. The first large-scale glassmaking was instituted by the Pennsylvania ironmaster Stiegel about 1768. Before his enterprise broke down, it produced some fine ware which still interests connoisseurs. In 1771 another factory in the neighborhood of Philadelphia conducted a town establishment called the American Glass Warehouse. There was also some activity in pottery. In 1767 certain Pennsylvania products were advertised as possessing "beauty of colours and elegance of figure" superior to any imported from England. Paper making centered about Philadelphia, where Franklin was interested in several mills. The best-known New England venture was at Milton near Boston.[2]

Occasional approaches to the factory system were to be found. Some workers were assembled in the "Manufactory House" in Boston and in the linen factory of the New York Society of Arts. Such projects, inspired by educational or philanthropic motives, gained popular support from the current political controversies which emphasized the need of economic independence. But

[1] C. S. Boyer, *Early Forges and Furnaces in New Jersey* (Phila., 1931), 26-33; Kathleen Bruce, *The Virginia Iron Manufacture in the Slave Era* (N. Y., 1931), 12-16; Rowland, *Carroll,* I, 60.

[2] Clark, *History of Manufactures,* I, 98, 116, 165-169; H. E. Gillingham, "The Cost of Old Silver," *Pa. Mag. of History and Biog.,* LIV, 32-51; Sam Briggs, *The Essays, Humor and Poems of Nathaniel Ames, Father and Son, . . . from Their Almanacks* (Cleveland, 1891), 373, 409.

as business enterprises they possessed only a passing importance.[1]

As to the outlook for American manufactures opinions varied. William Eddis, a minor British official, expected no substantial development in the near future. He believed the textile industry would be handicapped by the inferior quality of American wool. Moreover, with free land diverting "ingenious artisans from their crafts" and making wages high, Americans could more profitably import "almost every article of use or ornament" than make it themselves. At some distant time the colonies might rival Britain in certain products, but in woolen manufactures, "the grand staple," Britain would remain "*single* and *pre-eminent*." Hasenclever was one of those who distrusted patriotic promoters, "economists and manufacturers in theory, but little in practice." Even the patriotic Ames almanac for 1774 suggested that agriculture and "other rich resources of America" would prove more profitable than manufacturing, which might well be left to "Britains and Hybernians."[2]

Others were more optimistic. Though as a colonial agent Franklin tried to quiet English fears of American competition, he took a different line during his examination in the House of Commons in 1766, when he declared that he knew of no article then imported which Americans could not "either do without or make for themselves." The Scotch traveler, Lord Adam Gordon, observing in 1765 the general wearing of homespun, regarded it as the natural consequence of disturbing the West Indian trade by which Americans got specie to pay for British manufactures. A British merchant long resi-

---

[1] Clark, *History of Manufactures*, I, 188-193.
[2] William Eddis, *Letters from America* (London, 1792), I, 139-145; Clark, *History of Manufactures*, I, 211, 217; Briggs, *Ames . . . Almanacks*, 447-448.

dent in Virginia reported "no grand manufactury," but added, "all the people do manufacture." He, too, believed they could easily get on without British wares.[1]

Industrial progress obviously required an adequate supply of skilled and inventive workers, imported or native. Examples of the former were Hasenclever's German ironworkers, Stiegel's glassmakers, and the Welsh craftsman who is credited with introducing improvements into the Lynn shops. That the British legislation against the emigration of skilled workers was not always effective may be judged from the fact that in January, 1772, the *Pennsylvania Gazette* announced the expected coming of "a master in several large manufactures for linen, cotton, and calico printing," bringing six journeymen. Suitable machines had been shipped secretly. A few months later John Hewson arrived, and in 1774 he opened calico-print works near Philadelphia, promising goods equal to those imported. At Norwich, Connecticut, in 1773, Thomas Harland, a "London craftsman," was ready to make watches and clocks of all kinds, and presently built up an extensive business.[2]

A few Americans were already interested in steam-driven machinery. The Pennsylvania gunsmith, William Henry, who had known Watt in England, experimented with a steamboat. Oliver Evans, of Delaware, was interested in steam power as early as 1772. Applying his inventive talent first toward improving machinery for woolen and flour mills, he became afterwards the outstanding steam-engine builder of his time. Another capable mechanic was the metal worker, John Fitch, who

[1] [Lord Adam Gordon], "Journal of an Officer's Travels in America and the West Indies, 1764-1765," N. D. Mereness, ed., *Travels in the American Colonies* (N. Y., 1916), 412.

[2] Hazard, *Boot and Shoe Industry*, chap. ii; H. E. Gillingham, "Calico and Linen Printing in Philadelphia," *Pa. Mag. of History and Biog.*, LII, 97-110.

later managed a gun factory during the Revolutionary War, but was subsequently better known as a pioneer in developing the steamboat. Though the actual achievements of such men during this period were not remarkable, they illustrate the mechanical ingenuity which helped to win independence and made possible future industrial progress.

CHAPTER IV

SOCIAL RELATIONS

STATISTICS of population of the thirteen colonies are only approximations. In 1763 they had perhaps two million people; twelve years later the total probably stood between two and a half and three million. The number south of the Mason and Dixon line was about equal to that north of it. Virginia still ranked first; next in order came Massachusetts (including Maine), Pennsylvania, North Carolina and Maryland. New York, the future "Empire State," and Connecticut competed for sixth place. There were roughly half a million Negroes in the colonies in 1775, perhaps a fifth of the whole population. Probably not more than one out of seven lived north of the Mason and Dixon line.[1]

In the decade or so before the war began some important shifts of population took place. Between 1765 and 1775 the interior counties of Massachusetts grew three times as fast as those on the seaboard. Settlement advanced along the Merrimac and thousands of persons followed the Connecticut Valley up into New Hampshire and Vermont. In New York the principal gains occurred in the upper Hudson Valley and in New York City. In Pennsylvania, Philadelphia was growing steadily, but the most striking movement of people was northward in the Delaware Valley and westward along the Maryland boundary. Farther south, Maryland population was increasing chiefly about the new urban center of Baltimore and in the frontier county of Fred-

[1] Population estimates are based chiefly on E. B. Greene and Virginia D. Harrington, comps., *American Population before the Federal Census of 1790* (N. Y., 1932).

erick. Similar changes were occurring in the Virginia piedmont, the Shenandoah Valley and the Carolina backcountry.

The cities were small by modern standards. Boston remained nearly stationary during these years. Next door, in Rhode Island, Newport and Providence contained hardly a quarter of the whole population. New York City grew faster than the province as a whole; between 1756 and 1771 the population of New York County rose from thirteen thousand to nearly twenty-two. Otherwise the province was almost wholly rural, as were also New Jersey and Delaware. In 1775 some thirty thousand Pennsylvanians, or about one in every ten, lived in Philadelphia; next came the inland town of Lancaster. Baltimore and Charleston were the largest urban communities in the South, with approximately six and twelve thousand respectively in 1775. Though Charleston was gaining, the South Carolina backcountry was increasing much faster. Of the other Southern capitals neither Annapolis nor Williamsburg numbered more than a few hundred permanent residents.

A major factor in the rapid growth of colonial population was the custom of early marriages and the resulting high birth rate. Families of from six to ten children were usual, while larger ones were not uncommon. Two Virginia Carters possessed respectively seventeen and twenty-three. Among Revolutionary leaders Charles Carroll had seven; Henry Laurens, twelve or more; and William Livingston, thirteen. Chief Justice John Marshall, born in 1755, was the eldest of fifteen children. The high birth rate was to some extent offset by the appalling mortality among infants and young people generally. Of Carroll's seven offspring four died in childhood; of Livingston's thirteen only seven survived him; and of Laurens's children only four reached maturity. Unhealthy climatic conditions in South

Carolina and Georgia made for exceptionally high death rates, but eighteenth-century mortality tables indicate that even in Hingham, Massachusetts, more than a third of the youngsters died before the age of five.[1]

Immigration, interrupted by the war, began again, not only from England and Scotland but also from Ireland and Germany. Official lists show, for instance, that in a single week in December, 1773, a hundred and seventeen persons, all servants, left London for the colonies, mainly bound for Virginia. During one fortnight in January, 1774, two hundred and sixty-four persons sailed from London for Maryland, Pennsylvania or the Carolinas; and the movement continued during the early months of 1775. Though most of these migrants came from English homes, some set forth from Scotland or Ireland.[2] The Scots were largely from the Highlands and the northern islands, but the Lowlands also sent a substantial number. Among their reasons for moving were "racking rents," "arbitrary and oppressive services," failing crops and the inclosure of commons. The bulk of them landed in New York, Philadelphia, North Carolina and Virginia. Available lists for 1774 and 1775 show more than a thousand persons departing for New York from Scotland alone, while others embarked at English ports. Though most of the Scots were poor they included a few men of means. In 1771 about five

[1] Benjamin Franklin, *Writings* (Albert Smyth, ed., N. Y., 1907), III, 63 ff.; [Lord Adam Gordon], "Journal of an Officer's Travels in America and the West Indies, 1764-1765," N. D. Mereness, ed., *Travels in the American Colonies* (N. Y., 1916), 406; D. D. Wallace, *Henry Laurens* (N. Y., 1915), chap. v; U. B. Phillips, *Life and Labor in the Old South* (Boston, 1929), 224, 228; Kate M. Rowland, *Life and Correspondence of Charles Carroll of Carrollton* (N. Y., 1898), II, 54; Theodore Sedgwick, *A Memoir of the Life of William Livingston* (N. Y., 1833), 446; Edward Wigglesworth, "Observations on the Longevity of the Inhabitants of Ipswich and Hingham," Am. Acad. of Arts and Sci., *Memoirs*, I (1785), 565.

[2] Emigration lists, Public Record Office, T. 47/9, 10, 11 (transcripts in American Antiquarian Society); M. L. Hansen, *The Atlantic Migration, 1607-1860* (A. M. Schlesinger, ed., Cambridge, 1940), 52.

hundred persons sailed with a "gentleman of wealth and merit" of an old family in their neighborhood.[1]

The Irish influx seems to have reached a high point during this period. According to one contemporary estimate, more than forty thousand persons sailed from five northern ports between 1769 and 1774. Departures from southern Ireland were also considerable. Agrarian troubles and the depression in the linen industry stimulated emigration, while religious discrimination against Catholics and dissenters supplied additional motives. In 1765 the *Pennsylvania Journal* advertised the arrival of servants from Dublin and County Connaught, and in 1773 Daniel Carroll of Maryland settled immigrants from Galway on his land, suggesting that Washington do the same. He thought Irish Catholics might be attracted by providing a glebe for their priests.[2]

According to the most scientific analysis so far made of the eighteenth-century American population, about three fifths of the whites enumerated in the federal census of 1790 were of English stock, a ratio probably not very different from that of 1775. Most definitely English in origin were the inhabitants of New England and the Chesapeake tidewater. Of the remaining two fifths about half may be credited to other parts of the British Isles: Wales, Scotland and Ireland. These included some Gaelic-speaking people, but most of them used English with dialectal variations not much greater than in different English counties. In both Scotland and Ireland

---

[1] [Janet Schaw], *Journal of a Lady of Quality, 1774 to 1776* (Evangeline W. and C. M. Andrews, eds., New Haven, 1921), app. i; S. C. Johnson, *A History of Emigration from the United Kingdom to North America, 1763-1912* (London School of Econs. and Polit. Sci., *Monograph Ser.*, no. 34), 2 ff.; emigration lists, Public Record Office, T. 47/12.

[2] Johnson, *Emigration from the United Kingdom*, 1-2; *Pa. Journal*, Jan. 3, Aug. 8, 1764; David Macpherson, *Annals of Commerce* (London, 1805), III, 528; S. M. Hamilton, ed., *Letters to Washington* (N. Y., 1898), IV, 256-257.

there had been a mingling of Celtic, Anglo-Saxon and Scandinavian strains, the Celtic element being strongest in the Scotch Highlands and in the south and west of Ireland. Of the Irish immigrants to America, a majority had come from the north, which had been largely colonized from Scotland in the seventeenth century, and somewhat more than a third from the more Celtic south and west. There was also a religious differentiation between these two groups, the former being preponderantly Protestant, the latter mainly Catholic.[1]

Of the Continental Europeans, the Germans were by far the most numerous, including probably between eight and ten per cent of the colonial whites. In Pennsylvania, however, they numbered about a third of the total population. They were also strong in the Middle region generally and in the Southern backcountry. New England had very few. More than any other foreign group, the Germans preserved their native language and culture, whether in separate communities or through separate churches in the larger towns.

Unlike the Germans, the early Dutch, Swedish and French settlers had not been substantially reënforced by later comers and hence formed a steadily diminishing proportion of the inhabitants, often scarcely distinguishable from their English neighbors. Though Swedish was still used in a few churches on the Delaware, it was gradually disappearing. The Dutch element, largely concentrated in New York and New Jersey, maintained their identity more successfully and the language continued to be used in a few communities until long after the Revolution. Some Dutch Reformed churches had to provide English services for their young people in order to avoid dwindling congregations. Intermarriage

[1] Committee on Linguistic and National Stocks in the Population of the United States, "Report," Am. Hist. Assoc., *Ann. Rep. for 1931*, I, 107-125, and "Annexes"; J. T. Adams, *Provincial Society, 1690-1763* (*A History of American Life*, III), 171-173.

played a large part in hastening assimilation.   Dutch blood flowed in the veins of Morrises and Livingstons, while Schuylers and Van Cortlandts had British as well as Dutch ancestors.   In the case of the French the melting-pot process was almost complete.   Though a few congregations, as in Charleston and New York, conducted French services, they were quite exceptional. Such names as those of Bowdoin, Revere, Jay and Laurens indicate a Gallic origin, but none of these men belonged to a sharply differentiated national group.[1]

The influence of the non-English stocks, especially in politics, was hardly in proportion to their numbers, partly because the social patterns had been largely fixed by earlier English settlers, partly because of the poverty of many of the newcomers, and partly also because they were less numerous on the seaboard, where political control was principally centered.   Though social discontent among the less fortunate immigrants contributed to the break with Britain, most of the Revolutionary leaders, with their more articulate followers, thought of themselves as transplanted Englishmen demanding English liberties.   After the Revolution, however, the immigrant stocks tended to become more influential.   It is suggestive that the first speaker of the United States House of Representatives was the son of an immigrant German pastor.

Social conventions in the colonies were the product of the interplay of Old World traditions and American conditions.   Thus marriage, in England as in Catholic Europe, was regarded as peculiarly within the jurisdiction of the church and of ecclesiastical courts.   Even in those colonies, however, where the Anglican Church was established, there were modifications of the English practice.   Under Virginia law the established clergy had the exclusive right of performing the marriage ceremony,

[1] M. L. Hansen, "The Minor Stocks in the American Population of 1790," Am. Hist. Assoc., *Ann. Rep. for 1931*, I, 360 ff.

but the absence of a resident bishop made necessary also governmental action. The provincial assembly regulated the conditions of marriage, the governor issued licenses, and lay judges determined matrimonial cases. In Maryland and North Carolina marriages might be celebrated by civil magistrates. In general, however, the Southern colonies, following Anglican tradition, made no provision for absolute divorce.[1]

Puritan New England departed radically from English precedents, treating marriage as a civil contract and referring matrimonial questions to secular courts. Though the ceremony was usually conducted by ministers, they acted as agents of the state, and a purely civil marriage was permissible. Secular courts granted not only legal separation but absolute divorce. Between 1760 and 1774 the Massachusetts governor and council, sitting as a court, heard thirty-six cases, and in a majority of them granted absolute divorce. Acceptance of divorce did not, however, imply an indulgent attitude toward marital infidelity, which was severely dealt with by both church and state.[2]

The Middle colonies pursued no uniform practice. In New York, marriages were usually celebrated by ministers. No church, however, had a monopoly and civil services were legal. The Pennsylvania Friends required their members to marry "in meeting," but made no attempt to impose their ideas on outsiders. The law required registration and due notice, leaving any denomination to set standards for its communicants. Though divorce had been permitted in New Netherland and later in Pennsylvania, British policy was against it,

[1] G. E. Howard, *A History of Matrimonial Institutions* (Chicago, 1904), II, chap. xiii.
[2] *Ibid.*, 121-139; Thomas Hutchinson, *The History of the Colony and Province of Massachusetts-Bay* (L. S. Mayo, ed., Cambridge, 1936), I, 375.

and in 1773 a new royal instruction specifically forbade legislation for that purpose.[1]

Provincial laws prohibited the intermarriage of whites and blacks, but illicit relations between master and slave were evidenced by the large mulatto population of the South. A few references to the legal marriage of slaves occur in Quaker and Anglican records, but for most Negroes legal wedlock did not exist. The permanence of any union depended on their masters; and a considerate owner might take pains to keep families together. Even a white servant could not marry without his master's consent.[2]

Though court proceedings and church records may suggest a gloomy view of sex morality, most European travelers were impressed by the comparative soundness of colonial society, a condition characterized by freedom and informality before marriage and a fundamental respect for the institution itself. "Gallant adventures" seemed less common than in Europe, and marital infidelity more severely judged, even though the offender were "protected by wealth, position or other advantage." Conversely, Americans abroad commented on the laxity of European manners.[3]

As to the position of women, most eighteenth-century Americans did not differ fundamentally from their European contemporaries. "By the Law of God, as well as that of the English Government," said the Philadelphia lawyer, Joseph Galloway, "a wife is enjoined to be Obedient and Subject to her Husband." No less conservative was Oliver Ellsworth, the future chief justice of

[1] Howard, *Matrimonial Institutions*, II, chap. xiv; L. W. Labaree, ed., *Royal Instructions to British Colonial Governors, 1670-1776* (N. Y., 1935), I, 154.

[2] Phillips, *Life and Labor in the Old South*, 203-205; Howard, *Matrimonial Institutions*, II, 215-216; Adams, *Provincial Society*, 158.

[3] J. D. Schoepf, *Travels in the Confederation, 1783-1784* (A. J. Morrison, ed., Phila., 1911), I, 100.

the United States, who defended the common-law rule
that a married woman could not bequeath her estate.
Public policy required the maintenance of this principle
"because the government" was "not placed in her
hands." An example of comparatively liberal action
was the Massachusetts law of 1763, which enabled a
woman living apart from her husband to convey real
estate independently. A similar measure in Virginia
was, however, disallowed by the crown since it altered
"the Law in so Settled and Known a point." [1]

Large families gave matrons ample opportunity to
display managerial capacity, especially when they had to
direct numerous slaves. Widows sometimes took over
the stores, taverns or printing shops of their husbands.
Others engaged in the familiar feminine occupations of
seamstress, nurse and dame-school teacher. Occasional
women managed large business enterprises. A Mrs.
Bowling was reputed to own half the town of Petersburg, Virginia, with tobacco warehouses and an establishment for making millstones and bolting machines;
"lively, active, and intelligent," she knew "perfectly
well how to manage her immense fortune." [2] In general, however, most provincials would probably have
agreed with the following lines in the *American Magazine* for July, 1769:

> A woman's noblest station is retreat:
> Her fairest virtues fly from public sight.

Probably about a third of the people were legally
unfree in 1763. For nearly all the Negroes this servile
status was permanent and hereditary. Some forty years
before the Revolution a Virginia court held that, while

[1] R. B. Morris, *Studies in the History of American Law* (Columbia
Univ., *Studies*, no. 316), chap. iii; W. G. Brown, *Oliver Ellsworth*
(N. Y., 1905), 113-115.
[2] Marquis de Chastellux, *Travels in North-America* (London, 1787),
II, 131-136.

for certain purposes slaves were classified as real estate, they could be taken for debt as chattels, "considered no otherwise than Horses or Cattle." Thomas Jefferson, however, reported a decision of 1772 asserting the hereditary and human association of the slave with his master and with the land. Blacks, it said, were "not the subject of perpetual transfer from hand to hand, but live in families with us, are born and die on our lands, and, by their representatives may continue with us as long as the lands themselves." Though slave codes were naturally most severe where Negroes were numerous, Massachusetts and Connecticut resembled the South in discouraging manumission and subjecting Negroes to special police control. In criminal cases there was a special procedure for colored defendants, and in South Carolina, where the death penalty might be imposed by two justices and three freeholders, Quincy was told that "for killing a negroe ever so wantonly—there could be nothing but a fine." In 1775, however, the *Virginia Gazette* approved the capital punishment of a white man for beating a Negro to death, as a "warning to others to treat their slaves with more moderation." Even in the Lower South, there was some frank criticism of slaveholders. A letter in the *South-Carolina Gazette* in 1772 spoke of "people who boast an attachment to Freedom; yet are mean enough to beget children that must follow the condition of their mothers." [1]

White servitude was most prevalent between the Potomac and the Hudson, and especially in Maryland and Pennsylvania. Broadly speaking, the legal status of the men and women involved was much the same everywhere. The indentured servant, the most familiar

---

[1] Helen T. Catterall, ed., *Judicial Cases Concerning Slavery and the Negro* (Carnegie Inst., *Publs.*, no. 374), I, 83-84, 93; U. B. Phillips, *American Negro Slavery* (N. Y., 1918), esp. chaps. vi, xxi-xxiii; Josiah Quincy, "Journal," Mass. Hist. Soc., *Proceeds.*, XLIX, 446; *Va. Gazette*, April 21, 1775; *S.-C. Gazette*, Sept. 24, 1772.

type, was commonly an immigrant, though sometimes a poor inhabitant who found in such employment the best cure for his troubles. The length of service usually varied between one and four or five years. One instance of nineteen years is on record. The law required the master to supply food, clothing and shelter to the servant and at the expiration of the period to make allowances known as "freedom dues."

Besides the redemptioners and other indentured servants, there were transported convicts generally serving for seven years. These "Seven Year Passengers" or "King's Passengers" were especially numerous in Maryland. Colonial legislation to check their importation by tariff duties was usually, though not always, disallowed. Thus in 1775 a tax of forty shillings a head was held to be in "direct opposition" to the authority of Parliament. Another group of the unfree consisted of defaulting debtors and vagrants sold by court order. On a somewhat higher level were the apprentices and also the indentured workers who received fixed wages and differed only slightly from free wage-earners. Apprenticeship at its best provided vocational education, arranged by parents for their children or by public authority for orphans. White servants enjoyed some protection against ill treatment by their masters. Thus in Maryland a servant might bring his complaints into court, summon witnesses and demand a jury trial.[1]

Of the many who at one time or another passed through some form of unfree status, a certain number of the less fit became "poor whites" or lawless frontiersmen, but many others graduated into self-supporting artisans or small farmers. Indentured service might thus be a kind of initiation into colonial life. Once established

[1] E. I. McCormac, *White Servitude in Maryland, 1634-1820* (Johns Hopkins Univ., *Studies*, XXII, nos. 3-4), esp. chaps. iv, vi, viii; C. A. Herrick, *White Servitude in Pennsylvania* (Phila., 1926), chaps. vi-xiv.

as a landowner, even on a small scale, a former European without political privileges might become a citizen and a voter. Many servants, however, enjoyed the initial advantage of knowing a trade. Some were schoolmasters and one was said to be the pastor of a Lutheran congregation.[1]

Of free wage-earners the number was limited, partly by the ease with which men could become independent farmers or master workmen and partly by the competition of unfree labor, including slaves hired out by their masters. A familiar example of the rural wage-earner is the New England hired man, who supplied the labor largely provided elsewhere by slaves or white servants. On the smaller farms of the Middle colonies conditions resembled those in New England; but on large New York estates hired men worked along with slaves and white servants. Southern plantations also employed wage-earners. Washington paid expert mowers by the day, a joiner for a year's service and a stonecutter by the month.[2]

In the towns unskilled persons toiled as carters and boatmen and performed all sorts of rough labor. Higher in the social and economic scale were the skilled workers —weavers, tailors, shoemakers, house carpenters and cabinetmakers—with no clear line between the capitalist-workman, who had his own shop and tools, and the simple employee of a master workman. The leaders of the Philadelphia Associated Carpenters were not ordinary wage-earners; and the New York Friendly Society of Tradesmen, House Carpenters, was not strictly a labor union. The conflicts in which the latter society engaged were not between employers and workmen, but rather between the local industry and competing coun-

[1] Ibid., 267-273.
[2] George Washington, Diaries, 1748-1799 (J. C. Fitzpatrick, ed., Boston, 1925), I, 214, 276, 282, 366.

try carpenters who paid no city taxes. On one occasion
the organization also complained of municipal building
regulations.[1]

Even when legally free, many wage-earners lacked
the suffrage qualifications. Some could vote, as in New
York, where certain of them qualified as "freemen"; but
in Philadelphia the number excluded by property tests
was sufficient to make the extension of the franchise a
political issue. Radical factions enlisted the workers.
Through "mechanics'" tickets at elections Samuel
Adams in Boston and Christopher Gadsden in Charleston
furthered patriotic measures. Even nonvoters were useful in popular demonstrations.

As against the ruling classes, the small farmers had
something in common with the city workers. In 1765
Governor Colden divided the free inhabitants of New
York into four classes, of which the first three were
privileged groups: large landowners, well-to-do merchants and professional men. Below these he put the
mechanics and small farmers.[2] By contrast, New England yeomen occupied a more favorable position. Owning small farms and working independently or with one
or two hired men, they lived among neighbors much
like themselves. Similar conditions prevailed in parts
of the Hudson-Delaware country, though certain New
York counties were dominated by a few great landlords.
The Southern tidewater, as we have seen, had many
small farmers living close to the margin of decent exist-

[1] T. J. Wertenbaker, *The Founding of American Civilization, the
Middle Colonies* (N. Y., 1938), 244-250; A. E. Peterson and G. W.
Edwards, *New York as an Eighteenth Century Municipality* (N. Y.,
1917), 289-291; Samuel McKee, *Labor in Colonial New York, 1664-
1776* (Columbia Univ., *Studies*, no. 410), chap. i. For a tailors' strike,
see I. N. P. Stokes, *Iconography of Manhattan Island* (N. Y., 1915-
1928), IV, 784.

[2] Cadwallader Colden, *Letter-Books* (N. Y. Hist. Soc., *Colls.*, IX-X),
II, 68 ff.

ence or below it, but also "middle-class" farmers, small slaveholders living in fair comfort.

How some of the humbler Southern freemen felt toward the landed aristocracy may be seen in the autobiography of Devereux Jarratt, the son of a carpenter-farmer in tidewater Virginia. From "gentlemen as beings of a superior order" he kept "a humble distance" and his folk took for granted the distinction between "gentle" and "simple." Politically the small farmer suffered a disadvantage, even though many of them owned enough land to qualify as voters. In New England town meetings their "rude democracy" could assert itself, and in Virginia the number of white persons actually voting in provincial elections seems to have been proportionately larger than in Massachusetts. In Virginia, however, viva-voce elections exposed voters to social pressure from the "gentry." [1]

The ruling elements in the pre-Revolutionary era consisted mainly of the great planters, the more substantial merchants, and such predecessors of our later "captains of industry" as the ironmasters, shipbuilders, flour millers and distillers. Drawn largely from this aristocracy of wealth were the officeholders, provincial and local. The social standing of these classes was commonly shared by the clergymen, lawyers and physicians. The high status of the clergy dated from early colonial times, but the lawyers and physicans were now gaining in number and influence.

Several factors gave the legal profession greater prestige. One was British policy, which sought through royal instructions and the disallowance of colonial statutes to harmonize colonial practice with the common law. Another was the fact that more royal officials,

---

[1] Devereux Jarratt, *Life* (Balt., 1806), 13-15; A. E. McKinley, *The Suffrage Franchise in the Thirteen English Colonies in America* (Univ. of Pa., *Ser. in History*, no. 2), 47, 357.

particularly chief justices of the higher courts and attorneys-general, had received legal training in England. At the same time the increase of wealth offered larger opportunities for lawyers, who could protect their clients before judges accustomed to English precedents. Nevertheless, a comparatively small number were primarily lawyers. In Virginia, for instance, plantation owners who had studied some law took fees for legal advice, while only a few, like George Wythe, were full-time practitioners. Even many judges were laymen.

A definitely professional class naturally developed chiefly in the larger towns. In South Carolina most members of the provincial bar were Charlestonians. Massachusetts on the eve of the Revolution had some forty "barristers" and a less qualified group of "attorneys." Most of the barristers lived in Boston and other seaboard towns, very few in the country. In New York and Philadelphia, lawyers were probably somewhat more numerous. Nevertheless, some Boston lawyers were already complaining that the profession was overcrowded.[1]

An increasing number of colonists studied at the London Inns of Court, though the instruction received need not be taken too seriously. Charles Carroll thought nothing "more absurd than the usual manner of young gentlemen's studying the law." They read "Coke Little," whom they could "not possibly understand," and visited the courts with similar lack of understanding; soon discouraged, they gave themselves up to dissipation. Yet many such Americans returned to become leaders of the provincial bar, notably in South Caro-

---

[1] M. N. Stanard, *Colonial Virginia* (Phila., 1917), 160; Edward McCrady, *History of South Carolina under the Royal Government, 1719-1776* (N. Y., 1899), chap. xxiv; Emory Washburn, *Sketches of the Judicial History of Massachusetts from 1630 to the Revolution in 1775* (Boston, 1840), 199-201, 305; John Adams, *Works* (C. F. Adams, ed., Boston, 1856), II, 197.

lina, which had the most entries at the Inns, including the two Rutledges, future delegates to the Continental Congress, and the two Pinckneys—Thomas and Charles Cotesworth.   Josiah Quincy, meeting Edward Rutledge in Charleston, took pains to copy his manuscript law reports.   He noted also that one of the Pinckneys appeared to have been "improved" by his Temple training.   Other distinguished Americans who studied at the Inns were John Dickinson and Daniel Dulany.[1]

Training at home for the bar was usually secured through apprenticeship in a lawyer's office.   In New York, William Livingston, who had himself been apprenticed to James Alexander, complained that practitioner-teachers gave pupils too much routine, neglecting instruction.   But other New York youths apparently fared better, learning more law than many who went abroad.   In Massachusetts, John Adams served a two-year apprenticeship with James Putnam of Worcester. Thomas Jefferson entered Wythe's law office, carrying through under his guidance a remarkably broad plan of reading.   All three had previously received a college education—Livingston at Yale, Adams at Harvard and Jefferson at William and Mary.   Most leaders of the Massachusetts bar were Harvard graduates.   Of the younger lawyers elsewhere James Duane and John Jay had graduated from King's College, while Oliver Ellsworth and William Paterson were Princetonians.   Patrick Henry, however, began his profitable practice with little formal education or legal instruction.[2]

Professional standards were gradually advancing. John Adams's diary throws light on preparation for

[1] Rowland, *Carroll*, I, 53-54; E. A. Jones, *American Members of the Inns of Court* (London, 1924); Quincy, "Journal," 446.

[2] P. M. Hamlin, *Legal Education in Colonial New York* (N. Y., 1939), 43, 167-170; Adams, *Works*, II, 30; Gilbert Chinard, *Thomas Jefferson* (Boston, 1929), chap. ii; W. W. Henry, *Patrick Henry* (N. Y., 1891), I, chap. i.

the Massachusetts bar. After leaving Putnam's office he was sponsored by a leading Boston lawyer who vouched in court for the young man's character and legal knowledge. Adams was then admitted to the status of an "attorney" with the right to practise in the inferior courts, "shook hands with the bar" and invited them to drink punch with him. After three years' further study he became a barrister. The final ceremony was held in 1761 in the superior court, then presided over by Thomas Hutchinson, where the prospective lawyers presented themselves duly garbed with gowns, bands and tiewigs. In 1766 Adams noted that the bar, in an effort to stiffen requirements, had "at last introduced a regular progress to the gown" with a seven-year "probation." The New York supreme court in 1767 issued rules requiring candidates, with some exceptions, to show satisfactory service as clerks to a "sworn attorney"— for three years in the case of college graduates and five years for others. In Virginia applicants appeared before an examining board, but apparently with no prescribed period of study or apprenticeship. Patrick Henry was admitted after a few weeks' study, while Jefferson qualified after several years of serious preparation. In South Carolina, admission to the bar without entry at the Inns was said to be exceptional.[1]

Until Blackstone's first volume was published in 1765, Coke was the most generally recommended authority. Jeremiah Gridley told Adams that he "began with Coke-Littleton and broke through," and Adams himself declared that "whoever is master of his [Coke's] writings is master of the laws of England." But Coke made hard reading. Jefferson wished the devil had him, while to William Paterson he was the "pedantic, rambling, helter-skelter Master Coke." A new epoch in legal education

---

[1] Adams, *Works*, II, 49, 133, 197; Hamlin, *Legal Education*, 39; McCrady, *South Carolina under Royal Government*, chap. xxiv.

started with Blackstone, whose fame reached the colonies even before the first volume of his *Commentaries* appeared. Adams heard of his Oxford lectures in 1759, and a little later a New York merchant wrote of "a Professor at Oxford, who they say has brought that Mysterious Business to some System." The *Commentaries* was promptly advertised in America and as early as 1773 the first volume was reprinted at Philadelphia. Legal classics were supplemented by various practical manuals. Both Adams and Jefferson displayed interest in legal history and a select few knew about such medieval writers as Bracton and Glanville. Duane told Adams he had been reading the English *Yearbooks*. Adams also read Roman law. Significant in this connection was the forming of such organizations as the New York "Moot" to discuss legal topics, and the Boston "Sodality" which inspired John Adams to write his "Dissertation on the Feudal and Canon Law." [1]

Then, as now, lawyers' incomes varied widely. Jefferson's annual earnings perhaps averaged £3000 for some time and those of Charleston practitioners are said to have ranged from £2000 to £3000; Adams understood that they were lower in Boston. Many lawyer-politicians ranked among the more prosperous members of the community, though their incomes did not always derive from strictly legal business. Adams, who thought he had for a time the largest practice in his neighborhood and "the very richest clients," remained comparatively poor, while John Sullivan of New Hampshire throve on a combination of law and business, including investments in real estate, notes and mortgages. Legal practice, then largely concerned with disputed titles, was often accompanied by

---

[1] Adams, *Works*, II, 36, 46-47, 80, 100, 103, 146-150, 429; IX, 432; Thomas Jefferson, *Works* (P. L. Ford, ed., N. Y., 1904-1905), I, 436; W. J. Mills, *Glimpses of Colonial Society* (Phila., 1903), 28; John Watts, *Letter-Book* (N. Y. Hist. Soc., *Colls.*, LXI), 13; Hamlin, *Legal Education*, 96.

land speculation, as in the careers of Duane, the Dulanys and Henry. The law also offered the prospect of public patronage. Peyton Randolph, first president of the Continental Congress, had been a Virginia king's attorney; while Jared Ingersoll of Connecticut was successively king's attorney, stamp collector, and vice-admiralty judge. Among Adams's Massachusetts contemporaries, Benjamin Pratt became chief justice of New York and Jonathan Sewall held several important offices under the crown. Adams thought the judicious distribution of patronage frequently made Tories of promising young lawyers.[1]

Legal practice entailed hardships. In Massachusetts, judges and lawyers had to travel on circuits which included remote counties in Maine. Adams complained of the consequent interference with his reading, reflection and business; but the occupation might also bring agreeable social intercourse, as when Virginia lawyers met at county courts or attended the general court at Williamsburg. When Adams "took a pipe after supper" with his landlord, he probably also learned much that was useful to an aspiring politician.[2]

Debt collections for local clients and creditors at a distance furnished much of the lawyer's practice. Joseph Hawley in western Massachusetts helped Boston merchants collect accounts in Rhode Island, Connecticut and New York. Besides land litigation, increasing wealth brought profitable employment in probate business. Clients were rarely numerous enough to encourage specialization, but there was a limited amount. Henry was an eloquent advocate rather than a profound lawyer, and Jefferson, not being an easy speaker, was better as a

---

[1] Chinard, *Jefferson*, 36; Adams, *Works*, II, 197, 232, 251; X, 192; John and Abigail Adams, *Familiar Letters during the Revolution* (C. F. Adams, ed., Boston, 1875), 2-4; Quincy, "Journal," 446, 449.

[2] Adams, *Works*, II, 208-209, 240-247.

consultant.   Occasionally a specialty was advertised.
One Philadelphia lawyer aimed to limit himself to con-
veyancing, and a former student of Clement's Inn, London, proposed to "decline the Practice of the Courts"
and concentrate on office business.[1]

The more prosperous lawyers usually maintained close
connections with well-to-do landowners and merchants.
Governor Colden complained that in New York the
landed magnates found in the lawyers "the surest support of their iniquitous claims."   But sometimes antagonism disturbed the relations of lawyers and merchants.
In the New York elections of 1768 the merchants and
traders were asked to oppose the lawyers, "whose sole
study it is . . . to divide the Gain of the industrious
Merchant and Mechanick if possible among themselves."
A popular slogan was "No lawyer in the Assembly!"
On the other hand, Pennsylvania radicals attacked lawyers as allies of the mercantile aristocracy.   The common man's attitude toward the profession was often one
of suspicion.   The Ames almanac for 1765 denounced
"Pettyfoggers" who took up "the most trifling Causes,
exciting Quarrels." [2]   John Adams agreed that many
attorneys engaged in "dirty and ridiculous litigations."
A bit of contemporary doggerel betrays similar feeling:

> Anoint the lawyer, grease him in the Fist,
> And he will plead for thee, even what thou list.[3]

---

[1] E. F. Brown, *Joseph Hawley, Colonial Radical* (N. Y., 1931),
chap. iv; *Pa. Journal*, Dec. 26, 1765; *N.-Y. Mercury*, Feb. 16, 1761.

[2] E. B. O'Callaghan and Berthold Fernow, eds., *Documents Relative
to the Colonial History of the State of New-York* (Albany, 1856-1887),
VII, 705; Colden, *Letter-Books*, I, 230-231, 395-398; Stokes, *Iconography of Manhattan*, IV, 783; C. H. Lincoln, *The Revolutionary Movement in Pennsylvania, 1760-1776* (Univ. of Pa., Ser. in History, no. 1),
84; Sam Briggs, *The Essays, Humor and Poems of Nathaniel Ames,
Father and Son, . . . from Their Almanacks* (Cleveland, 1891), 361-
362.

[3] *Bickerstaff's Boston Almanack for 1774*; Adams, *Works*, II, 90.

The medical profession also made progress, though it still had to meet much nonprofessional competition. Many people patronized a motley assortment of drug sellers, bonesetters and plain quacks, while obstetrics fell largely to midwives. Perhaps not one in eight or ten of the three or four thousand practitioners in the colonies held a medical degree. Some others, however, had received passable instruction from older physicians. The Ames almanac for 1765 denounced the failure to protect the public against so-called doctors who had "the audacity to practice their Butchery on the human Race." [1] The methods of even the more intelligent physicians left much to be desired. Dr. Theodorick Bland of Virginia, after study at Edinburgh and London, treated a slave for epilepsy by bleeding, purging and, when these failed, giving the patient an electric shock. Heavy medication was general, and the doctor was usually himself a drug seller. Dr. John Kearsley, a leading Philadelphia practitioner, indorsed "Keyser's Pills" as a "wonderfully efficacious" panacea for rheumatism, "leprosies," "stiff joints," gout and "dry gripes." [2]

Until 1765 medical instruction in the colonies could be acquired only through apprenticeship. As in the case of legal training, the practitioner-teacher often failed in professional competence or in consideration for his pupils. Dr. John Bard of New York, a pupil of Dr. Kearsley, who prepared many provincial physicians, complained of the menial services, which left little time for study. On the other hand, Dr. John Redman of Philadelphia, who had taken his doctorate at Leyden and also studied in Edinburgh, London and Paris, was

[1] F. R. Packard, *History of Medicine in the United States* (rev. edn., N. Y., 1931), I, 284 ff.; Briggs, *Ames . . . Almanacks*, 361, 413.

[2] Stanard, *Colonial Virginia*, 160-163; James Rivington to Henry Knox, Mass. Hist. Soc., *Proceeds.*, LXI, 269 and *n.*; *Pa. Gazette*, Feb. 8, 1775.

highly praised by his pupils, including Dr. John Morgan and Dr. Benjamin Rush, who became medical professors in Philadelphia College. In Boston Dr. Joseph Warren gave stimulating and fairly systematic instruction to his students. An important advantage enjoyed by Philadelphia as a medical center was the Pennsylvania Hospital, founded in 1751, which was as yet the only general institution of its kind in British America.[1]

An increasing number of young men went abroad for study, at Leyden, Paris and particularly at Edinburgh and London. In the three decades beginning in 1758 sixty-three Americans graduated from the Edinburgh medical school which, though comparatively young, had a distinguished faculty and attracted foreign as well as British students. Among the colonials who wrote glowing reports of their Edinburgh instructors were the Philadelphians, Morgan and Rush, and Samuel Bard of New York. Rush warmly admired Dr. William Cullen, the "idol of his pupils," who unfolded "each day some new secret to us in Animal economy." Bard described his final examinations at Edinburgh, in which the candidate had to comment in writing on "aphorisms" from Hippocrates, discuss two cases in practice, and defend a thesis—all in Latin.[2]

[1] Michael Kraus, *Intercolonial Aspects of American Culture on the Eve of the Revolution* (Columbia Univ., *Studies*, no. 302), 143; Packard, *History of Medicine*, I, chaps. v-vi; T. F. Harrington, *The Harvard Medical School* (N. Y., 1905), I, 46-50; G. W. Norris, *Early History of Medicine in Philadelphia* (Phila., 1886), 30-35; T. G. Morton, *History of the Pennsylvania Hospital* (Phila., 1895), *passim*.

[2] H. E. Hayden, "American Graduates in Medicine at the University of Edinburgh," *New England Hist. and Geneal. Register*, XLI, 391; Samuel Lewis, "List of American Graduates in Medicine in the University of Edinburgh," *ibid.*, XLII, 159-161; John Morgan, *A Discourse upon the Institution of Medical Schools in America* (Phila., 1765), 28-29; Benjamin Rush, *A Memorial Containing Travels through Life or Sundry Incidents* (Phila., 1905), 20; M. H. Thomas, "Dr. Samuel Bard," *Columbia Univ. Quar.*, XXIII, 120; Rush as quoted in Joseph Carson, *History of the Medical Department of the University of Pennsylvania* (Phila., 1869), chap. vi.

In London, where young Americans supplemented their Edinburgh training by "walking the hospitals," they found two distinguished practitioners: William Hunter, a leading authority on obstetrics, and his brother John, known to posterity as "one of the three greatest surgeons of all time." Other contacts proved equally broadening. Franklin delighted to introduce his countrymen to celebrities, and for a time Rush was "domesticated in Dr. Franklin's family." Another good friend of Americans was the distinguished and generous Dr. John Fothergill. Rush also met the great Dr. Samuel Johnson, Oliver Goldsmith, David Hume, Sir Joshua Reynolds and John Wilkes. Some Americans traveled on the Continent. Morgan studied anatomy in Paris and was admitted to the Académie Royale de Chirurgie. He met Giovanni Morgagni, the famous Italian anatomist, and talked with Voltaire. In Paris Rush heard a company at Mirabeau's house discussing Dickinson's *Letters from a Pennsylvania Farmer* and Diderot.[1]

Edinburgh graduates took the lead in founding the first American medical schools. After consulting his British friends, Cullen, Fothergill and Hunter, Dr. Morgan drafted a plan which he submitted to the trustees of the College of Philadelphia, who promptly elected him professor of the theory and practice of medicine. Shortly afterward, William Shippen, jr., who had been lecturing on anatomy in Philadelphia since 1762, accepted the chair of anatomy and surgery. Formal instruction began in 1765, with Dr. Thomas Bond presently giving clinical lectures at the hospital. The curriculum led first to the degree of bachelor of medicine, that of M.D. being reserved to graduates who should, after an interval of at least three years, "write and defend a

[1] Rush, *Memorial*, 31 ff.; John Morgan, *Journal* (Phila., 1907), *passim*; F. H. Garrison, *An Introduction to the History of Medicine* (3rd edn., Phila., 1921), chap. x.

thesis publickly in college." In 1768 ten bachelors graduated, and three years later four graduates, having presented Latin theses, received the doctorate.   By this time there were two more professors: Rush in chemistry and Adam Kuhn, a pupil of Linnæus, in materia medica and botany.[1]

Two years later than Philadelphia, a medical department was introduced at King's College.   Of the initial faculty, which included young Samuel Bard, two had studied at Leyden, two in Scotland and one each in Ireland and France.   The first bachelors graduated in 1769 and the first doctors in 1770.   The New York school was at a disadvantage as to clinical instruction since the hospital there was not in operation before the Revolution.[2]   At Harvard proposals for medical training were considered, but no action was then taken.

Morgan's inaugural *Discourse upon the Institution of Medical Schools in America* (1765) suggests a remarkably liberal view of his profession.   He advocated a liberal education, including the classics, as the foundation.   In Greek literature were "the rich original treasures of ancient medical science," Latin constituted the common language of scholars, and French was needed for current professional literature.   Mathematics and natural philosophy were also essential.   The strictly medical curriculum should include anatomy, botany for materia medica, chemistry, physiology, pathology and the "Practice of Medicine."   He favored greater professional specialization, maintaining that the physician should not be an apothecary and that medicine should be differentiated from surgery.   Finally, Morgan emphasized research, recalling the great men who, "pushing

---

[1] Packard, *History of Medicine*, I, chaps. v-vi; Carson, *Medical Department of the University of Pennsylvania*, chap. iv; M. W. Jernegan, "The Birthday of Medical Honors in America," Society of Medical History of Chicago, *Bull.*, IV, 151-155.

[2] Thomas, "Doctor Samuel Bard," 114-130.

their researches into the bosom of nature," had "extended
the bounds of useful science." For such studies America,
a largely unexplored continent, offered unique opportunities.

Other colonial physicians also showed interest in scientific research, medical or otherwise. In the *Transactions*
of the American Philosophical Society for 1769 Dr.
Lionel Chalmers of South Carolina published essays on
botany, meteorology and the prevalent diseases of his
neighborhood. Dr. Alexander Garden of Charleston,
after whom the gardenia is named, was a capable naturalist and a member of the Royal Society. Though such
contributions were of minor value, Morgan and his associates did much to enlarge American knowledge of European medical progress. Some physicians were also
prominent in public life. Notable examples are Morgan
and Rush in Philadelphia, the Bards in New York and
Joseph Warren in Boston.

One handicap to professional instruction was the
popular opposition to the dissection of human bodies.
Though there had been earlier instances of dissection,
Shippen was the first American to make systematic use
of it in teaching. As a result, his students were charged
with grave-robbing and he himself was publicly denounced. He explained that the only corpses were those
of suicides and criminals, with an occasional one from
the potter's field. While insisting on the great scientific
value of the practice, he promised to "preserve the utmost
decency with regard to the dead." Shippen also introduced the scientific teaching of obstetrics into this
country.[1]

For the first time, too, the provincial governments
endeavored to improve professional standards. A New

[1] Packard, *History of Medicine*, I, 322; *Pa. Gazette*, Jan. 11, 1770;
Carson, *Medical Department of the University of Pennsylvania*, 217;
Norris, *Early History of Medicine in Philadelphia*, 44-45; Adams, *Pro-
vincial Society*, 125-126.

York statute of 1760 provided for physicians' licenses after certification by an examining board; in 1775 such a certificate was signed by two members of the King's College faculty. New Jersey took similar action in 1772. Though Connecticut forbade the sale or administration of drugs by "mountebanks" at public exhibitions, it failed to adopt a licensing system in spite of appeals from enlightened physicians. Elsewhere there was no legal regulation of medical standards.[1]

Nevertheless, something was accomplished through the coöperation of the better practitioners. In 1755 Charleston physicians had organized a "Faculty of Physic," intended primarily to regulate fees. The Philadelphia Medical Society, formed in 1765, merged with the American Philosophical Society after a separate existence of three years. In 1770 the American Medical Society was established at Philadelphia by "students who had assembled . . . to hear the lectures of the medical professors." Lasting until 1792, it served to promote discussion and publish papers. A pioneer state organization was the New Jersey Medical Society (1766). Though interested in proper compensation and the regulation of fees, this group also sought to advance medical science and raise professional standards. Practitioners who had not received proper training "either at some university, or under the direction of some able masters" were discountenanced; secret nostrums were regarded as "inconsistent with the generous spirit of the profession."[2] There is little information about professional incomes. A Williamsburg doctor is said to have charged a governor's wife the conventional British fee of a guinea a visit, but

[1] Packard, *History of Medicine*, I, chap. iii; certificate, 1775, in Pennsylvania Historical Society (reference contributed by C. H. Vance).

[2] McCrady, *South Carolina under Royal Government*, 432; Norris, *Early History of Medicine in Philadelphia*, 115-117; Packard, *History of Medicine*, I, 341 ff.; Stephen Wickes, *History of Medicine in New Jersey* (Newark, 1879), 43-48.

that was exceptional. Joseph Warren, who had among his patients Hancock, Josiah Quincy and John Adams, charged an average fee of three shillings, including drugs. Rush estimated his annual professional earnings at nine hundred pounds.[1]

Supplementing the advice of physicians were manuals for laymen. Two popular handbooks were those of the Scotch physician, William Buchan, and André Tissot, a medical authority of Lausanne. Buchan's *Domestic Medicine* aimed to show people what could be done by "Regimen and Simple Medicines." Tissot's *Avis au Peuple sur la Santé*, which was translated into several languages, was well known in the colonies, partly through extracts in English printed in *Bickerstaff's Boston Almanack* (1768) and in Thomas's *Royal American Magazine* (1774). Other advice—sensible, harmless or pernicious—appeared in newspapers, periodicals and almanacs.[2]

Common professional interests were not the only reasons for forming social groups. Urban gregariousness manifested itself in a variety of ways. Among the clubs in Philadelphia was the Junto, of which Franklin wrote affectionately in 1765: "'Tis now perhaps one of the oldest clubs, as I think it was formerly one of the best in the King's Dominions. . . . We are grown Grey together, and yet it is too early to part." In Charleston, Quincy met with the Friday-night Club, whose members were "substantial gentlemen" of the older set; the Monday-night Club, which entertained itself at a tavern with "cards, feasting, and indifferent wines"; and the Sons of St. Patrick. Boston also had such groups, in-

[1] Stanard, *Colonial Virginia*, 161-163; Garrison, *History of Medicine*, 391; Harrington, *Harvard Medical School*, I, 48; H. R. Viets, *A Brief History of Medicine in Massachusetts* (Boston, 1930), 92; Rush, *Memorial*, 53-56.

[2] *Pa. Gazette*, Jan. 11, 1775; Garrison, *History of Medicine*, 380; Packard, *History of Medicine*, I, chap. vii.

cluding the Fire Club to which John Rowe belonged. In New York, William Livingston's wit enlivened a club of gentlemen at "Mother Brock's" tavern. Societies representing particular British nationalities—St. George's, St. Andrew's, St. Patrick's and St. David's—combined charitable service with good-fellowship.[1]

Many prominent colonists also belonged to Masonic lodges, which sometimes existed in smaller towns as well as in the cities. Some lodges were affiliated with the Grand Lodge of England; others were of Irish or Scotch origin. There were also "Atholl Masons," called "Ancients" to distinguish them from the "Moderns" associated with the English Grand Lodge. Rowe described his installation as grand master at St. John's Lodge in Boston as a "very solemn ceremony," followed by a procession to Trinity Church. It is difficult to generalize about the religious and political attitudes of the colonial Free Masons. Their ritualistic language, once distinctly Christian, was now sufficiently general to accommodate Deists and freethinkers, but American Masonry included clerical as well as lay members. Representative Masons also differed politically. Rowe was a cautious Whig while Warren, another Mason, was a radical. Over against such Whigs as Franklin and Washington may be set a strong Loyalist element in the South Carolina lodges. In general, the "Ancients" tended to be more liberal than the "Moderns." In any case, connections formed through Masonry probably facilitated intercolonial acquaintance and that interchange of ideas without which the Revolution could hardly have succeeded.[2]

[1] Franklin, *Writings*, IV, 386; Quincy, "Journal," 448 ff.; Rowe, *Letters and Diary*, 174; Sedgwick, *Livingston*, 153.

[2] J. H. Tatsch, *Freemasonry in the Thirteen Colonies* (N. Y., 1929); John Rowe, *Letters and Diary* (Annie R. Cunningham, ed., Boston, 1903), 141, 176, 180; H. W. Smith, *Life and Correspondence of the Rev. William Smith* (Phila., 1880), I, 107; II, 11, 347, 409.

The most fashionable social institution for both sexes was the dancing assembly. At such a gathering in Annapolis a royal official fresh from England was impressed by the "affability and propriety" of the ladies as well as by their modish appearance. The Philadelphia assembly also enjoyed great prestige. In Boston John Rowe was apparently a kind of *arbiter elegantiarum*, and when his Cambridge friends gave a "Genteel Ball" at the town house, he was asked to serve as "Master of the Ceremony." Some people, however, had misgivings—not only New England Puritans but also good Presbyterians and Philadelphia Quakers. Abigail Adams's sister and brother-in-law after seeing a Harvard commencement concluded that "all such as learn to dance are so taken up with it, that they can't be students." Adams himself said he had never known a good dancer to be good for anything else; some "men of sense and learning . . . could dance . . . but none of them shone that way . . . ."[1]

Taverns and coffeehouses played an important part in urban social life. At Philadelphia's London Coffee House patrons could drink punch and hear of "everything that is done, or to be done." Another Philadelphia resort, later frequented by delegates to the Continental Congress, was the City Tavern. Williamsburg had its Raleigh Tavern with the beautiful Apollo Room, famous for peace-time gayeties and even better known for its Revolutionary associations. In New York one may still lunch at the Fraunces Tavern of colonial days where Washington said farewell to his fellow officers in the Continental army.[2]

In one important respect voluntary associations performed what is today regarded as a governmental func-

---

[1] Rowe, *Letters and Diary*, 104, 119; William Eddis, *Letters from America* (London, 1792), 7-9, 112-115; Adams, *Works*, II, 288-289.
[2] William Gregory, "Journal," *William and Mary College Quar.*, XIII, 227; Adams, *Works*, II, 400, 402.

tion. For fire protection, towns still depended on volunteers, though by 1772 New York City's eleven companies were directed by a municipal fire chief. Fire risks emphasized the need of building regulations. In 1761 the New York assembly enacted a law, to take effect in 1766, making stone or brick, with slate or tile roofs, compulsory for new houses in the business section of Manhattan; but the opposition proved strong enough to prevent enforcement. In Charleston, restrictions on the building of wooden houses were said to be generally ignored. In 1762, however, John Adams noted the prosecution of several Bostonians for using wooden shingles.[1]

Such community services as water supply, sewerage and lighting were generally primitive. In 1774 the New York common council authorized the young Irish engineer, Christopher Colles, to construct a well with a pumping system and wooden pipes to distribute the water; but the work was not finished before the Revolution. The Moravians at Bethlehem forced water from the Lehigh River to a tower from which it was piped through the town. In the matter of wastes, even so enterprising a town as Philadelphia made a bad showing. Graydon told of walking to school through a street which resembled "a filthy uncovered sewer." On the other hand, one British observer commented on the well-paved Philadelphia streets with footwalks on both sides. He found New York streets irregular and narrow, but so graded as to be "washed by every rain, which makes it clean and wholesome." Public lighting was improving. In 1774 Boston installed a new system of street lamps, and somewhat earlier New York had an imperfect municipal lighting service. In 1772 a citizen complained that no lamp had been lighted for three months,

[1] Peterson and Edwards, *New York as an Eighteenth Century Municipality*, 330-336; [Gordon], "Journal," 398; Adams, *Works*, II, 138.

apparently because of an oil shortage. The Charleston system was operated for the city by private contractors.[1]

In contrast to earlier times provincial society was more highly organized. But class distinctions continued to be conspicuous, notably in the case of the numerous unfree persons, black and white, and of those men who lacked property qualifications for voting. A Philadelphia assemblyman complained of inconsiderate treatment because he had once been a "Tradesman." He insisted that "true nobility" could as often be found among "honest Farmers, Mechanics and Tradesmen . . . as among those who affect the character of Gentlemen and Assume the Airs of Quality." Jarratt's youthful experience of the distinction between "gentle" and "simple" was shared by many colonials, and modes of dress were more significant of social status than in later days.[2]

Yet, apart from the Negro slave, New World conditions facilitated the movement of individuals from lower to higher levels and lessened, though they did not destroy, class feeling. A familiar example of antidemocratic prejudice is Gouverneur Morris's remark: "The mob begin to think and to reason. Poor reptiles! . . . they bask in the sunshine, and ere noon they will bite, depend upon it. The gentry begin to fear this." John Adams, later denounced as a partisan of the "wellborn," now resented the pretensions of the "first families." Was it not a pity, he asked in 1772, "that a brace of so obscure a breed" as the two Adamses "should be the only ones to defend the household, when the generous mastiffs and best-blooded hounds" were taking

[1] Peterson and Edwards, *New York as an Eighteenth Century Municipality*, 324-326, 339-341; Adams, *Familiar Letters*, 240; Schoepf, *Travels*, I, 169; Alexander Graydon, *Memoirs of His Own Time* (J. S. Littell, ed., Phila., 1846), 43; [Gordon], "Journal," 411, 415; Justin Winsor, ed., *Memorial History of Boston, 1630-1880* (Boston, 1880-1881), III, 152; *S.-C. Gazette*, Oct. 24, 1772.

[2] *Pa. Gazette*, Jan. 10, 1765; Lincoln, *Revolutionary Movement in Pennsylvania*, chap. v.

the Tory side? Yet there was already a certain fastidiousness in his republicanism. Passing through Connecticut and having to sit at the table with his hostess's carpenter, who "might be smelled from one room to another," he wrote in his diary: "these republicans are not very decent or neat." [1] The elder Charles Francis Adams, who as a youth was familiar with a New England society not far removed from that of his grandfather's time, made this suggestive comment on social relations. There were, he thought, "more of admitted distinctions" in the old days but more "general equality." What most impressed contemporary European observers of the American scene was not the "admitted distinctions," but their lessened importance, comparatively speaking, in colonial life. [2]

These last years of the provincial régime were thus marked not only by steady expansion but also by progress toward a maturer social order and by a social outlook increasingly differentiated from that of the mother country. The rapidly growing population contained a large proportion of non-English elements, a development partially offset, however, by the fusion of earlier migrants. One mark of a maturing society was the improved position of the legal and medical professions. Judged by European standards, the Americans had advanced far toward an equalitarian order, though over against that advance must be set the servile status of a substantial minority.

[1] Jared Sparks, *Life of Gouverneur Morris* (Boston, 1832), I, 23-25; Adams, *Works*, II, 273, 295.
[2] Abigail Adams, *Letters* (C. F. Adams, ed., 4th edn., Boston, 1848), xxi; Eddis, *Letters*, 128; Marquis de Chastellux to Mr. Madison, Chastellux, *Travels*, II, 344-346; Franklin, *Writings*, V, 362.

CHAPTER V

PREREVOLUTIONARY RELIGION

THOUGH political relations with England grew more and more strained as the Revolution approached, religion continued to play an important part in colonial life. The toleration of Protestant dissenters was now a fixed principle of British policy. Church-state connections continued in the majority of the colonies; but even where this relationship was approved in principle, uniformity could no longer be effectively enforced.

The Anglican establishment was most powerful in Virginia, where dissenters were taxed for its support. Nonconformity was further hampered by registration and licensing requirements for preachers and meeting places. Though the Presbyterians had lately secured some relief, Baptists were still fined or imprisoned for taking part in unauthorized gatherings. In 1774 James Madison wrote that several "well-meaning men" in his neighborhood were in jail because of their "religious sentiments." [1] Nevertheless, the dissenting churches steadily gained as a result of immigration, the revivalism of "New Light" preachers and the anticlericalism of many Anglican laymen. When the assembly required the clergy to accept money in place of tobacco at what they considered an unfair ratio, they succeeded in getting the law disallowed by the crown and sued for recovery of their salaries on the old basis. Their attitude was widely resented, however, and the verdict of the jury in the famous "Parson's Cause," in which Patrick Henry skill-

[1] James Madison, *Writings* (Gaillard Hunt, ed., N. Y., 1900-1901), I, 19-23.

fully exploited popular feeling, practically defied the royal order.[1] Meantime, Madison returned from President Witherspoon's teaching at Princeton an earnest advocate of religious liberty, and there was an unorthodox circle at Williamsburg of which Jefferson was a junior member.

In Maryland also the Church of England had long been established; but its adherents were in a minority and its position was weakened by the unfortunate character of some of its clergy. In the Carolinas and Georgia the Anglican establishments were similarly confronted by dissenting majorities. North of Maryland, the Church of England had no establishment except a partial and ineffective one in four New York counties. In the province as a whole it faced a majority of hostile and suspicious dissenters. In the North generally the Anglicans, while enjoying a certain social prestige in the large towns, counted as only one of several competing denominations; in New England it was commonly regarded as an intrusive dissenting sect. As a result of this unsympathetic environment, however, the Episcopal clergy tended to be more aggressive than their Southern brethren.[2]

In the North, as in the Carolinas, the missionaries of the Society for the Propagation of the Gospel helped to strengthen the Anglican position, though they were not adequately supported by the authorities in England. The society and its colonial representatives urged the appointment of American bishops, but the opposition of dissenters on both sides of the Atlantic and the indifference of British politicians prevented action.

Though the Puritan establishments had lost ground,

[1] M. C. Tyler, *Patrick Henry* (J. T. Morse, jr., ed., *American Statesmen*, III, rev. edn., Boston, 1898), chap. iv.

[2] Herbert and Carol Schneider, eds., *Samuel Johnson, President of King's College. His Career and Writings* (N. Y., 1929), I, 379.

they were well rooted and most of their pastors had behind them several generations of New England ancestry. In Boston, Samuel Mather had a clerical forbear in every generation from the days of John Cotton, while Jonathan Mayhew was the son, grandson and great-grandson of Congregational ministers. These clergymen had commonly studied at Harvard or Yale, where the curriculum, though not exclusively planned for them, was fairly adapted to their requirements as then understood. For more definitely professional training, aspirants relied mainly on the older ministers. Once installed, a preacher could generally count on a long tenure. Clerical influence, though diminished, was still important, especially in rural communities.[1]

Except in Rhode Island, Congregational ministers were generally supported by public taxation. Both Massachusetts and Connecticut reluctantly exempted from church taxes Baptist and Quaker members of local congregations; and the law provided that those paid by Episcopalians might go to their own ministers. Persons not affiliated with these denominations were still expected to pay such taxes and attend church services. The Baptists were the most vigorous champions of religious equality; but in Connecticut especially, the tax issue was complicated after the Great Awakening by the formation of "New Light" or "Separate" Congregational churches, whose members did not at first receive the concessions made to Baptists and Episcopalians. Soon, however, most of the "Separates" either joined the Baptists or were reunited with the Congregationalists.[2]

[1] Mary L. Gambrell, *Ministerial Training in Eighteenth-Century New England* (Columbia Univ., *Studies*, no. 428); Alice M. Baldwin, *The New England Clergy and the American Revolution* (Duke Univ., *Publs.*, 1928), chap. i.

[2] J. C. Meyer, *Church and State in Massachusetts from 1740 to 1833* (Cleveland, 1930), chaps. ii-iii; Maria L. Greene, *The Development of Religious Liberty in Connecticut* (Boston, 1905), chaps. ix-xi.

Though the New England nonconformists were increasing, they were still, except in Rhode Island, outnumbered by their fellow citizens who, if not members or adherents of the "standing order," at least acquiesced in it. More serious than the competition of the dissenters were the divisions within the established churches, which during this period included three distinct elements. The followers of Jonathan Edwards, commonly known as "Edwardians" or "New Divinity" men, stood for a freshly interpreted Calvinism, touched with a new emotional quality.[1] Though largely engaged in refining and systematizing the "New England theology," they were not wholly occupied with theological subtleties. Among others, Samuel Hopkins and the younger Edwards were ardent antislavery men. A second group, the "Old Calvinists," distrusted the "New Divinity" and the emotionalism of the Edwardian revival. Satisfied with the ancient ways, they took less interest in dogmatic controversies. A third group resembled the "Old Calvinists" in disliking the "New Divinity," but its members were turning away from Calvinist teaching altogether. Some of them, rejecting more or less definitely the historic doctrine of the Trinity, prepared the way for Unitarianism.

In Rhode Island and the Middle colonies the voluntary principle of church support prevailed. In New York and New Jersey most church members belonged to one of the Calvinist denominations. The Dutch Reformed Church was still supported by many families of Dutch descent. Though associated with the state church of Holland, the American branch showed an increasingly independent spirit, but it was weakened by the gradual Anglicizing of the Dutch stock. Other Calvinist groups in this region were the German Reformed, a few French

[1] For Edwards's teachings, see J. T. Adams, *Provincial Society, 1690-1763* (*A History of American Life*, III), 282-283.

Protestants and the Presbyterians. This last denomination had grown rapidly through the fusion of Puritans from New England with Scotch and Irish Presbyterians, with some recruits from the non-English Reformed churches. Other elements in the ecclesiastical complex were the Anglicans—numerically weak though politically influential—the German Lutherans, smaller groups of Quakers, Moravians and Baptists, and a Jewish synagogue in New York City.

In southern New Jersey and Pennsylvania the Quakers exerted a strong religious influence and were also an important factor in politics. They had long been embarrassed by imperial opposition to their scruples about oaths and military service. The first of these issues was finally compromised by permitting them to substitute an affirmation for an oath in all cases, though the more conscientious adherents were barred from serving as judges because they were not willing to administer oaths to other persons. Military legislation caused more trouble, especially during the recent French war when Quaker members avoided responsibility by resigning from the assembly. The Pennsylvania Friends were conspicuous in humanitarian activities. Two of them, John Woolman and Anthony Benezet, strove for greater justice for the Indian and the Negro. Woolman, who died in 1772, was largely responsible for the agitation which in 1776 led the Philadelphia yearly meeting to exclude slaveholders from membership in the Society of Friends. Benezet, through his publications and his correspondence with British sympathizers, crusaded against the slave trade.[1]

---

[1] W. T. Root, *The Relations of Pennsylvania with the British Government, 1696-1765* (Univ. of Pa., Publs., 1912), chap. viii; Isaac Sharpless, *A Quaker Experiment in Government* (Phila., 1902), pt. i, chaps. v-viii; E. R. Turner, *The Negro in Pennsylvania* (Am. Hist. Assoc., Prize Essays, 1911), chaps. iv-v; Carl and Jessica Bridenbaugh, *Rebels and Gentlemen* (N. Y., 1942), 253-260.

In Philadelphia the Church of England, to which the proprietary family now belonged, enjoyed a certain prestige. The old antagonism between Quakers and Anglicans was less intense and the latter tended to be less militant here than in other Northern colonies. The Anglicans were, however, outnumbered by the Presbyterians, who, while strong in Philadelphia, were especially aggressive in the backcountry where, faced by Indian troubles, they naturally disliked Quaker pacifism. Most of the Germans belonged to one or the other of the two Protestant state churches of the fatherland, Lutheran or Calvinist. Among these people, as in other German sects, there was a strong pietist element which reacted against formalism and emphasized the inner life of the believer. Heinrich Mühlenberg, the chief Lutheran leader, sympathized with this attitude and coöperated with kindred spirits in other denominations. In 1770 George Whitefield spoke to a large audience from Mühlenberg's pulpit.[1]

Generally speaking, the minor German sects advocated a return to primitive Christianity, and many of them were pacifists. Though usually inactive politically, they could not be ignored by the politicians, and they commonly sided with the Quakers.[2] Especially important among these groups was the Moravian Church or *Unitas Fratrum*, then directed from headquarters in Germany. Their chief colonial center was in and about Bethlehem, Pennsylvania, but they had congregations elsewhere, as at Philadelphia and New York City; they also had a group of villages in North Carolina known as Wachovia. Strongly pietist in religion, they were friendly, tolerant,

---

[1] C. H. Maxson, *The Great Awakening in the Middle Colonies* (Chicago, 1920), 126.

[2] P. G. Mode, ed., *Source Book and Bibliographical Guide for American Church History* (Menasha, Wis., 1921), 172-173; Thomas Balch, *Letters and Papers Relating Chiefly to the Provincial History of Pennsylvania* (Phila., 1855), 208-212.

and practical in their communal enterprises. They were also conspicuous for courageous and humane missionary work among the Indians and for the high quality of their church music. Mennonites and Dunkers, whose parents or grandparents had come to Penn's colony long before, held their ground in the central counties, particularly Lancaster; still spoke German exclusively; cherished their belief in special revelations; abhorred war, oaths, politics and, for the most part, secular learning.

In the South religious diversity was becoming almost as marked as in the Middle provinces. South Carolina had long had French Protestant, Congregational, Presbyterian and Lutheran congregations as well as Anglican parishes. Similar conditions existed in Georgia and in the Southern backcountry generally. By 1775 Presbyterianism was an important force throughout the South not only in religion but also in education and politics. Its ministry, at first recruited largely from Scotland and Ireland, was now mainly native-born, with the college at Princeton as a principal source of supply. Though the American presbyteries had no organic connection with those of Scotland and Ireland, they accepted the doctrinal standards of the Scotch Church as "their pattern in general," while seeking to adapt themselves to American conditions.[1]

In the South as well as in the North the Baptists were gaining rapidly, especially among the "plain people." In theology they differed among themselves, some accepting certain Calvinistic tenets, while others emphasized the principle of free will. They agreed, however, in limiting baptism to converted adults and in practising the rite of immersion. Both these doctrines were well adapted to the psychology of the Great Awakening, which continued longer in the South than in New England. Though Rhode Island had been the first Baptist

[1] C. A. Briggs, *American Presbyterianism* (N. Y., 1885), 328.

stronghold, Philadelphia was now the principal base. Accepting the Congregational theory of church government, the Baptists acknowledged no central authority; but their Philadelphia Association was an effective missionary agency, through whose efforts several churches were organized in Virginia and grouped in a new association. Even earlier there had been an association in South Carolina.[1]

More aggressive than the "Regular Baptists" were the "Separate Baptists," an outgrowth of the Great Awakening in New England, where a marked growth of the denomination had occurred. Two of the most successful New England evangelists, Shubal Stearns and Daniel Marshall, carried their preaching into Virginia and North Carolina. Their strenuous revivalism was especially attuned to the common folk, who, according to another Baptist preacher, would often "cry out, fall down, and for a time lose the use of their limbs." In Virginia these itinerant exhorters suffered more than the Presbyterians from the restrictions imposed on dissenting preachers. They and their followers were frequently fined or imprisoned, sometimes on charges of vagrancy or disorderly conduct. As the most active opponents of church establishments wherever found, the Baptists gave a definite impulse to the democratic movement.[2]

To this period also belong the origins of organized Methodism in the colonies. Though American Methodism owed something to George Whitefield, the British evangelist, who was well known all along the seaboard, his permanent influence counted for less than that of John Wesley. The latter, in contrast with Whitefield's Calvinist ideas, emphasized the doctrine of divine grace

[1] A. H. Newman, *A History of the Baptist Churches in the United States* (Philip Schaff and others, eds., *The American Church History Series*, N. Y., 1893-1897, II), 284-310.

[2] W. M. Gewehr, *The Great Awakening in Virginia, 1740-1790* (Duke Univ., *Publs.*, 1930), chap. v.

freely offered to all men for their acceptance or rejection. Though stressing personal religion and the necessity of conversion, the Methodists combined their emotional appeal with a remarkable practicality and organizing power. Their first American societies were formed in New York City, where a chapel was built in 1768, and in Maryland. A picturesque early disciple of Wesley was Thomas Webb, a retired British officer who impressed John Adams by his eloquence.[1]

From these modest beginnings Methodism gradually expanded. Presently Wesley sent out several lieutenants, including the future bishop, Francis Asbury. At the third conference of colonial preachers in 1775 the Methodists claimed over three thousand members. With "circuits" in New York, New Jersey and Pennsylvania they had their greatest following in Maryland and Virginia. Notwithstanding that Wesley was a clergyman of the Anglican Church, his adherents were coldly received by most of his fellow churchmen in America. Nevertheless, the Methodists during these years did not establish a distinct church. In general, the crowds who were stirred by these pioneer preachers consisted mainly of comparatively uneducated persons, including many Negroes. Among the few upper-class converts was one of Asbury's Maryland supporters, who was said to possess a large fortune.[2]

The Catholics still formed a small minority. Shortly before the Revolution the English vicar apostolic who supervised the colonial clergy estimated the number of Catholics at about sixteen thousand in Maryland and six or seven thousand in Pennsylvania, making a total of twenty-two or twenty-three thousand. Even after the

---

[1] J. M. Buckley, A History of Methodists in the United States (Schaff and others, American Church History Series, V), chaps. iv-vi; John Adams, Works (C. F. Adams, ed., Boston, 1856), II, 401.
[2] Buckley, History of Methodists, 149, 155; Gewehr, Great Awakening, chap. vi.

Revolution Bishop John Carroll thought there were only about that number in the thirteen states. There were, of course, persons of Catholic sympathies in places without organized congregations, where their public worship was prohibited. Catholic interests were cared for by Jesuit missionary priests. In Maryland they held services in private chapels, but in Pennsylvania they were free to worship publicly. When in 1773 the Jesuit order was dissolved by the pope, its members were seriously embarrassed.[1]

The Maryland Catholics, though subject to serious legal disabilities, included socially important families. The Carrolls, for example, contributed both a signer of the Declaration of Independence and the first Catholic bishop in the United States. Elsewhere the adherents were mainly recent immigrants from Ireland and Germany, often distrusted by their neighbors and likely, according to a Catholic contemporary, to "become in general, poor and dejected." Anti-Catholic feeling stemmed partly from the wars between Protestant England and the Catholic governments of France and Spain; but one important factor was the activity of the Jesuits in extending French influence among the Indians. Few Americans before 1776 knew a Catholic priest or had seen a Catholic service; but in 1773 and 1774 two representative New Englanders attended services in Philadelphia with mingled feelings of admiration and disapproval. Josiah Quincy noted "the deepest solemnity of worship and musick: the greatest sanctity of countenance and gesture," whereby "reason lost part of her influence." John Adams, similarly impressed, wondered "how Luther ever broke the spell."[2]

---

[1] Peter Guilday, *The Life and Times of John Carroll* (N. Y., 1922), 225-226.

[2] *Ibid.*, 59-72; Josiah Quincy, "Journal," Mass. Hist. Soc., *Proceeds.*, XLIX, 472-474; John and Abigail Adams, *Familiar Letters during the Revolution* (C. F. Adams, ed., Boston, 1875), 46.

No one can say how far in any church personal convictions harmonized with the professed tenets. Even authentic records of individual thought and feeling may not be really typical. For some church members religion meant primarily a means of maintaining social morality and public order; and though many were led by zealous preaching or long usage to emphasize sectarian dogmas, others in the same groups took little interest in such distinctions.

Sophisticated older communities were affected by European attitudes associated with the Age of Enlightenment, and particularly with the rationalistic philosophy of Deism. This in turn was related to the changed outlook on the physical universe resulting from the recent developments in natural science, represented in England by the work of Sir Isaac Newton. Even for men who like Newton desired to harmonize the new theories with the older faith, some readjustment seemed inevitable. Men wondered how far the conception of a universe governed by fixed laws was consistent with supernatural occurrences. The thoroughgoing Deists rejected miracles and such historic dogmas as the Incarnation and the Trinity. They insisted also that truth was to be determined by the human reason rather than by any special divine revelation in the Scriptures. They had, however, their own "natural religion" with its "Supreme Being" or "Supreme Architect of the Universe," and generally believed that in a future state virtue would be rewarded and vice punished. Many of them, indeed, were ready to accept a simplified Christian teaching stripped of "superstitions."

Though British Deism probably reached its high point in the first half of the eighteenth century, it became influential in America somewhat later. John Adams found Deistic literature in the country town of Worcester and reported that his lawyer-teacher was skeptical about the

New Testament narratives. Of three outstanding leaders in the Revolution, Franklin and Jefferson may fairly be called Deists, and Adams was certainly far from orthodox, though he valued the social influence of the churches. President Samuel Johnson of King's College considered New England in danger both from the vagaries of religious "enthusiasm" and from "infidelity." As for Philadelphia, Quincy observed that "the more influential, opulent and first characters rarely attended any public worship." It is only fair, however, to note the conservative religious outlook of such Revolutionary leaders as Samuel Adams, Patrick Henry and Henry Laurens.[1]

The tendency toward a more secular outlook was displayed in various ways: the diminishing proportion of college graduates attracted to the ministry; the large number of academic theses dealing with secular topics; and the shift of interest shown in contemporary publications. Regarding the American scene as a whole, however, it is difficult to generalize. Though in New England the Great Awakening had largely spent its force, elsewhere Presbyterian Calvinism had never been more widespread or vigorous. Significant also was the success of Baptists and Methodists in cultivating neglected areas and social classes. Even in New England the drift of sophisticated persons from traditional orthodoxy was partially offset by the evangelism of "Separates" and Baptists.

The churches made little progress in intercolonial organization. The Presbyterians had their synod of New York and Philadelphia; but the loose associations of Congregational churches were limited to particular

---

[1] Adams, Works, II, 1-36, passim; W. C. Ford, "Henry Knox and the London Book-Store in Boston, 1771-1774," Mass. Hist. Soc., Proceeds., LXI, 250-260; Schneiders, Samuel Johnson, III, 279; Quincy, "Journal," 476; H. M. Morais, Deism in Eighteenth Century America (Columbia Univ., Studies, no. 397), 70 and passim.

colonies, and the Anglican Church had no organic union on this side of the water other than the common dependence of the clergy on the authorities in England. There were, however, informal conventions of Anglican clergy from some of the Northern colonies to discuss such matters as the need for American bishops. Several other religious groups were, as we have seen, subject to oversea direction, including the Dutch Reformed and German Reformed churches, the Moravians and the Catholics. Colonial clergymen occasionally received academic honors from British universities. The Anglican churchmen, Samuel Johnson and Samuel Auchmuty, of Trinity Church, New York, held honorary doctorates from Oxford; and some New England ministers were similarly recognized by Scotch universities.[1]

The responsibility of the colonial churches for converting the Indians had long been acknowledged by philanthropic persons, though the work undertaken was on a distinctly smaller scale than that of the Spanish and French Catholics. On the eve of the Revolution the chief missionary activities centered in the Society for the Propagation of the Gospel (the S. P. G.), the New England Congregationalists with some Presbyterian coöperation, and the Moravians. Puritan efforts are especially associated with Eleazar Wheelock and his school at Lebanon, Connecticut, where Indian boys and girls were trained in agriculture as well as religion, and young colonials prepared for mission work. Conspicuous among the latter was Samuel Kirkland, who in 1764 began a long career of devoted service among the Oneida of northern New York. Especially admirable were the Moravian missions under the courageous leadership of David Zeisberger, first in Pennsylvania and later in what

---

[1] A. L. Cross, *The Anglican Episcopate and the American Colonies* (*Harvard Hist. Studies,* IX), chaps. vii, ix; Briggs, *American Presbyterianism,* cxix-cxxii.

is now eastern Ohio, where they gathered Indian converts in communities under paternalistic direction.[1]

The S. P. G. interested itself in the Negroes as well as the Indians; but for the most part the spiritual welfare of the blacks was neglected. Though the Quakers led in opposing slavery, the most significant religious work for Negroes during the Revolutionary era was probably that of the Baptists and Methodists. One serious proposal for missionary activity in Africa came, curiously enough, from the slave-trading town of Newport. There the two Congregational pastors, Ezra Stiles and Samuel Hopkins, took a zealous interest in their Negro parishioners. Stiles held special meetings for them. With Hopkins he launched an unsuccessful project for missionary service in Africa by two Newport Negroes.[2]

Then, as now, churches concerned themselves with problems of social control involving ethical issues. Most obviously related to religious teaching was the governmental regulation of Sabbath observance. In 1764 New York had a pillory for Sabbath-breakers; and in Charleston fines were imposed for walking the streets during Sunday services. In some respects William Livingston, the New York lawyer, and Henry Laurens, the Charleston merchant, were hardly less Puritan than Samuel Adams. Others, however, were not so austere. Franklin observed that the freedom of a Dutch Sunday did not seem to provoke "God's judgment" and concluded that the Deity was less disturbed about such matters than a New England justice. John Adams, riding through Rhode Island, found people there "much more gay and

[1] Edmund De Schweinitz, *The Life and Times of David Zeisberger* (Phila., 1870), 307-381.

[2] M. W. Jernegan, "Slavery and Conversion in the American Colonies," *Am. Hist. Rev.*, XXI, 504-527; Gewehr, *Great Awakening*, chap. x; Ezra Stiles, *Literary Diary* (F. B. Dexter, ed., N. Y., 1901), I, 39, 204, 213, 363-366; Mode, *Source Book*, 560-562.

social" on Sunday than in Massachusetts.   Young Philip Fithian noted differences in this respect between the Virginia planters and the New Jersey Presbyterians. While being rowed to Sabbath service, he saw the river "alive with boats," some people going to church, others fishing or "sporting."   People who came under the influence of dissenting preachers were said to be stricter in such matters.   According to Quincy, a Charleston Sunday was "a day of visiting and mirth with the rich, and of license, pastime and frolic for the negroes." [1]

Toward alcoholic beverages the clergy were comparatively indulgent.   Few persons advocated total abstinence, though efforts were made to check abuse of liquor on grounds of health and social welfare.   John Adams was disturbed by the corrupting effect of the business on local politics and favored reducing the number of licensed houses.   The Quakers Woolman and Benezet preached temperance, and among the Baptists and Methodists drunkenness was a frequent cause for penalties.   Wesley's *Book of Discipline* condemned the sale of spirituous liquors or their "use unless in cases of extreme necessity." Probably, however, most respectable colonials would have approved these lines in a contemporary almanac:

The Minister, the Merchant, and Physician,
The Lawyer, and the deep-schem'd Politician
Meet round the friendly Board, crown'd with the Bowl
Which drowns their Cares and recreates each Soul. [2]

[1] A. E. Peterson and G. W. Edwards, *New York as an Eighteenth Century Municipality* (N. Y., 1917), 308; Edward McCrady, *South Carolina under the Royal Government, 1719-1776* (N. Y., 1899), 101; Benjamin Franklin, *Writings* (Albert Smyth, ed., N. Y., 1907), IV, 185-186; Adams, *Works*, II, 35; P. V. Fithian, *Journal and Letters, 1767-1774* (J. R. Williams, ed., Princeton, 1900), 255; Quincy, "Journal," 455; Gewehr, *Great Awakening*, 260.

[2] J. A. Krout, *Origins of Prohibition* (N. Y., 1925), chap. iii; Adams, *Works*, II, 84-85, 96; Sam Briggs, *The Essays, Humor and Poems of Nathaniel Ames, Father and Son, . . . from Their Almanacks* (Cleveland, 1891), 352-354.

Clerical and lay opinion about lotteries was also tolerant, more so in Massachusetts than in earlier years when they had been condemned as "mischievous and unlawful games" tending to "the utter ruin and impoverishment of families." Lotteries were used to raise money for all sorts of private and public purposes. There were, however, a few objectors. In 1760, after warm debate, Woolman persuaded a Rhode Island Friends' meeting to take action discouraging the practice. As for other diversions, card playing, "mixed dancing" and the theater, though opposed by the stricter Puritans and Quakers, were generally free from legislative interference, with the conspicuous exception of the New England ban on the theater. While the New England code tended to relax, the Southern revivalists demanded greater rigor. Among their followers horse racing, cards, dice, "playing or dancing wanton tunes" and similar amusements became objects of church discipline. To the Virginia élite such people seemed to be "quite destroying pleasure." [1]

The clergy still formed the most important single class of educated men, notably among the New England Congregationalists, where a college degree was almost indispensable for ministerial standing. In spite of the much publicized deficiencies of the Anglican clergy in the South, many of them were English university graduates and may well have been more broadly cultivated than some of their Puritan contemporaries. The Presbyterians also emphasized the need of a "learned ministry." The Baptists were less interested, especially the "Separate Baptists," who feared that too much education might deaden religious zeal. Gradually, however, and particularly among the "Regular Baptists," the desir-

[1] John Noble, "Harvard College Lotteries," Colon. Soc. of Mass., Publs., XXVII, 162-186; John Woolman, Journal (Ernest Rhys, ed., Everyman's Library, N. Y., 1910), 90; Gewehr, Great Awakening, 260.

ability of an educated clergy gained more general recognition. Significant in this connection was the founding of Rhode Island College in 1764 as primarily, though not exclusively, a Baptist institution. The position of the Methodists resembled the earlier Baptist stand. Though Wesley was an Oxford graduate, he was dependent on the coöperation of comparatively uneducated preachers. Among the German and Dutch churches—Lutheran and Calvinist—tradition favored an educated ministry. The elder Mühlenberg and two of his sons in the Lutheran clergy had studied in German universities. In the colonial "coetus" or synod of the German Reformed Church, some thirty members had attended German universities.[1] The Dutch Calvinists, whose clergy had normally received similar training in the Netherlands, established Queen's College at New Brunswick, New Jersey, in 1766 to make such clerical education possible in America.

Many clergymen were active in promoting education, tutoring boys for college, conducting private schools and founding academies. The institutions of higher learning were still largely under clerical control and all their heads were ministers. Even at the nondenominational College of Philadelphia, the provost and vice-provost were respectively Anglican and Presbyterian divines. It was also the clergy—Baptist, Dutch Reformed and Congregational—who took the lead in founding the three new colleges of Rhode Island, Queen's and Dartmouth. The third of these was established in 1769 on the New Hampshire frontier. The intellectual interests of the ministry appeared in other ways as well. In a small New Hampshire parish Jeremy Belknap was beginning to write his excellent history of that colony. Several preachers were members of the

[1] J. H. Dubbs, *History of the Reformed Church, German* (Schaff and others, *American Church History Series*, VIII), 295.

American Philosophical Society, and much of Franklin's correspondence was with clergymen, several of whom shared his scientific curiosity. Stiles, while a Congregational pastor at Newport, showed himself to be one of the most energetic and active-minded Americans of his day. His diary records friendly conversations with a Jewish rabbi and a "romish priest," and though he denounced the Deists, he was ready "to come forth into the open field, and dispute the matter on even footing." One of his special interests was astronomy.[1]

In the field of religion generally there was an obvious continuance of trends apparent in the preceding period, notably the weakening of church establishments and the growing strength of dissent. In matters of thought and feeling there were, as before, clearly defined cross currents. One was the essentially "fundamentalist" emotionalism generated by the Great Awakening, now past its peak in New England but gaining strength in the South. Opposing this trend were the increasing secularism in many circles and a widespread intellectual revolt against orthodoxy, whether Puritan or Anglican.

[1] Stiles, *Diary*, I, 507; Abiel Holmes, *The Life of Ezra Stiles* (Boston, 1798), 79.

CHAPTER VI

PREREVOLUTIONARY CULTURE

How far the Americans of 1775 were literate, in the minimum sense of ability to read and write, is not easily determined. Undoubtedly overoptimistic was John Adams's claim that a native inhabitant who could not read was "as rare as a comet or an earthquake." But equally exaggerated was the comment of the British Lieutenant Thomas Anburey, while a prisoner in Massachusetts, that "very few" of the American sentinels could read. No exact statistics are available except of the most fragmentary sort. These indicate that the number of persons who had to sign their marks instead of their names was probably diminishing.[1]

In systematic provision for publicly supported schools New England was still in the lead, even though the statutory requirements were not always enforced. John Adams considered it one of the chief glories of Massachusetts "that the education of all ranks of people was made the care and expense of the public, and this in a manner unknown to any other people—ancient or modern." Though some of his fellow citizens regarded government support of schools as "an imposition upon the rich in favor of the poor," he insisted that the maintenance of this principle was more important to the community than "all the property of all the rich men in the country." Doubtless this emphasis on public re-

---

[1] John Adams, *Works* (C. F. Adams, ed., Boston, 1856), III, 456; Thomas Anburey, *Travels through the Interior Parts of America* (Boston, 1923), II, 48; M. N. Stanard, *Colonial Virginia* (Phila., 1917), 262-270. I am also indebted for information on this subject to notes prepared for me by Miss Mary S. Benson.

sponsibility, however imperfectly the theory may have been applied, fairly represents prevailing opinion among intelligent New Englanders. In Boston an outstanding annual event was the formal inspection of the town schools. In 1766 these exercises were conducted by the selectmen accompanied by clerical and lay dignitaries, who joined in a public dinner afterwards in Faneuil Hall.[1]

Outside New England, education was still considered as primarily the duty of the family or the church. In New York City the Dutch Reformed and Anglican denominations maintained charity schools. In 1765 the Dutch school was in charge of a master whom the consistory had brought from Holland. Besides teaching the catechism he also served as church clerk and chorister. Among its various activities the Society for the Propagation of the Gospel subsidized schoolmasters. In Pennsylvania and New Jersey the Friends displayed a warm interest in elementary education, while the German church schools tried to preserve the cultural traditions of the fatherland. Especially significant for the Middle colonies, though not peculiar to them, were the freelance teachers who advertised their services in the newspapers and were, sometimes at least, men of character and intelligence. Their offerings ranged from the most rudimentary to fairly advanced studies. A substantial number of men and women must have received some part of their education from such teachers.[2]

Though the South generally followed the English

[1] Adams, *Works*, III, 456-457; John Rowe, *Letters and Diary* (Annie R. Cunningham, ed., Boston, 1903), 100, 168.

[2] Hugh Hastings, comp., *Ecclesiastical Records of New York* (Albany, 1901-1916), V, 3614; VI, 3983. Compare W. W. Kemp, *The Support of Schools in Colonial New York by the Society for the Propagation of the Gospel in Foreign Parts* (Teachers College, Columbia Univ., *Contribs.*, no. 56), with R. F. Seybolt, *Source Studies in American Colonial Education: the Private School* (Univ. of Ill., Bur. of Educational Research, *Bull.*, no. 28).

tradition of parental rather than public responsibility for education, poor children were partially provided for through apprenticeship or on a charity basis. Rich planters could engage well-trained tutors for their off-spring. In Councilor Carter's family the tutor was a young Princeton graduate whose work ranged from teaching the youngest daughter her letters to reading Sallust with an older brother. Near by, in a plantation schoolhouse, an indentured servant from Scotland with a decent, if not extensive, education taught the children of the household and those of neighboring families. The South had occasional school endowments, and in the Carolinas Presbyterian ministers as well as the S. P. G. interested themselves in education. Local societies also raised money for schools. Charleston, like the Northern cities, had numerous free-lance teachers.[1]

How many families availed themselves of these various opportunities or gained an elementary education without formal schooling, we cannot say; but the experience of three Southern leaders is suggestive. Patrick Henry went to a "common English school" until he was ten, and though he attended no other school he received further instruction from his father. Of Washington's teachers we know little, but, besides the usual elementary subjects, he learned business forms and enough mathematics for surveying. Charles Carroll, like other wealthy Catholic boys, attended a Maryland Jesuit school before going abroad.[2] By contrast, Devereux Jarratt belonged

<hr/>

[1] M. W. Jernegan, *Laboring and Dependent Classes in Colonial America, 1607-1783* (Univ. of Chicago, *Social Service Monographs*, no. 17), chaps. x-xii; P. V. Fithian, *Journal and Letters, 1767-1774* (J. R. Williams, ed., Princeton, 1900), 50; John Harrower, "Diary," *Am. Hist. Rev.*, VI, 65-107; Edward McCrady, *South Carolina under the Royal Government, 1719-1776* (N. Y., 1899), chap. xxv.

[2] W. W. Henry, *Patrick Henry* (N. Y., 1891), I, 8-10; J. C. Fitzpatrick, *George Washington Himself* (Indianapolis, 1933), 19-31; Kate M. Rowland, *Life and Correspondence of Charles Carroll of Carrollton* (N. Y., 1898), I, 18.

to a humble family whose expectations did not rise beyond reading, writing and "some knowledge of Arithmetic." At eight or nine he went to a near-by school and continued his education with "great interruptions" until he was twelve or thirteen. Rounding out this instruction by private reading, he became a teacher himself.[1]

Though girls received less formal education than boys, the careers of such distinguished Massachusetts women as Abigail Adams and Mercy Otis Warren show that literary cultivation was not limited to men. Church schools in New York and Pennsylvania provided elementary instruction for both sexes, while tutors on Southern plantations taught girls as well as boys. In addition, advertisements of private teachers—masters and mistresses—offered girls training in "the common branches" and in such "accomplishments" as music and needlework.

Secondary education was available only for a small minority. Under the old seventeenth-century law Massachusetts towns were expected to provide "grammar schools," where boys could be prepared for college, but the requirement was not always met. In New England the best secondary school was probably the Boston Latin School, presided over by John Lovell, a Harvard graduate and a considerable personage. His seven-year classical curriculum emphasized Latin. At least three of his pupils later signed the Declaration of Independence. To prepare boys for Rhode Island College the Baptists founded a new academy in that colony. Connecticut had its Hopkins Grammar School at New Haven, where the future President Timothy Dwight once taught, and Nathan Tisdale's coeducational school at Lebanon, which attracted an intercolonial clientèle. An interesting illustration of tutoring by ministers was

[1] Devereux Jarratt, *Life* (Balt., 1806), 15 ff.

that of Oliver Ellsworth, later chief justice of the Supreme Court, who prepared for Yale with the famous Calvinist theologian, Joseph Bellamy.[1]

There were a few good secondary schools in the Middle colonies. When President Myles Cooper of King's College in 1763 complained that his students were ill prepared, the college established a new fitting school. Philadelphia had two creditable academies: the William Penn Charter School under Quaker auspices and the new academy promoted by Franklin. Near by was the recently founded Germantown Academy, where Greek and Latin were taught and both German and English were used in the teaching. Presbyterian ministers conducted schools on both sides of the Delaware River. One of them, at Newark, Delaware, had among its pupils the future secretary of the Continental Congress and two Delaware signers of the Declaration. Also under Presbyterian auspices were the grammar school connected with New Jersey College at Princeton and a new academy at Newark in the same colony. In such schools classical learning went along with Calvinist theology. Until the founding of Rhode Island College, the chief educational enterprise of the Baptists was probably their academy at Hopewell, New Jersey.[2]

Maryland's best-known secondary school was King William's, located at Annapolis. Nevertheless, Governor Horatio Sharpe declared in 1763 that the province had "not even one good grammar school." A law authoriz-

[1] E. E. Brown, *The Making of Our Middle Schools* (N. Y., 1903), chaps. v-vii; anon., "Master Tisdale and the Lebanon School," *Am. Journ. of Educ.*, XXVIII, 793-797; W. G. Brown, *The Life of Oliver Ellsworth* (N. Y., 1905), 12; R. F. Seybolt, *The Public Schools of Colonial Boston, 1635-1775* (Harvard Docs. in the History of Educ., 1935), 73-76.

[2] Herbert and Carol Schneider, eds., *Samuel Johnson, President of King's College* (N. Y., 1929), IV, 101-104, 156; Brown, *Making of Our Middle Schools*, 95, 102.

ing county schools proved ineffective.[1] Besides the Presbyterian academies of Hampden-Sydney in the piedmont and Liberty Hall west of the Blue Ridge, Virginia maintained a grammar school in connection with William and Mary College; but classical training was commonly supplied elsewhere by individual clergymen, Jefferson being among those so taught. The Carolinians also had clerical schoolmasters, Anglican or Presbyterian. Some Southern boys went to Northern schools while others were sent abroad. Among the latter, Arthur and Richard Henry Lee and Thomas Nelson, jr., the later Virginia war governor, attended English schools; John Laurens went to a Protestant school in Geneva; and Charles and John Carroll studied at Jesuit schools on the Continent. James Delancey of New York and East Apthorpe of Boston were Northern examples, the former attending Cambridge and the latter Oxford. In brief, a fair proportion of the Revolutionary leaders received some classical education.

Interest in modern subjects was growing. The Philadelphia Academy had an English division along with the Latin school. Hampden-Sydney, though continuing the classical tradition, gave special attention to mathematics as a preparation for science and to English, geography and history. Instruction in such courses was also offered by free-lance schoolmasters. French, for instance, was advertised as a desirable accomplishment and also for its use in business. Among the definitely practical subjects announced were bookkeeping, surveying and navigation, with geometry and trigonometry and occasionally even architecture.[2]

On the eve of the Revolution higher education was

[1] N. D. Mereness, *Maryland as a Proprietary Province* (N. Y., 1901), 137-145.
[2] W. M. Gewehr, *The Great Awakening in Virginia, 1740-1790* (Duke Univ., *Publs.*, 1930), 227; Seybolt, *Source Studies*, chaps. i-ii.

provided by nine colonial colleges: Harvard, Yale, William and Mary, King's at New York, the College of New Jersey at Princeton, the College of Philadelphia, Rhode Island College, Queen's and Dartmouth. There were also unrealized projects for new colleges in Massachusetts, Maryland and South Carolina. The most interesting of these, the proposed "Queen's College" in western Massachusetts, was blocked by Harvard influence in the legislature. The line between secondary and higher education was not, however, always clearly drawn. Jefferson complained that William and Mary was full of "children," and certainly many undergraduates were very young.[1] Among the eight Harvard signers of the Declaration, John Adams left college under twenty and five others at eighteen or less. Of Princeton alumni in the Federal Convention at least three finished their course before they were eighteen.

Perhaps one out of every thousand colonists in 1775 had been to college at some time or other. Information as to the areas from which students were drawn and the distribution of graduates is too fragmentary for exact statistical statement, but certain generalizations are possible. Harvard attracted nearly all its students from Massachusetts and New Hampshire, and few of its graduates settled outside New England. Similarly, William and Mary College was almost wholly a college for Virginians as King's College was for New Yorkers. Yale students, though drawn chiefly from Connecticut, came also from western Massachusetts, with a fair number from New York; and Yale alumni included several influential leaders in the last province. Philadelphia College because of its central location enjoyed an intercolonial constituency, limited, however, almost wholly to the Delaware Valley and Maryland. From this standpoint

[1] Thomas Jefferson, *Works* (P. L. Ford, ed., N. Y., 1904-1905), IV, 67.

the institution at Princeton was the least localized of the older colleges, whether in respect to the territory from which its students came or the spread of its alumni. New England and the Southern colonies were both substantially represented in its student body. Of its alumni, roughly a quarter found careers south of the Mason and Dixon line, and another quarter went to New England. The influence of personal associations, formed in student days, was an important factor in broadening the outlook of men who were to become leaders in widely scattered communities, whether within the same colony or across provincial boundaries.[1] It is highly significant that of the fifty-four signers of the Declaration of Independence at least eighteen had attended college—eight at Harvard, four at Yale, three at William and Mary, two at Princeton and one at Philadelphia.

Though, in general, the curricula gave central importance to the classics, some interest was displayed in modern subjects. There was a substantial collection of physical apparatus at Harvard, where losses by fire in 1764 were repaired by contributors on both sides of the Atlantic. The most eminent college teacher of science was Harvard's John Winthrop, a member of the American Philosophical Society, a fellow of the Royal Society and an honorary doctor of the University of Edinburgh. Winthrop taught mathematics, astronomy and physics with "Philosophic Experiments." Among his students was one destined to become a distinguished scientist, Benjamin Thompson. Shortly before the Revolution, chairs of science were provided at Yale, Princeton and King's College. The corresponding professorship at William and Mary, established many years earlier, was given in 1773 to James Madison, a kinsman of the better-known statesman of that name. John Adams, on

[1] Estimates in this paragraph are based on material in alumni lists and biographical dictionaries collected by Mary S. Benson.

a visit to Princeton in 1774, admired its planetarium, constructed by David Rittenhouse, and also its electrical apparatus.[1] At Philadelphia, Provost William Smith lectured on natural philosophy, but the chief scientific work there was that of the medical faculty, which extended its charge over botany and chemistry.

No college possessed a chair of modern foreign languages or made any provision for them in the regular curriculum. In English and public speaking there were "disputations" and other literary exercises. At Yale two vigorous young tutors, John Trumbull and Timothy Dwight, stimulated interest in literature as President John Witherspoon did at Princeton. Provost Smith at Philadelphia also seems to have done much to encourage young writers. The Philadelphia commencement of 1770 illustrates the kind of literary effort favored. Besides Latin parts, the program included "forensic disputes" in English on such topics as: "Whether Self-love and the Pursuit of Self-interest be the ultimate end of all human actions," and "Whether resistance of the Supreme Powers of Government be in any Case lawful." In a "Dialogue in Verse," referring to the pending controversy between Britain and the colonies, students professed ardent faith in the American future: "It seems decreed that Empire, Freedom, Arts, and their refulgent train should urge their course, Glorious from East to West." [2] The political and social sciences were largely by-products of instruction in the classics and moral philosophy. Witherspoon's Princeton lectures on moral philosophy included politics, but he also announced lec-

---

[1] Josiah Quincy, *History of Harvard University* (Cambridge, 1840), II, apps. xi, xxvi; Ezra Stiles, *Literary Diary* (F. B. Dexter, ed., N. Y., 1901), I, 77, 84; John Maclean, *History of the College of New Jersey* (Phila., 1877), I, 357-367; Brander Matthews and others, eds., *A History of Columbia University, 1754-1904* (N. Y., 1904), 22; Adams, *Works*, II, 356.

[2] *Pa. Gazette*, June 14, 1774.

tures on "chronology and history, civil as well as sacred." At Philadelphia College, Provost Smith seems to have discussed the works of Grotius, Pufendorf and Locke.[1] Contemporary criticism of the colleges found expression in John Trumbull's *Progress of Dulness*, which satirized pedantic teachers who

> Read ancient authors o'er in vain,
> Nor taste one beauty they contain.[2]

Innovators, however, faced difficulties. When William and Mary was urged to follow the example of Princeton under Witherspoon, a defender of the old order scored the New Jersey faculty for attempting too much. "Your Nassaus alone," he wrote, "can boast the truly magic art of forming, in a year or two, the classic, the mathematician, the moral philosopher, and the patriot."[3] Though college libraries were usually small and apparently not much used by students, the case may be overstated. Harvard in 1773 owned a well-balanced collection, much of it given by Thomas Hollis, the English liberal. The works on theology and philosophy represented various shades of opinion, Anglican, Puritan and Deistic. Treatises in politics included some by Grotius, Locke, Pufendorf, Vattel, Montesquieu, Burlamaqui, Beccaria and Blackstone. Along with volumes on British history by Hume and Robertson were such standard treatises of Continental European and Asiatic history as Rollin's *Ancient History*, the Jesuit *Lettres Édifiantes*, histories of France, Spain, Holland and Poland, and the important works on China and Japan by

[1] John Witherspoon, *Works* (Phila., 1800), III, 268 ff.; W. A. Whitehead and others, eds., *Archives of the State of New Jersey* (Newark, 1880-1905), ser. 1, XXVI, 303 ff.; H. W. Smith, *Life and Correspondence of the Rev. William Smith* (Phila., 1879), I, 126-127.

[2] John Trumbull, *Poetical Works* (Hartford, 1820), II, 17.

[3] Rind's *Va. Gazette*, quoted in *William and Mary College Quar.*, II, 107.

Duhalde and Kaempfer. There is some interesting information about the books used by Dartmouth students and teachers from 1773 to 1777. In most frequent demand was Rollin's *Ancient History;* Pope stood first in English literature; and Locke's *Essay on the Human Understanding* was apparently more called for than his *Treatises of Civil Government.* Other authors chosen were Jonathan Edwards, Richard Baxter, John Bunyan and Bishop Butler.[1]

Student discipline was adapted to young boys. At King's College undergraduates who went over the fence to swim were kept in bounds for a time and required to translate four pages of a sermon into Latin. Complaints of food in college commons led to the Harvard "Butter Rebellion" of 1766, and an uprising at Yale precipitated President Thomas Clap's resignation. Deference to superiors was enforced by tradition and sometimes by college rule, and social status was considered in listing Yale and Harvard students, though both colleges abandoned the practice shortly before the Revolution. Extracurricular activities centered in student clubs. Harvard had three new ones in the seventeen-seventies, all interested in public speaking. Yale had its Linonian Society and Brothers in Unity, and Princeton its Cliosophic and Whig societies. Undergraduates were also interested in plays. At Harvard in 1765 the "Day of Judgment" was "acted in a very shocking manner," arousing fears in some quarters that the college would suffer unless the "profane wretches" who participated were expelled.[2]

---

[1] Harvard College, *Catalogus Librorum* (Boston, 1773) ; H. D. Foster, "Webster and Choate in College," in his collected *Papers* (n. p., 1929), 236.

[2] S. E. Morison, *Three Centuries of Harvard* (Cambridge, 1936), chap. vi; F. B. Dexter, *A Selection from the Miscellaneous Historical Papers of Fifty Years* (New Haven, 1918), 269; M. H. Thomas, ed., *Black Book; or Book of Misdemeanors in King's College, New York, 1771-1775* (N. Y., 1931), 4; Dennys de Berdt, "Letters" (Albert Matthews, ed.), Colon. Soc. of Mass., *Publs.*, XIII, 320.

Most of the colleges had some governmental connections. All the lay members of the Harvard board of overseers, which included the governor, represented the provincial authorities. Harvard, Yale, King's, Philadelphia and Dartmouth obtained more or less support from their respective governments. William and Mary received a standing revenue from the Virginia assembly, the provincial governor was a member of the governing board, and the college elected a representative in the house of burgesses. In other respects, also, these institutions were objects of general interest. The Harvard commencement had somewhat the character of a public holiday in that neighborhood, and the festivities were attended by the governor and other officials. In 1771 Governor John Wentworth of New Hampshire led an imposing cavalcade from Portsmouth to the Dartmouth commencement.[1]

The colleges continued to seek and obtain British patronage. After the burning of a Harvard building, as we have seen, the college secured contributions in money, books and apparatus. The New York and Philadelphia institutions raised several thousand pounds in England, and even the young colleges at Providence and Hanover secured British gifts. There were also intercolonial campaigns for funds in which some Northern institutions went as far afield as South Carolina and the West Indies.[2]

As an instrument of popular education the newspaper supplemented the schools and colleges, and attained a greater importance than ever before known in America.[3]

[1] Rowe, Letters and Diary, 103; Morison, Three Centuries of Harvard, 119 ff.; L. S. Mayo, John Wentworth (Cambridge, 1921), 114.

[2] Quincy, Harvard University, II, 113-116 and app. xi; Matthews and others, History of Columbia University, chap. iii; McCrady, South Carolina under Royal Government, 499.

[3] For the earlier story of the colonial newspaper press, see J. T. Adams, Provincial Society, 1690-1763 (A History of American Life, III), 264-268.

By 1775 there were about thirty newspapers, against
twenty in 1763, and before the war there was one in
every colony except New Jersey and Delaware. Each of
the four principal towns had three or more of these week-
lies; Philadelphia had seven. Circulation statistics are
scanty. James Rivington's *New-York Gazetteer* was
said to have thirty-six hundred subscribers in 1774; but
that, if true, was probably exceptional. Rivington's
contemporary, Isaiah Thomas, estimated that in 1754
the average circulation of the four Boston papers did not
exceed six hundred apiece. William Goddard began
the publication of his *Pennsylvania Chronicle* in 1767
with seven hundred subscribers, a figure soon raised to
more than a thousand. Most newspapers had readers in
other colonies. Goddard employed subscription agents
in Delaware, New Jersey, Maryland and Virginia. Hugh
Gaine boasted that his *New-York Mercury* went to all
the "Capital Places" and many rural communities in the
colonies and to the West Indies as well.[1]

The colonial newspaper was of tabloid size, and usually comprised four closely printed pages without head-
lines or pictures. A characteristic make-up was that of
the *Pennsylvania Gazette* on January 6, 1763. The
whole first page was given to a poem and certain legal
documents. Of the next page about a third consisted
of European items; the remainder, of miscellaneous notes
from Boston and Salem, shipping news from New York
and legislative proceedings in Jamaica. The last two
pages contained advertisements and two paragraphs of
shipping news. Since the sheets appeared once a week
and were handicapped by slow communications, the
editors found it difficult to provide fresh news. The

[1] *N.-Y. Gazetteer*, no. 78, Oct., 1774; Isaiah Thomas, *The History
of Printing in America* (Am. Antiquarian Soc., *Archæologia Americana*,
Trans. and Colls., V-VI, Albany, 1874), II, 8; J. F. Watson, *Annals
of Philadelphia and Pennsylvania, in the Olden Time* (Phila., 1845),
II, 461; Hugh Gaine, *Journals* (P. L. Ford, ed., N. Y., 1902), I, 41.

Pennsylvania Gazette of January 3, 1765, carried no
English or Irish advices later than September, 1764;
Jamaica reports were over two months old; all the
Charleston items but one had November dates; and
Boston notices were at least two months old. The latest
European entry in the *South-Carolina Gazette* of Sep-
tember 24, 1772, was dated July 14. The *Gazette*
sometimes postponed an issue, awaiting news from an
incoming vessel.[1]

The publisher-editor was generally a printer or printer's partner, frequently a bookseller, sometimes a postmaster. Often he held government printing contracts.
Family connections were important in the history of
certain journals. Descendants of Samuel Green, the
pioneer Cambridge printer in 1649, ran papers in the
eighteenth century at Boston, New London, Norwich,
New Haven and Annapolis.[2] New England newspaper
men were usually native-born, trained as apprentices to
older men. Elsewhere there were more British-born
journalists. Two of the ablest editors in all the colonies
were Hugh Gaine, a former printer's apprentice in Ireland, and James Rivington, a member of the English
book-publishing family of that name, who conducted
papers in New York City. Several Southern newspapers, including Purdie and Dixon's *Virginia Gazette,*
the *South-Carolina and General American Gazette* and
the *Georgia Gazette,* were published by Scots. In addition to the English-language journals in Pennsylvania,
German-language papers were edited by Christopher
Sauer and John Henry Miller. Sauer's outlook was
pietist, pacifist and conservative, while Miller was a
Whig.

Politics received increasing attention in the newspapers
as the Revolution approached. The *Pennsylvania*

[1] Thomas, *History of Printing,* II, 170.
[2] J. C. Oswald, *Printing in the Americas* (N. Y., 1937), chap. vii.

Gazette of December 26, 1765, gave nearly half its space to the stamp-act controversy. The colonial printers, who were directly burdened by the stamp tax, acted with greater unanimity than at any later time, aiding powerfully the propaganda for repeal. The chief Whig journals in New England were the *Boston Gazette,* published by Benjamin Edes and John Gill, and Isaiah Thomas's *Massachusetts Spy,* founded in 1770. The former printed the "Novanglus" essays of John Adams. Aiming to reach a wider constituency by using "common sense in common language," Thomas claimed that his circulation exceeded for a time that of any other New England paper. By contrast, Draper's *Massachusetts Gazette and News-Letter,* which published Daniel Leonard's Loyalist essays, was moderately conservative. The more aggressive Toryism of the *Boston Chronicle* (1767-1770) resulted in its suspension.[1]

In New York John Holt's *Journal* was strongly Whig, while Gaine in the *Mercury* and Rivington in the *Gazetteer,* though claiming to be nonpartisan, leaned to the government side. Vigorous Tory communications in the *Gazetteer* antagonized the patriots and in 1775 led to the destruction of Rivington's press by a mob. Philadelphia had no thoroughgoing Tory organ, while William and Thomas Bradford's *Pennsylvania Journal* and John Dunlap's *Pennsylvania Packet* were vigorously Whig. Jefferson declared after the Revolution that Purdie and Dixon's *Virginia Gazette,* having been given the public printing, was unwilling to admit anything "disagreeable to the governor"; so the opposition imported William Rind, a Maryland printer, to "publish a

---

[1] *Pa. Gazette,* June 14, 1770; A. M. Schlesinger, "Colonial Newspapers and the Stamp Act," *New England Quar.,* VIII, 63-83, and "Propaganda and the Boston Newspaper Press, 1767-1770," Colon. Soc. of Mass., *Publs.,* XXXII, 396-416; Thomas, *History of Printing,* I, xlv and *passim;* Justin Winsor, ed., *Memorial History of Boston, 1630-1880* (Boston, 1880-1881), III, chap. iii.

free paper." One Charleston paper was issued by the Loyalist printer and bookseller, Robert Wells, and the other two by Whigs.[1]

Less successful than the Whigs at propaganda, the government authorities from time to time considered measures to muzzle the patriot press. In 1765 the New York attorney-general held that the author and publisher of a communication in the *New-York Gazette* might be prosecuted for sedition; but the provincial council, while regarding the article as "highly culpable," favored waiting for "a more seasonable time," which never came. Governor Colden later complained of an opposition pamphlet "to render the Government odious and Contemptible," but again without result. In Boston Governor Sir Francis Bernard unsuccessfully urged the arrest of Edes and Gill, and in 1771 a provocative article in the *Spy* led to an attempt to indict Thomas, but this move also failed. As the movement of resistance developed, the chief threat to free discussion came from the radicals rather than the conservatives, and through extralegal measures.[2]

With all its limitations the newspaper press helped to broaden mental horizons. In the opinion of an anonymous writer in the *New-York Journal*, April 19, 1770,

> 'Tis truth (with deference to the college)
> Newspapers are the spring of knowledge;
> The general source throughout the nation
> Of every modern conversation.
> What would this mighty people do

---

[1] Thomas, *History of Printing*, I, 336 n. and *passim*; V. H. Paltsits, "John Holt," N. Y. Public Library, *Bull.*, XXIV, 483-499; A. M. Schlesinger, "Politics, Propaganda, and the Philadelphia Press, 1767-1770," *Pa. Mag. of History and Biog.*, LX, 309-322.

[2] Cadwallader Colden, *Letters and Papers* (N. Y. Hist. Soc., *Colls.*, L-LVI), VII, 38, 62; I. N. P. Stokes, *Iconography of Manhattan Island* (N. Y., 1915-1928), IV, 780; Thomas, *History of Printing*, I, xlvii-liii.

If there alas were nothing new?
A newspaper is like a feast,
Some dish there is for every guest:
. . . Our services you can't express
There's not a want of human kind,
But we a remedy can find.

Rivaling the newspaper in importance was the almanac. "Our business," wrote one almanac maker, "is
looked upon by many as low and vulgar . . . yet there
are no Works so essential to the Well-being of the community, so universally beneficial, so constantly purchased
as ours. . . . The most accurate Scholar has recourse
to us and we are read by Multitudes who read nothing
else." Probably the most important of these publications in this period was the one taken over in 1764 by
Dr. Nathaniel Ames of Dedham, Massachusetts, from
the elder Nathaniel; but it had numerous competitors,
German as well as English. Sauer's *Hoch-Deutsch
Americanische Kalender* and another issued by John
Henry Miller had an intercolonial circulation.[1]

The almanacs faithfully reflected current trends in
economics and politics. The Ames almanac, which in
1766 reported the Americans happy "under as good a
King as ever reign'd," printed six years later a portrait
of John Dickinson, "The Patriotic American Farmer"
who defended American liberties "with Attic Eloquence
and Roman Spirit." *Bickerstaff's Boston Almanack*
presented cover-page pictures of both American patriots
and British sympathizers. Below the cut of John
Wilkes in 1769 were placed open volumes of Locke and
Sydney, "in whom the Spirit of the antient Republics
revived." James Otis was so honored in 1770 and the
Earl of Chatham in 1772. The Ames almanac for 1775

---

[1] *Bickerstaff's Boston Almanack for 1774*, preface; Oscar Kuhns,
German and Swiss Settlements of Colonial Pennsylvania (N. Y., 1901),
133-134.

contained an appeal to Americans to champion their
"Country's cause," and implemented it with an essay
on making gunpowder. Science also received attention.
One almanac of 1768 printed "A Chronological Table
of the Discovery of the Arts and Sciences." The Ames
almanac eulogized Franklin's scientific accomplishments
and paid tribute in verse to Locke and Newton.[1]

For magazines educated Americans still relied largely
on the English periodicals. Those published in the colonies were few and imitative. In 1763 there were none,
and in the next twelve years only three lasted long
enough to make any impression at all: Lewis Nicola's
American Magazine (January to September, 1769);
Isaiah Thomas's *Royal American Magazine* (Boston,
1774-1775); and Robert Aitken's *Pennsylvania Magazine* (1775-1776). Perhaps the most significant feature of the *American Magazine* was the attention paid to
scientific topics, including selections from the publications of the Royal Society and the early transactions of
the American Philosophical Society. Like Nicola's publication, the *Royal American Magazine* consisted mostly
of British material, though it exhibited an ardent Americanism in such titles as "Address of America's Genius to
the People in the American World" and "A Prophecy
of the Future Glory of America," and also in its engrav-
ings, which were chiefly by Paul Revere. The issue for
March, 1774, contained a portrait of John Hancock
"supported by the Goddess of Liberty and an Ancient
Briton." At the time of the Boston port bill, Revere's
engraving showed a doctor pouring tea on a helpless

[1] C. N. Greenough, "New England Almanacs, 1766-1775, and the
American Revolution," Am. Antiquarian Soc., Proceeds., n.s., XLV, 288-
316; Sam Briggs, *The Essays, Humor and Poems of Nathaniel Ames,
Father and Son, . . . from Their Almanacks* (Cleveland, 1891), 347,
372-373, 387, 402, 437; *Bickerstaff's Boston Almanack,* 1768 and
later.

patient. In March, 1775, "America in Distress" was pictured with British politicians as "Evil Physicians" and "Wicked Councellors." The *Pennsylvania Magazine* printed some fresh American matter from the pens of John Witherspoon, Francis Hopkinson and Thomas Paine. Along with political essays, there was lighter material, including poetry and Hopkinson's allegories.[1] Every sizable town had one or more booksellers. Among those who were also journalists were Robert Wells in Charleston; William Bradford and John Dunlap in Philadelphia; Hugh Gaine and James Rivington in New York; and John Mein of the *Boston Chronicle*, whose London Bookstore for a time outshone all his competitors in Massachusetts. Other representative dealers were Henry Knox, the future general, also of Boston, and the much more important Robert Bell. After some experience in Glasgow and Dublin, the latter established himself at Philadelphia, where he held book auctions with printed catalogues and developed an intercolonial trade. He was also a noted wit and a publisher, in the latter capacity issuing the first American editions of Robertson's *Charles the Fifth*, Blackstone's *Commentaries* and Paine's *Common Sense*.[2]

Of the earlier lending libraries, that of the Charleston Library Society in South Carolina now numbered six or seven thousand volumes.[3] Franklin while in London was an active buyer for the Philadelphia Library Company. New York had the library of the New York

[1] L. N. Richardson, *A History of Early American Magazines, 1741-1789* (N. Y., 1931), chaps. vi-vii, pp. 362 ff. See also issues of *American Magazine or General Repository*, June, Sept., 1769, and *Royal American Magazine*, Jan., March, June, 1774; March, 1775.

[2] L. C. Wroth, "Book Production and Distribution from the Beginning to the War between the States," Hellmut Lehmann-Haupt and others, *The Book in America* (N. Y., 1939), 55; Carl and Jessica Bridenbaugh, *Rebels and Gentlemen* (N. Y., 1942), 82-86.

[3] For earlier library development, see Adams, *Provincial Society*, 115-119.

Society and some smaller towns had similar membership ventures. Characteristic of New England was the institution known as the "Social Library." Such a collection at Salem belonged to a club of which the Loyalist Samuel Curwen was a member. Booksellers occasionally conducted circulating libraries. In 1763 that of Garratt Noel in New York was said to contain several thousand volumes.[1]

There were some considerable private collections as well. In the South, Councilor Carter owned more than a thousand books. George Mason used the library of his stepfather, John Mercer, which was said to embrace over fifteen hundred volumes. Among the Boston lawyers Jeremiah Gridley, James Otis and John Adams all had substantial collections. Thomas Hutchinson's important library suffered damage from the stamp-act riots. One of the most serious consequences of the burning of Charlestown in 1775 was the destruction of the Mather library built up through four generations. At that time the merchant-politician, James Bowdoin, owned a well-selected collection of twelve hundred volumes.[2]

Though colonial readers still depended mainly on British publications, colonial imprints were increasing. Between 1765 and 1774 they rose from less than four hundred to nearly seven hundred, though many of the issues were newspapers, pamphlets or broadsides, or

[1] McCrady, South Carolina under Royal Government, 508-512; Benjamin Franklin, Writings (Albert Smyth, ed., N. Y., 1907), V, 315; A. B. Keep, History of the New York Society Library (N. Y., 1908), chaps. i-iii; C. K. Bolton, "Social Libraries in New England," Colon. Soc. of Mass., Publs., XII, 332-338; Samuel Curwen, Journal and Letters (G. A. Ward, ed., Boston, 1842), chap. i; Stokes, Iconography of Manhattan, IV, 737; Lehmann-Haupt and others, Book in America, 361.

[2] John and Abigail Adams, Familiar Letters during the Revolution (C. F. Adams, ed., Boston, 1875), 76; J. H. Tuttle, "The Bowdoin Library," Mass. Hist. Soc., Proceeds., LI, 362-368; Stanard, Colonial Virginia, 297-307; Gilbert Chinard, Thomas Jefferson (Boston, 1929), 39; Helen Hill, George Mason, Constitutionalist (Cambridge, 1938), 12.

American reprints of European books.[1] Of the total amount of reading matter, theological works, though less prominent than in earlier years, still bulked large. Among David Hall's book importations at Philadelphia in 1763 were numerous religious titles, Anglican, Calvinist and Quaker. The Philadelphia Library Company advertised for sale Foxe's *Book of Martyrs*, Bunyan's works, Anglican treatises by Jeremy Taylor and Archbishop Tillotson, and volumes by such Deistic or skeptical writers as Hume, Bolingbroke, Voltaire and Rousseau.[2]

The classics still ranked high with cultivated readers. In the controversial essays of Charles Carroll Latin authors were freely quoted. Jefferson was apparently influenced by reading Homer and, through Cicero, by Stoic philosophy. George Wythe, writing to Adams, quoted Greek lines from the *Odyssey*. Though Adams made no special claim to classical scholarship, he continued to read Latin authors after leaving college, including Horace, Pliny's letters, Cicero's *De Officiis* and Ovid. Otis was reputed to be "a passionate admirer of the Greek poets." Plutarch's *Lives*, available in English translation, helped to form American notions of ancient personages and ideals. The *Ancient History* of the French scholar Charles Rollin was also well-known. There was nevertheless some skepticism about classical training, as in the case of Franklin. Henry Laurens thought the classics had "often been impediments to the success of young men," and another contemporary maintained that English literature offered more than "all the boasted treasures of antiquity." [3]

[1] Charles Evans, *American Bibliography* (new edn., N. Y., 1941-1942), III.-V.

[2] *Pa. Gazette*, Jan. 6, 1763; March 15, 1770.

[3] Maryland Invoices and Letters, 1772-1787 (MSS., Library of Congress); Rowland, *Carroll*, I, app. a; Chinard, *Jefferson*, 26; Adams, *Works*, II, 3, 37, 86; III, 197; William Tudor, *The Life of James Otis*

In English literature, Shakespeare and Bacon were read less than the later seventeenth-century authors such as Milton and Dryden among the poets, and these in turn less than the writers of the "Augustan Age." Interest in the *Spectator* was continuous from the days of Franklin's youth. Some Americans knew Dean Swift and the dramatist Congreve while the favorite poet was Pope. The mid-eighteenth-century novelists— Richardson, Fielding, Smollett—were widely advertised in the press. Richardson was generally considered the most edifying; but in spite of some misgivings about Fielding and Smollett, they were read even in Puritan Boston. Sterne's *Sentimental Journey*, Goldsmith's *Vicar of Wakefield* and Chesterfield's *Letters* were known, and, among the British historians, Clarendon, Burnet, Hume and Robertson. Very popular, though now almost forgotten, was Catherine Macaulay's Whiggish *History of England*.[1] Most influential of all was John Locke's *Two Treatises of Civil Government*. Through the "intellectuals"—lawyers, politicians and clergy—Locke's ideas were passed on to the plain people in pamphlets, newspapers and sermons. Sydney's seventeenth-century republican *Discourses Concerning Government* was also highly regarded and so was Milton's political writing. Harrington's seventeenth-century account of an ideal commonwealth was still read, and Coke gave Americans an argument for fundamental law as transcending ordinary legislation.[2]

(Boston, 1823), 16; D. D. Wallace, *Henry Laurens* (N. Y., 1915), 182; *Royal American Magazine*, April, 1774.

[1] Advertisement in *American Magazine* or *General Repository for 1769*; Stanard, *Colonial Virginia*, 299 ff.; Tuttle, "Bowdoin Library," 362 ff.; Hall's advertisement in *Pa. Gazette*, Jan. 6, 1763; Adams, *Familiar Letters*, 143, 153, 161, 196; Adams, *Works*, IX, 331-333.

[2] C. H. Van Tyne, *The Causes of the War of Independence* (Boston, 1922), 343-344; C. F. Mullett, *Fundamental Law and the American Revolution* (N. Y., 1933), chaps. i-ii.

Of the modern literature of Continental Europe, Americans knew less, though some could read French in the original. John Adams, Carroll, Franklin and Jefferson illustrate varying degrees of proficiency in this respect. A number of standard French books were, of course, also available in translation. Rabelais and Montaigne were probably the best-known sixteenth-century French writers. Rabelais was advertised by the Philadelphia Library Company and was in Bowdoin's private collection. Councilor Carter owned Montaigne's *Essays*. In 1774 William Paterson of New Jersey wrote to his Virginia friend, Henry Lee, that Montaigne's manner was "Full of himself yet ever agreeable." The plays of Corneille, Molière and Racine were advertised in a Boston almanac for 1769. Mrs. John Adams sent a copy of Molière's plays to Mercy Warren, though she feared he had "ridiculed vice without engaging us to virtue." Boileau, Bossuet, Pascal and Fénelon were also known, the last because of his ideas on education.[1]

Notwithstanding Voltaire's unorthodox views he found many readers. *Bickerstaff's Boston Almanack* (1769) listed his works for sale and Bowdoin had them in his library. Josiah Quincy read them, we know, as did Jonathan Mayhew, who without indorsing Voltaire's religious views lingered over him "with high delight." Rousseau was probably best known through the educational philosophy of his *Émile* rather than for his *Contrat Social* (1762), though John Adams quoted the latter in 1765. Adams considered Rousseau "too virtuous for the age and for Europe," but Charles Carroll called him "that restless, fantastical Philosopher." Especially important in influencing American

---

[1] *Pa. Gazette*, March 15, 1770; Tuttle, "Bowdoin Library," 362 ff.; Stanard, *Colonial Virginia*, 299 ff.; W. J. Mills, *Glimpses of Colonial Society* (Phila., 1903), 69, 135; *Bickerstaff's Boston Almanack for 1769*; Mrs. John Adams, *Letters* (C. F. Adams, ed., Boston, 1848), 11.

political theory was Montesquieu's *Esprit des Lois.*[1] Aside from the French, the Continental European writers on politics most frequently mentioned were the Dutch Grotius, the Swiss Burlamaqui and Vattel and the German Pufendorf, whose *Law of Nature and Nations* could be had in English translation. Among the politicians who cited at least two of them were the Adamses, Otis, Galloway, Dickinson, James Wilson and Alexander Hamilton.

But the colonists did not draw all their intellectual sustenance from abroad. To an increasing degree they were striking out for themselves. Political pamphlets by Stephen Hopkins and James Otis were printed on both sides of the Atlantic; Daniel Dulany's argument against the stamp act won the approval of William Pitt; and John Dickinson's *Letters from a Pennsylvania Farmer* were translated into French. In history, also, works dealing with American themes were under way. In 1769 Ezra Stiles started a book, never completed, on the "Ecclesiastical History of New England and British America." Isaac Backus's *History of New England, with Particular Reference to the Denomination Called Baptists,* begun before the Revolution, is still important for American religious history. The most scholarly product of this period was Governor Thomas Hutchinson's *History of the Colony [and Province] of Massachusetts Bay.* The first two volumes and a collection of documents appeared before the Revolution; the third, dealing with the stormy years 1750-1774, was finished while the author was a Loyalist exile. The earlier volumes, based on original sources, were well written and

[1] H. M. Morais, *Deism in Eighteenth Century America* (Columbia Univ., *Studies,* no. 397), 48-53; Josiah Quincy, "Journal," Mass. Hist. Soc., *Proceeds.,* XLIX, 455-468; Mayhew to Hollis, Jan. 7, 1766 (Bancroft Transcripts, N. Y. Public Library); Adams, *Works,* II, 148; III, 454-455; Adams, *Familiar Letters,* 349; Charles Carroll, *Unpublished Letters* (T. M. Field, ed., U. S. Catholic Hist. Soc., *Monograph Ser.,* I), 131.

impartial and, in spite of partisanship in the last volume, Hutchinson is fairly entitled to first place among colonial historians.

For fiction Americans still depended on British novelists. Poetry, though attempted, possessed for the most part little merit. At Philadelphia young Thomas Godfrey in 1759 had composed a poetic tragedy, "The Prince of Parthia," the first play by a native dramatist to be presented by a professional company of actors, and Francis Hopkinson wrote graceful verse in the manner of seventeenth-century English lyrics. There were also literary efforts at New Haven. Besides the satiric poetry of *The Progress of Dulness*, John Trumbull prepared for a Yale commencement exercise some lines predicting an American literature comparable with that of England. When the Revolution came on, he turned to politics, and in his *M'Fingal* (1775), a burlesque epic, the central figure was a Tory. It ran into thirty editions. Another literary figure was Philip Freneau. Of French-Huguenot stock, he had the advantage in youth of a family library and a Latin-school training. As an undergraduate at Princeton he wrote verse and for his commencement composed, with Hugh Henry Brackenridge, a poetic dialogue entitled *The Rising Glory of America*. This was followed in 1772 by the *American Village*, contrasting the melancholy scene of Goldsmith's *Deserted Village* with an America which should

> With rising pomp divine
> In its own splendor and Britannia's shine.[1]

Colonial creative talent met with greater success in natural science. The American outlook was naturally

[1] A. H. Quinn, *A History of the American Drama from the Beginning to the Civil War* (N. Y., 1923), 16; M. C. Tyler, *The Literary History of the American Revolution, 1763-1783* (2nd edn., N. Y., 1898-1900), I, chaps. viii-ix, xx; F. L. Pattee, ed., *The Poems of Philip Freneau* (Princeton, 1902-1907), I, iii-xcii.

conditioned by developments in Europe, and notably by the gradual establishment of Newtonian science with its conception of a world governed by physical laws ascertainable through observation and experiment, a "universe of inconceivable size and of amazing regularity." [1] Among the recent scientific advances were the invention of the Leyden jar and a somewhat better understanding of electrical phenomena. In astronomy public interest had been excited by the reappearance in 1759 of Halley's comet and also by the coöperation of British and Continental scholars in world-wide observations of the transit of Venus (1761 and 1769). Though Lavoisier's major contributions to modern chemistry came later, some progress was made in this field before 1775, notably in the work of three British scientists—Black, Rutherford and Priestley—in distinguishing the constituents of air.

The great names in biology were those of the Swede Linnæus, whose classification was the starting point of modern systematic botany, and the Frenchman Buffon, whose *Natural History* popularized scientific facts about animal life. Buffon's studies also familiarized educated persons with the notion of geologic ages extending over immense periods of time. Similarly, geographical knowledge was enlarged by notable voyages including those of Captain James Cook in the Pacific, and a marked improvement in cartography resulted from more accurate instruments for determining latitude and longitude. Through the publication of encyclopædias the new information was made more generally available. Especially significant were the French *Encyclopædie* of Diderot and d'Alembert (1751-1772) and the first edition of the *Encyclopædia Britannica* (1768-1771). Important also were the increased activity of learned socie-

[1] Preserved Smith, *A History of Modern Culture* (N. Y., 1930-1934), II, 148.

ties and academies and the development of scientific collections.[1]

The American Philosophical Society at Philadelphia, organized in its present form in 1769, reflected the European conception of learned academies.[2] It had a membership extending from New England to Georgia and the West Indies. Among the Americans who kept abreast of scientific developments in the Old World Franklin was, of course, outstanding. His British correspondents included the president of the Royal Society, the astronomer royal and the principal librarian of the British Museum. A member of the Royal Society, he had received its Copley Medal for his electrical experiments. He knew personally such British savants as Black, Cavendish and Priestley and carried on a correspondence with Continental scientists. In 1772 he became one of the eight foreign associates of the French Academy of Science. To Professor John Winthrop he wrote of European scientific apparatus and of a proposed American expedition to Lake Superior to observe the transit of Venus. He also from time to time supplied the American Philosophical Society with learned publications. Among Franklin's Philadelphia neighbors was John Bartram, who collected botanical specimens for British clients and acquired through his English friends, Peter Collinson and John Fothergill, some familiarity with the Linnæan system. In 1765, as "Botanist to the King," he undertook an expedition to Florida. Another Philadelphian was David Rittenhouse, largely self-trained as a mathematician and astronomer. By 1775 four professors of the Philadelphia medical faculty had studied abroad.[3]

[1] *Ibid.*, chaps. ii-iv.
[2] For its earlier history, see Adams, *Provincial Society*, 263-264.
[3] Franklin, *Writings*, V, 136-142 and *passim*; Benjamin Franklin, *Benjamin Franklin's Electrical Experiments* (I. B. Cohen, ed., Cambridge, 1941), *passim*; Bridenbaughs, *Rebels and Gentlemen*, chap. ix.

Next in significance to the Philadelphia circle was the Boston-Cambridge group with Winthrop as the leading figure. In 1766 he became a fellow of the Royal Society, to whose *Transactions* he contributed eleven papers. In New York, Lieutenant Governor Colden, an important amateur scientist, had earlier published essays in botany, physics and philosophy and now, in his old age, he kept in touch with kindred spirits, including Alexander Garden of Charleston, who wrote of "happy hours" spent in hearing the old governor "Expatiate on the amazing works of the Great Architect and Contriver of nature." Garden, a student of the Linnæan system, carried on a correspondence with his Swedish master, as did also the Virginian, John Clayton, a competent botanist some of whose work was embodied in the *Flora Virginica* (second edition, 1762) of the Dutch scholar Jakob Gronovius. Other intellectuals in Virginia were William Small, the Scotch professor of mathematics, who gave Jefferson his "first views of the expansion of science," and Governor Francis Fauquier, a member of the Royal Society. From this environment the future Bishop James Madison, after election to the chair of natural philosophy and mathematics at William and Mary, went abroad for further study.[1]

Of the various branches of science, astronomy attracted particular attention. Several American students took part in observing the transit of Venus in 1769, including Rittenhouse, Winthrop and Stiles. Winthrop's chief contributions lay in this general field. An early student of Newton's *Principia*, he is also credited with being the first American college teacher of the calculus and with conducting "the first laboratory of experi-

[1] F. E. Brasch, "The Royal Society of London and Its Influence upon Scientific Thought in the American Colonies," *Scientific Mo.*, XXXIII, 337-355, 448-469; Colden, *Letters and Papers*, VI, 283-285; Jefferson, *Works*, I, 6.

mental physics in this country." His studies of electricity supplemented Franklin's earlier ones, and he popularized the subject in public lectures. Chemistry was taught chiefly in the medical faculties of Philadelphia and New York.[1]

It seemed to the Philadelphian, Dr. John Morgan, that botany, because of its relation to materia medica, was an especially appropriate field for American research. Stimulated by the conquest of the trans-Appalachian country and the Floridas, Bartram eagerly explored the new acquisitions, where he hoped to find in six months "more curiosities" than the English, French and Spaniards had in "six score of years." In 1762 he visited the backcountry of the Carolinas and Georgia, and shortly afterwards his expedition to Florida resulted in a journal of travel and observation (London, 1769) which is a classic of American botany.[2]

By contrast, pre-Revolutionary America knew little of modern geology, though the New England earthquake of 1755 resulted in Harvard lectures by Winthrop, who has been called "our first seismologist." Geography and travel had a wider appeal. During this period two British engineer-officers, W. G. De Brahm and Bernard Romans, made important surveys of the South Atlantic and Gulf coasts. The journals of Robert Rogers and Jonathan Carver, colonial officers in the French war, gave new information about the Northwest. There were some college courses in geography, and Ames's almanac advocated a knowledge of the sub-

[1] Franklin, *Writings*, V, 226, 270-271; Stiles, *Diary*, I, 12; Brasch, "Royal Society of London," 453-457; Stokes, *Iconography of Manhattan*, IV, 738-741, 760; Michael Kraus, *Intercolonial Aspects of American Culture on the Eve of the Revolution* (Columbia Univ., *Studies*, no. 302), 163.

[2] William Darlington, *Memorials of John Bartram and Humphrey Marshall* (Phila., 1849), 256, 422, 425; Bridenbaughs, *Rebels and Gentlemen*, 310-317.

ject for the "common people," especially from an economic standpoint.[1]

Of the fine arts, the most significant during these years were architecture and painting. The former usually followed English models, at least for the more pretentious buildings. These were generally planned by owners or master builders using standard English manuals rather than by professional architects. The governor's mansion at Newbern, North Carolina, completed in 1770, was, however, apparently the work of a British architect. An extremely skillful designer of Maryland and Virginia houses was William Buckland, who built George Mason's Gunston Hall (1758) and the Hammond house in Annapolis (1774). In Philadelphia the Carpenters' Company helped maintain good architectural standards. Probably no public building erected at this time equaled Independence Hall, completed some years earlier. Of special interest, however, is Carpenters' Hall built in 1771 and soon afterwards used by the Continental Congress. Church edifices were represented by St. Paul's Chapel (1766) in New York, constructed in the Italian Renaissance style then popular in England; the Brattle Square Church (1772) in Boston; and the First Baptist Meeting House (1775) of Providence. A good example of a country meetinghouse was that of Wethersfield, Connecticut (1761). Growing interest in the stage was reflected in new theaters at New York, Philadelphia, Annapolis and Charleston.[2]

More important, on the whole, than public architec-

---

[1] Brasch, "Royal Society of London," 455; Briggs, Ames . . . Almanacks, 382-383.

[2] Fiske Kimball and Gertrude S. Carraway, "Tryon's Palace," N. Y. Hist. Soc., Quar. Bull., XXIV, no. 1, 13-24; Hill, George Mason, 18-26; T. J. Wertenbaker, The Founding of American Civilization, the Middle Colonies (N. Y., 1938), 244 ff.; Morgan Dix, ed., A History of the Parish of Trinity Church in the City of New York (N. Y., 1898-1906), I, 315-318; Winsor, Memorial History of Boston, IV, 470; Quinn, History of the American Drama, I, chap. i.

ture was domestic architecture. The finer private dwellings were still usually in the Georgian style. Notable in New England were the Jewett house (1774) in South Berwick, Maine; the residences at Portsmouth, New Hampshire, which favorably impressed a French visitor; the homes of prosperous shipowners on the North Shore of Massachusetts; and certain country houses in western Connecticut. Of the dwellings then being built on Manhattan the only survivor is that of Roger Morris, with its high portico and interesting octagonal room. In the Chesapeake colonies, Annapolis constructed an attractive group of Georgian houses, two owned by signers of the Declaration of Independence. The best examples of Virginia Georgian were built earlier. Significant for the future development of American architecture was Jefferson's house at Monticello, to which he brought his bride in 1771-1772 and on which he continued to work for many years, adapting classical ideas to American requirements. Also of this period was the three-story Charleston home of Miles Brewton, said to have been designed by a London architect. Josiah Quincy thought it "most superb." [1]

In household furnishings well-to-do provincials tended to follow English styles, depending partly on imported work and partly on native craftsmanship. From abroad came Oriental rugs, Chinese wallpaper, Chinese and English porcelain and occasional furniture. Yet when Samuel Powel needed furniture for his new Philadelphia house, he was told he could do as well at home as abroad and at less cost. Americans did some excellent work; but they usually followed contemporary English patterns, notably those of the London designer,

[1] Fiske Kimball, *Domestic Architecture of the American Colonies and the Early Republic* (N. Y., 1922), chap. ii; Architects Emergency Commission, *Great Georgian Houses of America* (N. Y., 1937); Marquis de Chastellux, *Travels in North-America* (London, 1787), II, 232, 234; Quincy, "Journal," 443-445.

Thomas Chippendale, whose *Gentlemen's and Cabinet Maker's Director* was widely used. The general tendency was toward decorative effects: the curved instead of the straight line, as in the cabriole leg for chairs and tables, and elaborate carving. Americans also did well in silverware. Paul Revere was a successful Boston silversmith several years before his famous ride, and when Harvard's graduating class of 1763 wished to honor a college tutor, they gave him a silver teapot made by Samuel Minot. Similar craftsmen were active in other colonies.[1]

To plain folk the homes of their prosperous fellow citizens seemed magnificent. John Adams thought that Nicholas Boylston's Boston mansion with its Turkish carpets, painted hangings and "rich beds with crimson damask curtains" was fit for "a prince." Later he saw furniture in New York "as rich and splendid as any at Mr. Boylston's," and he was similarly impressed by Philadelphia houses. At Charleston, Quincy admired the "magnificent plate" of the Brewton home.[2]

In painting, Benjamin West enjoyed the greatest reputation, though, on the whole, he seems rather a British than an American artist. Born in Pennsylvania, he went abroad in 1763 before doing any important pictures, and he never returned. In London he was aided by royal and fashionable patronage, ultimately becoming president of the Royal Academy. Nevertheless, West is significant for American art as the friend and teacher of younger American painters who found their way to England.

[1] R. T. H. Halsey and C. O. Cornelius, *Handbook of the American Wing* (5th edn., N. Y., 1932), 99 ff.; W. C. Lane, "Early Silver Belonging to Harvard College," Colon. Soc. of Mass., *Publs.*, XXIV, 174; Adams, *Works*, II, 179; Esther Forbes, *Paul Revere and the World He Lived In* (Boston, 1942), chaps. i-v.

[2] Adams, *Works*, II, 179, 349-351, 360-400; Quincy, "Journal," 446.

The best colonial work was in portraiture. With the accumulation of wealth and the improvement of taste, more families could now recognize competent work and pay good prices. John Singleton Copley, the Boston artist, wrote of his New York patrons, "The Gentry of this place distinguish very well, so I must slight nothing."[1] Philadelphia, being centrally placed, offered special advantages to painters. One of the ablest was Matthew Pratt, a pupil of West's in London, whose picture, "The American School" (now in the Metropolitan Museum in New York), shows the master teaching a group of his countrymen. Besides being patronized by Pennsylvania notables, Pratt in 1771 painted a likeness of Governor Colden for the New York Chamber of Commerce. A recent critic credits him with more "knowledge of values" than most eighteenth-century artists. Henry Benbridge, another Philadelphian who returned to America after studying abroad, executed a portrait of the Corsican patriot Pascal Paoli for James Boswell. Better known than either of these was Charles Willson Peale. Helped by wealthy Maryland friends, he also studied with West in London, where he did a likeness of the Earl of Chatham. Returning to America, Peale became the principal delineator of Virginians, Marylanders and Pennsylvanians, beginning during these prewar years a series of portraits of Washington.[2]

But the outstanding pre-Revolutionary artist was Copley, a young man still in his thirties when his American career ended. At twenty-seven he painted his much admired "Boy with the Squirrel," which was exhibited in London in 1766, and he was presently chosen a fellow of the Society of Artists. Encouraged by West to

[1] John Singleton Copley and Henry Pelham, *Letters and Papers, 1739-1776* (Mass. Hist. Soc., *Colls.*, LXXI), 174.
[2] C. C. Sellers, *The Artist of the Revolution, the Early Life of Charles Willson Peale* (Hebron, Conn., 1939), chaps. v-vii.

go to England, he at first declared that he was doing very well at home. Not until 1774 did he remove to London, where he settled permanently. Notwithstanding Copley's important place among British artists, he performed much of his best work in America, and even among his later portraits were those of Americans, notably John and John Quincy Adams.[1]

American interest in music was marked chiefly by indications of improving taste. The use of church organs was increasing. Trinity Church in New York City imported a new one from England in 1764 and employed a paid organist. Even in New England, where organ music had a doubtful repute among Puritans, a pipe organ was acquired by the First Congregational Church of Providence. Instrumental music was much cultivated by the German sects. The Lutheran Church in Lancaster installed an organ which had been built by a neighboring German craftsman. The Moravians maintained at Bethlehem a *Collegium Musicum*, which under John Frederick Peter's direction performed the work of outstanding European composers as well as of the director himself. The North Carolina Moravians, who used various instruments in their services, obtained a new organ in 1772. John Adams, who heard Catholic music in Philadelphia, described it as "exquisitely soft and sweet." An interesting figure in New York's musical history was William Tuckey, a newcomer from England who described himself as formerly "Vicar Choral of the Cathedral Church of Bristol." He directed the Trinity choir, taught music in the church school and invited subscriptions for "a compleat sett of church service." At the same time the New Englanders, William Billings and Josiah Flagg, were trying to lighten the monotony of

---

[1] F. W. Bayley, *The Life and Works of John Singleton Copley* (Boston, 1915), esp. 5-18.

psalm singing. Billings's compositions, however, were more lively than dignified.[1]

Performances of secular music could occasionally be heard in Boston, New York, Philadelphia and Charleston. The St. Cecilia Society of Charleston paid its principal performers and even advertised for musicians in a Boston paper. At one of its concerts Quincy thought a French violinist played "incomparably better" than anyone he had ever heard. Boston, too, had a concert hall, where in 1769 John Rowe found a "large genteel Company." He also attended performances directed by David Propert, organist of Trinity Church, and at a musical evening in Rowe's home Propert played the spinet.[2]

There are glimpses, too, of family music. In Franklin's household Scotch songs were sung to the accompaniment of his daughters on the harpsichord and of his own "armonica." In Virginia the Carters of Nomini Hall were especially musical, using a variety of instruments. Besides playing the "Forte-Piano," the father collected scores and "made great advances in the Theory, and Practice of music." Jefferson, on the eve of his marriage, ordered a clavichord from Hamburg, though later he decided instead on a "forte-piano."[3] Washington played the flute. There were newspaper advertisements of music teachers and of collections of popular songs, some imported and others printed in the colonies. Among them were *The American Mock-Bird* (New

[1] Dix, *Trinity Church*, I, 263-300, 305, 309; Stiles, *Diary*, I, 57-58; Adelaide L. Fries, ed., *Records of the Moravians in North Carolina* (N. C. Hist. Comn., *Publs.*, 1922-1930), II, 661, 830; Adams, *Works*, II. 395.

[2] O. G. Sonneck, *Early Concert Life in America, 1731-1800* (Leipzig, 1907), 18 and *passim*; McCrady, *South Carolina under Royal Government*, 525-529; Quincy, "Journal," 441-442; Rowe, *Letters and Diary*, 180-188, 213.

[3] Franklin, *Writings*, IV, 210; Stanard, *Colonial Virginia*, chap. xii; Fithian, *Journal and Letters*, 82, 132, 225; Jefferson, *Works*, II. 5, 12.

York, 1760), *Masque, a New Song Book* (New York, 1767), and the *American Syren* (Williamsburg, 1773). Knowledge of the better European composers was spreading. The best known was doubtless Handel.[1] Interest in the theater was growing, also. After peace returned in 1763 the "American Company," then directed by the actor-manager David Douglass and composed of British actors, presented plays in various places. During the winter season of 1763-1764 at Charleston this company gave three performances a week for two months to crowded houses, with nightly receipts said to average more than a hundred pounds sterling. After a short sojourn in England the troupe began in 1766 a period of almost continuous activity. Washington was an ardent playgoer; during one week in 1770 he attended the theater five times. In the North opposition to the stage still proved strong. No theater was permitted in Boston while in New York and Philadelphia public opinion was sharply divided. When a benefit performance was given for the New York Hospital in 1773, President Myles Cooper of King's College wrote the prologue; but a writer in the *New-York Journal* protested that theatrical productions were "against the inclinations of all the most sober and respectable inhabitants," and William Livingston forbade his daughters to attend them. Several religious groups in Philadelphia took a similar stand and the provincial assembly in 1767 received a protest against the opening of the Southwark Theater. Both there and in New York, however, the cause of the drama made progress.[2]

[1] *Pa. Gazette,* Jan. 5, 1764; titles of songbooks in Evans, *American Bibliography,* III-IV.

[2] G. O. Seilhamer, *History of the American Theatre* (Phila., 1888), I, *passim;* Colden, *Letters and Papers,* VI, 281-283; Theodore Sedgwick, *A Memoir of the Life of William Livingston* (N. Y., 1833), 102; Stokes, *Iconography of Manhattan,* IV, 781; George Washington, *Diaries, 1748-1799* (J. C. Fitzpatrick, ed., Boston, 1925), I, 384.

Shakespearean plays were frequently given, though often in eighteenth-century adaptations. Six of them marked the first season of the Southwark Theater. Other dramatists represented on the provincial stage were Otway, Addison, Congreve, Farquhar, Rowe, and Gay with his "Beggar's Opera." Among contemporary English plays promptly reproduced in the colonies were Cumberland's "West Indian," first given in London in 1771 and performed the same year at Williamsburg, and Goldsmith's "She Stoops to Conquer," first presented at Covent Garden in 1773 and seen a few months later in New York.[1]

Young Lewis Hallam, son of an earlier actor on the American stage, played leading Shakespearean rôles and seems to have been a fair performer. Graydon complained of his "mouthing or ranting" in tragic parts, but thought him a "thorough master of all the tricks and finesse of his trade" with a manner both "graceful and impressive." John Henry, a native of Dublin, began his American career in 1767, though his chief successes were to come later. His Irish characterizations were especially popular. Leading female parts were taken by Margaret Cheer and by her successor, a cousin of Hallam's, who also had ardent admirers. A writer in the *Maryland Gazette* expressed his enthusiasm in verse:

> Ye Gods! 'Tis Cytherea's face;
> 'Tis Dian's faultless form;
> But hers alone the nameless grace
> That every heart can charm.[2]

At Annapolis and Williamsburg the players could always count on large and appreciative audiences, and even smaller places in Virginia and Maryland saw occa-

[1] Seilhamer, *American Theatre*, I, 153-156, 282.
[2] *Ibid.*, 155-157, 198, 204-208, 214-215, 278-281, 346-347; Alexander Graydon, *Memoirs of His Own Time* (J. S. Littell, ed., Phila., 1846), 86-87.

sional performances. Notwithstanding legal prohibitions, New Englanders were not wholly uninterested in the drama. In 1765 John Rowe witnessed Otway's "Orphan" "miserably performed" before a Boston audience. Five years later he heard the reading of a contemporary English farce, "The Mayor of Garratt." At the Boston Concert Hall the "Beggar's Opera" was read with some of the music. Away from home Quincy visited the New York theater and thought that if he lived there he would attend "every acting night." [1]

This story of pre-Revolutionary culture is mainly one of gradual advance on lines previously indicated. New schools and colleges were founded, with some reconsideration of educational programs, and the graduates of the colleges were contributing significantly to political leadership. Meantime there was a notable expansion of the newspaper press, which was increasingly active politically. For progress in science, letters and the arts Americans were almost inevitably dependent on their contacts with Europe. Important in this mediatory service were such men as Winthrop, Garden and, above all, Franklin, with his Philosophical Society associates. American achievements in literature and art perhaps most nearly achieved distinction in the best of the political pamphlets and in Copley's portraits.

[1] Seilhamer, *American Theatre*, I, 32-33; Rowe, *Letters and Diary*, 77, 197, 200; Quincy, "Journal," 478-479.

CHAPTER VII

THE OLD WEST AND NEW FRONTIERS

THOUGH the comparatively mature communities of the seaboard supplied most of the leaders of the Revolution and the early republic, the story of these years cannot be told without taking into account "freshwater" America. The "Old West," as Frederick Jackson Turner called it, was the inland country east of the Alleghanies. In the South it lay above the falls of the eastward-flowing rivers. At the close of the first colonial century this region was largely unoccupied. Its real development proceeded from the middle decades of the eighteenth century.

In New England the original lines of settlement had followed the coast from Maine to Connecticut and the Connecticut Valley from Long Island Sound to northern Massachusetts. Between these two zones much of central Massachusetts long remained untenanted. The Berkshire country, crossing over into Connecticut, did not attract many people until after the conquest of Canada. The occupation of the northern New England back-country was checked by border warfare. Not until after 1760 did settlement spread with rapidity in the upper Merrimac Valley and the Connecticut Valley north of Massachusetts. Of five New Hampshire counties in 1769 three fell wholly within this newly colonized area and a fourth largely so. Meantime, migrants from New Hampshire, Massachusetts, Connecticut and New York were pioneering in Vermont. By 1771 they were said to number nearly five thousand. New settlements were also forming in Maine, where between 1765 and 1·776

Lincoln County, adjoining the old French frontier, more than quadrupled in population. Thus, at the beginning of the Revolutionary War, a substantial proportion of the New Englanders lived in communities not far removed from the pioneering stage.[1]

In New York comparatively recent settlements had been made on the west bank of the Hudson, on the lower Mohawk, on a southern branch of that river, the Schoharie, and on the upper Susquehanna. Some New Englanders had lately moved into eastern New York near the border. Across the Hudson in northern New Jersey there were also newly colonized areas. In Pennsylvania three new counties had been formed as early as the second quarter of the eighteenth century to take care of the westward movement: Lancaster (1729), York (1749) and Cumberland (1750). Then twenty years later, in 1771, came Bedford County on the eastern slopes of the Alleghanies. Northward expansion followed the north branch of the Susquehanna and the Delaware and its tributaries. Somewhat detached was the Susquehanna Company's Connecticut outpost in the Wyoming Valley. On the eve of the war the people of these new communities, mainly frontiersmen or the sons of frontiersmen, outnumbered those of the older counties on the Delaware.[2]

In the Chesapeake provinces occupation of the piedmont also occurred mainly in the eighteenth century. Though in 1700 nearly all the organized Virginia counties had been in the tidewater, half a century later most of the present counties on the eastern side of the Blue

[1] E. B. Greene and Virginia D. Harrington, comps., *American Population before the Federal Census of 1790* (N. Y., 1932), 12-51; Lois K. Mathews, *The Expansion of New England* (Boston, 1909), chap. v.

[2] Ruth L. Higgins, *Expansion in New York* (Ohio State Univ., Contribs., no. 14), chaps. vii-viii; W. R. Smith, "Sectionalism in Pennsylvania during the Revolution," *Polit. Sci. Quar.*, XXIV, 208-235; Greene and Harrington, *American Population*, 117.

Ridge had been formed, with some in the Great Valley. Here and in Maryland the inland movement was marked by the rise of market towns at the heads of river navigation or even farther up. One such settlement, Frederick, Maryland, contained more inhabitants before the Revolution than Annapolis, ranking next to Baltimore, which had developed mainly as an outlet for the wheat of the backcountry. Even more striking was the progress in North Carolina. In 1740 nearly all its people had dwelt in counties facing the ocean or one of its larger estuaries, but thirty years later a majority lived in the interior counties. Similarly in South Carolina most of the communities above the fall line were peopled within twenty years before the Revolution, and contemporary estimates indicate that by 1775 the bulk of the whites were to be found in these newer settlements.[1]

Relations between older and newer districts varied. In New England the eighteenth-century communities were formed mainly by descendants of seventeenth-century colonists. Exceptional groups like the Scotch-Irish in central Massachusetts and southern New Hampshire comprised a comparatively small minority. Place names in New Hampshire and Vermont frequently reproduced those of towns in southern New England. In Virginia, too, there was a considerable migration from tidewater to piedmont. Though numerous Scotch-Irish and Germans settled in the Northern Neck between the Rappahannock and the Potomac, for instance, the dominant planter class of English stock established folkways much like those of the lower country.[2]

Elsewhere, however, a sharper antithesis existed be-

---

[1] *Ibid.*, 123 ff.; C. A. Barker, *The Background of the Revolution in Maryland* (*Yale Hist. Publs. Miscellany*, XXXVIII), 12; W. A. Schaper, "Sectionalism and Representation in South Carolina," Am. Hist. Assoc., *Ann. Rep. for 1900*, I, 250, 335.

[2] Mathews, *Expansion of New England*, 79-80; Fairfax Harrison, *Landmarks of Old Prince William* (Richmond, 1924), I, preface.

tween older and newer settlements. From Pennsylvania southward the inland counties were largely peopled from Scotland, Ireland and Germany. Though the inhabitants of Pennsylvania had from the first been drawn from various sources, the crowding of recent immigrants into the interior emphasized sectional differences, notably between the British Quakers, who dominated the east, and the Scotch-Irish Presbyterians of the backcountry. Thus Pennsylvania sectionalism differed markedly from that of New England. As non-English immigrants moved through Pennsylvania into the western parts of Maryland, Virginia and the Carolinas, they also introduced elements of discord. To most of these newcomers the traditions of the tidewater were quite alien. Aside from differences of origin were others of an economic or religious kind. Nowhere were these distinctions so great as in the Carolinas, where difficulties of communication were serious. In 1768 a journey of two hundred and sixty-four miles from Newbern in the North Carolina tidewater to Salisbury, then the most important backcountry town, took ten days on horseback, mainly through sparsely settled country. One traveler reported going forty miles without seeing a house. Inland communities in this province could sometimes trade more conveniently with Philadelphia or Charleston than with their own seaboard.[1]

Though this pre-Revolutionary West contained a society less marked by class distinctions than that of the East, inequalities existed even here. The capitalist-promoter played a part in the process of expansion. New England had its proprietors, absentee or resident, whose interests often clashed with those of the ordinary settler. The interior South possessed landed magnates like Lord

[1] U. B. Phillips, ed., *Plantation and Frontier* (J. R. Commons and others, eds., *A Documentary History of American Industrial Society*, Cleveland, 1910-1911, I-II), II, 236-238.

Fairfax in Virginia and like Lord Granville, the absentee landlord of a great tract in North Carolina. Washington himself had rent-paying tenants in the backcountry. In western Maryland the Dulanys controlled a numerous tenantry; and in New York even Revolutionary leaders like James Duane, Philip Schuyler and the Livingstons carried the leasehold system into newly settled areas.[1]

Alongside the yeoman farmers, the western edges of the piedmont also had their large plantation owners, including such champions of the backcountry as Jefferson and Madison. It has been estimated that Jefferson during "most of his mature life" owned "approximately ten thousand acres of land and from one to two hundred slaves." Another example was Richard Henderson, the North Carolina judge who planned the proprietary colony of Transylvania. In the seventeen-seventies a Moravian preacher noted sharp contrasts of this kind on the Virginia-North Carolina border. One of his hosts owned great tracts, but in the same region he found a poverty-stricken Irish settlement of "robbed and plundered people." Between these extremes were numerous farmers with moderate holdings. Even in western Massachusetts there were some considerable landholders. In Pittsfield the wealthy William Williams, an influential politician and officeholder, became one of the original proprietors of Bennington, Vermont.[2]

[1] F. J. Turner, *The Frontier in American History* (N. Y., 1920), chap. iii; William Eddis, *Letters from America* (London, 1792), 98-102; Barker, *Background of the Revolution in Maryland*, 23; E. W. Spaulding, *New York in the Critical Period* (D. R. Fox, ed., *N. Y. State Hist. Assoc. Ser.*, I), 54-55; George Washington, *Diaries, 1748-1799* (J. C. Fitzpatrick, ed., Boston, 1925), II, 66, 144-145.

[2] Dumas Malone, "Thomas Jefferson," Allen Johnson and Dumas Malone, eds., *Dictionary of American Biography* (N. Y., 1928-1937), X, 17-35; Archibald Henderson, "The Creative Forces in Westward Expansion," *Am. Hist. Rev.*, XX, 95; Adelaide L. Fries, ed., *Records of the Moravians in North Carolina* (N. C. Hist. Comn., *Publs.*, 1922-1930), II, 791-794; J. E. A. Smith, *History of Pittsfield* (Boston, 1869), 78.

One characteristic of the backcountry was the mobility of its inhabitants. Though some settlers, securing legal rights by purchase or lease, established permanent homes, others, more restless or less industrious, soon shifted to fresh tracts. Even in New England the residents of new towns tended to migrate more freely than those of older communities. The careers of certain Pennsylvania delegates to the state ratifying convention of 1787 are suggestive. Two of the chief leaders of the backcountry anti-Federalists were natives of Ireland while the third was the son of a Scotch-Irish immigrant. All three had tried an older section of the interior country before transferring to newer settlements. Another delegate of Irish birth had lived for a time in Lancaster County, then went west into the Cumberland Valley and later died in a town on the Juniata River. Thomas Marshall, father of the chief justice, who had been born in the Northern Neck of Virginia, changed residence several times thereafter, living for a period in one of the valleys of the Blue Ridge and ultimately settling in Kentucky. Daniel Boone, a native of what was then frontier country near Reading, Pennsylvania, went successively to the Shenandoah Valley, the North Carolina piedmont and Kentucky. James Robertson, who grew up in the Virginia backwoods, moved on to North Carolina, eastern Tennessee and the Cumberland Valley.[1]

The rural economy of the "Old West" was not all of a kind. In New England its agriculture did not differ radically from that of many older communities. In the Middle region and the Chesapeake provinces, however,

---

[1] John Adams, *Works* (C. F. Adams, ed., Boston, 1856), II, 278; sketches of William Findley, John Harris, John Smilie and Robert Whitehill in J. B. McMaster and F. D. Stone, eds., *Pennsylvania and the Federal Constitution, 1787-1788* (Phila., 1888), 727-729, 733, 752-753, 756-757; R. G. Thwaites, *Daniel Boone* (N. Y., 1902), *passim*.

the backcountry farmer possessed an important export staple. His wheat and flour went out through Philadelphia, Baltimore, Fredericksburg and Alexandria. Though upper Carolina had no staples comparable with the rice and indigo of the lowlands, its cattle might be driven to Philadelphia as well as to Southern ports. In all parts of this interior region wagoners transported farm products and skins to storage and market centers on the fall line, whence they could be floated to the seaboard. The result was a marked development of inland towns. Typical examples in Pennsylvania are Lancaster, York and Carlisle; in Maryland, Frederick and Hagerstown; in Virginia, Richmond, Fredericksburg, Falmouth and Alexandria on the fall line and also the Valley towns of Winchester and Staunton; and in the Carolinas, Hillsborough, Salisbury, Cross Creek at the head of navigation on the Cape Fear, and Camden. At such points the farmers could exchange produce for manufactured goods.[1]

The most advanced of these communities was Lancaster. Situated on important westward and southward routes, it became a considerable manufacturing town, where craftsmen gathered to serve the surrounding country. At Frederick grain was collected for shipment to Baltimore, warehouses were built, and imported goods sold—"elegancies" as well as necessities. A Scotch storekeeper at Falmouth, Virginia, in the seventeen-sixties and seventies imported goods from Glasgow, London and Bristol, and traded them with Shenandoah Valley farmers for flour. He had a partner in Winchester. One wagoner employed by this firm was the future Revolutionary general, Daniel Morgan. Washington as a young surveyor enjoyed at Winchester "a good Dinner"

[1] Leila Sellers, *Charleston Business on the Eve of the American Revolution* (Chapel Hill, 1934), chap. iii.

with "Wine and Rum Punch in Plenty; and a good Feather Bed with clean sheets." [1]

Of Cross Creek in North Carolina William Bartram tells us that its mills attracted promoters who sold lots and built houses for the artisans, while merchants profited by the "brisk commerce" in country produce brought for shipment down the Cape Fear to Wilmington. There were also overland connections with Philadelphia. At Camden, South Carolina, were to be found storehouses, gristmills, sawmills, a bakery and a distillery. From this point flour, tobacco and skins went downstream or overland to Charleston. The contents of Joseph Kershaw's "Pine Tree Store" in 1774 were valued at over fifteen thousand pounds; two branch establishments were worth nearly eighteen thousand. Kershaw was also a partner in Charleston firms and politically influential. Thus the Carolina backcountry had its capitalists as well as those who made their living by cultivating the soil. [2]

In this inland development the Germans played an important rôle. Apparently regarding themselves "as better and more orderly economists" than their neighbors, they tilled many prosperous farms in the Valley of Virginia and also in the Lower South, where they seemed to succeed better than most of their neighbors. Especially interesting was the colony of Moravians at Wachovia, whose gristmills and stores served a considerable area. Their wagons, laden with produce, went not only to other North Carolina settlements, but also to Charleston and Pennsylvania. They had their

---

[1] V. S. Clark, *History of Manufactures in the United States* (Carnegie Inst., *Contribs. to Am. Econ. History*, rev. edn., N. Y., 1929), I, 89, 185, 186; Eddis, *Letters*, 98-102; M. S. Malone, "Falmouth and the Shenandoah," *Am. Hist. Rev.*, XL, 693 ff.; Washington, *Diaries*, I, 6.

[2] William Bartram, *Travels through North & South Carolina, Georgia, East & West Florida* . . . (Phila., 1791), 477-478; Sellers, *Charleston Business*, 87-91.

trained craftsmen: tanners, potters, blacksmiths and gunsmiths.[1]

Outside the towns extremely primitive houses were still usual. In western Maryland, in fairly well-cultivated country, they were described as of "rude construction." A British traveler in Virginia during the Revolution observed that about Charlottesville only the better dwellings were lathed and plastered within. Most of them had wooden chimneys and wooden shutters without glazed windows. More ambitious were the homes of Madison at Montpelier and of Jefferson at Monticello. Comparable with these were some attractive residences in western Connecticut. Backcountry travel, with poor taverns or none at all, was uncomfortable, but there was some simple hospitality in private houses. A Moravian preacher told of a leading citizen in upper North Carolina who built a tavern to relieve his home from "the constant stream of visitors." [2]

Regarding religion on this newer frontier three facts stand out: the weakening of the older churches; the highly emotional evangelism required for unsophisticated folk; and, sometimes, a more tolerant outlook. Among the pioneers there was not so much intellectual dissent from orthodox theology as the disuse of religious habits enforced by public opinion in their old homes. This relaxation of ecclesiastical traditions, however, was less marked in New England, where grants made to the founders of new towns commonly directed them to support an "orthodox minister." Though itinerant preachers made proselytes and organized dissenting

[1] J. D. Schoepf, *Travels in the Confederation, 1783-1784* (A. J. Morrison, ed., Phila., 1911), II, 22-23; W. H. Gehrke, "The Ante-Bellum Agriculture of the Germans in North Carolina," *Agricultural History*, IX, 143-160; Fries, *Records of the Moravians*, II, passim.

[2] Eddis, *Letters*, 129-134; Thomas Anburey, *Travels through the Interior Parts of America* (Boston, 1923), II, 187; Fries, *Records of the Moravians*, II, 796.

churches, the proportion of such congregations does not seem during this period to have been radically different in the backcountry from what it was in the older communities.   In Vermont, Congregational churches were formed rapidly during the early years and before long this kind of orthodoxy was stronger there than in eastern Massachusetts.[1]

As we have seen, the religious variety characteristic of the older settlements in the Middle provinces reappeared in the backcountry.   The chief difference, in Pennsylvania especially, was in the weakness of the Friends and Anglicans and the comparative strength of the Scotch-Irish Presbyterians with their vigorous hostility to Quaker and Moravian pacifism.   In the South the ecclesiastical divergence of tidewater and backcountry was even more striking.   Though the Church of England was legally established, its adherents in the inland communities were far outnumbered by nonconformists of divers denominations.   Even in legally organized parishes vestries might be controlled by dissenters, as in certain Scotch-Irish settlements in Virginia.   In Wachovia in 1773 the freeholders of Dobbs Parish actually chose Moravian churchwardens.   In much of the interior country no organized churches or settled pastors were to be found.   Hence the religious life in these parts depended on itinerant preachers, Moravian, "New Side" Presbyterian or Baptist.   One Baptist preacher had a circuit of four counties, including both slopes of the Blue Ridge.[2]

[1] Mathews, *Expansion of New England*, 80 ff., 91-95; Williston Walker, *A History of the Congregational Churches in the United States* (Philip Schaff and others, eds., *The American Church History Series*, N. Y., 1893-1897, III), 309; A. H. Newman, *A History of the Baptist Churches in the United States* (same ser., II), 268.

[2] H. L. Osgood, *The American Colonies in the Eighteenth Century* (N. Y., 1924), III, 470; Fries, *Records of the Moravians*, II, 746; W. M. Gewehr, *The Great Awakening in Virginia, 1740-1790* (Duke Univ., *Publs.*, 1930), chap. v.

Two instances may serve to illustrate the mingling of religious groups. Frederick, Maryland, possessed not only an Anglican Church, but also "several chapels for the accommodation of the Germans and other dissenters," while in Loudon County, Virginia, a prospective settler could choose between "the Church" and Presbyterian or Anabaptist meetinghouses. Sometimes, however, communities were formed on the basis of a common faith and worship, as in the case of the Moravians and of the Presbyterians who dominated the neighborhood of the Waxhaws in northern South Carolina. There were also puritanical elements in these forest settlements. Mid-eighteenth-century court records in the Valley of Virginia show the prosecution of one man "for driving hogs on the Blue Ridge on the Sabbath day" and of another for "unnecessarily traveling ten miles" on Sunday. In general, the tolerance of the "Old West" was due less to theological liberalism than to the practical necessity of mutual adjustment.[1]

Education naturally suffered under pioneer conditions, though something may be said on the credit side. In Massachusetts the setting apart of a school lot was a usual condition of grants for towns, and town appropriations for education came early. In 1762 the new Berkshire town of Pittsfield voted for school support, and before the Revolution it had five schoolhouses. Peterborough, New Hampshire, gave forty pounds for education at its first regular town meeting.[2]

While New England extended to the backcountry a school system already established by law, that was not the case in those colonies where education had been

[1] Eddis, Letters, 98-102; Pa. Gazette, Jan. 25, 1775; Edward McCrady, South Carolina under the Royal Government, 1719-1776 (N. Y., 1899), 315-317; Phillips, Plantation and Frontier, II, 287.

[2] Mathews, Expansion of New England, chap. v; Smith, History of Pittsfield, chap. vii; Albert Smith, History of the Town of Peterborough (Boston, 1876), chap. x.

mainly left to churches, private philanthropy or family initiative. A few schools existed in the freshly settled areas of New York; a Presbyterian minister is credited with founding the first New York grammar school west of Albany. In inland Pennsylvania the Moravians conducted schools at Nazareth and Bethlehem, while others were maintained by clergymen. One of the latter, at Carlisle, offered to teach Greek and Latin "in the most concise and perfect manner." In the Virginia piedmont John Marshall read Horace and Livy with a young Scotch clergyman. There were also, as we have seen, the piedmont and Valley academies of Liberty Hall and Hampden-Sydney. The Moravians of Wachovia maintained schools for boys and girls, and in both the Carolinas Presbyterian ministers did their part.[1]

Maladjustments between seaboard and backcountry proved important in the political and social life of these times. In Virginia such tension was not yet troublesome, but obvious differences in outlook existed between slave-owning planters and yeoman farmers, between the aristocratic older families and the more democratic newer settlements, between Anglicans and dissenters. Though Jefferson in 1782 noted the inadequate representation of the interior counties in the legislature, the issue was not pressed until after the Revolution.[2]

In Pennsylvania, on the other hand, the inland counties actively complained of the unfair legislative apportionment. Easterners and Westerners also disagreed about Indian policy. If the people a little west of the Susquehanna had been able to put their true weight into provincial policy, they might have brought protection to the frontier. As it was, the Philadelphia Quakers

[1] W. W. Campbell, *Annals of Tryon County* (N. Y., 1924), 8; Fries, *Records of the Moravians*, II, 710, 744, 827; McCrady, *South Carolina under Royal Government*, 315-317.

[2] Thomas Jefferson, *Works* (P. L. Ford, ed., N. Y., 1904-1905), IV, 18.

persisting in their traditional pacifism refused to vote adequate defense, while some Philadelphia merchants were accused of making swollen profits out of selling fire-arms to the warlike savages. Raids from the Western tribes had penetrated Pennsylvania in 1763, sowing broad destruction. The menace was brought home to Shippensburg, Carlisle and other settled places by the arrival of hundreds of refugees. Utterly disgusted by Eastern indifference, and madly bent on destroying Indians—any Indians—fifty-seven rangers from the town of Paxton fell upon the peaceful and defenseless Conestoga, living by their handicrafts near Lancaster, and killed twenty in cold blood. Local magistrates were so sympathetic with the rioters that Governor John Penn's command to bring them to trial had no effect. The following year six hundred armed "back inhabitants" marched on Philadelphia to enforce redress. It required all the diplomacy of Benjamin Franklin to dissuade them from civil war.[1]

The most violent sectional disturbances, however, took place in the Carolinas. The Regulator movement in North Carolina was mainly a protest against Easterners who controlled the assembly, the revenue system and the courts. The Western counties complained of unequal taxation, excessive court fees, land administration in the interest of Eastern politicians, and a marriage law discriminating against dissenting ministers. Among other things they demanded freer paper-money issues, the trial of debt cases without lawyers by a jury of freeholders, and the ballot in place of viva-voce voting. At the "Battle of the Alamance" in May, 1771, about two thousand poorly armed Regulators were dis-

[1] C. H. Lincoln, *The Revolutionary Movement in Pennsylvania, 1760-1776* (Univ. of Pa., Ser. in History, no. 1), esp. chap. iv; W. R. Smith, "Sectionalism in Pennsylvania," *Polit. Sci. Quar.*, XXIV, 208-235; B. J. Wallace, "Insurrection of the Paxton Boys," *Presbyterian Quar. Rev.*, VIII, 627-677.

persed by Governor William Tryon and the provincial militia led by several future leaders in the Revolution. A similar but less serious rising in South Carolina was directed against the Charleston government for not providing adequate law-enforcement agencies. When the decent elements in the backcountry resorted to lynch law for their protection, they clashed with the provincial authorities. Fortunately, however, the assembly proved conciliatory and established new courts. No such spectacular outbreaks occurred in New England, though there already existed some of that antagonism between the mercantile seaboard and the rural interior which later flamed up in the Shays Rebellion.[1]

While new societies were thus growing up between the coastal region and the mountains, many Americans were looking hopefully toward the recently acquired trans-Appalachian empire. This land of the "Western Waters" had long been known to adventurous individuals and plans for its exploitation had precipitated the last intercolonial war; but its vast resources were hardly realized. Many provincials of 1763 were, however, attracted by the prospect of an expanding fur trade. Others knew of agricultural resources in the bottom lands of the Ohio and Mississippi, and speculators were planning new colonies.

Nevertheless, the victors over France in the late war had hardly more than a quitclaim deed to the greater part of this area. Most numerous among its human occupants were the Indians, perhaps two hundred thousand in all. Behind the Northern colonies the principal group was still the Iroquois Confederacy.[2] Though its

[1] J. S. Bassett, "Regulators of North Carolina," Am. Hist. Assoc., Ann. Rep. for 1894, 141-212; W. L. Saunders, ed., Colonial Records of North Carolina, 1662-1776 (Raleigh, 1886-1890), VIII, 75-80; Schaper, "Sectionalism in South Carolina," 334-338.

[2] See J. T. Adams, Provincial Society, 1690-1763 (A History of American Life, III), 35-36.

base lay in the Mohawk Valley, it had to be reckoned
with in the trade and warfare of the farther West. To
the south were the Delaware, then being pushed back
into the Ohio Valley. Unlike the Iroquois, most of
whom had favored the British in the recent war, the
Delaware, formerly allied with the French, were troubled both by colonial frontiersmen and by Iroquois
claims to overlordship. Also in the Ohio Valley were
the Shawnee, whose raids disturbed the frontier settlements of Pennsylvania and Virginia.

In the southern Appalachians, the Gulf Coast and the
lower Mississippi Valley dwelt four important tribes or
confederacies numbering perhaps fifteen thousand war-
riors: the Cherokee to the rear of the Carolinas and the
Creek, Chickasaw and Choctaw in the present Gulf
states. All these had to be carefully handled and clashes
with the settlers resulted from lawlessness on both sides.
Conflicting tribal claims complicated land cessions, and
hostilities between northern and southern Indians also
made trouble for outlying white settlements. More remote from the English colonists than these bands were
those of the upper Mississippi Valley and the Great
Lakes region. Among them were the Chippewa and the
Ottawa whose chief was Pontiac. Half a century passed
before the larger part of the Northwest could be effectively occupied.[1]

Less numerous as well as less troublesome than the
Indians, but hardly negligible, were the king's "new
subjects." The chief French settlements in the Northwest were Detroit, with minor posts in the Great Lakes
region, Vincennes on the Wabash, and a few villages in
the Illinois country. In the South some French remained
east of the Mississippi, notably at Mobile. In addition
there were Spaniards in the Floridas. Many of the

[1] For varying estimates of the number of Indians, see Greene and Harrington, *American Population*, 194 ff.

French in the Northwest were attached to the soil, raising crops for themselves and for export to New Orleans. They were governed by local commandants, with certain elected village officers, and the priests played an important part in local affairs. For these people adjustment to the new order was still imperfect when the Revolution began.[1]

While traders, land speculators and prospective settlers looked forward to a general advance beyond the mountains, the westward trek was checked by "Pontiac's Conspiracy." The prime factor in this outbreak was the belief of the savages that the English were less satisfactory neighbors than the French. The "King's subjects," wrote Sir William Johnson, were "very ill Calculated to Cultivate a good understanding with the Indians." The French had been more adaptable and Johnson saw little hope that the English would "treat the Indians with the like kindness and Civility." Meantime, in the matter of trade regulation, the provincial governments and the imperial superintendents of Indian affairs worked at cross-purposes, the traders being guilty of such objectionable practices as the indiscriminate sale of arms and liquor and actual cheating. Another source of trouble was the intrusion of settlers into the Indian country. While the whites challenged the right of a comparatively few savages to hold great tracts of land, the latter naturally regarded the colonials as unwarrantable trespassers.[2] Early in 1763 the storm broke. Western posts were seized by the Indians, Detroit and Pittsburgh narrowly escaped capture and many frontier settlements were broken up. By the end of 1763, however, the main force of the uprising was broken, though

[1] C. W. Alvord, *The Illinois Country, 1673-1818* (C. W. Alvord, ed., *The Centennial History of Illinois*, Springfield, 1920, I), chap. x.
[2] William Johnson to the Lords of Trade, C. W. Alvord and C. E. Carter, eds., *The New Régime, 1765-1767* (Ill. State Hist. Library, Colls., XI), 117-122.

border warfare continued for a time. The captured posts were presently recovered and British soldiers now took over the French villages on the Mississippi and the Wabash.

Peace of a sort was restored, but serious problems remained. It was not easy to reconcile the conflicting views of British statesmen and American colonials, of provincial conservatives and impatient frontiersmen, not to speak of differences between rival colonies. British policy was indicated by the royal Proclamation of 1763, which provided for three new continental provinces: Quebec for the St. Lawrence Valley, and East and West Florida in the Gulf region. To avoid trouble with the Indians, the rest of the trans-Appalachian country was for the present closed to settlers. No provision was made, however, for the civil government of the French in the Northwest or for effective control of unauthorized persons entering the Indian country. The board of trade, in consultation with the Indian superintendents, proceeded to draft an elaborate plan for imperial regulation of the Indian trade: the superintendents were to be given greater powers and those of the provincial governments restricted. The home government was not prepared, however, to supply funds for carrying out this program. Another obstacle was the opposition of certain colonies to interference with their own schemes. So the imperial plan was abandoned and the trade problem left largely to the independent and often conflicting measures of provincial governments.

As to the future occupation of the West opinion was divided. For a time, influential British officials were willing to consider new colonies centering about the former French posts, as, for instance, at Detroit and in the Illinois country; but this policy was eventually rejected on the ground that such remote communities would become economically self-sufficient and therefore be out of harmony with the old colonial system. It was thought better to encourage the peopling of such comparatively undeveloped seaboard areas as Nova Scotia, Maine and the Floridas. Nevertheless, the government proved willing to make Indian treaties permitting settlements adjoining the older colonies. In the North this was done in 1768 by the treaty of Fort Stanwix with the Iroquois, and in the South similar agreements were negotiated with the Cherokee.

Numerous schemes were now proposed for new colonies, especially on the southern side of the Ohio. Of these, the so-called Vandalia colony had the most influential supporters, including such provincials as Sir William Johnson and Benjamin Franklin along with British politicians and financiers. In 1773 favorable action by the crown seemed probable; but as the controversy between the colonies and the home government became acute, the project collapsed. Meantime, royal instructions looked to the systematic survey and sale of unoccupied lands. Provincial governments were to make thereafter no grants without accurate surveys, and lands were to be sold at public auction with fixed minimum prices. This plan of 1774, reasonable enough in itself and similar to that adopted later by the Confederation, was generally condemned in the colonies as an arbitrary attempt "to prevent the population of these states."

Americans also differed among themselves as to Western policies. Pennsylvania frontiersmen were so distrustful of Eastern merchants supplying Indians with arms that in 1765 some of them attacked a party bound for the Illinois country bearing trading goods and presents for the Indians. Virginia and Pennsylvania had conflicting claims to the upper Ohio Valley, including Pittsburgh; and the Old Dominion, claiming under its charter all territory "west and northwest" to the Mississippi, denied the right of Northern promoters to found a new colony within those limits.[1]

After Pontiac's defeat traders again advanced into the Indian country; but the results proved disappointing to the merchants of the older Northern colonies. Most of the furs from the Lake region moved, as before, down the St. Lawrence, to the advantage of British and Canadian dealers. Though certain Philadelphia merchants tried to combine the fur traffic in the Illinois country with the sale of supplies to the Western garrisons, they could not compete with French and Spanish traders across the Mississippi, who sent pelts down the river to New Orleans. But in the Southwest, where shipping points within English territory—Charleston, Savannah, Pensacola and Mobile—were more accessible, British traders fared better. In 1769 deerskins stood third among Charleston exports, while shipments from Savannah, Pensacola and Mobile were increasing.[2]

Some of the traders in the Indian country operated on a considerable scale with numerous employees. Of this type was James Adair, who wrote an important *History of the American Indians* (1775) in which, on the basis of long experience among the Southern tribes, he described such a trading post. It embraced a group of houses in or near an Indian town, with a storehouse for goods to be sold to the natives and for peltry received in exchange. Adair was an intelligent and sympathetic observer. "I sat down," he said in his book,

[1] On this and preceding paragraphs, see C. W. Alvord, *The Mississippi Valley in British Politics* (Cleveland, 1917), I-II; E. B. O'Callaghan and Berthold Fernow, eds., *Documents Relative to the Colonial History of the State of New York* (Albany, 1856-1887), VIII, 193; L. W. Labaree, *Royal Instructions to Colonial Governors* (New Haven, 1935), II, 533-537; Max Savelle, *George Morgan* (N. Y., 1932), 21.

[2] W. E. Stevens, *The Northwest Fur Trade, 1763-1800* (Univ. of Ill., *Studies*, XIV, no. 3), chap. i; Virginia D. Harrington, *The New York Merchant on the Eve of the Revolution* (Columbia Univ., *Studies*, no. 404), 235 ff.; Savelle, *George Morgan*, chaps. ii-iii; Sellers, *Charleston Business*, 169 ff.

"to draw the Indians on the spot—had them many years standing before me, and lived with them as a friend and brother." The savages, he held, should neither be cheated nor spoiled, but dealt with firmly; "a mean submissive temper can never manage our Indian affairs." [1]

While such men as Adair helped to maintain tolerable relations between the races, the average Indian trader had a bad reputation. General Thomas Gage declared most of them were "as wild as the Country they go in, or the People they deal with, and by far more vicious and wicked." Franklin, too, called them "vicious." Adair himself denounced the less responsible of his fellow traders as "abandoned, reprobate white savages." A notorious evil was the traffic in rum and its abuse in bargaining with the Indians. Major Robert Rogers described such an unscrupulous bargainer in his play of *Ponteach*:

> A thousand Opportunities present
> To take Advantage of their Ignorance;
> But the Great Engine I employ is Rum.

Such traders were largely responsible for border warfare.[2]

Many of the early trans-Alleghany pioneers were people of the older frontier who had been prepared for similar undertakings in the newer West. The actual settlements in these years were chiefly in western Pennsylvania and the present West Virginia, with smaller ones in eastern Kentucky and Tennessee. By 1765 there were a few permanent residents about Fort Pitt with the soldiers and traders, and during the next ten years a rush

[1] James Adair, *The History of the American Indians* (S. C. Williams, ed., Johnson City, Tenn., 1930), xxxvi, 395, 442 ff.
[2] Thomas Gage, *Correspondence with the Secretaries of State, 1763-1775* (C. E. Carter, ed., New Haven, 1931-1933), I, 124; Adair, *American Indians*, 306 ff.; Robert Rogers, *Ponteach* (Allan Nevins, ed., Chicago, 1914), 180-181; J. A. Adams, "The Indian Trader of the Upper Ohio Valley," *Western Pa. Hist. Mag.*, XVII, 163-174.

of pioneers occurred into southwestern Pennsylvania, where two new counties were organized by 1773. Other migrants passed farther down the Ohio Valley, settling on or near the Ohio, Monongahela and Kanawha rivers. From such outposts developed the West Virginia cities of Wheeling, Morgantown and Charleston. Here was a fighting frontier frequently traversed by Indian war parties. North of the Ohio, except for a few old French communities, lay Indian country.[1]

In Kentucky, Daniel Boone acted as the agent of that energetic North Carolina promoter, Judge Richard Henderson, who secured from the Indians a dubious title to a large tract of land on which he proposed to found the colony of Transylvania. Boone, who was sent to blaze the way, established the "station" of Boonesborough on the Kentucky River. Near by, James Harrod of Pennsylvania had begun an independent settlement at Harrodsburg. Shortly afterwards, Henderson held at Boonesborough a convention of delegates from the four existing communities and set up a fairly liberal proprietary government. Virginia refused, however, to recognize his title, and Transylvania soon became a part of that province, receiving a county government in 1776. Somewhat in advance of the Kentucky settlers, other pioneers, largely Virginians, followed tributaries of the Tennessee River into northeastern Tennessee, then supposed to be a part of Virginia. There, setting up a simple government, they were soon joined by a few other persons from Virginia and North Carolina.[2]

The Northern migration to the West came largely from Pennsylvania and New Jersey—overland to the

[1] A. T. Volwiler, *George Croghan and the Westward Movement* (Cleveland, 1926), 209-259.

[2] Henderson, "Creative Forces in Westward Expansion," 86-107; T. D. Clark, *A History of Kentucky* (Carl Wittke, ed., *Prentice-Hall History Series*; N. Y., 1937), chaps. iv-v; T. P. Abernethy, *From Frontier to Plantation in Tennessee* (Chapel Hill, 1932), chap. i.

upper Ohio and thence downstream. Virginians and Carolinians generally traveled either by the Ohio and its branches or by land through the Cumberland Gap. The volume of this human stream can only be conjectured. In 1770 George Croghan stated that the previous year had seen between four and five thousand families settle beyond the mountains, and "all this spring and summer," he added, "the roads have been lined with wagons moving to the Ohio." In 1771 it was estimated, perhaps optimistically, that ten thousand families dwelt along the Ohio and its tributaries. In the words of Governor Dunmore, "the emigrating Spirit of the Americans" could not be controlled. The chief base for Western enterprises—trading, military or colonizing— was Pittsburgh, with its motley assemblage of soldiers, traders, adventurers and farmers.[1]

The people in these westward-moving throngs were of many sorts. Judge Henderson and George Washington were promoters rather than settlers: they and their agents surveyed sites for others to live on. Yet no sharp line can be drawn between speculators and settlers. Arthur St. Clair, after resigning from the British army and marrying into a well-to-do Boston family, moved to western Pennsylvania, where he acquired a large estate. A representative promoter-settler in Kentucky was James Harrod who after founding Harrodsburg became a leading citizen of the new commonwealth. The careers of Tennesseans like James Robertson and John Sevier further illustrate the success of frontier leaders with a flair for promotion. Sevier was a particularly active speculator.

Of course, not all settlers were community builders. For some the master interest was hunting and trapping

---

[1] Alvord, *Mississippi Valley in British Politics*, II, 112-114; R. G. Thwaites and Louise P. Kellogg, eds., *Documentary History of Dunmore's War, 1774* (Madison, 1905), 371.

—the "call of the wild." But far more important were the obscure men and women who tilled the farms, founded homes and built ordered communities. For such people the establishment of secure titles to their homesteads was often difficult. Provincial land offices were generally far from the frontier, adequate surveys were lacking, and land warrants frequently conflicting. A considerable number were squatters without titles, staking out claims by clearing the land, building primitive cabins and planting crops. As Jefferson later said, many people were "appropriating lands of their own authority, and meditating to hold them by force . . . ." Such folk usually had the sympathy of their neighbors when newcomers with formal titles contested possession. In the end, the Virginia legislature found it necessary to give way to the torrent and accept the principle of preemption, or preference to actual settlers. Other states took similar action during the Revolution. A North Carolina statute gave the occupant the preference "even against a prior certificate of entry." According to Jefferson, a liberal policy would ultimately be more profitable to the government since the frontiersmen would "settle the land in spite of everybody." [1]

Life in the trans-Alleghany settlements resembled that in backcountry homes east of the mountains, with one-room log cabins scantily furnished. Corn and pork formed a large part of the diet, varied with game and vegetables. The men dressed in a combination of Indian and European modes, with garments of cloth or deerskin, moccasins, and caps or ordinary hats. The women were clothed in loose gowns and large sunbonnets. Wearing moccasins in winter, they commonly went barefoot in summer. The men hunted, did some farm work

[1] Jefferson, *Works*, II, 239-240; III, 4-8; Henry Tatter, "State and Federal Land Policy during the Confederation Period," *Agricultural History*, IX, 176-186.

and guarded their families against the savages, while the women performed the household tasks, reared the children, made the family clothing and commonly hoed corn. Cabins in exposed situations were inclosed by stockades to which near-by settlers resorted when fearing Indian attacks.[1]

None can doubt the heroism of the eighteenth-century pioneers who built the new commonwealths—their courage, self-reliance and democratic spirit. But the frontier experience was not pure gain. The settlers lacked not only the material comforts of an older society but some of the higher values as well. Border warfare was brutalizing; children often grew up with little or no schooling; religion, if not wholly neglected, tended to be crudely emotional. Itinerant preachers occasionally found their way across the mountains. John Adams heard one preach in Philadelphia "with no learning, no grace of action or utterance, but an honest zeal."[2]

The responsibility of lawless frontiersmen for many Indian troubles is clear. Brutal treatment of the red man was partly the work of normally decent men outraged by the killing of wives, children and friends; but there were also vicious characters like Daniel Greathouse, a leader in the Yellow Creek massacre in which white men wantonly murdered the family of Chief Logan. Another was Simon Girty, "the Great Renegade," who even encouraged the torture of white captives. The "Bulltown Massacre" of Indians by whites in 1772 was, according to one historian, "accompanied by atrocities as repulsive" as any charged against the redskins.[3] Alexander Withers, a sympathetic chronicler who knew many of the pioneers, admitted a lowering of moral

[1] Thwaites, *Daniel Boone,* chap. iii.
[2] Adams, *Works,* II, 401.
[3] A. S. Withers, *Chronicles of Border Warfare* (R. G. Thwaites, ed., Cincinnati, 1895), 128-149 and *passim.*

standards. This he regarded as "the certain result of circumstances, which they could not control." He thought it remarkable that "their dereliction from propriety" was no greater.

CHAPTER VIII

EMERGING AMERICANISM

THE Frenchman Crèvecœur, writing during the
Revolutionary War after some twenty years' residence
in the colonies, recorded his conviction that the people,
despite their divergent origins, possessed certain characteristics that differentiated them from Europeans and
which might fairly be called American.[1] Many elements
of this underlying unity may be easily perceived. The
men politically and socially influential were English-
speaking and chiefly of British stock. Governmental
institutions everywhere rested on such fundamental notions as popular representation, trial by jury and other
common-law safeguards of liberty and property. The
eighteenth century brought about a more general acceptance of common-law principles than earlier. This was
the natural result of a more settled society, a bench and
bar increasingly familiar with English precedents, and
imperial insistence on the harmonizing of colonial legislation with English law.[2] The rapid expansion of the
newspaper press also promoted unity through intercolonial circulation and exchanges. Nor were religious
differences seriously divisive. Except for small Catholic
and still smaller Jewish minorities, the British Americans, so far as they were religious at all, were Protestant
Christians. Within particular denominations there were

[1] J. Hector St. John [de Crèvecœur], *Letters from an American Farmer*
(new edn., London, 1783), esp. 51-53.

[2] R. B. Morris, *Studies in the History of American Law with Special
Reference to the Seventeenth and Eighteenth Centuries* (Columbia Univ.,
Studies, no. 316), chap. i. For the earlier conditions, see J. T. Adams,
Provincial Society, 1690-1763 (*A History of American Life*, III),
14-17, 277-278.

some intercolonial associations, as in the Presbyterian synod, the Friends' meetings and the correspondence or occasional conferences among the Anglican clergy.

The recent intercolonial war with France affected Anglo-American patriotism in opposite ways. The unequal response of provincial assemblies to appeals for financial and military support showed the strength of particularism, as did also the prevalence of trade with the enemy. The friction between British regulars and provincial troops worked to the same end. Nevertheless, many Americans thought of the conflict as a national enterprise in whose outcome they were deeply concerned. They acclaimed such leaders as William Pitt and Lord George Augustus Howe and, when Howe fell at Ticonderoga in 1758, Massachusetts erected a monument to him in Westminster Abbey. The Puritan clergy ardently supported the "Protestant succession," regarding England as a bulwark against Catholic France and Spain. In 1759 a Connecticut parson referring to the British Constitution declared there was "none that exceeds, perhaps none that, in all Respects, equals it in Excellency." After General James Wolfe's victory at Quebec, the Ames almanac printed lines expressing pride in a common effort:

> Fame stood amaz'd at our victorious Troops
> When proud Quebec unto their Capture stoops.

So also Franklin wrote in 1760: "No one can more sincerely rejoice than I do, on the reduction of Canada; and this is not merely as I am a colonist, but as I am a Briton." [1]

Anglo-American patriotism continued after the war.

[1] Alice M. Baldwin, *The New England Clergy and the American Revolution* (Duke Univ., Publs., 1928), 83; Sam Briggs, *The Essays, Humor and Poems of Nathaniel Ames, Father and Son, . . . from Their Almanacks* (Cleveland, 1891), 341; Benjamin Franklin, *Writings* (Albert Smyth, ed., N. Y., 1907), IV, 4.

Oxenbridge Thacher, while vigorously opposing parliamentary taxation, "exulted in the name of Briton" and hoped that "the whole English empire, united by the strongest bonds of love and interest," might "happily possess immortality." John Adams in his "Essay on the Canon and Feudal Law" (1765) urged his fellow Americans to remember their "British ancestors who have defended for us the inherent rights of mankind." In the song, "Virginia Hearts of Oak," printed shortly after the repeal of the stamp act, there was a similar note of British patriotism:

> Though we feast and grow fat on America's soil
> Yet we own ourselves subjects of Britain's fair isle;
> And who's so absurd to deny us the name
> Since true British blood flows in every vein.

In 1766 young Francis Hopkinson, a future signer of the Declaration of Independence, said in a commencement essay: "We in America are in all respects Englishmen, notwithstanding that the Atlantic rolls her waves between us and the throne to which we all owe our allegiance." More familiar are the frequent references of colonial spokesmen to "the rights of Englishmen." [1]

Though many American visitors to England were disillusioned by its society and politics, other comments were sympathetic. Franklin, returning from London in 1763, wrote warmly of the old country and those whom he had met there, "No friend could wish me more in England than I do myself." A few years later Benjamin Rush was deeply moved by his last view of "the white cliffs of Britain," enjoying "in silence this pensive retrospect of the finest country in the world." Arthur Lee considered taking up professional practice in this

[1] M. C. Tyler, *The Literary History of the American Revolution, 1763-1783* (2nd edn., N. Y., 1898-1900), I, 52-56, 228; John Adams, *Works* (C. F. Adams, ed., Boston, 1856), III, 462; *Va. Gazette*, May 2, 1766.

"Eden of the world and the land of liberty and independence." His brother William became enough of a
Londoner to be chosen sheriff and alderman of the
metropolis.[1]

In their formal publications Americans expressed
themselves in English much like that used across the
Atlantic. Even in the colloquial speech the differences
were apparently less than might be supposed. Lord
Adam Gordon found the language of Bostonians quite
like that of the "old country." Visiting Philadelphia,
he declared that English was "spoken by all ranks, in a
degree of purity and perfection, surpassing any, but the
polite part of London." William Eddis, whose experience was chiefly in Maryland, said "the pronunciation
of the generality of people" had an "accuracy and elegance" which must gratify "the most judicious ear."
Considering the mixed origin of the inhabitants, he
thought it remarkable that the spoken language should
show so few divergences. The young English traveler,
Nicholas Cresswell, was also surprised to find the speech
of colonials as good as it was and the variations no
greater. "In general," he believed, they used "better
English than the English do."[2]

There were, of course, immigrants from Continental
Europe who spoke either their own native tongue or a
hybrid speech, and other differences were due to the

---

[1] Franklin, *Writings*, IV, 207; Benjamin Rush, *A Memorial Containing Travels through Life or Sundry Incidents* (Phila., 1905), 49-50;
B. J. Hendrick, *The Lees of Virginia* (Boston, 1935), 145-146, 218.

[2] Other testimony to the good quality and comparative uniformity of
American English came from the Tory parson, Jonathan Boucher, and the
German physician, Johann D. Schoepf. [Lord Adam Gordon], "Journal
of an Officer's Travels in America and the West Indies, 1764-1765,"
N. D. Mereness, ed., *Travels in the American Colonies* (N .Y., 1916),
411, 449; William Eddis, *Letters from America* (London, 1792),
59-61; Nicholas Cresswell, *Journal* (N. Y., 1924), 271; Jonathan
Boucher, *Reminiscences of an American Loyalist, 1738-1789* (Jonathan
Bouchier, ed., Boston, 1925), 61; J. D. Schoepf, *Travels in the Confederation, 1783-1784* (A. J. Morrison, ed., Phila., 1911), II, 62.

survival in America of forms which had become archaic in England. The colonial vocabulary also included words taken over from the Indians as well as from non-English white neighbors.[1] There were, besides, minor local divergences. Philip Fithian, for instance, noted that Virginians spoke of a "sale" instead of a "vendue," the New Jersey term, and of an "ordinary" instead of a "tavern." A Virginian would have called a horse "vicious" when the Jerseyman would have said "mischievous." Regarding colonial speech Franklin was probably a better judge than most Americans because of his broader experience. He believed that, on the whole, the colonists spoke well and that informed Englishmen agreed with him. Though the people of different counties in the homeland could be distinguished by dialectal peculiarities, one could not so "distinguish a North American." President John Witherspoon thought the common man in the colonies spoke better than an Englishman of the corresponding class, while the language of educated Americans was less correct than that of educated Englishmen. Nevertheless, one hopeful colonial maintained that the "highest perfection" of the English tongue was "reserved for this Land of light and freedom." He proposed, therefore, the choice of "Fellows of the American Society of Language" to "correct, enrich and refine" the speech.[2]

A genuine English loyalty was sometimes associated with an equally real Americanism that was conceived within the framework of the empire in which America was to grow increasingly important. Thus Franklin wrote to Lord Kames: "I have long been of opinion,

[1] See Adams, *Provincial Society*, 288-290.
[2] G. P. Krapp, *The English Language in America* (N. Y., 1925), II, 49 ff.; P. V. Fithian, *Journal and Letters, 1767-1774* (J. R. Williams, ed., Princeton, 1900), 147; Franklin, *Writings*, V, 208-210; John Witherspoon, *Works* (Phila., 1800), IV, 460; *Royal American Magazine*, Jan., 1774, 6-7.

that the *foundations of the future grandeur and stability
of the British empire lie in America . . . .*" Less provincial
than most of his compatriots, Franklin constantly
displayed his concern with America's long-range interests.
Though in 1767 he still favored union with Great
Britain, he considered it more advantageous to the mother
country than to the colonies. In any case, "America, an
immense territory . . . with all advantages of climate,
soil, great navigable rivers, and lakes, &c. must become a
great country, populous and mighty; and will, in a less
time than is generally conceived, be able to shake off
any shackles that may be imposed on her . . . ." According
to Charles Carroll, the power of Britain, an
island with limited territory, had already reached its
zenith, while that of America was destined to be "as
unbounded as our dominions are extensive." Contemporaries
noted the psychological effect of this large-scale
physical environment. By contrast, William Eddis
found the Thames "reduced to a diminutive stream."
A French visitor was similarly impressed by the geographic
extent, immense resources and rapidly increasing
population. All seemed to foreshadow independence,
which he found already the subject of general
conversation.[1]

Nevertheless, as Josiah Quincy observed, there was a
"prevalent and extended ignorance" in the colonies about
one another's concerns, while mutual prejudices and
clashing interests also worked against a common American
feeling. Quincy himself resented Southern pretensions
and thought the "hospitality and politeness" of
Virginians greatly exaggerated. He noted among the
Philadelphia Quakers a general "disliking" of New England.
Young William Paterson of New Jersey charac-

[1] Franklin, *Writings,* IV, 4; V, 20-22; Kate M. Rowland, *Life and
Correspondence of Charles Carroll of Carrollton* (N. Y., 1898), I, 75;
Eddis, *Letters,* 6; A French Traveller in the Colonies, "Journal," *Am.
Hist. Rev.,* XXVII, 84.

terized the Yankees as an "odd, inquisitive kind of beings," while Southerners accused them of hypocrisy. Lewis Morris expressed a general opinion among New Yorkers when he objected to having his son educated in Connecticut lest he acquire the "lowe craft and cunning so incident to the people of that country." Connecticut folk reciprocated by complaining of "frauds and unfair practices" by New York merchants. Similarly Bostonians charged New Yorkers with being profiteers and inordinate money lovers.[1]

Such animosities were sharpened by boundary controversies and mutual business suspicions. New Yorkers disputed the Vermont country with grantees from New Hampshire and Massachusetts and with aggressive Connecticut settlers. Pennsylvanians resented Connecticut's intrusion in the Wyoming Valley and came to blows with Virginians on the upper Ohio. Rhode Island inflation disturbed relations with Massachusetts, and there were other intercolonial trade quarrels. In the preliminaries of the Revolution nonimportation agreements were weakened by mutual recriminations among merchants in different provinces. To some observers such antagonisms seemed insuperable obstacles to union. The English clergyman, Andrew Burnaby, who visited the colonies in 1759-1760, maintained that, if the colonies became independent, "there would soon be a civil war from one end of the continent to the other."[2]

Some intelligent politicians also feared the possible divisive effect of provincial prejudices. When John Adams went to the First Continental Congress, Joseph

[1] Josiah Quincy, "Journal," Mass. Hist. Soc., *Proceeds.*, XLIX, 467, 477, 481; anon., *Glimpses of Colonial Society and the Life at Princeton College, 1766-1773* (W. J. Mills, ed., Phila., 1903), 133; Edward Channing, *A History of the United States* (N. Y., 1905-1925), III, 468.

[2] Adams, *Works*, II, 276; Andrew Burnaby, *Travels through the Middle Settlements in North America in the Years 1759 and 1760* (London, 1775), 92.

Hawley told him that Massachusetts men, especially Bostonians, had an unfortunate reputation for "inward vanity and self-conceit." Adams was advised that there would be fellow delegates "fully equal" to New Englanders, including Southerners with "as much sense and literature as any we can or ever could boast of." New Englanders needed also to respect the feelings of men of "Dutch, or Scotch, or Irish extract." [1]

One factor in the rise of Americanism was an increasingly detached and critical attitude toward British society. By 1772 Franklin was emphasizing the imperfections of a social system which depressed "multitudes below the Savage State that a few may be rais'd above it," and a little later he noted the "extream Corruption prevalent among all Orders of Men in this old rotten State." Virtuous America should avoid too close association with so vicious a society. This notion of Old World decadence, urged on both sides of the Atlantic, may be illustrated by a reprint from the *London Gazette* in the *American Magazine* of Philadelphia. Like Macaulay's New Zealander, "two North-American Travellers" in 1944 found the British metropolis in ruins. An Anglican dignitary told William Samuel Johnson that the colonies might become an asylum "from the boundless impiety and approaching destruction" of a "dissolute and abandoned" mother country. England, said the elder Charles Carroll of Doughoregan, was corrupt, and "corruption and freedom" could not "long subsist together." His son advised an English friend to leave a land marked by "the symptoms of general decay." Henry Laurens thought chastity was "out of fashion" in England. Even Loyalists were not always happy there. Samuel Curwen complained of "vicious indulgences of every kind" as well as of "the deplorable

[1] Adams, *Works*, IX, 344-345.

venality" in politics. When the Revolutionary War ended, he gladly returned to Massachusetts. Ward Chipman, a Harvard graduate who served in the British army, declared that life in England, even with a full purse, did not offer "half the rational social enjoyments" of colonial society.[1]

As an eighteenth-century interpreter of Americanism perhaps no one surpassed Crèvecœur. Its chief characteristics, he thought, were a comparatively simple and democratic society and an expansive outlook. In America the European peasant, accustomed to work for princes or nobles and lacking political privileges, might easily become a freeholder and a citizen. There was a change of scale also: "two hundred miles formerly appeared a very great distance, it is now but a trifle." In this bracing atmosphere men were inspired to undertakings which would never have occurred to them in Europe: "Thus Europeans become Americans." [2] Crèvecœur's picture was somewhat idealized, for America, too, had its class distinctions and the colonial franchise was quite undemocratic. In terms of contemporary Europe, however, his analysis was essentially sound.

The idea that culture, like "the course of Empire," was likely to move westward appears occasionally in provincial literature. John Trumbull hoped that American prose and verse might rival the works of Addison and Pope, of Shakespeare and "lofty Milton." One ardent patriot looked forward to the day when "Art's fair Empire" would "grace Ontario's Shore," when

---

[1] Franklin, *Writings*, V, 363; VI, 312; *American Magazine or General Repository*, July, 1769, 207-208; Charles Carroll, *Unpublished Letters* (T. M. Field, ed., U. S. Catholic Hist. Soc., *Monograph Ser.*, I), 77-79, 96-97; D. D. Wallace, *Henry Laurens* (N. Y., 1915), 185; Samuel Curwen, *Journal and Letters* (G. A. Ward, ed., Boston, 1842), 33; Edward Gray, "Ward Chipman, Loyalist," Mass. Hist. Soc., *Proceeds.*, LIV, 340.

[2] [Crèvecœur], *Letters*, letter iii.

America might have its own Locke and Newton and "Another Shakespeare" appear on the banks of the Ohio River.[1]

Emotion as well as reason contributed toward a revolutionary psychology. This state of mind stemmed partly from causes other than the grievances which provided the immediate occasion for extreme measures. Discontent arising from any source was sometimes directed against persons and policies not primarily at fault. Evidences of social unrest may be found first in the older countryside. In rural New England existed survivals of the ancient antagonism between town proprietors and nonproprietary inhabitants, and that between country debtors and merchant-creditors who had opposed such agrarian measures as the land bank and the expansion of paper currency. Here the British government was also involved since Parliament had suppressed the land bank and checked the issue of legal-tender paper. Elsewhere quitrents, royal or proprietary, accounted for some discontent, though these payments, irregularly collected, were hardly a major issue. In some provinces, however, efforts to enforce them had led to acrimonious controversies, notably among the tenants of Lord Granville who had inherited extensive proprietary rights in North Carolina. In New York many great landowners paid only nominal quitrents; but their tenants complained of oppressive dues and during the seventeen-sixties uprisings on Hudson Valley estates were not suppressed without some bloodshed. In the South, parliamentary restraints on tobacco exports to Continental Europe limited the planter's market, but the chief object of complaint was the British creditor and his agents on whom was blamed the accumulating debt

---

[1] Trumbull, quoted in Tyler, *Literary History*, I, 210; Briggs, *Ames . . . Almanacks*, 402.

burden at a time when the plantation economy was declining through soil exhaustion.[1]

Though rural discontent helped to prepare the way
for radical proposals, mercantile grievances were at first
more conspicuous. The difficulties of the colonial merchant did not arise wholly from government policies:
one factor was the transition from war to peace after
1763. Privateering was over, army contracts were
smaller and the exceptional profits of enemy trade were
ended. Governmental action did, however, complicate
the situation through stricter enforcement of existing
trade regulations, especially those affecting commerce
with the foreign West Indies. The navy coöperated
with the customs service, seizures of suspected vessels
increased, trade fell off and, as we have seen, an acute
depression set in. Then came the new parliamentary
measures which further depressed colonial business.
Customs officials and admiralty courts received additional
powers for the enforcement of commercial regulations.
In 1764 and 1765 followed the sugar act, the sweeping
prohibition of legal-tender paper, and the stamp act.[2]

Though radicals and conservatives agreed in condemning the obnoxious legislation and, as General
Thomas Gage said, "differed only in the means to be
pursued," that difference became increasingly important.
Radicals were ready for violent resistance, while others,
fearing its effect on the masses, favored methods less
obviously illegal. Nevertheless, wealthy merchants sat
in the Stamp Act Congress, supported the boycott of
English goods and, with more or less misgiving, acqui-

[1] Irving Mark, *Agrarian Conflicts in Colonial New York, 1711-1775*
(Columbia Univ., *Studies*, no. 469), chaps. iv-v; A. O. Craven, *Soil
Exhaustion as a Factor in the Agricultural History of Virginia and Mary-
land, 1606-1860* (Univ. of Ill., *Studies*, XIII, no. 1), 52-56.

[2] A. M. Schlesinger, *The Colonial Merchants and the American Revolution, 1763-1776* (Columbia Univ., *Studies*, LXXVIII), chaps. i-ii; Virginia D. Harrington, *The New York Merchant on the Eve of the Revolution* (same ser., no. 404), 328.

esced in the riotous proceedings of the Sons of Liberty. The business depression survived the repeal of the stamp tax and the modification of the sugar act; and before long the merchants were again protesting against parliamentary measures.[1]

The Townshend acts of 1767 brought a further tightening of the enforcement machinery directed against illicit trade, while the taxation issue was revived through "external" duties on glass, paper, painters' colors and tea. Again the merchants responded with nonimportation agreements; but the experience of the stamp-act riots and the consequent disturbance of business led to more emphasis on orderly procedures, as in Dickinson's *Letters from a Pennsylvania Farmer*. Intercolonial cooperation proved difficult, however, and it was not until 1769 that the three principal Northern ports were united in nonimportation agreements. In Charleston the merchants acted reluctantly under pressure from the "mechanics and tradesmen." Even so, the various mercantile communities feared loss of trade and were mutually suspicious. When, therefore, all the Townshend duties except that on tea were repealed, many merchants accepted this as substantial, if not complete, redress, with the result that the nonimportation program broke down. In 1770 business was reviving and there was a tendency to let well enough alone rather than risk the consequences of radical appeals to the masses.[2]

Two other urban groups, the lawyers and the printers, were directly affected by the stamp act. The lawyers disliked the tax on legal documents and some of them became vigorous opponents of the statute. After it was repealed, however, they lacked a specific class grievance and thereafter did not display a similar consensus of

[1] *Ibid.*, 319; Thomas Gage, *Correspondence with the Secretaries of State, 1763-1775* (C. E. Carter, ed., New Haven, 1931-1933), I, 81.
[2] Schlesinger, *Colonial Merchants*, chaps. iv-vi.

opinion. Much the same thing was true of the printer-publishers, who especially resented the stamp duties on newspapers and advertisements and naturally took a conspicuous and effective part in the opposition propaganda, printing the arguments and filling their columns with inflammatory appeals. Some journals temporarily quit publication, while others defiantly continued to appear without stamps. The *Pennsylvania Journal* announced its prospective suspension by a funereal front page, death's heads and the words, "Adieu, adieu to the Liberty of the Press." After the repeal, however, the printers, like the lawyers, differed among themselves and in later crises took no uniform stand.[1] Freedom of the press cannot, in general, be regarded as a significant issue in the Revolution.

From the standpoint of class feeling a more important group was that commonly known as the "mechanics and tradesmen"—small traders, clerks, artisans, seamen, carters and common laborers. At the upper levels a fair number of these people could vote, being "freemen" pursuing recognized occupations or owners of sufficient property to meet minimum suffrage requirements. Many others, however, could not qualify or, if they could, lacked effective organization. Of employer-labor conflicts comparable with those of later times we hear little, though in 1768 the *New-York Journal* reported a strike of journeymen tailors whose wages had been reduced. More common were such other indications of class consciousness as resentment at social pretensions and demands for a larger share in public affairs. The latter appeared, for instance, in Philadelphia, where a close corporation directed the city government and the suffrage was so sharply restricted that few even of the taxpayers could vote. In the *Pennsylvania Journal* (1773)

[1] A. M. Schlesinger, "The Colonial Newspapers and the Stamp Act," *New England Quar.*, VIII, 63-83.

"Mechanic" denounced the upper-class "Junto" who might pose as friends of liberty but could not be trusted. Another newspaper communication, from "Citizen," complained that, though the "laborious Farmer and Tradesman" had always been the support of liberty, the ruling class did not wish them to "intermeddle in State affairs."[1]

The urban working class counted heavily in the Revolutionary movement. Public meetings repeatedly occurred in which suffrage requirements did not apply or were not enforced. In New England, royal officials complained of "town meetings," regular or irregular, where "the lowest Mechanics" could discuss "the most important points of government, with the utmost freedom."[2] Conservatives regarded such gatherings, guided by a "few hot and designing men," as a "constant source of sedition." In New York, where mass meetings in the interest of particular candidates had long been familiar, they were used to bring forward mechanics' tickets. When mercantile opposition to British measures seemed too cautious, the mechanics here and elsewhere had their radical spokesmen, not necessarily members of their own class, but commonly skillful politicians like Samuel Adams, Christopher Gadsden and the New York triumvirate of Lamb, Sears and McDougall. Adams was a Harvard graduate; Gadsden, a substantial business man; John Lamb, a moderately prosperous wine merchant; Alexander McDougall was fairly well off; and Isaac Sears was an early member of the New York Chamber of Commerce.

[1] I. N. P. Stokes, *Iconography of Manhattan Island* (N. Y., 1915-1928), IV, 784; C. H. Lincoln, *The Revolutionary Movement in Pennsylvania, 1760-1776* (Univ. of Pa., *Ser. in History*, no. 1), chap. iii, pp. 91-93; A. E. McKinley, *The Suffrage Franchise in the Thirteen English Colonies in America* (same ser., no. 2), 290-292.

[2] L. H. Gipson, *Jared Ingersoll* (*Yale Hist. Publs. Miscellany*, VIII), 270.

In short, the mechanic-tradesman group offered combustible material which might be effectively directed in critical situations. In New York it forced conservatives to accept measures about which they felt misgivings. In Charleston it turned the tide in favor of the nonimportation agreement of 1769. A corresponding group was active in the Boston Tea Party, and in 1776 combined in Pennsylvania with backcountry farmers to overcome the conservativism of the legislature. In the larger capitals especially, urban radicalism could exert pressure on provincial assemblies and officials.

There were also, as we have seen, dissatisfied elements in the "Old West," jealous of the overrepresentation of the East in the colonial legislatures. Along the New York border a petty warfare of a dozen years had developed partly out of the territorial claims of Massachusetts and partly from the resentment of native tenants against the Livingston, Van Rensselaer and Van Cortlandt landlords. These difficulties came to a head in 1766. It was a conflict, as a recent writer has said, "that extended its glowing front for a distance of nearly a hundred and fifty miles, that gathered mobs of two hundred to two thousand men who had to be dispersed by royal troops, that carried the torch of destruction through forests and fields, barns and homes, that pitted the poor against the rich perhaps more dramatically than any struggle in previous colonial times, that set a pattern of strife between Yankees and Yorkers which left little to be invented in the later controversies in Vermont." [1] By the action of the soldiers and of the London government the direct westward expansion of Massachusetts was checked and the New York system of land tenure saved for the rest of the provincial period. The three great manor lords involved took the Whig side in the Revolution, and that temporarily assuaged the class feel-

[1] D. R. Fox, *Yankees and Yorkers* (N. Y., 1940), 140.

ing between landlords and tenants; but apparently the
latter felt, and quite rightly, that a successful revolution would in some way improve their status.

There were further sources of discontent in the problems of the trans-Alleghany country. Both the frontiersmen themselves and the land speculators or promoters were involved. Each group resented more or
less keenly the restrictive policies of the home government in relation to the newly acquired territory. Two of
the grievances listed in the Declaration of Independence
dealt with this Western situation: the complaint against
the new regulations for taking up Western lands and the
denunciation of the Quebec act.

To the friction resulting from economic grievances
were added less material factors. Efforts to exploit
religious feeling may not always have been sincere,
but they would hardly have been made if the feeling
had not widely existed. In New England the political
influence of Puritanism was clearly recognized by Whigs
and Tories alike. The inheritors of that tradition had
been generally loyal to the Hanoverian dynasty as the
symbol of Protestant victory over Jacobites and
"papists," but now their attitude gradually changed,
partly because of the frequent association of Loyalism
with Anglican churchmanship. Though rigid Calvinism
had weakened, even unorthodox ministers like Jonathan
Mayhew and Charles Chauncy were aggressively Protestant, resembling their Puritan ancestors in repudiating
Anglican theories of divine right. No Revolutionary
leader appealed more effectively to such sentiments than
Samuel Adams. Among the grievances which he listed
in 1772 for the Boston town meeting and for circulation in the country towns, one dealt at length with the
proposed Anglican episcopate, reminding the people that
their fathers had crossed the sea to preserve religious and
political liberties now endangered. Many years later

John Adams declared that "the apprehension of Episcopacy" had stimulated "close thinking on the constitutional authority of parliament." [1]

The Puritan conception of the Anglican Church as a "half-way house to Rome" appeared in the discussion of the Quebec act, which established the Roman Catholic Church in Canada. In Isaiah Thomas's *Royal American Magazine* for October, 1774, a cartoon entitled "The Mitred Minuet" pictured the supposed alliance of "Popery" and "Prelacy." The famous resolves of Suffolk County, Massachusetts, denounced the Quebec act as a menace to Protestantism and the "civil rights and liberties of all *America,*" a sentiment presently echoed by the Continental Congress. In 1775 an Englishman in Boston observed that the radicals were exploiting this anti-Catholic feeling. A similar attitude existed among the Presbyterians, who resented even the comparatively weak Anglican establishment in New York, especially when it opposed charters to dissenting churches. The designation in that province of conservative and radical parties as "Church" and "Presbyterian," though not exact, indicates a real relation between political and ecclesiastical attitudes. The Tory rector, Charles Inglis of New York, regarded the Presbyterians as a subversive influence, insisting that the grand object of the dissenters was "an abolition of the Church of England." The idea that religious as well as political rights were involved in the Revolution appears also in the South. In short, religious grievances contributed to the emotional attitudes which helped to make many men responsive to radical propaganda. [2]

---

[1] Baldwin, *New England Clergy,* chaps. vii-ix; Samuel Adams, *Writings* (H. A. Cushing, ed., N. Y., 1904-1908), II, 367-368; John Adams, *Works,* X, 185.

[2] Suffolk Resolves in Peter Force, comp., *American Archives* (Wash., 1837-1853), ser. 4, I, 778; Margaret W. Willard, ed., *Letters on the American Revolution, 1774-1776* (Boston, 1925), 67; A. J. Riley,

Though the importance of political theories in the Revolution may easily be exaggerated, the slogan "No taxation without representation" was not mere camouflage. Assembly journals long before the Revolution show that the essential doctrine, whatever the various forms in which the issue was raised, was deeply rooted in the colonial mind. It rested on a reasoned belief in the power of the purse as an essential safeguard of self-government and of the right of a community to deal freely with its own problems. Though many, probably most, men fight for specific and immediate interests, some at least of the American leaders had a longer perspective, recognizing that the assertion of principle, even though the interest directly involved was slight, might in the end prove highly practical. Nor, when all is said, can we ignore that emotional factor called "the spirit of liberty."

Catholicism in New England to 1788 (Catholic Univ., Studies, XXIV), 88-90; Charles Inglis, "State of the Anglo-American Church," E. B. O'Callaghan, ed., The Documentary History of the State of New York (Albany, 1849-1851), III, 1049-1066; E. F. Humphrey, Nationalism and Religion in America, 1774-1789 (Boston, 1924), 78-81.

CHAPTER IX

THE PARTING OF THE WAYS

SOCIAL discontent in given groups or areas did not always determine the final choice of individuals between Whigs and Tories. Furthermore, party lines were not definitely drawn once and for all at any stage of the controversy. The alignment of 1774 differed from that of 1765, and other changes followed successively the outbreak of hostilities in 1775, the Declaration of Independence and the veering fortunes of war. The sequence of events during the five years immediately preceding the appeal to arms sheds considerable light on these shifts of attitude.

The year 1770, marked by the so-called Boston Massacre on the one hand and the partial repeal of the Townshend duties on the other, began, as we have seen, a period of rapid recovery from economic depression. The small surviving tax on tea seemed hardly worth fighting. Tea drinking was a popular diversion even among radicals, who did not always ask too curiously whether the obnoxious duty had been paid. Meantime, however, the radical leaders, especially in Boston, refused to let matters rest and, aided by the tactical mistakes of their opponents, continued to remind their fellow citizens that their liberties were still in danger. One of the most effective devices for this purpose was the series of orations on the anniversary of the Boston Massacre.[1]

In 1772 the Boston town meeting appointed a com-

[1] John Adams, Works (C. F. Adams, ed., Boston, 1856), II, 255; J. S. Loring, ed., The Hundred Boston Orators (4th edn., Boston, 1852), 1-155. For types of patriot propaganda, see Philip Davidson, Propaganda and the American Revolution (Chapel Hill, 1941).

mittee of correspondence dominated by Samuel Adams, on whose recommendation the town adopted a declaration of colonial rights with a formidable list of "infringements"—parliamentary claims to unlimited legislative and taxing power, the extension of admiralty jurisdiction, restrictions on colonial manufactures and the dreaded Anglican episcopate. This document was widely distributed and presently Adams had an effective network of coöperating town committees. Popular feeling could be more readily excited as the enforcement of customs regulations was stiffened under the new American board of commissioners. Seizures of contraband provoked resistance, as in the spectacular case of the revenue vessel *Gaspee,* destroyed in June, 1772, in Narragansett Bay. The proposal to transport the guilty parties in that affair to England for trial further aroused public wrath, and in 1773 Virginia radicals led by Patrick Henry, Richard Henry Lee and Thomas Jefferson induced the house of burgesses to appoint a provincial committee of correspondence, an example soon followed in other colonies.[1]

Nevertheless, there was still general reluctance to adopt extreme measures until the passage of a new tea act, which, while making tea cheaper for the colonists by removing certain duties in England, kept the tax issue alive by retaining the threepenny duty payable in America. The act also antagonized colonial merchants by authorizing the East India Company to export directly to American agents, thereby enabling them to undersell independent traders. As a result the radicals were reënforced by a considerable body of moderate men. Though the latter group deprecated violence, the radi-

---

[1] Samuel Adams, *Writings* (H. A. Cushing, ed., N. Y., 1904-1908), II, 350 ff.; A. M. Schlesinger, *The Colonial Merchants and the American Revolution, 1763-1776* (Columbia Univ., *Studies,* LXXVIII), 253-278; W. W. Henry, *Patrick Henry* (N. Y., 1891), I, 159 ff.

cals in December, 1773, took matters into their own hands in the Boston Tea Party, which not only defied Parliament but alienated many colonial adherents of public order and property rights. Though other ports also adopted hostile measures, the Boston resistance was the most destructive affair and the most objectionable to conservatives both in England and America.[1] Even some American Whigs favored compensation to the East India Company.

Just as the Boston proceedings were threatening to divide the colonial opposition, parliamentary action helped to close the broken ranks. The series of measures seemed to Americans not only unfair but revolutionary. Three of them—the act closing the port of Boston, the Massachusetts government act and the act for the "impartial administration of justice"—aroused sympathy throughout British America because of their extreme severity and the precedents set for arbitrary interference with local self-government. The reconstruction of the Massachusetts constitution, placing it on substantially the same footing as other royal governments, implied Parliament's right to revoke charter privileges. Similarly, the administration-of-justice act, though limited to Massachusetts, suggested the possibility that royal officials in conflict with colonial authorities elsewhere might claim trial in other provinces or in England.

The two remaining statutes had a more general application. One authorized the quartering of soldiers without action by provincial assemblies. The other, the Quebec act, aimed primarily to solve Canadian problems, but it excited widespread antagonism for three reasons. The well-founded concessions made to the Canadian Catholics aroused strong anti-Catholic feeling. Further-

[1] Schlesinger, *Colonial Merchants*, chap. vii.

more, the organization of Quebec province without a representative assembly, and the acceptance of the French law permitting trial without jury in civil cases, were said to foreshadow attempts at similar government elsewhere. Finally, the inclusion of the Northwest within the boundaries of Quebec disturbed those colonies which had claims in the trans-Alleghany country.

During the summer and early autumn of 1774 events moved rapidly. General Thomas Gage succeeded Hutchinson as governor of Massachusetts and proceeded to enforce the coercive acts. The port of Boston was closed, "mandamus" councilors replaced those formerly elected and town meetings were restricted. The people, however, proved recalcitrant. "Mandamus" councilors resigned under the pressure of public opinion, and the house of representatives, having refused to work with the governor, managed to choose delegates to a Continental Congress before being dissolved. Gage's government, supported by the military, controlled Boston and its vicinity; but elsewhere the real power passed rapidly to a *de facto* government consisting of a provincial congress and of a committee of safety which served as a central executive with the backing of local committees. Taxes were paid to this extralegal government and most of the courts of justice were suspended.

Parallel with this development in Massachusetts was the activity of committees in other colonies in enforcing the tea boycott and collecting supplies for the relief of suffering Boston. Such contributions were partly a natural expression of popular sympathy, but they also helped to bind the colonies more closely together. There was continuous discussion in conventions, committees and the press of appropriate modes of resistance. New nonimportation agreements were adopted, and finally local activities came to a head in the First Continental

Congress, to which every colony but Georgia sent delegates.[1]

When the members assembled at Philadelphia on September 5, 1774, they all agreed on the need of uniting in defense of colonial rights, but differed as to the method to be pursued. New England radicalism, though distrusted by men from other sections, was nevertheless supported by such Southerners as Patrick Henry, Richard Henry Lee and Christopher Gadsden. The conservatives favored the plan proposed by Joseph Galloway, which would have required the concurrent action of Parliament with a general American legislature on measures involving the colonies. Its adoption would have marked a distinct advance in the colonial system. Though supported by some cautious Whigs, this scheme was rejected. The conservatives met a further defeat when Congress approved the revolutionary proceedings in Massachusetts. Congress's declaration of principles was, however, a compromise between those who denied to Parliament any legislative authority in the colonies and those who admitted some parliamentary control outside the field of taxation, especially in the regulation of trade.[2]

Most significant of all was the congressional plan known as the Association, which included nonimportation, nonexportation and nonconsumption agreements against British trade. To protect the Southern staple-producing planters, the enforcement of nonexportation was postponed until September 1, 1775, but nonimportation was to start within a few weeks. To replace imports, native industry was to be stimulated and sheep conserved for woolen manufactures; and profiteers were to be boycotted. The execution of such measures re-

[1] Schlesinger, *Colonial Merchants,* chaps. viii-ix.
[2] W. C. Ford and others, eds., *Journals of the Continental Congress* (Wash., 1904-1937), I, 43-73 and notes; E. C. Burnett, ed., *Letters of Members of the Continental Congress* (Wash., 1921-1936), I, 1-89; E. C. Burnett, *The Continental Congress* (N. Y., 1941), 22-54.

quired not only the support of popular opinion but an
adequate organization. For this purpose provincial and
local committees were to be further developed to deal
with violators of the Association, who were to be publicly denounced as "enemies of American liberty." Here
were the elements of a far-flung *de facto* government
whose orders, though not legally enforceable, would
none the less have the effect of law. As a directing
agency for the provincial and local organizations, the
Second Continental Congress was to assemble in May,
1775.[1]

From now on, party lines were more sharply drawn.
The supporters of the Association, who called themselves
Whigs, were denounced by their opponents as "republicans," "Cromwellians" and the like, while the conservatives were variously characterized as "friends of
government," Loyalists or Tories. Both parties engaged
in vigorous propaganda through public meetings and in
the press. On the conservative side Galloway, a leader
of the Philadelphia bar and speaker of the Pennsylvania
assembly, enjoyed an intercolonial repute. While recognizing colonial grievances he denounced the Association
as a menace to both public order and individual liberty.
He insisted on the supreme authority of Parliament,
which should, however, be asked to coöperate in a new
constitutional union with an American legislature em-
powered in certain cases to approve or reject acts of
Parliament.[2]

Samuel Seabury, an Anglican clergyman who wrote
over the signature of "A. W. Farmer" or the "Westchester Farmer," also attacked the Whig congresses and
committees, and hoped for redress of colonial wrongs

[1] Ford and others, *Journals*, I, 75-80; Schlesinger, *Colonial Merchants*,
chap. x.
[2] Joseph Galloway, *A Candid Examination of the Mutual Claims of
Great-Britain, and the Colonies* (N. Y., 1780), 14, 54-68.

through appeals to Parliament by the regular provincial assemblies. He emphasized the hardship imposed by nonimportation and nonexportation on the ordinary farmer, who must pay more for "the little conveniences and comforts of life" while getting less for what he sold. Furthermore, congressional measures would end in war, with probable defeat for the colonists followed by "slaughter, Confiscations, and Executions"; if the Americans won, civil war and anarchy might be expected. Seabury's essays exasperated the Whigs, and a meeting in Ulster County, New York, ordered one of his pamphlets to be publicly burnt, characterizing its author and publisher as "enemies to their Country." A Virginia county committee denounced his "slavish doctrines . . . impudent falsehood and malicious artifices to excite divisions among the friends of *America*." [1]

Another vigorous Tory advocate was Daniel Leonard, a king's attorney in Boston, who published a series of newspaper essays signed "Massachusettensis." He saw no middle ground between the sovereignty of Parliament and absolute independence which, even if won, would destroy the indispensable balance of monarchy, aristocracy and democracy. As for the Whig propaganda organization, it had planted the "small seed of sedition" now become "a great tree"; it should be cut down at once, for if it fell "suddenly by a stronger arm" it might "crush its thousands in the fall." [2]

John Adams, who as "Novanglus" answered "Massachusettensis," and other Whig leaders such as Jefferson and James Wilson exceeded the cautious language of

---

[1] Samuel Seabury, *Free Thoughts, on the Proceedings of the Continental Congress* (N. Y., 1774), 7 and *passim*; same author, *The Congress Canvassed* (N. Y., 1774), 27 and *passim*; Peter Force, comp., *American Archives* (Wash., 1837-1853), ser. 4, II, 131-133, 234-235.

[2] John Adams and Daniel Leonard, *Novanglus, and Massachusettensis* (Boston, 1819), 159, 168-174, 182. In this edition the name of Jonathan Sewall mistakenly appears on the title page in place of that of Leonard.

the Continental Congress by definitely contesting the legislative as well as the taxing power of Parliament. They were beginning to think of the empire as a personal union in which allegiance to the crown might be acknowledged without admitting parliamentary control of American affairs. What king and Parliament were to Great Britain, king and assembly were to Virginia or Massachusetts. So far, however, even the radicals generally disclaimed, in public at least, a desire for separation.

On neither side was there any readiness to hear opposing views. Whigs had no more regard than Tories for free discussion, and it was generally safer to speak ill of Parliament than to criticize patriot congresses and committees. James Rivington in New York was denounced for printing Loyalist communications in his paper even though he agreed to do the same for the Whigs. Why, wrote a Philadelphian, should "that base fellow" be allowed to publish such "vile calumnies"? Another writer held a Tory pamphleteer to be as dangerous as a violator of the nonimportation agreements and equally punishable. Freedom of the press, said a Newport committee, was needed to defend liberty, but must not be used to support improper measures or excite discord. On the other hand, the Tories thought it absurd that men who were "eternally declaiming on freedom of thought" would not let "an opponent open his mouth on the subjects in dispute, without danger of being presented with a coat of tar and feathers." It is worth noting, however, that William Hooper, a Whig member of Congress, condemned the suppression of a Loyalist pamphlet, declaring it "a strange freedom that was confined to one side of a question." [1]

[1] Force, *American Archives*, ser. 4, I, 1011, 1036, 1233; II, 12-13; Hooper in Deane Papers (N. Y. Hist. Soc. MSS.; contributed by Dr. Michael Kraus).

Meantime the coercive machinery of the Association was being vigorously used. Everywhere committees ordered violators of the Association publicly listed so that they might be cut off from "all commercial intercourse and connection whatsoever." In Maine tenants of the Loyalist landowner, Sir William Pepperell, were advised not to renew their leases. A Virginia agent of a Scotch firm was disciplined for refusing to allow inspection of his books without his principal's consent. Profiteers were punished for raising prices unduly or "engrossing" essential commodities. In short, these bodies were exercising governmental functions. There were, undoubtedly, cases of unfair discrimination or of extreme cruelty, but the injury to persons and property was probably less than might have been expected in a revolutionary movement.[1]

When war began, the royal and proprietary governors in most instances were wielding hardly more than a nominal authority. Virginia public affairs were for the most part controlled by a convention which replaced the house of burgesses and was largely directed by former members of the provincial assembly and county governments. While the royal governor remained at Williamsburg, the convention sat at Richmond and the regular courts were suspended. In North Carolina, also, the old administration was nearly powerless.[2] In Pennsylvania the framework of proprietary government was maintained with a conservative assembly, but the real power was passing to revolutionary committees. The royal governments most nearly held their own in Georgia and New York, both of which had strong Loyalist elements. Neither Rhode Island nor Connecticut needed an extra-

---

[1] Force, *American Archives*, ser. 4, I, 983-985, 1138; Schlesinger, *Colonial Merchants*, chaps. xii-xiii.

[2] H. J. Eckenrode, *The Revolution in Virginia* (Boston, 1916), chap. ii; C. L. Raper, *North Carolina* (N. Y., 1904), chap. x.

legal government since their officers were already chosen
directly or indirectly by the voters.

In view of this state of affairs an appeal to force
seemed almost inevitable. With this in mind the Whigs
proceeded to build up their own military companies. In
Massachusetts the provincial militia had been directed
by the governor and many of its officers were Loyalists.
So a popular militia of "minutemen" was organized
which took orders from the provincial congress and the
committee of safety. Early in April, shortly before the
fight on Lexington common, the Massachusetts provincial congress went farther and formed an "army of observation" under new regulations. Similarly in Vir-
gina volunteer military companies replaced the old
militia. In the various provinces, also, military stores
were collected and the committees of correspondence supplied an intelligence service.[1]

The Loyalists were less effectively organized. In
Massachusetts, Brigadier Timothy Ruggles, a veteran of
the French war, formed an association whose members
pledged themselves to oppose interference by Whig committees. Such a group at Marshfield, when attacked by
Plymouth minutemen, received aid from British regulars
in Boston. "Now," said a Loyalist sympathizer, "every
faithful subject to his King dare freely utter his thoughts,
drink his Tea, and kill his Sheep as profusely as he
pleases." In the end, however, the Ruggles plan failed.
A Loyalist gathering at Ridgefield, Connecticut, resolved
that Congress's measures were unconstitutional and "subversive of our real liberties," to which a Whig convention responded by declaring nonintercourse with the
town's inhabitants. In New York, Dutchess County
Loyalists established an association, and Ulster County
Tories set up a royal standard with an inscription de-

[1] Allen French, *The First Year of the American Revolution* (Boston,
1934), chap. iv; Eckenrode, *Revolution in Virginia*, 109-110.

nouncing "Republican government." There was also some intercolonial correspondence among members of this party. Early in 1775 a Philadelphia sympathizer reported hopefully that Rivington's pamphlets were changing public opinion and that Loyalist associations were increasing. Though this opposition to Congress was certainly widespread, it could not compete with the Whigs in technique of organization and propaganda.[1]

So matters stood in April, 1775, when a British attempt to seize some Whig military stores at Concord, Massachusetts, precipitated civil war. That this was no mere local incident was soon evident. News of the fight, sent on the nineteenth, reached the New York committee on the twenty-third and was immediately forwarded to Philadelphia. A later message arrived in New York on the twenty-fifth, Philadelphia on the twenty-sixth, Baltimore on the twenty-seventh and Virginia on the twenty-eighth, though it did not reach Charleston until three weeks after the engagement.[2] During the next two months the Massachusetts troops were expanded into a New England army and Congress provided for an intercolonial force with a Virginian at its head.

Of the subsequent political history up to the Declaration of Independence only the principal steps need be noted. Of prime importance was the gradual elimination of provincial governments. Most of them had disappeared before Congress in May, 1776, formally decreed the end of all authority under the crown. This meant that, except in Rhode Island and Connecticut, a new governmental structure had to be built and a new basis for civil authority laid to replace the old allegiance. Meantime, the normal processes of law protecting life

[1] Force, *American Archives*, ser. 4, I, 802, 1057, 1068, 1164, 1177, 1208, 1211, 1239.
[2] *Ibid.*, II, 364-370.

and property were interrupted. For the responsible Whig leaders this proved a source of real anxiety. One argument for independence was the need of a new public law based on the principle of popular rule.

The first year of the war brought a gradual change of objective. At first, most responsible leaders asked only for self-government within the empire, with the traditional rights of Englishmen. They claimed simply to be resisting unconstitutional measures of Parliament and the ministry. Actual warfare, however, sharpened antagonism, especially after the king's rejection of a conciliatory petition sent by Congress. But even when George III accused the insurgents of aiming to establish "an independent empire," the charge was not yet true of most of the congressional leaders. During the following winter, however, the radical minority grew steadily. Thomas Paine's *Common Sense*, more than any other single piece of writing, set Americans to thinking of the possibility and desirability of an independent place among the nations. Shortly afterwards Washington declared he was ready "to shake off all connections with a state so unjust and so unnatural." The opposition, however, still continued strong. Many who accepted separation as inevitable did so reluctantly and often under pressure. Paine's "new mode of thinking" required difficult emotional and intellectual adjustments.[1]

But the drift of opinion was indicated by the steps toward governmental reconstruction taken before the official declaring of independence. A solid foundation was available in the local governments. Virginia justices of the peace and New England selectmen did not necessarily forget their responsibility for law and order when they became members of revolutionary committees.

[1] [William Cobbett], *The Parliamentary History of England* (London, 1806-1820), XVIII, 696; George Washington, *Writings* (J. C. Fitzpatrick, ed., Wash., 1931-1940), IV, 318-323; Burnett, *Continental Congress*, 129-137.

Nevertheless, such emergency organizations could not meet the needs of a healthy society. Less than a month after the war began, Massachusetts turned to Congress for counsel "respecting the taking up and exercising the powers of civil Government," noting the risk of raising armed forces "without a civil power to . . . control them." In response Congress advised the conduct of government under the terms of the province charter with the executive power vested in the elected council; and this course was taken. New Hampshire, after consulting Congress, adopted a provisional constitution, and South Carolina took similar action in March, 1776. Meanwhile, three colonies moved toward settled governments. A North Carolina committee outlined a state constitution, but differences of opinion delayed further action with the result that Virginia and New Jersey were the first to adopt permanent constitutions before the Declaration of Independence.[1]

Two other developments preceding formal independence are also significant. Before the end of 1775 both the Continental Congress and Parliament, each for its own reasons, had prevented normal commerce within the empire. This involved the greater part of colonial oversea trade and created a difficult situation not only for private business but also for the revolutionary governments which needed to exchange American exports for war materials. So Congress in April, 1776, opened American ports to the vessels of all nations, a trade hitherto illegal. Parallel with the discussion of commercial policy Congress and the states had to consider how to curb actual or potential enemies within their own communities. With Whigs and Tories oftentimes neighbors the task of distinguishing between friend and foe

---

[1] Force, *American Archives*, ser. 4, II, 622, 955; Allan Nevins, *The American States during and after the Revolution* (N. Y., 1924), chap. iii; W. L. Saunders, ed., *Colonial Records of North Carolina* (Raleigh, 1886-1890), X, 1033-1037.

was not always easy. So far as possible, however, the Loyalists had to be identified, kept under surveillance and disarmed. The states had already done much along this line, but Congress now recommended systematic action.[1]

As the radical program developed, the political alignment correspondingly changed and many of the more conservative opponents of parliamentary policy became Loyalists or neutrals. The Continental Association, however, made a neutral position increasingly difficult. Those who supported the Association were now "patriots" and those who declined were penalized. The alignment altered again when the war began, for some who had accepted the Association in the hope of restraining the radicals refused to join in armed resistance. Another shift occurred when the Declaration of Independence raised the issue of secession from the empire. So it was with two representative New York merchants, Isaac Low and John Alsop. Low sat in the First Continental Congress and signed the Association, but opposed separation and was attainted as a Loyalist. Alsop, a member of the Second Continental Congress, withdrew when independence was voted because that action "closed the door of reconciliation." On the other hand, John Dickinson, Robert Morris and John Jay, who at first argued against independence, finally worked for it. Thus both parties were reënforced from the moderate or hesitant center group. Even later some changes took place. In enemy-occupied areas Loyalism often seemed the line of least resistance, while in other cases British depredations converted neutrals into supporters of the Revolution.[2]

No simple formula explains why particular classes

---

[1] Ford and others, *Journals*, IV, 18-20, 257-259.
[2] Burnett, *Letters*, II, 13; A. C. Flick, *Loyalism in New York during the American Revolution* (Columbia Univ., *Studies*, XIV, no. 1), 147.

or individuals chose to be Whig, Tory or neutral. Some students have assumed a clean-cut division between Tory aristocrats and liberty-loving, democratic Whigs who opposed imperial policies in the interest of self-government. Tories have further been conceived of as officeholders or closely related to that class, or else as temperamental conservatives under the spell of Old World traditions. More recently the class-conflict form of economic interpretation has made headway, while still other historians have emphasized religious affiliations. These explanations each contain an element of truth, but no one of them takes sufficiently into account the complexity of human motives.

In general, officeholders tend to support the existing order, and that was usually true of those who held important royal or proprietary commissions. The governors, whether sent from England or American-born, adhered to the home government. Wentworth in New Hampshire, Hutchinson in Massachusetts and Benjamin Franklin's son William in New Jersey—all members of old colonial families—were strongly Loyalist. Provincial councilors usually took this side, partly no doubt because they frequently held other profitable appointments. Sharper differences distinguished minor officials such as sheriffs, county justices and militia officers, who had to consider not only their official and legal obligations but also local opinion. In Massachusetts the county militia colonels were about evenly divided. Social connections also counted. Officials who were permanent residents usually had business and family ties with many persons whom they could influence.

The professional groups illustrate clearly the disruptive effect of the Revolution on colonial society. In eastern Massachusetts a large proportion of the leading lawyers became Tories. Among them were Jonathan Sewall, Samuel Quincy who was a marriage connection of John Adams, and Daniel Leonard, author of the "Massachusettensis" essays. Many years later, Adams spoke of these men as having been his "cordial, confidential, and bosom friends." Conspicuous lawyers who took the Whig side included Adams himself and John Lowell, afterwards a United States judge.[1]

Of the famous triumvirate of New York lawyers—William Livingston, John Morin Scott and William Smith—Smith became a Loyalist. A much more strenuous Tory was Judge Thomas Jones. Peter Van Schaack, another outstanding lawyer, though not an active partisan, refused to swear allegiance to the Revolutionary state government. Among the moderate Whig members of the bar were Duane and Jay, both of whom supported the conservative Galloway plan but later rendered good service to the Continental cause. Several prominent Philadelphia lawyers were Loyalists, neutrals or conservative Whigs. Joseph Galloway and Chief Justice William Allen were Tories, and Benjamin Chew was suspected of Loyalism and temporarily imprisoned. John Dickinson opposed the Declaration as premature, but once the decision was made he acquiesced. On the other hand, two of the ablest practitioners—James Wilson and Joseph Reed—were definitely Whig. Tory lawyers were scarcer in the South, where the profession furnished such conspicuous patriot leaders as George Wythe, Patrick Henry, Thomas Jefferson, James Iredell and the young Charlestonians: the Rutledges and Pinckneys.

In like fashion physicians were to be found on both sides. In Boston two conspicuous Loyalists were Drs. Jeffries and Lloyd, both of whom had studied in Britain. John Jeffries became a surgeon major in the British

---

[1] Adams, *Works*, X, 194; Emory Washburn, *Sketches of the Judicial History of Massachusetts from 1630 to the Revolution in 1775* (Boston, 1840), 214-218, 237-238.

army, while James Lloyd continued his professional practice in Boston. Among the Whig doctors were Joseph Warren, who died at Bunker Hill, and his brother John, who became an army surgeon.[1] In the King's College medical faculty Dr. John Jones coöperated with the Continental army while Samuel Bard and Peter Middleton were Loyalists. In Philadelphia the Whigs enlisted in the Continental service three of the most forward-looking physicians: John Morgan, William Shippen and Benjamin Rush. The outstanding medical man in Charleston was the Loyalist, Alexander Garden, but on the opposite side was David Ramsay, a young graduate of the Philadelphia medical school.

The political attitude of ministers depended partly on their denominational affiliations. In the North most of the Church of England clergy were Tories. Though mainly of colonial ancestry and often graduates of New England colleges, they accepted the church's tradition of loyalty to the crown. Among the Loyalist exiles were the three Anglican rectors in Boston. When the American army occupied New York, Episcopal services had to be suspended because the clergy refused to omit the prayers for the king. But from Pennsylvania southward the alignment of the Anglican preachers was less distinct. Their three principal functionaries in Philadelphia at first supported Congress and preached patriotic sermons even after the war began. One of them, Jacob Duché, was chosen as congressional chaplain. None of these men, however, really favored independence. Two of them subsequently became Loyalists while the third, Provost William Smith, was distrusted by the more ardent Whigs. On the other hand, William White, a future bishop of Pennsylvania, took the American side.

[1] E. A. Jones, *The Loyalists of Massachusetts* (London, 1930), 179-181, 197 and *passim*; T. F. Harrington, *The Harvard Medical School* (N. Y., 1905), I, *passim*.

In the Chesapeake provinces many of the clergy joined their Whig parishioners and supported the Revolution, some serving as army chaplains. The church suffered, however, through the Loyalism of some conspicuous representatives, notably the rector at Annapolis and the Tory clergy of William and Mary College. In Charleston also the churchmen were divided. The rector of St. Philip's Church was so strenuous a Whig that during the British occupation he was imprisoned and later banished.[1]

For reasons already indicated, most of the Congregational and Presbyterian ministers were Whigs, though even among the New England Congregationalists there were a few exceptions. The conspicuous clerical leaders of the Revolutionary party included Samuel Cooper and Charles Chauncy in Boston and the Presbyterians: President Witherspoon of Princeton, John Rodgers of New York, George Duffield of Philadelphia and David Caldwell in North Carolina. These two denominations contributed by far the largest number of chaplains in the Continental army.[2]

The Baptist preachers, in spite of the discrimination they suffered at the hands of their colonial neighbors, also generally supported the Revolution. Democratic in their social philosophy, they hoped for fairer treatment under the new governments. With the Methodist preachers, often newcomers from England, Loyalism proved stronger—naturally enough, in view of John

---

[1] Justin Winsor, ed., *Memorial History of Boston, 1630-1880* (Boston, 1880-1881), III, 128; Morgan Dix, ed., *A History of the Parish of Trinity Church in the City of New York* (N. Y., 1898-1906), I, chap. xxii; list of clergy in E. L. Goodwin, *The Colonial Church in Virginia* (Milwaukee, 1927), 245-319; Edward McCrady, *History of South Carolina under the Royal Government, 1719-1776* (N. Y., 1899), chap. xxiii.

[2] Alice M. Baldwin, *The New England Clergy and the American Revolution* (Duke Univ., Publs., 1928), chaps. ix, xi; C. A. Briggs, *American Presbyterianism* (N. Y., 1885), chap. ix.

Wesley's condemnation of independence. The Dutch and German Protestants were divided in opinion with the younger Muhlenbergs conspicuous among the Lutheran Whigs. Though the few Catholic priests in Maryland and Pennsylvania could hardly exert much political influence, Father John Carroll coöperated with a committee of Congress in the effort to win over the French Canadians.[1]

As for the educators, there is no reason to suppose that their political attitude differed from that of the communities in which they lived or the religious societies with which they might be affiliated. It happens, however, that three well-known school-teachers were Tories: John Lovell of the Boston Latin School; the Philadelphia Quaker, Robert Proud; and the Maryland clerical tutor, Jonathan Boucher. On the eve of the Revolution two heads of colleges were also Loyalists—Myles Cooper of King's and John Camm of William and Mary. Cooper fled to England, while Camm was dismissed in favor of a young Whig professor. At Philadephia the dubious position of Provost Smith almost broke up the college. The New England and New Jersey faculties, however, adhered to the patriot side.

In the political cleavages the position of the merchants is of special importance. Though generally opposed to the revenue measures of 1764-1765 and the Townshend acts of 1767, they had become increasingly troubled by the violence of the radicals, the interference of the Continental Association with private business, the taking up of arms against the king's representatives and the idea of separation from the empire. A representative statement was the address of the "Merchants and Traders" and others of Boston to Governor Hutchinson as he was

[1] On the conservatism of the elder Muhlenberg, see T. G. Tappert, "Henry Melchior Muhlenberg and the American Revolution," *Church History*, IX, 284-301.

leaving for England in 1774. These "addressers" disapproved the harsh provisions of the port bill, but they favored indemnification of the East India Company and denounced the radicals. During the next year the position of the conservatives grew more unhappy, and when Howe evacuated Boston some two hundred merchants became refugees, including members of solid old Massachusetts families. Nevertheless many substantial New England merchants remained. Typical of the cautious Whigs in this group was John Rowe. He called the Tea Party "a Disastrous Affair"; but, though he believed his fellow citizens had "done amiss" and favored compensation to the East India Company, he considered "the revenge of the Ministry . . . too severe." Staying on in Boston during the siege, he complained of misconduct by the British troops, and after Howe's withdrawal invited Washington to dinner. Though many of his intimates were Tory refugees, Rowe continued active in town affairs.[1]

In New York a majority of the members of the Chamber of Commerce seem to have been Tories, with perhaps a quarter out-and-out Whigs and the rest neutral. Loyalists and neutrals were influenced by family and official connections, profitable business relations with the government, and early British occupation of the city. Conspicuous on the Loyalist side was John Watts, for many years in the official circle. Isaac Low's Toryism may be contrasted with the opposite stand of his brother Nicholas. Other prominent Whig merchants were Philip Livingston and Francis Lewis, both signers of the Declaration of Independence. Many of the Philadelphia merchants were Quakers who, opposed on principle to armed resistance, refused allegiance to the Revolutionary

<hr>

[1] Schlesinger, *Colonial Merchants*, 316-317, 432-440, 591-606; John Rowe, *Letters and Diary* (Annie R. Cunningham, ed., Boston, 1903), 256-258, 273-304, 315.

state government. Though not necessarily Tories, they were naturally distrusted by the Whigs, who sent some of them away to Virginia when the British army approached in 1777. Some well-known merchants actively supported the Revolution, including General Thomas Mifflin, who was disciplined by the Quakers for taking up arms, and Robert Morris. Morris voted against independence on July 2, but two days later refrained from voting, making possible Pennsylvania's affirmative action. He subsequently signed the Declaration.[1]

Among the Charleston merchants Loyalism was strong, especially with the agents of British firms; but two of the wealthiest, Henry Laurens and Gabriel Manigault, were ardent patriots. In the other plantation provinces the merchants were usually Tories. In Virginia the Scotch traders formed the backbone of the Tory element; and farther south there were strong pro-British groups in and about Wilmington and Savannah. A typical Loyalist of Scotch background was Robert Hogg, member of an important Wilmington firm, who after coöperating for a time with the Whigs drew back as they took control of affairs, and left the province. On the other hand, the chief leader of the local radicals was also an outstanding merchant. In Savannah the Tory merchant, Joseph Habersham, had a son and a nephew on the American side.[2]

[1] Virginia D. Harrington, *The New York Merchant on the Eve of the Revolution* (Columbia Univ., *Studies*, no. 404), 349-351; Flick, *Loyalism in New York*, 34 and *passim*; Isaac Sharpless, *The Quakers in the Revolution* (*A History of Quaker Government in Pennsylvania*, Phila., 1898-1899, II), chaps. vi-vii.

[2] Edward McCrady, *History of South Carolina in the Revolution, 1775-1780* (N. Y., 1901), 172; Leila Sellers, *Charleston Business on the Eve of the American Revolution* (Chapel Hill, 1934), 235; D. D. Wallace, *Henry Laurens* (N. Y., 1915); Eckenrode, *Revolution in Virginia*, 114 ff.; [Janet Schaw], *Journal of a Lady of Quality . . . 1774 to 1776* (Evangeline W. and C. M. Andrews, eds., New Haven, 1921), 323; R. D. W. Connor, *Cornelius Harnett* (Raleigh, 1909), 166 ff.

Among the colonial business men the ironmasters formed a special group definitely affected by parliamentary restraints. In Pennsylvania at least, most of the important ones seem to have favored the Whigs. Nevertheless, in the colonies as a whole several of them were Tories, and in any given case it is hard to discover the determining motive. Apparently, then, a majority of the more substantial business men did not favor separation from the empire. Many who were not definitely pro-British tried to be neutral; others, like Morris, acquiesced in the vote for independence; and a fair number were zealous radicals.

Though the urban working classes were natural allies of the radicals, lists of Loyalists include many mechanics and tradesmen—"shopkeepers," shoemakers, blacksmiths, milliners, "servants" and "laborers." Still others were probably too obscure to be listed. But the great bulk sided with the radicals, making up for the lack of support from the "best people." Loyalists and conservative Whigs alike feared the increasing influence of the masses. The "mobility," to quote Gouverneur Morris, could not always vote, but they could join in popular demonstrations and attend town meetings where votes were not closely scrutinized.[1]

Rural communities exhibited similar contrasts. In New England some conspicuous Loyalists were to be found among the comparatively few "country gentry," but most of the farmers belonged to the Whig camp. Consequently, the division between the two parties caused no serious social cleavage.[2] In New York the proprietors of great landed estates, though naturally conservative and preponderantly Tory, included, on the

---

[1] Flick, *Loyalism in New York*, 35, 203; W. H. Siebert, *The Loyalists of Pennsylvania* (Ohio State Univ., Contribs., no. 5), chap. v; Jones, *Loyalists of Massachusetts, passim.*

[2] *Ibid., passim*, esp. 58-61, 215-217, 249-260, 297.

patriot side, the heads of four important manors: Cortlandt, Rensselaerswyck, Livingston and Morrisania.
Among the owners of large tracts not strictly manorial,
Roger Morris and the Delanceys were Tories, while Philip
Schuyler was a Revolutionary general. Several families
of this group were divided in allegiance. Thus of the
Morrisania Morrises two were Whig leaders and one became a British general. Even many tenants on the great
estates and some of the yeoman farmers were Tories;
but probably a majority of the latter vigorously supported the patriot cause. As a result, rural New York
was badly rent, with the situation further complicated
by British control of the lower Hudson during most of
the war. New Jersey, nearly all rural, had fewer consistent Tories than New York, but the Loyalists were
numerous enough to call for constant vigilance on the
part of the Revolutionary government. Pennsylvania
Tory and neutral landowners, many of them connected
with Philadelphia mercantile families, were strong in
the eastern counties, making up more than two thirds of
the attainted Tories in this state outside Philadelphia.
The inland farmers tended to be Whigs.[1]

In the Chesapeake tidewater region Loyalism proved
weaker than might have been expected in the case of
normally conservative landowners, though some among
them felt no enthusiasm for the Revolution. The weakness of Toryism here was due to the energy and prompt
organization of the Whigs; to Lord Dunmore's inept
leadership as governor of Virginia, including his threat
of slave insurrections; and to the lack of a strong British
force about which Loyalists could rally. The out-and-
out Tories among the planter class belonged chiefly to

[1] Flick, *Loyalism in New York*, 33, 34; Theodore Sedgwick, *A Memoir of the Life of William Livingston* (N. Y., 1833), 231-233; Siebert,
Loyalists of Pennsylvania, 34-37, 58; C. H. Lincoln, *The Revolutionary
Movement in Pennsylvania, 1760-1776* (Univ. of Pa., *Ser. in History*,
no. 1), *passim*.

the officeholding group. Of the Virginians who later
claimed British compensation for their losses, only eight
were planters, the majority being merchants. Among
the Virginia Whigs, however, a well-marked line separated radicals and moderates, though the division was
not wholly determined by economic status. Many of
the extremists stemmed from the large-planter class. A
good example is that of the Lee brothers.[1]

The Whiggism of the Virginia landholders may be
variously explained. One cause was the old antagonism
between the planter-debtor and his British creditor, with
the opportunity offered by the war to get rid of burdensome obligations. Early legislation enabled such debtors
to discharge their accounts by payments to the state in
depreciated paper. Aside from this and other specific
grievances, such as the regulations regarding Western
lands which had antagonized Virginia promoters, there
was the broad issue of self-government, the desire of a
community accustomed to a considerable measure of
autonomy to defend itself against interference from further external control. On this issue planters and farmers could and did agree. One factor that aided the
Loyalist cause in the North was absent in Virginia. In
this province there was no large urban community where
unprivileged groups directed by radical agitators aroused
the anxiety of the property-holding classes. The situation in Maryland resembled that in Virginia, but with
some special features, notably the parasitic character of
the Baltimore proprietorship. Though the Catholics
had legitimate grievances against their Protestant neighbors, most of them apparently followed Charles
Carroll's Whig leadership. While no effective pro-
British party existed either here or in Virginia, Tory
activities in both provinces proved temporarily disturb-

[1] Eckenrode, *Revolution in Virginia*, 26-27, 38-39, 119-129; I. S.
Harrell, *Loyalism in Virginia* (Durham, 1926), 62.

ing. Early in the war Lord Dunmore received aid from the Loyalists, and later Tory risings occurred on the eastern shore of Maryland.[1]

In eastern North Carolina the Whigs of the Edenton district included planters, merchants, lawyers and even some royal officeholders. One of their leaders was Samuel Johnston, Scotch-born nephew of a former royal governor, himself a substantial landowner with numerous slaves, a lawyer and royal official. In the Roanoke Valley the outstanding radicals were the well-to-do planters, Willie and Allen Jones, while in the Cape Fear Valley, with its commercial outlet at Wilmington, one of the foremost patriots was Robert Howe, a prosperous rice planter. An influential Loyalist element in this neighborhood consisted of the Scotch merchant-planter group. In South Carolina nearly all the conspicuous Whig leaders belonged to the socially and politically dominant class, including some who had held important royal appointments. The Revolutionary government was thus chiefly in the control of a fairly conservative group which disliked government by outsiders but wished to avoid extreme measures.[2]

Though the uprising was mainly directed by seaboard leaders, the backcountry people also played a part. In New England the newer country towns seem generally to have taken much the same stand as the farmers of eastern Massachusetts and Connecticut. In New York, however, Whigs and Tories faced each other in the Mohawk Valley as well as on the lower Hudson. The special significance of the inland settlements in relation

---

[1] *Ibid.*, 26-29; C. A. Barker, *The Background of the Revolution in Maryland* (*Yale Hist. Publs. Miscellany*, XXXVIII), 375; Burnett, *Letters*, II, 233; III, 179; G. H. Ryden, ed., *Letters to and from Caesar Rodney* (Phila., 1933), 178, 183.

[2] [Schaw], *Journal of a Lady of Quality*, appendices and *passim*; McCrady, *South Carolina in the Revolution, 1775-1780*, chaps. i, iii, vi; W. A. Schaper, "Sectionalism and Representation in South Carolina," *Am. Hist. Assoc., Ann. Rep. for 1900*, I, 380.

to the patriot cause is clearest in Pennsylvania, where they had long been refused adequate representation in the assembly by a conservative minority in the East. The Revolution here combined two distinct but connected objects: the dislodging of a provincial oligarchy, and a more aggressive opposition to British policies than the mercantile and landowning aristocracy of the East liked. A revolutionary organization and an extralegal "provincial conference" gave the interior inhabitants a better representation and forced the assembly into line on the question of independence. The way was now prepared for a more democratic state constitution. Though here as elsewhere the principal Whig leaders were Easterners, their support came largely from the backcountry. In no other province did the conflict between seaboard and interior so nearly parallel that on imperial issues.[1]

In Virginia no such fundamental cleavage divided tidewater and backcountry on the question of independence. As between moderate and radical Whigs, however, the inland counties inclined toward the latter. Henry and Washington lived on the eastern edge of the piedmont, Madison in one of its central counties and Jefferson among the foothills of the Blue Ridge. Washington had important interests in the Great Valley which gave him his first election to the house of burgesses. Jefferson was to become the most vigorous advocate of political and economic democracy.

In the Lower South the relation of the backcountry to the Revolution exhibited other features. The interior communities of the Carolinas were more isolated from the seaboard, took little part in the war at first and were much preoccupied with local problems. They also distrusted the tidewater Whig politicians, several of whom had supported the royal governor against the Regulators.

[1] Lincoln, *Revolutionary Movement in Pennsylvania*, esp. chaps. iv-v.

Moreover, the remoteness of the new settlements from one another and the variety of their foreign elements interfered with effective organization, while the proximity of this area to enemy-controlled East Florida further strengthened the backcountry Tories. For these reasons the Loyalists of this region were expected in 1776 to support the British sea attack on Charleston. In fact, a number of the prisoners taken by the Whigs after the battle of Moore's Creek Bridge were former Regulators, and though the Tory uprising failed, it might have succeeded with better leadership.[1]

Aside from the pacifism of the North Carolina Quakers and Moravians there were other difficulties confronting the patriot leaders. Differences in language and political traditions affected the attitude of the Germans. Having no serious quarrel with the old order, some of them feared the effect of a social upheaval on land titles. Another conservative element was the Scots, including traders and recently arrived Highlanders. Though a certain proportion of the latter had been Jacobites, they had later sworn allegiance to the king and they now supplied a number of Tory recruits. The Scotch-Irish seemed more promising for the Whigs. They had suffered from economic and religious disabilities in Ireland and their Presbyterian clergy commonly held Puritan ideas about the right to resist tyrannical rulers. Though many of them were inactive at first, they contributed largely to the later resistance to the British invasion. Among the Scotch-Irish who took an early part in the Revolution were those of Mecklenburg and adjoining North Carolina counties, the Waxhaws people in South Carolina and others in the frontier district of Ninety-Six.

[1] J. S. Bassett, "The Regulators of North Carolina," Am. Hist. Assoc., Ann. Rep. for 1894, 209-211; W. H. Siebert, Loyalists in East Florida, 1774 to 1785 (Fla. State Hist. Soc., Publs., no. 9), I, passim; Saunders, Colonial Records of North Carolina, X, 46, 90, 406.

In the end, the backcountry of the Lower South became the scene of peculiarly ruthless border warfare.[1]

Despite their distance from the principal centers of disturbance the trans-Alleghany folk also took sides in the conflict. So far as the promoters and speculators were concerned, they were divided. Franklin, Henry, Washington and many of their associates were Whigs; but others, including Joseph Galloway, Franklin's son William, and Lord Dunmore's agent John Connolly, were Tories. Their attitude, however, was not determined by their Western interests. More significant was the course pursued by the frontiersmen themselves. In this class, though not Westerners, were the Vermonters, whose problems somewhat resembled those of the trans-Alleghany pioneers. Dissatisfied with the royal decision awarding their territory to New York, they were naturally hostile to Whig speculators in that province. In 1775 they joined other New Englanders against the British and later applied for statehood; but they resented the failure of Congress to act and some of their leaders engaged in devious negotiations with the British. Nevertheless, most of the Vermonters were Whigs, however much they might dislike the New Yorkers or resent the unwillingness of Congress to set a precedent for secession from one of the original states.

In northern and western New York, Loyalists were active and the border fighting compared in bitterness with that of the Carolinas. In the Great Lakes region, where British posts—at Oswego, Niagara, Detroit and Mackinac—existed throughout the war, most of the pre-war traders and Indian agents were Tories. On the upper Ohio, then troubled by disputes between Virginia and Pennsylvania, the Tory Connolly tried to organize

[1] R. D. W. Connor and others, *History of North Carolina* (Chicago, 1919), I, 361; McCrady, *South Carolina in the Revolution, 1775-1780*, chap. ii.

an attack on the rear of the Southern colonies, and though this failed, some Loyalists remained in or about Pittsburgh. Not until this post was taken over by Congress did the more important of them withdraw. There were also some Tories among the West Virginia pioneers, but there and in Kentucky Whig sentiment prevailed. From the exposed Kentucky stations George Rogers Clark planned his famous expedition against the British posts in Illinois. Farther south, the British superintendent for the Southern Indians used his influence on the Tory side; but the Tennessee settlers, though chiefly occupied with frontier problems, occasionally cooperated with the Whigs east of the mountains, notably at the battle of King's Mountain in 1780 when they helped to defeat the British and Tories in upper Carolina.

Though it has been said that the alignment of parties betokened a struggle between affluent and privileged classes as against less fortunate groups, the various local situations show that this was only partly true. The Revolution helped to transfer power from provincial aristocracies to an economic middle class; but the shift may be exaggerated. The personnel of the Continental Congress included a substantial proportion of rich men. New England was represented by such well-to-do persons as John Hancock and the Rhode Islanders, Stephen Hopkins and Samuel Ward. Elbridge Gerry of Massachusetts was an important merchant, and John Adams a leader at the Boston bar. None of the four New York signers could be called poor; and, judged by colonial standards, Robert Morris, Charles Carroll, Washington and his Virginia colleague, Thomas Nelson, were all wealthy. John Adams's references to Whig leaders in New York and Philadelphia indicate comfortable and sometimes luxurious living. In the South especially, most of the outstanding patriots were men of social prestige, who lived well and with dignity.

Political differences oftentimes rent families. In the Massachusetts Quincy clan, Josiah was an ardent Whig while Samuel was a Tory refugee. The Virginia Loyalist, John Randolph, was the father of the young Whig leader Edmund, and his brother Peyton served as first president of the Continental Congress. In South Carolina, Lieutenant Governor William Bull stood by the crown, though three of his nephews supported the Revolution. Thomas Heyward, a South Carolina signer, was the son of a Tory. During the desperate fighting in upper Carolina, members of the same family sometimes faced each other across the firing line.[1] Though in such divided households the younger men were commonly the revolutionists, there were exceptions. Old Gabriel Manigault of South Carolina was a vigorous Whig while his son supported the old order. Loyalist Governor Wentworth of New Hampshire had a Whig father. Most striking of all was the case of Benjamin Franklin and his son William.

Though the effect of religious affiliations on the clergy has been considered, the question remains how far such affiliations governed the attitude of their parishioners toward the Revolution. In New England a large proportion of the Anglicans seem to have agreed with their ministers, less probably because of clerical influence than because so many of them belonged to the official and other naturally conservative classes. No outstanding New England Whig belonged to this church. In the Middle colonies, however, where Toryism and Anglican churchmanship were also commonly associated in the popular mind, several patriot leaders were Episcopalians. Most of the prominent Southern Whigs were at

[1] McCrady, *South Carolina in the Revolution, 1775-1780*, 29, 73, 173, 535.

least nominally of this communion. The Calvinist churches, as has been seen, were generally regarded by friends and enemies as active supporters of the Revolution, but there were exceptions even in New England.

Though the Quakers went on record officially against forcible resistance, they were not of one mind politically. Some were definitely Tory, a few out-and-out Whigs, sometimes to the extent of joining the army, while others were not active partisans on either side. How far Quaker attitudes resulted from pacifist principles and how far from the natural conservatism of the economic class to which many of them belonged, it is hard to say. Other pacifist groups also tried to keep aloof. Bishop John Ettwein of the Moravian Church was frankly a Loyalist at first, though later reconciled to the Revolution. In 1778 the North Carolina Moravians, while unwilling to renounce formally their allegiance to the crown, declared their "fidelity" to the new state and promised to refrain from aiding the enemy, hoping to "continue quiet and peaceable in the Places where Divine Providence has placed us." [1]

As to the relative strength of Whigs, Tories and neutrals one cannot go beyond plausible conjectures, especially since questions of definition are involved. Should an opponent of independence in 1776 who thenceforth remained passive be regarded as a Tory? What of the South Carolinians who after being associated with the Revolutionary government accepted protection from the British invader, or of the North Carolina Moravians who submitted to the Revolutionary government while refusing to renounce their old allegiance, or of the former

[1] J. T. Hamilton, "A History of the Unitas Fratrum, or Moravian Church, in the United States of America," Philip Schaff and others, eds., *The American Church History Series* (N. Y., 1893-1897), VIII, 472; Adelaide L. Fries, ed., *Records of the Moravians in North Carolina* (N. C. Hist. Comn., *Publs.*, 1922-1930), II, 850-851; III, 1373-1376.

Tories or neutrals who changed their attitude on account of British depredations?

On the basis of incomplete information one historian has estimated the total American enlistments either with the British regulars or in special Loyalist units at about fifty thousand. Including all the irregular fighters, the number of Tory combatants may well have been much larger. Available figures for civilians are even more fragmentary and uncertain. Lists of Loyalists named in confiscation acts or compensated by the British government for their losses tell something, but there were many other active or passive Tories too obscure to be enumerated. Roughly speaking, possibly a third of the population was Loyalist, a third definitely Whig, and a third not active on either side.[1]

The size of the opposing parties varied in different areas. In New England the Tory stronghold was mainly in eastern Massachusetts, but there were similar though smaller groups in New Hampshire, Rhode Island and western Connecticut. In New England, however, and also in Virginia the Tories constituted an inconsiderable minority. In the Middle colonies and the Lower South they were more numerous. The Whigs and Tories in New York seem to have been nearly equal in strength. Pennsylvania had fewer avowed Tories than New York, but more pacifists and neutrals. The historian Edward McCrady believed that in 1776 a majority of the South Carolinians disapproved of separation and that in 1778 they would have "gladly" accepted British proposals of concessions short of complete freedom. Yet many who held such opinions worked with the state government both before and after the Declaration of Independence.[2]

[1] Compare C. H. Van Tyne, *The Loyalists in the American Revolution* (N. Y., 1902), 183, with Edward Channing, *A History of the United States* (N. Y., 1905-1925), III, 216.

[2] Flick, *Loyalism in New York*, 180-182; McCrady, *South Carolina in the Revolution, 1775-1780*, 185, 263-265.

In all the colonies the success of the radicals in spite of their numerous opponents was due to their positive program, to efficient organization and to skillful propaganda. Important, too, was their ability to carry with them many moderate persons who, though not desiring independence, had so far coöperated with the radicals that they could not effectively withdraw.

CHAPTER X

SOLDIER AND CIVILIAN

BETWEEN the fight on Lexington common in April, 1775, and the formal cessation of hostilities in February, 1783, nearly eight years elapsed. Conditions approximating a state of war existed for even a longer time—from the autumn of 1774 until the British evacuation of New York in November, 1783. New England's contact with invading forces came early. During the winter of 1774-1775 both Gage's royal government and the *de facto* government of the provincial congress engaged in military preparations. Minutemen were drilled and military stores collected, and, as we have seen, the Massachusetts congress adopted a plan for a provincial army. Meanwhile there were exciting "incidents." As early as September, 1774, the seizure of powder by the British led to reports of soldiers and naval vessels firing on Boston. The whole country, wrote Gage, was "in Arms and in Motion" before the rumors were corrected. In February, 1775, an enemy expedition to seize military stores at Salem was successfully resisted. In New Hampshire insurgent citizens forced the surrender of munitions at Fort William and Mary.[1]

After the collision at Lexington and Concord and the British return to Boston a Massachusetts army was quickly gathered which formed the nucleus, first of a New England, and finally of a Continental, army. The

[1] Peter Force, comp., *American Archives* (Wash., 1837-1853), ser. 4, I, 1350-1355; Thomas Gage, *Correspondence with the Secretaries of State, 1763-1775* (C. E. Carter, ed., New Haven, 1931-1933), I, 371-377, 385-386, 389, 394: Edward Channing, *A History of the United States* (N. Y., 1905-1925), III, 156 n.

siege of Boston followed and the battle of Bunker Hill. During the siege regular communication between town and country was suspended, Loyalists came in from neighboring areas, and Whigs withdrew or were under close surveillance. In the surrounding country there were frequent alarms. The "constant roar of the cannon," wrote Abigail Adams from Braintree, rendered people unable to "eat, drink or sleep." After the British evacuation in March, 1776, conditions became more normal. In spite of some "abominable ravages" Mrs. Adams found Boston in a better state than she had expected.[1]

Howe's army was the last considerable enemy force seen in Massachusetts. Thereafter, except for a few minor skirmishes on the seaboard, the presence of British men-of-war off the coast and the temporary disturbance of Vermont by a detachment from Burgoyne's army, Massachusetts and northern New England suffered chiefly from the war's interference with commerce and the deep-sea fisheries. Southern New England was less fortunate. Newport, taken by the British in 1776, was held for three years with disastrous results for Rhode Island commerce. In 1778 an American attack on the city, supported by the French navy, failed after some fighting with few casualties. Soon afterward the British evacuated Newport in 1779 and French troops were landed. Connecticut, though near the British headquarters in New York, fared better, with no territory permanently held by the foe. In 1777 British troops seized military stores at Danbury and burned the place. Two years later they raided towns on the Sound and destroyed property but few lives. In 1781 a hostile force under Benedict Arnold attacked Groton and New London.

[1] Allen French, *The First Year of the American Revolution* (Boston, 1934), 122-128, chap. xxii; John and Abigail Adams, *Familiar Letters during the Revolution* (C. F. Adams, ed., Boston, 1875), 68, 149.

Fortunately, few of the country towns were disturbed. Except, then, for the first year of the war and the long enemy occupation of Newport, New England saw little of British soldiery. The interests adversely affected were chiefly commerce and the fisheries.[1]

New York and New Jersey suffered more severely. Nowhere else was the war brought so constantly and closely home to civilians, and nowhere, except in the Lower South, were Whigs and Tories so evenly matched. Though in the first year New York was comparatively quiet, both sides were preparing for action. The provincial congress organized regiments and in the autumn of 1775 New Yorkers took part in the invasion of Canada. By that time Governor Sir William Tryon had retired to a warship and the Continental army held the city, which was thenceforward under continuous military occupation, American or British. The Loyalist historian, Thomas Jones, credits the American troops in New York with more respect for property than was later shown by the British; but the city was not a comfortable place for Tories, many of whom departed.[2] When the enemy took control, the Whigs went out; and finally, on the British evacuation in 1783, there was an exodus of Loyalists. During the British occupation some civilians arrived with the army on public or private business; but many persons, including influential merchants, managed to remain through these changing régimes. The area of the enemy's continuous effective occupation coincided roughly with the present Greater New York, but the foe also dominated most of Long

---

[1] Charles Stedman, *The History of the Origin, Progress, and Termination of the American War* (London, 1794), I, 279-281; II, 142-144, 402-404; H. B. Carrington, *Battles of the American Revolution* (N. Y., 1876), 448, 468-476, 625-630.

[2] Thomas Jones, *History of New York during the Revolutionary War* (N. Y., 1879), I, 136-410; O. T. Barck, *New York City during the War for Independence* (Columbia Univ., *Studies*, no. 357), chap. ii.

Island and much of Westchester County. General Sir William Howe's victory at Brooklyn Heights in August, 1776, was followed by engagements on northern Manhattan and in Westchester, and by autumn the American forces had withdrawn to New Jersey. During these operations the environs of New York City suffered from both armies. Howe's adjutant general admitted that British soldiers, "Hessians in particular," had "unmercifully pillaged" the country. "No wonder," he wrote, "if the country people refused to join us." Meantime, the state committee of public safety complained of lawless conduct by American troops.[1]

After 1776 the counties immediately north of New York City endured petty warfare, with regular and irregular fighters on both sides. Many Whig and Tory guerrillas were mainly interested in looting or in gratifying personal animosities. In the upper Hudson Valley the new state government preserved order as well as it could, while local committees aided the military forces and dealt with actual or suspected Tories. Though some fighting occurred here, this area suffered less than the "neutral ground" near the British lines. The sparsely settled country beyond Albany experienced more of the conflict, especially in and about Ticonderoga which the Americans took in 1775 only to lose it to the British in 1776. Burgoyne's invasion ended a little to the north of Albany, but few settlements came into immediate contact with his army. More serious for civilians was the fighting between the Whigs and the Tories along the Mohawk and the upper Susquehanna. In 1777 Tories and Indian allies attacked Fort Stanwix, the western outpost of the Whigs on the Mohawk, but they were decisively beaten by troops under the German frontiersman, Nicholas Herkimer. In 1778 Tory and Indian raids on

[1] Otto Hufeland, *Westchester County during the American Revolution* (N. Y., 1926), chaps. vii-viii.

both sides of the New York-Pennsylvania boundary involved the massacring of men, women and children. In spite of Sullivan's retaliatory expedition against the Iroquois, fighting continued in the Mohawk Valley until the last year of the war, and many farms were abandoned.[1]

New York's experience was unique. For seven years the enemy controlled its chief center of population and wealth and enjoyed military support from many of the inhabitants. Moreover, the state was peculiarly exposed to attack from both north and west. The disturbance of normal society was therefore serious. The British occupation of New York Harbor also deprived northern New Jersey of its regular trading outlet. Furthermore, New York proved a convenient base for raiding into the Jerseys and securing supplies or news from Loyalists and neutrals.

The direct impact of armies on New Jersey proved greatest in the autumn and winter of 1776-1777. Washington's retreat across the state was followed by the establishment of a thin line of British garrisons between New York and Philadelphia; but after the American victories at Trenton and Princeton these outposts were withdrawn. At no time thereafter did the enemy hold any considerable part of the state. While they had the upper hand, however, the inhabitants suffered severely. "Atrocities" are often exaggerated, but the contemporary British historian of the war admitted that civilians, including Loyalists, had been badly treated. There were lawless elements in the Continental army, also, but the misdeeds of the Hessians made the deepest impression. An American officer predicted that, as a result of the British occupation, New Jersey would become "the most

---

[1] A. C. Flick, "The Sullivan-Clinton Campaign of 1779," A. C. Flick, ed., *History of the State of New York* (N. Y., 1933-1937), IV, 185-214; also same vol., *passim*.

Whiggish colony on the Continent." The British control of Philadelphia in 1777-1778 disturbed western New Jersey, and on Clinton's return to New York a major battle was fought at Monmouth. Otherwise the fighting was largely confined to raids from across the Hudson and naval attacks on American privateer bases on the sparsely settled coast. In 1777 and again in 1779-1780 Washington's headquarters were for several months in northern New Jersey at Morristown.[1]

No British army entered Pennsylvania until Howe's invasion in September, 1777, and his subsequent taking over of Philadelphia after defeating Washington on the Brandywine and at Germantown—the last considerable engagements in this state. Though many Philadelphia Whigs had to flee, the city as a whole, with its numerous Tories and neutrals, came through the British occupation better than the other principal towns. Washington's army was encamped less than thirty miles away at Valley Forge, but many Pennsylvania farmers did a good business supplying the British army with provisions in exchange for hard money.

In the Chesapeake country Maryland saw little actual warfare except when Howe's army passed through on its way to Philadelphia. Neither Annapolis nor Baltimore was ever held by the enemy, but here, as in Virginia, trade suffered through British control of the sea. In Virginia the only significant military operations before 1781 were in and about Norfolk, where Lord Dunmore and the Tories tried to keep a foothold. The town endured a naval bombardment and was later ravaged by the Whigs. British privateers appeared in Chesapeake Bay and the enemy temporarily occupied Portsmouth.

[1] Leonard Lundin, *Cockpit of the Revolution* (*Princeton History of New Jersey*, II; Princeton, 1940), 171-177, 420-422, 431; G. H. Ryden, ed., *Letters to and from Caesar Rodney* (Phila., 1933), 152; Stedman, *American War*, I, 225, 232.

But inland Virginia went almost wholly undisturbed until 1781, when British troops raided up the James Valley to Richmond and did considerable damage. One force reached Charlottesville, near the Blue Ridge. These troubles ended, however, with Cornwallis's surrender at Yorktown later in the year.[1]

The Lower South had a harder time. Before the end of 1775 Whigs were fighting British sympathizers in the northwest corner of South Carolina and shortly afterwards the North Carolina Whigs defeated the Tories of the Cape Fear Valley at Moore's Creek Bridge. In June, 1776, the Charlestonians repulsed a formidable naval and military assault with few casualties and no damage to the town. Soon, however, more serious trouble developed in the backcountry, where a Cherokee attack caused a general panic. Before the Indians were defeated, farms were abandoned and several hundred settlers massacred.[2] In 1778 the British took Savannah, the Whig government of Georgia almost disappeared, and savage partisan warfare followed. For a time the best security for persons and property in that state seemed to lie in accepting British control.

In 1779 the British turned again to South Carolina, seizing Beaufort, ravaging the coast plantations and nearly capturing Charleston. The next year they succeeded in taking Charleston and the Revolutionary government almost broke down. After the American defeat at Camden the conquest seemed nearly complete. Soon, however, harsh British measures produced a reaction, causing a general rising in the backcountry with ruthless strife between Whigs and Tories and widespread destruction of property. A historian of South Carolina

[1] H. J. Eckenrode, *The Revolution in Virginia* (Boston, 1916), esp. chaps. iii, x-xi.

[2] Edward McCrady, *History of South Carolina in the Revolution, 1775-1780* (N. Y., 1901), *passim*.

lists a hundred and thirty-seven engagements between November, 1775, and November, 1782, chiefly in 1780 and 1781. The most significant battles occurred at Camden, King's Mountain and Cowpens and in the Greene-Cornwallis campaign of 1781.[1] The British invasion of North Carolina, begun late in 1780, was nearly over by the following spring, though Wilmington and its neighborhood held out a few months longer. Some of the worst partisan warfare, however, came after the withdrawal of the British and Continental regulars, producing a reign of terror over wide areas. Thus by the winter of 1780-1781 the three principal ports of the Lower South had been taken by the enemy, who held Wilmington for nearly a year, Charleston for two years and a half and Savannah still longer. Throughout the war, also, British forces in East Florida menaced Georgia and the Carolinas.

In brief, then, the blows of the war fell with different weight on different areas. All the chief seaports except Baltimore experienced British occupation for periods ranging from less than a year in Philadelphia to more than seven in New York. On the other hand, much of the countryside, including that of New England and the great wheat-growing areas of Pennsylvania, Maryland and Virginia, suffered comparatively little from the contending armies. Quite different, however, was the tragic experience of the rural population in the Lower South.

In the frontier region, as we have seen, the Whigs had to contend mainly with Tories and Indians, who were frequently directed by British agents. Beyond the mountains the savages were the chief enemies though some Loyalists were active here also. In the Valley of the Ohio and its tributaries were the exposed settlements begun shortly before the war. To the north this fron-

---

[1] *Ibid.*; Edward McCrady, *History of South Carolina in the Revolution, 1780-1783* (N. Y., 1902), app. B.

tier was guarded by a Continental garrison at Pittsburgh. Though efforts were made to secure the neutrality of the Western tribes, it was hard to control the frontiersmen and in any event most Indians favored the British. Among the worst outrages on both sides was the murder of the Shawnee chief, Cornstalk, by lawless whites. In 1777-1778 Indian raids forced many frontiersmen to take refuge in stockaded posts.

In Kentucky the settlers on outlying farms were likely to be killed or captured as a result of Indian forays encouraged by the British at Detroit. It was to protect their settlements that George Rogers Clark undertook his expedition to the Illinois country and planned a more ambitious one against Detroit. Though remote from the principal war zone, the Tennesseans, including a new settlement on the Cumberland, had their difficulties also. There were frequent Indian attacks and an especially dangerous one in 1780. In that year, too, Tory activity in the hill country of western Carolina led the Tennesseans to join in defeating the Tory forces at King's Mountain.

Besides being a harsh and sometimes tragic experience, war was a business which had to be learned by both civilians and fighting men. Tory writers had insisted that the colonists could not cope with British armies. "War," said one of them, "is no longer a simple, but an intricate science." Against trained soldiers the Americans could oppose only the "tumultuary rage" of "a militia unused to service, impatient of command, and destitute of resources." Moreover, how would they secure munitions with the British navy patrolling the sea; what would happen to their commerce and fisheries; and how could the war be financed? Meanwhile, the Whigs displayed something of the "valor of ignorance." Their numbers included, said John Adams, hardy countrymen accustomed to Indian warfare. If provincial militia in the French wars had seemed ill disciplined, it might have been the fault of unintelligent British officers. Though Tories disparaged the "new fangled" Whig militia of Massachusetts, Adams insisted that its officers were abler than those chosen through the favoritism of a royal governor. Furthermore, American-made fire-arms were "as good as any in the world" and explosives could be easily manufactured. Even if American sea-ports should be destroyed, the people would hold out. Obviously neither Tory nor Whig expectations were justified. Loyalist advocates exaggerated the efficiency of British generals and administrators and failed to ap-preciate the difficulty of long-range strategy directed from London. The patriots were in turn forced, after painful experience, to realize that their own problems were far from simple.[1]

The starting point of the Revolutionary army was the colonial militia, many of whose regimental officers had served in earlier wars. Except in Rhode Island and Con-necticut they held commissions from royal or proprietary governors and were often, as we have seen, politically conservative. The Whigs therefore organized their own companies of minutemen. Then gradually such impro-vised organizations gave way to more orderly arrange-ments. Until after Bunker Hill in June, 1775, the troops around Boston were loosely associated contingents from the four New England colonies. Already, how-ever, Massachusetts had asked the Continental Congress for direction since the colonial forces were fighting for the general defense of colonial rights. Congress voted to supply gunpowder for the "Continental" army; and on June 15 it chose Washington as "General and Com-mander-in-chief of the Forces raised and to be raised in

[1] John Adams and Daniel Leonard, *Novanglus, and Massachusettensis* (Boston, 1819), 31-33, 226-227. In this edition the name of Jonathan Sewall mistakenly appears on the title page in place of that of Leonard.

defence of American liberty." Thirteen other general officers were then appointed, all but four of whom were New Englanders, and presently Congress took action to enlist riflemen in Pennsylvania, Maryland and Virginia to serve in "the American Continental Army." [1]

When Washington assumed command at Cambridge in July, 1775, the Massachusetts "army" embraced perhaps 12,000 men. With accessions from other colonies the New England troops numbered roughly 17,000 with fluctuating strength. During the latter half of the year an army, Continental in fact as in name, gradually took shape on the basis of one-year enlistments, observance of the Articles of War and other conditions which many early volunteers would not accept. Though the Continental army at the beginning of the new year had less than ten thousand men, it became the backbone of the fighting hosts which won independence. "This day," wrote Washington in his general orders for January 1, 1776, "giving commencement to the new army, which, in every point of view is entirely Continental; The general flatters himself, that a laudable Spirit of emulation, will now take place, and pervade the whole of it . . . ." [2]

It is impossible to say even approximately how many Americans actually engaged in military service. Of those whose names appear in army and militia lists a large proportion served but a few months. Even in the Continental army most enlistments were for only a year, though bounties and promises of Western lands caused some to be for the duration. Outside the Continental army were many more militiamen, besides irregular fighters who spent only a few weeks or months in the field.

---

[1] French, *American Revolution*, esp. chaps. iv-vii, xviii, xxxi; Force, *American Archives*, ser. 4, II, 620, 1847-1854.

[2] French, *American Revolution*, 86; L. C. Hatch, *The Administration of the American Revolutionary Army* (*Harvard Hist. Studies*, X), 17; George Washington, *Writings* (W. C. Ford, ed., N. Y., 1889), III, 311 n.

Including the American soldiers on both sides and all those who served at all, whether actual combatants or not, there was, perhaps, a fair proportion of participants to the total number of males of military age.

Available statistics of men in service at any given time, however, present a different picture. Washington's army during 1776 ranged roughly from 27,000 to 10,000; in December those actually fit for duty were fewer than 5000.[1] When Washington prepared to attack Trenton, he had only 2400 men, "all that were left of the Continental regulars." In the Saratoga campaign in 1777 the entire number of Americans involved was over 20,000, including emergency volunteers who helped to block the British advance, but Horatio Gates's immediate army of regulars and militia comprised perhaps half as many. In November, 1779, Washington's summary of state muster rolls, excluding South Carolina and Georgia, showed a paper total of about 27,000, with fewer than 15,000 enlisted for the whole war. At Yorktown in 1781 there were, according to official returns, about 5500 American regulars, 3500 militia and 7000 Frenchmen, omitting an undetermined number of Virginia militia in the neighborhood who doubtless contributed to the final result.[2]

Relative to the male population of military age the proportion of trained men engaged for any length of time in serious combat service seems small. Comparatively raw troops occasionally fought well; but they proved more useful in irregular fighting, as in operating on the flanks of Burgoyne's army, interrupting com-

[1] Force, *American Archives*, ser. 4, VI, 1119; ser. 5, I, 331, 764; II, 449, 907.

[2] J. C. Fitzpatrick, *George Washington Himself* (Indianapolis, 1933), 278; various estimates of numbers at Saratoga in Channing, *History*, III, 267; C. H. Van Tyne, *The War of Independence* (Boston, 1929), 434; Hoffman Nickerson, *The Turning Point of the Revolution* (Boston, 1928), app. ii; H. P. Johnston, *Yorktown Campaign* (N. Y., 1881), 108-116.

munications and cutting off supplies. Recruiting was stimulated by Continental and state bounties, and when state quotas were not readily filled, drafts were resorted to, though well-to-do persons could hire substitutes. The strain on particular communities sometimes proved severe. In September, 1776, Abigail Adams reported a shortage of farm labor, with more than half the men between sixteen and sixty in the army. If more enlisted, she said, the women would have to do the harvesting. That summer there were similar complaints in Connecticut.[1]

As to the quality of the rank and file contemporary testimony varied. A British ship's surgeon visiting the New England army early in 1775 called it "nothing but a drunken, canting, lying, praying, hypocritical rabble, without order, subjection, discipline, or cleanliness," which would soon "fall to pieces of itself." Another English observer spoke of the Americans as "ragged, dirty, sickly and ill-disciplined." Nor were Washington's early impressions of the army at Cambridge encouraging. Yet after Bunker Hill an enemy "Officer of Rank" admitted that the colonists when "equally well commanded" were "full as good soldiers" as the British. One of Burgoyne's officers later declared the Americans whom he had observed were "never contemptible in the eye of a soldier," fighting with "great courage and obstinacy." A German officer who saw Gates's troops when Burgoyne surrendered said that in spite of their nondescript appearance "they stood like soldiers." "The whole nation," he thought, had "much natural talent for war and military life."[2]

[1] Adams, *Familiar Letters*, 230; Force, *American Archives*, ser. 5, I, 938.

[2] Margaret W. Willard, ed., *Letters on the American Revolution, 1774-1776* (Boston, 1925), 120, 133; Nicholas Cresswell, *Journal* (N. Y., 1924), 159, 163; French, *American Revolution*, chap. xxix; Van Tyne, *War of Independence*, 394; R. W. Pettengill, ed., *Letters from America, 1776-1779* (Boston, 1924), 110-113.

The selection of officers presented difficulties. As we have seen, veterans of the colonial wars and militia officers were often Loyalists. Oliver De Lancey, who had led New York troops in the last French war, headed a Loyalist brigade in the Revolution; and a well-known Tory commander in South Carolina had been a provincial militia colonel. Besides, many colonial veterans were too old for effective service. Nevertheless, eight of the first fourteen Continental generals belonged to this group, though none had previously ranked higher than a colonelcy. Before the war was half over, Washington was the only colonial veteran who still held a high command. Much was expected of three former officers in the British regular army: Charles Lee, Horatio Gates and Richard Montgomery. Unhappily Montgomery, an able young officer, was killed in Canada in December, 1775; Lee failed to coöperate loyally with Washington; and Gates's reputation, enhanced by the Saratoga victory, suffered, justly or unjustly, from his crushing defeat in the South. Next to Washington, the most capable of the original list of generals was probably Nathanael Greene. With little professional training or experience, he was a serious student of military technique and his organizing talent gave him the command of the Rhode Island contingent at Cambridge.

Representative officers who came to the front later were Henry Knox, the Boston bookseller who without previous war experience had during his service at Cambridge so impressed the commander in chief that he became head of the Continental artillery; Benedict Arnold, a New Haven merchant and militia captain; and William Smallwood, a Maryland veteran of the French and Indian War. Among four brigadiers who were made major generals as the war ended, John Stark of New Hampshire and James Clinton of New York had been subalterns against the French, while Anthony Wayne was a tannery owner in Pennsylvania, and John Peter Muhlenberg, a Lutheran minister.   Conspicuous among the officers who never became Continental generals were three partisan commanders in the Carolinas: William Davie, a young law student, Francis Marion, a planter, and Thomas Sumter, a crossroads storekeeper.   The last two had been Indian fighters.[1]

The Revolutionary army owed much to certain other officers for specialized help.   When the war began, its principal engineer was Richard Gridley of Massachusetts, who resigned half-pay status in the British army to become successively chief engineer in the state and Continental services.   He was succeeded by the French officer, Louis Duportail.   Better known is the Polish soldier, Kosciusko, who acted as engineer in the Saratoga campaign and fortified West Point.   The most important European expert was General Steuben, a former captain on the Prussian general staff, brought to America through the good offices of the French government.   In 1778 he was made inspector general, and, in the opinion of his most recent and competent biographer, gave the American army "a technical training and equipment that was unknown in either the French or the British armies," making it "battalion for battalion the equal in discipline and skill of the best British regulars."[2]   While many foreign volunteers were not helpful, the half-German, half-French Johann Kalb and the Polish cavalry commander, Casimir Pulaski, deserve honorable mention. Lafayette's chief service consisted in promoting mutual understanding between his French countrymen and his American friends.   The finally decisive contribution of

---

[1] Army lists in F. B. Heitman, *Historical Register of Officers of the Continental Army during the War of the Revolution* (Wash., 1914).

[2] J. M. Palmer, *General von Steuben* (New Haven, 1937); quotation from Palmer's article in Allen Johnson and Dumas Malone, eds., *Dictionary of American Biography* (N. Y., 1928-1937), XVII, 601-604.

France to Continental victory was, of course, that of Rochambeau's army and the French navy.

As the war proceeded, the professional standards of the American officers improved. At first Washington was sharply critical of the New England officers, charging them with poor discipline, lack of steady public spirit and even dishonesty. In the end, however, he had a group of loyal and competent associates, few of whom enjoyed his confidence more fully than the New Englanders, Greene and Knox. A handful of the commanders were more or less serious students of military tactics and strategy. Washington had read professional treatises before the Revolution and in 1775 sent a list of books on the art of war to a Virginia colonel. Greene bought a work on Turenne's campaigns and Knox said he began his military studies in his bookshop. It is significant that the most competent contemporary historian of the war, the British officer Charles Stedman, was, on the whole, not unfavorable to the quality of the American leadership. He noted the resourcefulness of the Continental generals, praising Washington's "sagacity" at critical times as well as his "daring" expedients. He spoke highly also of Greene's strategy in the Carolina campaign.[1]

Besides the land soldiers there were the sea fighters in the state and Continental navies and on privateers. Eleven states had their own navies, and, in addition, Congress early in the war authorized the building of thirteen frigates. The Providence sea captain, Esek Hopkins, was commissioned as "Commander in chief of the fleet," together with four captains and several first lieutenants, including John Paul Jones, a recently arrived Scotch shipmaster. Hopkins had commanded a privateer

[1] Fitzpatrick, *Washington*, 149, 179; Marquis de Chastellux, *Travels in North-America* (London, 1787), I, 133, 140; O. L. Spaulding, "The Military Studies of George Washington," *Am. Hist. Rev.*, XXIX, 675-680; Stedman, *American War*, I, 167, 230-243; II, 448.

in the French war, and one of his captains, Nicholas Biddle, had been a British midshipman. Another officer, not in this first list, was the young Irish shipmaster, John Barry, who rivaled Jones in brilliant accomplishment. The total personnel of the Continental navy and marine service at its maximum strength probably did not exceed about three thousand. The most numerous sea fighters were the privateersmen, perhaps seventy thousand in all on the American side. The great expansion of privateering under Continental and state commissions sometimes interfered with army and navy recruiting. Yet its special attractions enlisted many adventurous individuals, who inflicted serious damage on British shipping.[1]

Behind the combat services was the civil administration, headed by the Continental Congress, which appointed the principal army and navy officers, regulated organization and discipline and, with state coöperation, supplied munitions, food and clothing. This proved a heavy responsibility for men few of whom had had much administrative experience. At the opening of the Second Continental Congress in 1775 Benjamin Franklin, the former deputy postmaster-general, was the only member to have held an important intercolonial office. Two Rhode Islanders had been governors with very restricted powers, and few had even been colonial councilors. Many delegates, however, had served in judicial or legislative positions and thus acquired a limited acquaintance with governmental problems. Other members could apply to financial questions a special knowledge of business. John Hancock, Elbridge Gerry, Stephen Hopkins and Silas Deane of New England, Philip Livingston and Francis Lewis of New York, Robert Morris of Philadelphia, Thomas Nelson of Virginia and, later, Henry

---

[1] French, *American Revolution*, chap. xxv; G. W. Allen, *A Naval History of the American Revolution* (Boston, 1913), I, esp. 29, 38-52, chaps. ii, vi.

Laurens of Charleston were all practical business men. So also were some of the well-to-do plantation owners. Among the successful lawyers available for legislative drafting were John Adams, Jay, Duane, R. R. Livingston, Dickinson, Wythe and John Rutledge. In short, this was no mere gathering of political agitators. As the war went on, able delegates took other posts, ceasing to sit in Congress. Washington, Schuyler and Mifflin entered the army. Deane, Franklin, John Adams and Jay were sent abroad. Robert Morris and R. R. Livingston respectively directed finance and foreign affairs. Notable for length of service among the numerous war-time members were Samuel Adams and Elbridge Gerry of Massachusetts, William Ellery of Rhode Island, James Duane of New York and John Witherspoon of New Jersey. Congressional administrative committees sometimes employed outsiders who proved capable civil servants, as, for instance, Richard Peters of Pennsylvania, secretary of the board of war.[1]

The state and local governments also played a significant part in the struggle. As in the case of Congress, these officials suffered from inexperience in dealing with new and difficult problems. Generally the state constitutions closely limited the executive power, but a man of vigor and initiative could render important service. Among the outstanding governors were Trumbull of Connecticut, Clinton of New York and Livingston of New Jersey. Jonathan Trumbull, functioning under the colonial charter, remained chief executive throughout the war. George Clinton and William Livingston were also continuously in office after the inauguration of their respective state governments. Another successful executive was John Rutledge of South Carolina, who had charge of affairs while much of the state was con-

[1] Lists of members in successive volumes of E. C. Burnett, ed., *Letters of Members of the Continental Congress* (Wash., 1921-1936).

trolled by the enemy. These governors, their agents and their legislatures coöperated with Continental authorities in recruiting, appointing minor military officers, furnishing supplies, checking enemy trade and maintaining public morale.

Much military business fell to private individuals, such as contractors for army materials and transport service. Many of them undoubtedly drove hard bargains, for this war, like others, had its profiteers. Of contemporary English contractors Edmund Burke wrote, "The merchants begin to snuff the cadaverous *haut gout* of lucrative war." [1] Washington and his associates uttered similar complaints of Americans who charged exorbitant prices. Among other essential allies in the war effort were the ironworkers, who were exempted from military service in order to make munitions. The women, too, shouldered substantial duties because of the absence of their men. Abigail Adams directing farm work under difficulties was typical of many of her sex. They do not seem to have served ordinarily as army nurses, and the exceptional cases of female combatants or spies, though picturesque, are hardly significant. Some women visited hospitals with delicacies for soldiers, while others made army shirts. The ladies of Trenton and Philadelphia formed committees to raise funds for army relief. [2]

Fundamental to the war effort was the problem of financing it. Not only did Congress lack the taxing power, but the states had inadequate revenue systems. Hostilities went on for two years before Congress assessed

[1] Quoted in E. E. Curtis, *The Organization of the British Army in the American Revolution (Yale Hist. Publs. Miscellany, XIX)*, 99.

[2] Adams, *Familiar Letters*, 152; James Thacher, *Military Journal during the American Revolutionary War* (Boston, 1823), 239-242; Frank Moore, ed., *Diary of the American Revolution* (N. Y., 1860), II, 296; A. M. Schlesinger, *New Viewpoints in American History* (N. Y., 1922), 132.

requisitions upon the states; but even then compliance could not be enforced, and the greater part remained unpaid. Borrowing was therefore necessary, but it proved difficult for a government with ill-defined powers and no certainty of survival. In the absence of banks the fluid capital available was small. John Adams calculated that investors, who could normally get six per cent, would not be apt to lend for less when "doubtful of the existence of the State." Congress, having unsuccessfully tried four per cent, advanced the rate to six. Though some domestic loans were attempted, especially after American credit was supported by French loans or subsidies, the total secured through this channel was less than eight million. There was also a mass of floating indebtedness, including certificates issued for property or services impressed by the army. Under these circumstances Congress had to look abroad. France helped through subsidies and loans based on political rather than commercial considerations. This was also true of the Spanish loans, but Dutch credits secured near the end of the war rested more nearly on a business basis.[1]

In the early years of the contest an attempt had been made to finance it largely with paper money, in increasing amounts and depreciating value. By 1780 Congress admitted that forty dollars in Continental currency were not worth more than a dollar in specie. "New tenor" interest-bearing notes payable in specie within five years were then issued in exchange for the depreciated currency. The latter practically ceased to circulate and little of it was ever redeemed. Thus the Continental paper issued amounted in effect to public taxation paid in varying proportions by those who originally received it for goods or services and by later recipients in successive

---

[1] D. R. Dewey, *Financial History of the United States* (A. B. Hart, ed., *American Citizen Series*; rev. edn., N. Y., 1939), chap. ii; Adams in Burnett, *Letters*, II, 248.

stages of depreciation. Besides this paper, an almost equal amount was issued by the states. However unfortunate the results, most hard-pressed governments have pursued a similar course and usually with less excuse than this Congress without taxing power.[1]

In the face of these financial difficulties Congress had somehow to supply war materials. Something could be done at home. Gunsmiths were numerous, rifles were made in many backcountry settlements, and capable ironmasters turned out cannon and small arms for the Continental army. But the total production fell far short of the requirements. A certain amount of material came from the capture of enemy vessels and some English artillery was taken at Ticonderoga; but much more was needed. A few weeks before the battle of Saratoga General Philip Schuyler reported that his army had "little ammunition and not a single piece of cannon." It has been estimated that during the first two and a half years of the struggle less than a tenth of the powder required was produced in this country; the rest had to be imported, chiefly from France. Because of the danger from British cruisers and privateers, such supplies came largely through the French and Dutch West Indies. A prime factor in Congress's revoking the nonexportation policy and opening American ports to foreign vessels was the dearth of munitions. To pay for them the government authorized its agents to collect tobacco and other export staples.[2]

During the greater part of the contest the army was badly clothed. Notwithstanding the prevalence of homespun textiles the country was embarrassed by the interruption of shipments from Britain, and some clothing

---

[1] Dewey, *Financial History*, 36-41.

[2] V. S. Clark, *History of Manufactures in the United States* (Carnegie Inst., *Contribs. to Am. Econ. History*; rev. edn., N. Y., 1929), I, chap. x; O. W. Stephenson, "The Supply of Gunpowder in 1776," *Am. Hist. Rev.*, XXX, 271-281.

contractors charged exorbitant prices. To a large extent uniforms had to be imported. During the early years many of the Continental troops presented a motley appearance, sometimes lacking even the elementary requirements for health and decency. At Valley Forge, Washington reported nearly four thousand of his men unfit for duty for this reason. A British agent predicted his defeat if the flow of European woolen goods could be stopped. Uniforms in actual use varied. One New York order called for a coat, deerskin waistcoat and breeches, felt hat, two pairs each of stockings and shoes, and a blanket. A later Continental uniform was blue, with facings differing according to states and branches of the service. Toward the end of the war the supply of apparel improved under a new clothier general. Tents of sailcloth or "country linen" sometimes provided shelter. During the winter of Valley Forge, where canvas tents were used at first, the men suffered badly from the cold, but later they were a little better housed in log cabins.[1]

The food supply was hampered by transportation difficulties, poor administration and fluctuating prices. Subject to the direction of Congress and its committees, the two principal officers in this branch were the quartermaster general and the commissary general. During the first year of the war Washington took occasion to compliment Commissary General Joseph Trumbull of Connecticut. "Few Armies," he wrote, "have been better and more plentifully supplied than the Troops under Mr. Trumbull's care." At Valley Forge, however, the provision services were in bad order, with tragic consequences. The situation temporarily improved later,

[1] Van Tyne, *War of Independence*, chap. vi; Hatch, *Administration of the Army*, chap. vi; J. C. Fitzpatrick, *The Spirit of the Revolution* (Boston, 1924), chap. viii; Force, *American Archives*, ser. 5, I, 203; C. K. Bolton, *The Private Soldier under Washington* (N. Y., 1902), 74-76, 98-99; Thacher, *Military Journal*, 158.

with General Greene as quartermaster general and Jeremiah Wadsworth in charge of the commissariat. Soon, however, there was more trouble in these offices and the army again suffered. The experiment of asking the states to furnish "specific supplies" having failed, soldiers were for a time reduced to half rations. In 1781, with Superintendent Robert Morris in charge of contracts, the army fared better; but there were still complaints of profiteering and of insufficient and inferior food.[1]

At Valley Forge the army ration consisted of a pound and a half of flour or bread per day; beef, fish or bacon; sometimes peas or beans; and a gill of spirits. On occasion, however, the men went for days without meat or even bread. Some critics also noted the lack of vegetables. Greene maintained that "putrid fever" resulted from an undue proportion of meat: "vegetables would be much more wholesome." In Congress, Gerry declared that the physical condition of the British troops profited by a suitable allowance of vegetables and vinegar and that the United States would "never have a Healthy and Vigorous Army without them." John Adams added his objections. "Our frying-pans and gridirons," he wrote, "slay more than the sword." The provision of liquor also excited comment. Rum was a normal part of the army ration and Washington once complained of an inadequate supply. Dr. Benjamin Rush, however, favored milder beverages.[2]

The Continental medical corps must not, of course, be judged by twentieth-century standards. Though the British fared better, they too had many inexperienced surgeons. The American service made a bad start, with

[1] George Washington, *Writings from the Original Manuscript Sources* (J. C. Fitzpatrick, ed., Wash., 1931-1940), V, 192; Hatch, *Administration of the Army*, chap. vi.
[2] Bolton, *Private Soldier*, chap. iii; Force, *American Archives*, ser. 5, I, 195; Burnett, *Letters*, II, 191; Curtis, *Organization of the British Army*, 91.

its first director, Dr. Benjamin Church, soon dismissed for treasonable correspondence. Congress then appointed Dr. John Morgan, who stood high in the profession, but who was hampered by inadequate equipment and by jealousies complicated by his own defects of temper. The regimental surgeons were often incompetent, and some of them, according to Washington, were "very great rascals." Morgan was followed by Dr. William Shippen, whose administration also bristled with acrimonious controversies. In 1781 a change for the better came with Dr. John Cochran, a former British army surgeon. Under the director general were regional directors. The pioneer Pennsylvania Hospital was turned over to the army and navy and there were other considerable military hospitals. By 1777 the one at Albany employed some thirty surgeons and surgeon's mates.[1]

The suffering of patients through inattention, lack of suitable diet and medicines and unsanitary housing proved serious. Without anæsthetics and modern antiseptics the mortality from disease and wounds was often appalling. Epidemics played havoc with the army. The prevalence of smallpox in 1777 caused widespread anxiety. There were, however, occasional comments of a favorable character. A German prisoner described a hospital, in which British soldiers were treated, as "well-equipped," providing even such luxuries as tea, sugar, chocolate and wine. Some surgeons were capable and conscientious. Young Dr. James Thacher of Massachusetts spent long days with his patients and was highly commended by his department chief. Though preventive medicine was undeveloped, Washington and his

[1] Curtis, *Organization of the British Army*, 10-12; T. G. Morton, *The History of the Pennsylvania Hospital, 1751-1895* (Phila., 1895), 57, 223; F. R. Packard, *History of American Medicine in the United States* (rev. edn., N. Y., 1931), I, chap. viii; Thacher, *Military Journal*, 112-115.

fellow officers did not overlook the importance of cleanliness. One of the army chaplain's duties was "to recommend cleenlyness as a virtue conducive to health."[1]

Congress and the commander in chief were also concerned about religion and morals in the army. Some delegates took a gloomy view, one complaining that in the "horrid sins of Cursing, swearing and other Vices" the American soldiers compared with the worst British troops. To improve morale chaplains were provided. The Congregationalists supplied the largest number, the Presbyterians stood next, and the Episcopalians third. There were also a few Baptists and German Protestants and at least one Catholic. These officers were expected not only to promote religion and morals but to assist in maintaining discipline and encouraging enlistments. Washington took a definite interest in the chaplain's work and his first general orders called on officers and men to attend the appointed religious exercises.[2]

In contrast to such painful conditions as those at Valley Forge there was some cheerful social intercourse, especially among the officers, as when Washington presided at dinner "with his lady" and two young women from Virginia, or when an army hospital staff took dancing lessons and met "amiable and accomplished ladies." A Yankee surgeon with a Virginia regiment recalled a Christmas season with daily social engagements and nights of "amusement and dancing."[3]

Every army has its undesirable characters and the Continental army was no exception. Its regulations, following the British model, penalized drunkenness, profanity, maltreatment of civilians and other offenses. Looting was punishable by whipping on the bare back, and more

[1] Burnett, *Letters*, II, 249, 376; Pettengill, *Letters from America*, 115; Thacher, *Military Journal*, 112 ff.

[2] Burnett, *Letters*, II, 376; statistics of chaplaincies compiled by Mary S. Benson; Fitzpatrick, *Washington*, esp. 130, 173.

[3] Thacher, *Military Journal*, esp. 154-160.

serious crimes entailed the death penalty. Nevertheless American as well as British soldiers were guilty of mistreating noncombatants. In one case of robbery two men were sentenced to be hung, one of whom was "pardoned under the gallows" and the other executed.[1]

As in other wars, also, "atrocities" occurred on both sides, sometimes in the heat of passion, sometimes through the deliberate policy or laxity of commanders, sometimes from inability to control vicious individuals. The British were charged now and then with refusing quarter, employing Indians and illtreating prisoners. Regarding Colonel Banastre Tarleton's slaughter of defeated Americans on one occasion, the British historian, Charles Stedman, admitted that "the virtue of humanity was totally forgot." Brutality commonly marked the border warfare between Whigs and Tories, with ruthlessness breeding cruel retaliation. On the other hand, Stedman commended the humane conduct of "Mad Anthony" Wayne's storming party at Stony Point, where under the accepted code he might have refused quarter; instead, no man "was put to death but in fair combat." Both sides employed Indians, but the British used them much more. In 1775 Massachusetts enlisted Stockbridge Indians and a few of the Penobscot tribe, and in 1776 the Continental Congress authorized similar action. Generally, however, the Americans favored keeping the savages neutral. However much the British tried to restrain their Indian allies, the latter could not reasonably have been expected to observe the rules of so-called civilized warfare.[2]

---

[1] William Winthrop, *Military Law and Precedents* (2nd edn., Boston, 1896), II, app., viii-x; Thacher, *Military Journal*, 186-188, 190, 195; Fitzpatrick, *Washington*, 330.
[2] Stedman, *American War*, II, 145, 193; Van Tyne, *War of Independence*, 398-403; Force, *American Archives*, ser. 5, I, 192; Burnett, *Letters*, I, 433, 508; French, *American Revolution*, 401-410, app. 35 and *passim*.

In an age when most penal institutions were barbarously managed, the inhumane treatment of military captives was not surprising. Difficulties of housing and shortage of supplies also were factors. Nevertheless, in the enemy prisons and more particularly in the prison ships there was often inexcusable neglect and cruelty. Philip Freneau's poem, "The British Prison Ship," reflects the impression made by such conduct on one sensitive personality. British captives had their complaints too. Stedman quoted Sir Archibald Campbell's protest against his Concord jail, "a dungeon of twelve or thirteen feet square . . . black with the grease and litter of successive criminals." But relations with the captor were sometimes more agreeable. The American Captain Alexander Graydon was courteously treated by Britons, whose kindness he was later able to reciprocate. Sterner patriots, however, entertained doubts about such amenities. Governor Livingston feared that as a result Americans might be "humanized" out of their liberties.[1]

In the coöperation of soldiers and civilians the unique contribution of the commander in chief is evident. Equally impressive is the devotion of the many men who fought loyally with him in times that tried men's souls. Behind the scenes, however, were incompetence, petty jealousies, slackness and profiteering. Undoubtedly some members of Congress and some disgruntled officers envied Washington's position or questioned his competence. Nevertheless, it was not necessarily unpatriotic, when affairs went badly, to wonder whether a change of leaders was desirable. Though there was a certain amount of defeatism and disloyalty, it is more

[1] W. A. Ganoe, *The History of the United States Army* (rev. edn., N. Y., 1942), 38-39; Thomas Anburey, *Travels through the Interior Parts of America* (Boston, 1923), II, 252-254; Stedman, *American War*, I, 169; Alexander Graydon, *Memoirs of His Own Time* (J. S. Littell, ed., Phila., 1846), 304-306; Theodore Sedgwick, *A Memoir of the Life of William Livingston* (N. Y., 1833), 337; Moore, *Diary*, II, 434-436.

significant that in the end the commander in chief was sustained. Congress certainly wasted energy through clumsy methods of doing business in general sessions or through numerous and often overlapping committees, instead of intrusting executive services to responsible heads. Allowance must, however, be made for comparatively inexperienced politicians who came from widely separated and mutually distrustful communities. If the states declined to give Congress adequate authority, they too faced unaccustomed responsibilities and the special difficulties of effecting the transition from provincial to republican institutions. The wonder is not that serious blunders were made, but rather that civilian and soldier should have done as well as they did in the unfamiliar business of waging war.

CHAPTER XI

THE WAR'S ECONOMIC EFFECTS

EVEN before the outbreak of hostilities the colonial merchant had to make drastic adjustments. The First Continental Congress had forbidden the importation of European and East Indian goods from Britain. Moreover, molasses could no longer be bought in the British West Indies or wine from the Portuguese islands or slaves from Africa. The export trade had more time for adjustment; but when nonexportation finally took effect in September, 1775, it closed most of the normal markets to colonial staples. Meantime British legislation reenforced congressional prohibitions. The "restraining acts" of March and April, 1775, barred the limited commerce previously permitted outside the empire. Especially serious for the New Englanders was the exclusion from the fisheries. When the war began, the commerce of the insurgent colonies became enemy traffic and ships engaged in it were liable to seizure by British warships.

It was soon realized that the Continental Association would have to be modified in order to secure munitions and other necessaries. "We are," said Robert R. Livingston, "puzzling ourselves between the commercial and the warlike opposition." The army, said James Duane, must have powder, and powder could not be had without "breaking the Association." Before the nonexportation agreement went into effect, shipments to Great Britain and the West Indies temporarily increased, those from New York and Philadelphia more than doubling in value. Congress now authorized unconditionally the exchange of American produce for munitions, "the non-exportation agreement notwithstanding." A "secret committee" was formed to facilitate this traffic and Congress itself acted in special cases. Under a contract between the committee and a group of merchants—all but one members of Congress—Congress was to appropriate funds to buy goods for export in return for needed supplies, the merchants receiving a five-per-cent commission. Thus the Browns of Providence held contracts with the secret committee for voyages to foreign ports from which they were to bring back munitions, if possible, otherwise drygoods, gold or silver. Finally, in April, 1776, as we have seen, Congress opened American ports to vessels of all nations other than Great Britain and her possessions.[1]

Business was also affected by enemy occupation of the chief commercial centers. In the case of New York City this interrupted normal trade with the upper Hudson Valley, with other colonies and, to some extent, with other countries. The city, however, received partial compensation from British army purchases and those of numerous Loyalist refugees. Many merchants remained throughout the war, importing and selling British goods. When the Chamber of Commerce was revived after a temporary interruption, a majority of the members who had attended the last meeting (1775) were still active. Meantime, an illicit trade in British goods went on through the military lines, and the city became a base for enemy privateers.[2]

---

[1] John Adams, *Works* (C. F. Adams, ed., Boston, 1856), II, 461; W. B. Weeden, *Early Rhode Island* (F. H. Hitchcock, ed., *The Grafton Historical Series*; N. Y., 1910), 338; A. M. Schlesinger, *The Colonial Merchants and the American Revolution, 1763-1776* (Columbia Univ., Studies, LXXVIII), 566-572; E. C. Burnett, ed., *Letters of Members of the Continental Congress* (Wash., 1921-1936), I, 372 ff.; W. C. Ford and others, eds., *Journals of the Continental Congress* (Wash., 1904-1937), IV, 257-263.

[2] New York Chamber of Commerce, *Colonial Records, 1768-1784* (J. A. Stevens, ed., N. Y., 1867), 201 ff.; O. T. Barck, *New York*

The much shorter British dominance of Philadelphia proved less unsettling. Until 1777 comparatively few business men left the city. But when Howe's army took possession, the more active Whig merchants withdrew and newcomers arrived, taking over their shops or establishing new ones. Among those who stayed through the enemy occupation were Robert Morris's partner, Thomas Willing, and Robert Bell, the bookseller. During this period profits accrued from army purchases and English goods could be bought more freely. Another shift came when the British army retired, with Tories going out and Whigs returning. Thereafter Philadelphia, as the seat of Congress, prospered through government business.[1]

Trade was also disturbed by the currency situation. Inflation and depreciation, with varying standards of value, had formerly been checked by imperial restrictions; but with these removed, a combination of circumstances—lack of specie, loss of normal export trade, military expenditures—led to an immense expansion of paper money. By 1779 Continental issues exceeded two hundred million dollars and the states had printed almost as much. Meantime, attempts were made to increase or maintain the supply of hard money. Early in the war Morris proposed a congressional committee to "bring in Gold and Silver and keep it in the country," reporting later that the treasury had only six thousand pounds. These efforts to halt specie exports were not, however, very successful.[2]

The final collapse of the Continental paper is a familiar story. A Philadelphian had predicted in the

City during the War for Independence (Columbia Univ., Studies, no. 357), chap. vi.

[1] Isaac Sharpless, A Quaker Experiment in Government (Phila., 1902), pt. ii. chap. vii; W. O. Mishoff, Business in Philadelphia during the British Occupation (seminar paper, Columbia University, 1928).

[2] Burnett, Letters, I, 276, 288.

summer of 1775 that these bills would at once be "as current as gold," but they were soon being accepted with great reluctance. According to New York and Philadelphia letters, the hoarding of specie began quickly notwithstanding that guilty persons were threatened with tar and feathers as "the least of their punishment." Robert Treat Paine, a good patriot, declared early in 1777 that the "glut of money" was "horrible" and he feared Rhode Island would "drown New England with paper." Though Massachusetts finance was more conservative, many creditors even there refused to take paper currency in payment of debts.[1]

Money lenders and investors naturally opposed inflation. Charles Carroll, much of whose income came from interest on loans, protested against a Maryland legal-tender act, urging that it should not be made retroactive. In 1777 John Adams estimated that a debt contracted four years earlier in gold and now paid in paper would give the creditor in purchasing value less than a quarter of what he had lent. Before the war ended, however, the currency situation had materially improved, partly through British and French hard money received for army supplies. Specie was also secured through foreign loans and export trade with Continental Europe and its West Indian dependencies. In January, 1781, a Massachusetts writer reported that hard money could be had without difficulty.[2]

How far rising prices were due to cheap money as compared with scarcity of goods and profiteering it is hard to say. At any rate there was a staggering in-

[1] Margaret W. Willard, ed., Letters on the American Revolution, 1774-1776 (Boston, 1925), 156, 260, 271; W. B. Norton, "Paper Currency in Massachusetts during the Revolution," New England Quar., VII, 43-69; Adams, Works, IX, 470.

[2] Kate M. Rowland, Life and Correspondence of Charles Carroll of Carrollton (N. Y., 1898), I, 200; Adams, Works, IX, 470; R. V. Harlow, "Economic Conditions in Massachusetts during the American Revolution," Colon. Soc. of Mass., Publs., XX, 183.

crease. In Massachusetts a bushel of corn climbed from
five shillings in the spring of 1777 to eighty dollars in
paper or four in hard money by the summer of 1779,
and beef from eight pence a pound to six or eight shillings. In 1780 Governor William Livingston of New
Jersey calculated that his salary of eight thousand pounds
in currency was worth no more than a hundred and fifty
pounds in silver.[1]

Advancing costs led to mutual recriminations.
Massachusetts farmers and merchants accused each other
of profiteering and there was a demand for price fixing.
The preamble of an act for this purpose attributed the
"exorbitant prices" of necessaries to the "avaricious conduct of many persons" and the increasing demands of
labor. Maximum rates were accordingly set for prices
and wages. These measures, however, proved ineffective and sharpened class antagonism. Robert Treat
Paine reported that they were "reprobated by many
and obeyed by few." In 1779, after a convention at
Hartford had recommended price regulation, Congress
indorsed the policy and a general convention was called;
but no delegate attended from Virginia or the Lower
South and no action was taken. Congress itself was
divided on the matter. Richard Henry Lee of Virginia
and Samuel Chase of Maryland thought price regulation
could be enforced, but several Northern delegates, including John Adams and James Wilson, strongly opposed it. "There are certain things," said Wilson,
"which Absolute power cannot do."[2]

One item on the credit side of the war-time account
was the new freedom of commerce with Continental
Europe, which not only opened some old markets but

[1] Harlow, "Economic Conditions," 168 ff.; Theodore Sedgwick,
A Memoir of the Life of William Livingston (N. Y., 1833), 355.
[2] Harlow, "Economic Conditions," 168 ff.; Burnett, *Letters*, II, 250-
253; IV, 514; V, 4, 16.

also offered fresh opportunities. Yankee skippers had long visited the Spanish ports of Bilbao and Barcelona and in 1777 Adams boasted that all Mediterranean ports permitted American trade. The mercantile house of Gardoqui and Sons at Bilbao was especially important for the Spanish trade. One vessel belonging to the Cabots is said for a time to have sailed between Beverly, Massachusetts, and Bilbao with almost the regularity of a packet.[1]

Pre-Revolutionary commerce with France had been subject to French as well as British regulations, though some trade, legal or illegal, had been carried on with Nantes and other western ports. Closer connections developed when the French government and its agent, Beaumarchais, promoted the shipment of war supplies to the United States. Among the ports most frequently mentioned were L'Orient, Nantes, Rochelle and Bordeaux. In February, 1777, a ship from Charleston carried to L'Orient five hundred barrels of rice and sixty thousand pounds of indigo, chiefly on state account. A little later a dozen or more vessels were reported as sailing from Nantes to Charleston. In 1781 the Browns of Providence imported a variety of goods through their Nantes agent, Elkanah Watson, who had a French partner. The French flag was soon familiar in many American harbors.[2]

Trade with Holland was a prime source of munitions and other commodities, the Dutch serving mainly

[1] *Ibid.*, II, 313; O. T. Howe, "Beverly Privateers in the American Revolution," Colon. Soc. of Mass., *Publs.*, XXIV, 366-368.

[2] Gaston Martin, "Commercial Relations between Nantes and the American Colonies during the War of Independence," *Journ. of Econ. and Business History*, IV, 812-829; Ralph Izard, *Correspondence* (N. Y., 1844), I, 242, 276 ff., 309; L. C. Gray, *History of Agriculture in the Southern United States* (Carnegie Inst., *Publs.*, no. 430), II, 578; Frank Monaghan, "Elkanah Watson," Allen Johnson and Dumas Malone, eds., *Dictionary of American Biography* (N. Y., 1928-1937), XIX, 541-542; Weeden, *Early Rhode Island*, 346.

as middlemen between Continental countries and the
United States. The admission of American vessels, including privateers, to their harbors was one cause of the
Anglo-Dutch war of 1781. Americans also visited
Hamburg and other ports. They faced difficulties, however: high insurance rates because of the danger from
enemy ships, the weakness of American credit, and differences in language and business methods. In 1780,
when the Bay of Biscay was said to be infested with
British privateers, John Jay thought it safer to trade by
way of the West Indies, where small fast ships could
exchange American produce for European goods brought
there in neutral vessels. Munitions came largely by this
route, with many other articles bartered for American
products. The rôle of the Dutch islands grew increasingly important late in the war when the French and
Spanish islands lost their neutral status. St. Eustatius
in particular was described by the British ambassador to
The Hague as the rendezvous for all clandestine commerce with the United States. When, however, the
Dutch entered the war, the island was taken by the
British.[1]

War-time trade with the foreign West Indies was
partly like that carried on by the American colonies during the wars with France; but much of it replaced the
former colonial commerce with the British Isles, as in
the case of tobacco exports and European goods previously brought by way of British ports. In time the
American traders adjusted themselves to the war situation, the shortage of European commodities was gradually made up and, with an active demand for luxuries

[1] J. F. Jameson, "St. Eustatius in the American Revolution," *Am.
Hist. Rev.*, VIII, 683 ff.; Friedrich Edler, *The Dutch Republic and the
American Revolution* (Johns Hopkins Univ., *Studies*, XXIX, no. 2),
42-62 and *passim*; John Jay, *Correspondence and Public Papers* (H. P.
Johnston, ed., N. Y., 1880-1893), I, 272, 294-295.

as well as necessities, some merchants reaped substantial profits.

As in the intercolonial wars, also, privateering was an important branch of business. In November, 1775, the Massachusetts provincial congress authorized the private owners of armed vessels properly bonded to seize hostile ships or merchantmen carrying supplies to the enemy, on condition that such vessels be taken into port for adjudication by a prize court, with whose approval they could be sold for the benefit of the captors. Early in 1776 Congress took similar action. Including both state and Continental privateers, probably more than two thousand were put into service, a majority of them with Continental commissions. The latter increased from thirty-four in 1776 to over three hundred in 1780 and to five hundred and fifty in 1781. These vessels varied in size from a Connecticut sloop of six guns with a crew of thirty to a ship carrying ten guns and more than two hundred men.[1]

This branch of service appealed strongly to adventurous merchants, ship captains and seamen. In August, 1776, John Adams wrote to his wife:

Thousands of schemes for privateering are afloat in American imaginations. Some are for taking the Hull ships, with woolens, from Amsterdam to Rotterdam; some are for the tin ships; some for the Irish linen ships; some . . . for Indiamen . . . and many for West India sugar ships. Out of these speculations many fruitless and some profitable projects will grow.[2]

---

[1] G. W. Allen, *Massachusetts Privateers of the Revolution* (Mass. Hist. Soc., *Colls.*, LXXVII), 25-35; G. W. Allen, *A Naval History of the American Revolution* (Boston, 1913), I, 45-57, 149, 180; II, 544-576; L. F. Middlebrook, *Maritime Connecticut during the Revolution* (Salem, 1925), II, 73, 98.

[2] John and Abigail Adams, *Familiar Letters during the Revolution* (C. F. Adams, ed., Boston, 1875), 208.

Massachusetts led the other states, with Pennsylvania next. It has been estimated that nearly twelve hundred prizes taken by Massachusetts privateers were brought into its courts, while similar captures, made in remote waters, were disposed of elsewhere. Besides Boston, other important bases in New England were Portsmouth, Newburyport, Gloucester, Beverly, Salem and Marblehead. Men and capital turned to this business from the fisheries and the coasting trade. Along the Sound, Providence and New London merchants were likewise engaged, and even Connecticut River towns participated. At Philadelphia there were frequent arrivals of privateers and prizes, and also in small New Jersey harbors. In the South, Charleston was the chief base during the early years of the war. As we have seen, these craft, besides preying on British merchantmen, carried their own commercial cargoes. New York, too, had privateers, but after 1776 they operated for the British. According to Governor Tryon, more than six thousand seamen served on such vessels. In one four-month period they brought in a hundred and forty-two prizes.[1]

Privateersmen were often lawless, and Congress complained of their "piratical" attacks on neutral ships as injurious to "the national honor of the States." According to a New Hampshire delegate, persons engaged in this service soon "lost all sense of right and wrong" and might even rob their own countrymen. One case debated by Congress was that of the Boston-owned schooner, *Eagle*, charged with seizing a brig of which a North Carolina Whig leader was part owner.[2]

This kind of warfare brought both large gains and heavy losses. The Cabots of Beverly, who owned nu-

---

[1] Allen, *Massachusetts Privateers*, 353, and his *Naval History*, I, 45, 48, 231; *Pa. Packet*, Aug. 4, 6, Nov. 7, 21, 1778; Barck, *New York City*, 130-133.

[2] Allen, *Naval History*, II, 699; Burnett, *Letters*, 199, 200, 411.

merous privateers, were highly successful. One of their ships, the *Pilgrim,* carried sixteen guns and a crew of a hundred and forty men. Commanded by a daring young Irishman, she took eight prizes in a six weeks' cruise off the Irish coast. The Salem fleet, of which Elias Hasket Derby was a principal owner, is said to have accounted for more than four hundred captures. When peace came, his war-time ventures had made him one of the richest merchants in New England. Nathaniel Tracy of Newburyport was less fortunate. Though prizes taken by his men were valued at four million, he finally lost most of his vessels and a large part of his wealth. According to one authority, a majority of the privateer owners in this vicinity lost more than they gained. A Connecticut ship, which went on four cruises in 1777-1779, took on its first voyage six valuable prizes; but later sailings proved less successful and finally the vessel was captured. Nevertheless, one of its prizes had a cargo worth twenty-five thousand pounds.[1]

Army contracting, another form of war business, also offered a combination of public service with private profit. Without such assistance the military forces could not have acquired necessary arms, food and clothing. The proportions in which patriotism and the profit motive were blended doubtless varied. On this point contemporary judgments, influenced by personal sympathies or animosities, cannot always be trusted. If the public interest was oftentimes sacrificed to selfish advantage, men might differ honestly about a fair return for service rendered, and the expectation of personal gain might go along with genuine, if not unalloyed, patriotism.

---

[1] Howe, "Beverly Privateers," 318-345, 352-354; S. E. Morison, "George Cabot," Johnson and Malone, *Dictionary of American Biography,* III, 395-396; R. E. Peabody, "Elias Hasket Derby," *ibid.,* V, 249-250; R. L. Jackson, "Nathaniel Tracy," *ibid.,* XVIII, 624; W. B. Weeden, *Economic and Social History of New England* (Boston, 1890-1891), II, 776-778; Middlebrook, *Maritime Connecticut,* II, 51-53.

Washington frequently complained of profiteering by army contractors; and though precise evidence is not always available, a number of them became "big-business" men in the postwar years. William Duer of New York is a conspicuous example. In 1777 Roger Sherman favored establishing maximum prices to save purchasing agents from "such a temptation as an honest man would not wish to be led into." Caesar Rodney of Delaware doubted whether he could buy army flour on satisfactory terms since speculators were "as Active and wicked as the Devil himself." [1]

One form of profiteering was the use of official position to advance private interest. Conspicuous among the merchants who fell under this suspicion was Robert Morris. John Adams gave an interesting contemporary estimate of him: "I think he has a masterly Understanding, an open Temper and an honest Heart . . . . He has vast designs in the mercantile way. And no doubt pursues mercantile ends, which are always gain; but he is an excellent Member of our Body [Congress]." The same year William Hooper of North Carolina noted the widespread appreciation in Congress of Morris's "burden of publick business" carried along with his "private concerns." "You may boast," he wrote to Morris, "of being the only man whom they all agree to speak and I really believe think well of." As the war proceeded, however, the difficulty of Morris's dual position became evident. While he was conducting congressional business, his firm held important public contracts, and he was associated with Silas Deane in personal as well as governmental transactions. Under the circumstances both men were sharply attacked by the Lees

[1] J. S. Davis, *Essays in the Earlier History of American Corporations* (*Harvard Economic Studies*, XVI), I, 394-395 and *passim*; R. A. East, *Business Enterprise in the American Revolutionary Era* (Columbia Univ., *Studies*, no. 439); Burnett, *Letters*, II, 315; G. H. Ryden, ed., *Letters to and from Caesar Rodney* (Phila., 1933), 324.

and their New England sympathizers.   In 1782 Arthur Lee charged that throughout the war Morris had made "his public trust subservient to his private Speculation" and thus "become as rich as a Jew." This was doubtless going too far, yet on one occasion Morris wrote to Deane, then in Europe, "It seems to me that the present oppert'y of improving our fortunes ought not to be lost, especially as the very means of doing it will contribute to the service of our country at the same time."   In spite, however, of the common talk about Morris's war profits, so careful an observer as James Madison thought no member of Congress could be "altogether insensible" of the value of his contributions to the common cause.[1]

Not only the government but the people at large complained of profiteering. Henry Laurens asserted that the country was taxed more heavily by profiteers than it could have been by Parliament, while "Knaves and fools" were "building enormous estates."   In May, 1777, a county convention in Massachusetts denounced the "avarice and extortion, which, like a resistless torrent, has overspread the land," and stated that even the necessaries of life were monopolized in order to boost prices.   There was a popular outcry against the merchants, and a Boston mob carted certain alleged offenders out of town.   Some men, however, noting the effect of currency inflation in raising prices, deprecated extreme charges which, by disparaging American patriotism, might "destroy it for ever." [2]

A special phase of war-time business, familiar in the intercolonial wars, was enemy trade.   Some of this was

[1] Burnett, *Letters*, I, 433; II, 195; VI, 368; John Adams, Samuel Adams and James Warren, *Warren-Adams Letters* (Mass. Hist. Soc., *Colls.*, LXXII-LXXIII), II, 184; T. P. Abernethy, "Commercial Activities of Silas Deane in France," *Am. Hist. Rev.*, XXXIX, 477-485.

[2] D. D. Wallace, *Henry Laurens* (N. Y., 1915), 287; Harlow, "Economic Conditions," 171; Adams, *Familiar Letters*, 261-263; Burnett, *Letters*, II, 251.

comparatively innocent, as when farmers in occupied territory could hardly help selling produce, or when Newport citizens had to supply the British fleet to save themselves from "immediate destruction." Congress itself consented at various times to an exchange of Virginia provisions for Bermuda salt. Other dealings with the foe were less excusable. After the British took New York, that neighborhood became deeply involved in such traffic. A German officer in 1780 reported "almost open trade" with the "rebels," apparently connived at by both parties. In New Jersey, where this business was said to have grown to an "enormous" height, the British bought fresh provisions with hard money, and Jersey shopkeepers received manufactured goods from New York. Similar intercourse went on across Long Island Sound. One vessel, built in New York but registered in Massachusetts and commanded by a Massachusetts man, was caught trading between two enemy ports. Sometimes there were collusive captures at sea. Illicit traffic was also covered by flags of truce for the exchange of prisoners or for other ostensibly legitimate purposes. One place notorious for such commerce was Bombay Hook Island in the Delaware, where it was said to be "most Villainous and distructive." Washington spoke of the "immense" amount of such intercourse and even proposed the death penalty for serious offenders. He suggested that the state governments were unwilling to let their neighbors get all the business. Notwithstanding some official connivance both sides made efforts to stop the trade. The British headquarters in New York took such action, and so did the legislatures of the near-by states, notably Connecticut and New Jersey.[1]

[1] Burnett, *Letters*, I, 297, 299; VI, 170, 180 ff.; Gray, *Agriculture*, II, 580 ff.; R. W. Pettengill, ed., *Letters from America, 1776-1779* (Boston, 1924), 232; Sedgwick, *Livingston*, 245; Middlebrook, *Maritime Connecticut*, II, 94, 139, 238; Edward Channing, *A History of the United States* (Boston, 1905-1925), III, 405 ff.; Adams, Adams

Another kind of enemy trade went on, directly or indirectly, through the West Indies with Europe. Southern tobacco was exchanged at St. Eustatius for British goods and there seem to have been some dealings even with the British West Indies. Enemy goods also reached the United States by way of Continental Europe. According to Lord Sheffield, Scotch thread was sent through France and Holland, American agents bought English cloth in Holland for army uniforms, and American privateers traded directly with the British Isles. Willing and Morris carried on some correspondence during the war with enemy houses; and in view of the numerous British agencies on the Continent, such relations between the two countries are not surprising. They may often have served the American cause.[1]

As a result of all this speculative trade, legal and illegal, there arose new business leaders, daring, adventurous and sometimes unscrupulous, causing a shift of power and wealth. Some of the pre-Revolutionary group had, as Loyalists, lost their estates and fled the country. In the words of a New England historian, "A new order of men came forward, and transacted the business incident to the new condition of the country." Property, said Robert Treat Paine, was thrown into fresh channels, increasing "little streams to overflowing rivers." "Rich and numerous prizes and the putting six or seven hundred per cent on goods bought in peace time" were "the grand engines." Meantime salaried men and persons living on fixed incomes were "suffering

---

and Warren, *Warren-Adams Letters*, II, 136-137; Ryden, *Letters to and from Caesar Rodney*, 195-197, 279; Barck, *New York City*, 130-133; George Washington, *Writings from the Original Manuscript Sources* (J. C. Fitzpatrick, ed., Wash., 1931-1940), XXI, 184-185.

[1] Channing, *History*, III, 405-408; Gray, *Agriculture*, II, 576-579; Lord Sheffield, *Observations on the Commerce of the American States* (6th edn., London, 1784), 10-11, 48, 155; Thomas Willing, *Letters and Papers* (T. W. Balch, ed., Phila., 1922), 53-57; Abernethy, "Commercial Activities of Silas Deane," 478.

exceedingly." The Loyalist exile, Samuel Curwen, corresponding with friends in America, noted the elevation of "base fellows" to "honors and great wealth." [1]

After Yorktown some men were not overanxious for peace. According to the French diplomat, the Marquis de Barbé-Marbois, the country people desired it, but not "the inhabitants of towns, whom commerce enriches," or the mechanics who were earning war-time wages. In 1782, during the peace negotiations, Gouverneur Morris declared an immediate end of the war was "not much for the interest of America." A little later, Robert Morris wrote, "The prospect of peace has given more general discontent than anything that has happened in a long time; particularly among the mercantile part of the community." [2]

For many merchants the war proved educational. Government business led to interstate coöperation and also to personal associations which bore fruit later in land speculation, schemes for internal improvements and banking projects. Similarly, war finance emphasized the need of agencies for mobilizing credit for public and private undertakings. In 1780 Gerry suggested an interstate alliance of merchants to support congressional finances. Shortly afterward a merchants' association was formed at Philadelphia, which, though not strictly a bank, was designed to supply war funds. Proposals for a real bank soon followed. In December, 1780, Congress, though uncertain of its authority, incorporated the Bank of North America. Thus real banking in the United States originated in war-time necessities. [3]

[1] Weeden, *Economic and Social History of New England*, II, 779; J. T. Austin, *Life of Elbridge Gerry* (Boston, 1829), I, 220; Samuel Curwen, *Journal and Letters, 1775-1784* (G. A. Ward, ed., N. Y., 1842), 416.

[2] Barbé-Marbois to Count de Vergennes in Mass. Hist. Soc., *Proceeds.*, VII, 262-266; Sedgwick, *Livingston*, 374 n.

[3] Burnett, *Letters*, V, 205, 220 n., 234, 239.

Educational also were the effects of the collapse of the Continental currency. Though cheap money did not end with that experience, mercantile opposition to currency inflation was strengthened and the way prepared for safeguards against it in the Federal Constitution. The war also stressed the desirability of a stable and uniform hard-money supply. Robert Morris outlined a plan for a national coinage based on the decimal system and Jefferson was studying the problem as early as 1776.[1] Significant, too, in its long-term effects was the issue of congressional and state certificates of indebtedness which the original holders were commonly forced to sell far below their face value. Even during the struggle a fairly compact group of men acquired such securities on a large scale, and trading in them was publicly advertised. At Philadelphia in 1782 brokers' advertisements were published by Isaac Franks, Haym Salomon, John Macpherson and Morris Cohen. Thus the exigencies of war greatly expanded this form of property and the practice of stock speculation.[2]

An educational result of a different kind was the new interest in communications. The imperial postal service had been replaced by a Continental administration, headed first by Franklin and later in succession by his son-in-law, Richard Bache, and Ebenezer Hazard. British occupation of important seaboard towns naturally complicated the mails, so much so that in 1781 a Rhode Island delegate declared that the scheme might well be abolished or suspended. But Congress busied itself with plans to improve the service and lessen its cost. In spite of handicaps the war-time government did establish a Continental system. At the same time

[1] Ibid., VII, 502 n.; W. G. Sumner, Financier and Finances of the Revolution (N. Y., 1891), II, 42-47.
[2] Pa. Packet, July 4, 6, 27, Sept. 12, 1782; Davis, History of American Corporations, I, 178-180.

tragic experiences like those at Valley Forge, when desperately needed supplies were almost unsalable only a short distance away, emphasized the need of better transportation. Though postwar internal-improvement projects cannot be wholly explained by war experience, it is at least suggestive that George Washington and other prominent Revolutionary leaders were active in such enterprises.[1]

War-time adjustments proved less difficult for industry than for commerce, partly because most manufactures were of a household character, carried on in rural and sparsely settled communities remote from battle areas. Nevertheless the war inevitably affected the situation. In response to the prewar propaganda for commercial retaliation and economic self-sufficiency, the Revolutionary organizations listed products which should be encouraged by premiums, bounties or loans, and the Second Continental Congress recommended the formation of societies to promote native industries. There were local efforts also, as, for instance, the Virginia convention's offer of premiums for textiles, textile machinery, nails and powdermills. Similar action was taken by Virginia counties. To conserve wool the Revolutionary governments discouraged the killing of sheep. Even so, the army had to rely largely on imports for uniforms. Other states also offered bounties for war materials. Daniel Roberdeau, president of a Pennsylvania company to establish textile manufactures, advocated economic independence both as a defense measure and on the ground that money could be saved by using home products. The wearing of homespun at weddings and college commencements became a favorite form of propaganda, and

---

[1] W. E. Rich, *The History of the United States Post Office to the Year 1829* (*Harvard Economic Studies*, XXVII), chap. iv; Burnett, *Letters*, V, 494; VI, 113; Channing, *History*, III, 395.

household manufactures expanded to meet the growing popular demand.[1]

More effective than propaganda was the interruption of European imports which, in spite of temporary increases in anticipation of the congressional boycott, soon dropped sharply, causing a serious dearth of commodities formerly imported. Later, however, as European goods came in more freely, native industry met with stiffer competition. Local manufacturers lost some prewar markets, as in the African demand for New England rum and in the sale of colonial ships in England. In both cases, however, American consumption had been relatively important. Sometimes a shortage of skilled labor occurred as a result of workmen being recruited for the army or the navy or allured by exceptional earnings into privateering. This diversion of man power was, however, partly avoided by exempting skilled workers from military service. Prisoners were also sometimes used, as in certain Pennsylvania ironworks.[2]

Shipbuilding, with the allied trades, was disturbed by the war's interference with the fisheries, intercolonial trade and normal commerce with the British. But these losses were at least partly offset by demands for other services, including privateering. Numerous vessels were built all along the seaboard, on the Delaware and in the South. Portsmouth, New Hampshire, constructed Continental warcraft carrying from eighteen to seventy-four guns and important Continental frigates were built in Massachusetts yards. John Peck of Boston has been called "the most scientific naval architect" then at work.

[1] Ford and others, *Journals*, IV, 222-225; V. S. Clark, *History of Manufactures in the United States* (Carnegie Inst., *Contribs. to Am. Econ. History*; rev. edn., N. Y., 1929), I, chap. ix; Peter Force, comp., *American Archives* (Wash., 1837-1853), ser. 4, II, 140 ff., 170-171, 563; Frank Moore, ed., *Diary of the American Revolution* (N. Y., 1860), I, 267.
[2] Clark, *History of Manufactures*, I, 219-220.

Philadelphia and Baltimore shipbuilders were also highly regarded, and of thirteen frigates ordered by Congress in December, 1775, four were assigned to Philadelphia yards. The replacement of tonnage destroyed by the enemy further helped to keep the shipyards busy.[1]

The iron industry boomed during the war. Though most of the colonial ironworks seem to have had Whig owners, some belonging to Loyalists were now confiscated. Virginia had its own small-arms factory at Fredericksburg and an establishment at Westham for casting cannon and cannon balls; and it also had contracts with the privately owned Hunter works. At Springfield, Massachusetts, weapons were manufactured first in private shops and later by the Continental authorities. Especially important for the Continental army were the New Jersey and Pennsylvania ironmasters. In New Jersey the German immigrant, John J. Faesch, cast large quantities of shot and shell. Though much of the iron industry was located inland, it was sometimes threatened by military operations. Before Washington encamped at Valley Forge, ironworks there had been destroyed by the British, who later demolished the Mount Holly concern in New Jersey. Desire to protect such establishments influenced Washington's Brandywine campaign. War demands also stimulated steel making, for which bounties were offered and new plants set up. Aside from military requirements, the demand for metal products such as nails and cards used in textile manufacturing rose to replace imports from England.[2]

[1] J. L. Bishop, *A History of American Manufactures from 1608 to 1860* (Phila., 1864), I, 42 ff., 55, 72, 80; Justin Winsor, ed., *Memorial History of Boston, 1630-1880* (Boston, 1880-1881), III, 186.

[2] A. C. Bining, *British Regulation of the Colonial Iron Industry* (Phila., 1933), 94-96, 110-113; Clark, *History of Manufactures*, I, 219 ff.; Kathleen Bruce, *The Virginia Iron Manufacture in the Slave Era* (N. Y., 1931), chap. i; Weeden, *Economic and Social History of New England*, II, 792.

By and large, agriculture proceeded more normally than commerce or manufactures. Though rural New England saw few enemy troops, even in peace time it had imported breadstuffs, and during the war it suffered from insufficient supplies, partly due to embargoes elsewhere. For certain farm products the war brought increased demands and rising prices, with Connecticut contributing substantial amounts to the army's food supply. In 1780, when beef was urgently needed, Congress called on New Hampshire, Massachusetts and Connecticut for a thousand head of cattle weekly. That year Connecticut's quota of forage grain exceeded any other state's except Pennsylvania and Maryland. New England also furnished draft horses. During the middle years of the conflict, the Yankee husbandmen prospered, paying off debts and living more comfortably. The subsequent period of deflation, however, told another story. Massachusetts then turned from paper money to specie, with increasing taxation of a kind that proved especially burdensome to the tiller of the soil. Retrenchment became necessary and, as might be expected, agrarian discontent followed.[1]

In rural New York many farmers lived within the enemy lines or in areas disturbed by armed strife. Though the British occupation of New York City deprived up-state farmers of their normal outlet for produce, they did not always find it easy to maintain a proper food supply. Recruiting, guerrilla warfare, army calls for draft animals and a shortage of agricultural implements—all these interfered with normal operations. As in Massachusetts, the farmers were sometimes accused of profiteering. By the end of the war depreciated paper had helped pay off their debts, and despite many difficul-

[1] Burnett, *Letters*, IV, 53, 60-62, 75-128; V, 185-188, 371 ff.; Harlow, "Economic Conditions," 177 ff.

ties they apparently came through the conflict better than some other economic groups.[1]

The New Jersey countryside also suffered seriously at times from military operations, especially during 1776-1778. At the end of the latter year John Jay reported that wheat crops in this and neighboring states had fallen far below the usual output. Nevertheless, if the war period be taken as a whole, the Jersey husbandmen, like those of Pennsylvania, plied a good business with the various armies. Two years after hostilities began, John Adams gave glowing accounts of the Pennsylvania and Maryland grain fields. Here, too, farmers were charged with profiteering and with refusing to sell to the American troops at army prices or in depreciated currency while willing to traffic with the enemy. Nevertheless, the Continental army drew its provisions and forage largely from this region. There was some concern about the distilling of liquor from grain when food conservation was important. John Adams heard that it might be "a question whether the people should eat bread or drink whiskey." In 1778 a congressional committee advocated state action to prevent the "converting of that Bread which was meant for the sustenance of Man into a Liquid poison for his Destruction." Insect pests also made trouble.[2]

In Virginia the farmers provided breadstuffs to supply the army or to ship abroad in exchange for war material; but with tobacco the story was different. The British market was now blocked despite some of the crop that slipped in indirectly. Though the government

---

[1] J. A. Krout, "Finance and Army Supplies," A. C. Flick, ed., *History of the State of New York* (N. Y., 1933-1937), IV, 125-127, 142-146; Division of Archives and History, *The American Revolution in New York* (Albany, 1926), 240; Burnett, *Letters*, III, 541.

[2] Adams, *Familiar Letters*, 238, 278; Ryden, *Letters to and from Caesar Rodney*, 327; Adams, *Works*, II, 433; Burnett, *Letters*, III, 492, 541; IV, 39, 61.

sent shipments abroad to establish credits, exports apparently declined, thanks partly to the increasingly effective blockade. In 1778 a congressional committee reported that large quantities of tobacco shipped to Continental agents had been lost. Later, Chesapeake Bay was said to be controlled by the enemy. A British prisoner in Virginia noted the glutting of the market because of enemy privateers. As a result of such complications Jefferson declared that his tobacco sold for a quarter or less of its normal price. Others of the farmers' difficulties stemmed from the fluctuating currency and the dearth of salt, much of it previously imported. Hoarded supplies of the latter were seized by exasperated persons who needed it for livestock and for preserving meat. Planters were also troubled about their slaves, some of whom ran away to the enemy. Toward the close of the war thirty of Jefferson's Negroes were said to have been carried off by the invading British army. It was estimated that Virginia lost some thirty thousand in all. In the last months before Yorktown one of Jefferson's plantations was occupied by the British for ten days. His tobacco barns were burned, his fields wasted, and his livestock killed or carried off.[1]

The South Carolina planters were also deprived of customary markets. Before the nonexportation regulation took effect in November, 1775, and in anticipation of the event, rice and indigo exports to Great Britain went up by nearly a half only to drop to negligible proportions. This decline was partially offset by shipments, direct or indirect, made to Continental Europe with the coöperation of Congress. A South Carolina historian has claimed that American credit abroad was principally sustained by these exports. Purchases for

[1] Gray, *Agriculture*, II, 577, 579, 586-596; Thomas Jefferson, *Works* (P. L. Ford, ed., N. Y., 1904-1905), V, 245, 247; Landon Carter, "Diary," *William and Mary College Quar.*, XX, 175-185; Nicholas Cresswell, *Journal, 1774-1777* (N. Y., 1924), 173-174.

the army and the French fleet also somewhat relieved the planters, though not enough to prevent serious privations. Here, too, slaves were lost and plantations seriously damaged.[1]

In the Southern uplands the experience was somewhat different. Piedmont and Valley farmers in Virginia and Maryland raised wheat and cattle much as usual, selling to the seaboard South, to New England and to the army. The stock raisers of the Carolina backcountry sent cattle northward in order to feed troops or provide leather; but in the later years of the war this region suffered badly from partisan strife.

In brief, then, agricultural conditions varied according to the fortunes of war and special marketing problems. Rural New England, the Shenandoah Valley and most of Pennsylvania went almost unscathed, profiting by new demands from the fighting forces, American, British and French. Other regions such as the "no man's land" in New York, the Jerseys at certain times and the Lower South during the British invasion, with its accompanying Whig-Tory feuds, suffered severely. Marketing problems proved particularly difficult for the Southern planters, whose oversea exports were reduced, notwithstanding some indirect trade with the enemy and the finding of new customers in Continental Europe.

[1] Gray, *Agriculture*, II, 593-596; Edward McCrady, *History of South Carolina in the Revolution, 1775-1780* (N. Y., 1901), 283.

CHAPTER XII

New Modes of Thinking

THE war experience brought "a new mode of thinking" in many ways. Friendships formed in the army and in the Continental Congress and its agencies gave men from widely scattered communities a broader outlook. This was true not only of major figures but also of lesser ones. Thus James Thacher, a young army surgeon who entered the service from Massachusetts, campaigned and shared hardships with New Yorkers on the Hudson and Virginians in New Jersey. Associations with foreign officers, beginning early and increasing after the French alliance, still further enlarged the horizons of many. There was a kind of intellectual shaking up through absence from familiar scenes and the necessary adjustment to novel situations.

One human interest greatly affected by the conflict was religion. Of all the sects the Church of England suffered most in material resources, popularity and morale. Outside the British lines a considerable number of its clergy closed their places of worship and some became refugees. In Virginia, where the Anglicans were strongest, disestablishment was not completed during the war, but compulsory tithes were abolished and, when peace came, less than a fourth of the ministers were at their posts, even though many of them had supported the Revolution. Deism and anticlericalism were contributing factors.[1]

The Quakers also lost ground though for different

[1] William Meade, *Old Churches, Ministers, and Families of Virginia* (Phila., 1857), I, 17.

reasons—their pacifism and their official stand against forcible resistance. Young men who enlisted were disowned and membership fell off. Prominent Friends were accused of Toryism, giving intelligence to the British or trying to discredit the Continental currency. The Moravians were similarly troubled, though some of them rendered noncombatant service, as in caring for wounded Continental soldiers. Methodism, too, experienced a temporary setback because of popular distrust of its leaders. John Wesley and some of his American preachers disapproved of the Revolution, and the future Bishop Francis Asbury refused for a time to swear allegiance to the Revolutionary government. Asbury, however, soon discreetly adjusted himself to the new order and the feeling against his followers diminished sufficiently to make possible a rapid advance of membership when the war ended.[1]

Among the Calvinist denominations the New England Congregationalists maintained their preferred legal status. Many ministers became army chaplains; some even served as combatants. Elsewhere the patriotic activity of such Presbyterian clergymen as John Witherspoon and John Rodgers enhanced the prestige of that church. Partly for this reason, however, the Presbyterians endured much at the hands of the enemy. Dr. Rodgers declared that more than fifty of their churches were destroyed.[2] The Baptists, while suffering somewhat from the general preoccupation with politics and

[1] E. C. Burnett, ed., *Letters of Members of the Continental Congress* (Wash., 1921-1936), II, 113, 485; J. M. Buckley, *A History of Methodists in the United States* (Philip Schaff and others, eds., *The American Church History Series*, N. Y., 1893-1897, V), chap. vii; G. H. Ryden, ed., *Letters to and from Caesar Rodney* (Phila., 1933), 219.

[2] Alice M. Baldwin, *The New England Clergy and the American Revolution* (Duke Univ., *Publs.*, 1928), chap. xi; Rodgers, quoted in E. F. Humphrey, *Nationalism and Religion in America, 1774-1789* (Boston, 1924), 99.

war, profited by the greater tolerance resulting from the need of coöperation in a common cause. During the struggle the Virginia Baptists gained freedom of worship and exemption from church tithes. In New England, however, the old discrimination against them continued, though on one occasion a Baptist, invited to preach an election sermon before the Massachusetts legislature, seized the opportunity to urge equal rights in religion.

The Catholics also gained from the war. The desire of Congress to win over the Catholic Canadians, France's participation in the conflict and the partial collaboration of Spain all helped to weaken, though they did not end, the traditional anti-Catholic feeling. Catholic chaplains arrived with the diplomatic and military representatives of France and Spain, and Protestant congressmen attended Catholic services on certain public occasions. Though the Tories tried to exploit the popular misgivings on this score—shared, indeed, by some patriots—most penal legislation against Catholics disappeared.[1]

Much was said, then and later, about the disintegrating effect of war on religion. The Massachusetts authorities early complained that the Sabbath was profaned by improper diversions and unnecessary business. Ecclesiastical historians of Virginia—Anglican, Presbyterian and Baptist—have noted the general "declension" of Christianity in that state. When the Marquis de Chastellux referred to religion among the inhabitants, he noted "the facility with which they dispense with it." In disturbed areas there and elsewhere, as we have seen, places of worship were dismantled and services suspended. In 1778 the Dutch Reformed clergy deplored

[1] *Ibid.*, 119; Sister Mary Augustina [Ray], *American Opinion of Roman Catholicism in the Eighteenth Century* (Columbia Univ., *Studies,* no. 416), chap. viii.

"the malicious and God-provoking" destruction of churches, scattering of congregations and the prevailing religious indifference. Army life also interfered with customary observances. Moreover, orthodox theology suffered. Among the American officers Charles Lee and Ethan Allen were hostile critics of traditional Christianity. In New England the reaction against Calvinist theology, apparent before the war, developed farther, whether as Deism or as incipient Unitarianism. Timothy Dwight regarded the Revolution as a period when "Infidelity began to obtain in this country an extensive currency and reception." [1]

Puritanical standards of conduct somewhat relaxed. At first, however, there was a natural emphasis on the need of subordinating amusements to patriotic duties. In 1774 Congress discountenanced balls and theatrical entertainments in the interest of economy and concentration of effort. Later it condemned army dramatics as "disagreeable to the sober Inhabitants" of Philadelphia. When pleasure lovers invited Mrs. Washington to a ball, a local committee objected and she withdrew her acceptance. James Warren felt unhappy about the "Magnificent Ball" given by John Hancock to the French officers in Boston and deplored the conduct of "Genteel People" with their "Assemblies, gameing, and the fashionable Amusements." On such matters Samuel Adams, the Puritan, and Christopher Marshall, the Quaker, agreed. According to Arthur Lee, Philadelphians were forgetting Quaker simplicity and losing

[1] Hugh Hastings, comp., *Ecclesiastical Records of New York* (Albany, 1901-1905), VI, 4302-4304; Marquis de Chastellux, *Travels in North-America* (London, 1787), II, 205-207; W. W. Henry, *Patrick Henry* (N. Y., 1891), II, chap. xxxi; W. M. Gewehr, *The Great Awakening in Virginia, 1740-1790* (Duke Univ., Publs., 1930), 136; Peter Force, comp., *American Archives* (Wash., 1837-1853), ser. 4, II, 1415; Dwight, quoted in R. J. Purcell, *Connecticut in Transition, 1775-1818* (Wash., 1918), 9.

"that unostentatious virtue" which should animate the "Infant republic." [1]

Dueling became more common, though the Continental army code, modeled on the British articles of war, prohibited the provoking of such affrays.[2] The challenger was penalized but not the other party. Among conspicuous examples of dueling were the encounters between General Charles Lee and Colonel John Laurens, Colonel John Cadwalader and General Thomas Conway, General Lachlan McIntosh and Button Gwinnett, and General Robert Howe and Christopher Gadsden. In the Lee-Laurens affair both Laurens, the challenger, and Hamilton, his second, belonged to Washington's staff. Though Southerners in general sympathized with the practice more than New Englanders, some of the latter also participated. In one case both principals were Massachusetts men. In another, acceptance of the challenge came after threats of ostracism. Among civilians Paine, Jefferson and Franklin condemned the custom. Paine, who called it "Gothic and absurd," advocated the death penalty for an aggressor who killed his opponent, and so did Jefferson. In spite of drastic legislation against dueling in Pennsylvania and three New England states either during the war or immediately after, the continuance of the practice illustrates the persistence of social convention.[3]

In other respects also men were concerned about the

[1] Christopher Marshall, *Extracts from the Diary Kept in Philadelphia and Lancaster during the American Revolution, 1774-1781* (William Duane, ed., Albany, 1877), 168; W. C. Ford and others, eds., *Journals of the Continental Congress* (Wash., 1904-1937), XII, 1001-1004; Burnett, *Letters*, III, 451-452; John Adams, Samuel Adams and James Warren, *Warren-Adams Letters* (Mass. Hist. Soc., *Colls.*, LXXII-LXXIII), II, 59, 82, 157, 184.

[2] For earlier dueling, see J. T. Adams, *Provincial Society, 1690-1763* (*A History of American Life*, III), 161-162.

[3] E. B. Greene, "The Code of Honor in Colonial and Revolutionary Times, with Special Reference to New England," Colon. Soc. of Mass., *Publs.*, XXVI, 367-388.

effect of the war on public morals. In 1775 the Massachusetts committee of public safety, reporting hard drinking among the soldiers, urged Washington to suppress the retailing of liquor in and about the camps. Notwithstanding complaints that gambling was on the increase, lotteries were still considered a suitable means of raising money and Congress publicly advertised its United States lottery office, whose tickets sold rapidly even in Boston.[1]   Crime flourished in areas not effectively controlled by either party.   There were also allegations of a decline in business morality.   In 1779 Samuel Blachley Webb wrote gloomily of paper "money depreciating, public Virtue totally damn'd—Morals of good men effected."   Mercy Warren considered war in many respects "unfriendly to Virtue" and called the deterioration of manners in her neighborhood unprecedented "in the History of Man."   In Virginia, Landon Carter expressed a similar opinion.   Elbridge Gerry, while agreeing that in this as in other revolutions morals suffered, took a longer view, holding that Americans had enough "Wisdom and Vertue" to save the day.[2]

Probably comments on "licentiousness" often covered dislike of a radicalism which seemed to threaten vested rights.   Samuel Adams early in the war found "everywhere" men who feared "a free Government" lest it become "a Cloke for Licentiousness. . . . as if anything were so much to be dreaded by Mankind as Slavery." His more conservative kinsman, John, was one who emphasized the need of "Decency, and Respect and Veneration" for men in authority.   Some Southerners, while accepting the new order, felt misgivings about a situation in which "everyone who bore arms, esteemed himself

[1] Force, *American Archives*, ser. 4, II, 1367; *Pa. Packet*, Aug. 1, 1778; Adams, Adams and Warren, *Warren-Adams Letters*, I, 297.

[2] S. B. Webb, *Correspondence and Journals* (N. Y., 1893), II, 226; Adams, Adams and Warren, *Warren-Adams Letters*, II, 54; Burnett, *Letters*, I, 417; III, 483.

upon a footing with his neighbor." Samuel Johnston of North Carolina complained that gentlemen were over-ridden by "a set of men without reading, experience, or principle to guide them."[1]

Of humanitarian legislation the war period produced little except as to the Negro. Congress's suspension of slave importations was a retaliatory measure directed against the British. State action flowed from broader considerations. Between 1774 and 1783 laws against importing slaves were enacted by Vermont, Connecticut, Pennsylvania, Delaware and Virginia. Only two states, however, at this time adopted emancipation, though the declaration of rights in the Massachusetts constitution (1780) was so interpreted by the courts in 1783. Vermont, which had practically no slaves, declared slavery a violation of natural rights, and Pennsylvania, which had comparatively few, provided for gradual liberation.[2]

Elsewhere, though many people felt that human bond-age violated Revolutionary principles, no legislative ac-tion followed. In 1774 a Providence town meeting resolved that gradual emancipation followed logically from American ideas of "natural rights" and "personal liberty." Citizens of Danbury, Connecticut, held it "a palpable absurdity to complain of attempts to enslave us while we are actually enslaving others." Even from Darien, Georgia, came a declaration that the retention of slavery would set "that liberty we contend for upon a very wrong foundation." Nevertheless, many men both North and South who, like Jefferson, were con-scious of this anomaly shrank from the practical diffi-culties of manumission. When a Massachusetts emanci-

[1] Adams, Adams and Warren, Warren-Adams Letters, I, 195-196, 234; Thomas Anburey, Travels through the Interior Parts of America (Boston, 1923), II, 214; G. J. McRee, Life and Correspondence of James Iredell (N. Y., 1857-1858), I, chap. ix, 338.

[2] W. E. B. Du Bois, The Suppression of the African Slave-Trade to the United States of America (Harvard Hist. Studies, I), app. A.

pation bill was shelved, John Adams hoped it would
"sleep for a Time" since there were already "causes
enough of Jealousy, Discord, and Division." Similarly,
when Governor Livingston asked the New Jersey legislature to "lay the foundation" for emancipation, no
action was taken.[1]

From the standpoint of culture the war years brought
both losses and gains. The effect upon education has
been described as "disastrous." In New England the
heavy taxes lessened public support with the result that
terms were shortened and some schools were closed.
Elsewhere private and church schools were abandoned.
Military operations interrupted instruction and destroyed or damaged buildings. Nevertheless many
teachers carried on. Free-lance schoolmasters continued
their advertisements in the press. The Friends' meetings
showed an active interest in maintaining and improving
their schools, and Robert Proud, the Quaker historian,
though a Loyalist, resumed his work as master in the
Penn Charter School at Philadelphia. In New York City
the charity school of Trinity Church had pupils during
the British occupation, and also in up-state New York
some teachers were at work. Likewise, the Virginia
academies of Liberty Hall and Hampden-Sydney and the
Moravian schools in North Carolina went on in spite
of the turmoil about them.[2]

Here and there forward steps were taken. The constitutions of Massachusetts, Pennsylvania, North Carolina, Georgia and Vermont recognized public responsibility for education, thus at least pointing the way to

[1] Force, *American Archives*, ser. 4, I, 334, 1135; Adams, Adams and
Warren, *Warren-Adams Letters*, I, 335-339; Theodore Sedgwick, *A
Memoir of the Life of William Livingston* (N. Y., 1833), 298-299.

[2] Thomas Woody, *Early Quaker Education in Pennsylvania* (Teachers
College, Columbia Univ., *Contribs.*, no. 105), 58, 71, 94, 149; O. T.
Barck, *New York City during the War for Independence* (Columbia
Univ., *Studies*, no. 357), 164; R. F. Seybolt, "New York Colonial
Schoolmasters," N. Y. Educ. Dept., *Fifteenth Ann. Rep.*, I, 666 ff.

future action. During the war Jefferson drafted his "Bill for the More General Diffusion of Knowledge" to give Virginia a public school system.[1] Though never passed, it showed the importance attached to education by an outstanding Revolutionary statesman. In New England a new type of academy began with those founded by members of the Phillips family at Andover, Massachusetts, and Exeter, New Hampshire, in 1778 and 1781. In 1782 the Andover institution had a pupil from Washington's home town of Fredericksburg, who was soon followed by some of his young relatives. Another war-time enterprise was Timothy Dwight's popular school for boys and girls at Northampton. In New York clergymen at Claverack and Salem founded academies.[2] There were also new secondary schools at Chester, Lancaster and York, Pennsylvania, the first two under Presbyterian auspices and the third conducted by an Episcopal clergyman. Provost William Smith revived an old school in Kent County, Maryland, which by 1782 was said to have a hundred and forty pupils. In 1777 a young Princeton graduate opened a classical school in the Northern Neck of Virginia, later incorporated as Warren Academy in memory of the Boston patriot. In North Carolina, James Hall, Princeton graduate and Presbyterian clergyman, opened "Clio's Nursery," which trained some influential laymen and many preachers.

All the colleges suffered in the war. For some it was calamitous. King's College virtually ceased to exist and the new Queen's College barely survived. Partly because Provost Smith was distrusted, the Whigs revoked the

---

[1] Thomas Jefferson, *Works* (P. L. Ford, ed., N. Y., 1904-1905), II, 414.

[2] C. M. Fuess, *Men of Andover* (New Haven, 1928), 1-3, 15 ff., 52, 54; L. M. Crosbie, *Phillips Exeter Academy* (Exeter, N. H., 1923), chaps. i-v; G. F. Miller, *Academy System of the State of New York* (Albany, 1922), 18.

Philadelphia College charter and incorporated a new institution: the University of the State of Pennsylvania. William and Mary College continued its work under a young Whig president. The dominant influence in the other colleges was definitely patriotic. In 1775, after the Massachusetts provincial congress ordered Harvard to dismiss members of the faculty who appeared to be "unfriendly to the Liberties and Privileges of the Colonies," the overseers presently reported that they were all politically sound.[1]

Most of the colleges were occupied for longer or shorter periods by armed forces. For about a year Harvard's buildings served as American army barracks. Nassau Hall at Princeton was badly damaged during the Trenton-Princeton campaign and the Americans subsequently used the college for barracks and hospital service. William and Mary College, which escaped enemy occupation until 1781, was temporarily Cornwallis's headquarters and after his surrender became a French military hospital.[2]

College incomes were seriously reduced. Harvard encountered difficulties because of Treasurer John Hancock's mismanagement of its finances, the depreciation of public securities, and a currency inflation resulting "in a fruitless endeavour to overtake . . . the vanishing value of paper currency." According to President Madison, the income of William and Mary was "almost annihilated." Similarly, Princeton lost much of its endowment. The revenue from college fees naturally fell off with reduced enrollments. Undergraduate enlistments seem, however, to have been less than might be supposed and state legislatures commonly exempted pro-

---

[1] S. E. Morison, *Three Centuries of Harvard* (Cambridge, 1936), 147.
[2] Josiah Quincy, *History of Harvard University* (Cambridge, 1840), II, chap. xxviii; John Maclean, *History of the College of New Jersey* (Phila., 1877), I, 321.

fessors and students from military service. Of nearly two hundred students at Harvard in 1775 very few entered the army before graduation. Apparently William and Mary College and Princeton furnished a larger proportion of recruits. All the colleges were, however, represented by alumni or teachers in war service, civil and military. Notable examples of faculty participation were John Witherspoon of Princeton and John Winthrop of Harvard. Timothy Dwight left a Yale tutorship for an army chaplaincy, three Philadelphia medical professors held important military posts, and Madison of William and Mary served for a time as a militia captain.[1]

But the war helped as well as hurt higher education. The most interesting effort to modernize the curriculum was that of Jefferson at William and Mary, where chairs in modern languages and law were substituted for those in classics and divinity. The new posts were given respectively to Charles Bellini and George Wythe. Medical education too had gains as well as losses. The King's College department disappeared and instruction at Philadelphia suffered from the conflict between the old college and the new "University." On the other hand, the Harvard medical faculty was a by-product of the war, and its chief founder, Dr. John Warren, had profited by army contacts with the Philadelphia faculty and with French military surgeons. In 1782 Warren became the first professor in the new school.[2]

For the medical profession the war proved educational also in other respects. As in the case of Warren, young

[1] Quincy, *Harvard University,* II, chaps. xxix, xxxi; Ezra Stiles, *Literary Diary* (F. B. Dexter, ed., N. Y., 1901), II, 447; Maclean, *College of New Jersey,* I, chaps. xv-xvi; S. F. Batchelder, *Bits of Harvard History* (Cambridge, 1924), chap. ii.

[2] Jefferson, *Works,* IV, 266 ff.; Stiles, *Diary,* II, 447; Edward Warren, *The Life of John Warren* (Boston, 1874), 253; T. F. Harrington, *The Harvard Medical School* (N. Y., 1905), I, 68-88.

doctors from several states came under the influence of the comparatively advanced group at Philadelphia and of European surgeons, British, German and French. Just as the war began, Dr. John Jones of the King's College faculty issued his *Remarks on the Treatment of Wounds and Fractures* (new editions, 1776, 1777), based on the teaching of British and French experts—the first American treatise on the subject. Publications by Drs. Morgan and Rush discussed the treatment of small-pox epidemics. Rush also printed an essay on the health of the army. Probably the most important war-time production by a Continental medical officer was Dr. William Brown's pharmacopœia (1778), the first ever published in the United States—a pamphlet of thirty-two pages in Latin. After the war several doctors wrote articles based on their field experiences.[1]

One step toward higher standards was the setting of examinations for the army medical service. According to Dr. James Thacher, an early test at Cambridge resulted in the rejection of six out of sixteen applicants. Dr. Morgan undertook to arrange state examining boards, a difficult task because of the attitude of the surgeons and the laxity of regimental commanders. Meantime a growing professional spirit led to the formation in 1781 of the important Massachusetts Medical Society. Though progress in preventive medicine was slight, there was some serious discussion, from this standpoint, of sanitation, the army ration and ventilation.[2]

But medicine was not the only branch of science to gain from war experience. Robert Erskine, the Scotch-born engineer and ironmaster who was appointed geographer and surveyor-general to the Continental army,

---

[1] E. B. Greene, "Some Educational Values of the American Revolution," Am. Philosophical Soc., *Proceeds.*, LXVIII, 188-192.

[2] *Ibid.*; James Thacher, *Military Journal during the American Revolutionary War* (Boston, 1823), 28; F. R. Packard, *History of Medicine in the United States* (Phila., 1901), app. B.

made important maps of the Hudson Valley. Better known is the American-born Thomas Hutchins, a former British engineer officer who served in Greene's Carolina campaign and in 1781 became "Geographer to the United States." He had previously published *A Topographical Description of Virginia, Pennsylvania and Carolina* (1778). Jefferson's *Notes on Virginia*, written during the war, shows a systematic interest in American geography, which also owes something to maps by European officers.

The war helped to promote scholarly coöperation. John Adams, who noted the reputation enjoyed by the American Philosophical Society abroad as well as at home, and who attended at least one session of the French Academy of Sciences, was eager to establish a similar organization in his own state. One result was a clause in the Massachusetts constitution of 1780 calling for the encouragement of scientific associations. Shortly afterward the legislature chartered the American Academy of Arts and Sciences at Boston. Founded to "cultivate every art and science which may tend to advance the interest, honor, dignity and happiness of a free, independent and virtuous people," the Academy soon began its still continuing series of publications. The preface of its first volume emphasized its war-time origin, and among its early contributors Surgeon Major Feron of the French navy wrote a survey of the Boston water supply; General Benjamin Lincoln, who had served in the Yorktown campaign, described "strata of earth and shells" in that neighborhood; and there were articles by army surgeons.[1]

War-time conditions reduced the output of the press.

---

[1] John and Abigail Adams, *Familiar Letters during the Revolution* (C. F. Adams, ed., Boston, 1875), 207; John Adams, *Works* (C. F. Adams, ed., Boston, 1856), III, 147; IV, 259-261; American Academy of Arts and Sciences, *Memoirs*, I, preface, 542 ff., 556 ff.; II, pt. i, 43, 170; American Philosophical Society, *Transactions*, II, 239-246.

The number of American imprints, which had reached a high point in 1774 and 1775, fell off steadily until 1782 when the number was less than half that for 1775. Aside from such items as newspapers, almanacs, recruiting posters and other broadsides the total was very small. Notable among the few war-time pamphlets were Paine's *Common Sense* and his *American Crisis*, which heartened soldiers and civilians in trying times. *Common Sense* also appeared in a German translation. Two English political essays were reprinted: Josiah Tucker's *True Interest of Great Britain*, advocating American independence in the interest of the mother country; and Richard Price's *Observations on the Nature of Civil Liberty*. Other imprints dealt with military technique.

Of literature in any exacting sense there was little. Some political poetry, Whig and Tory, appeared in newspapers; but apart from the pamphleteers, only two important names count in the literary history of this period: John Trumbull and Philip Freneau. Besides writing the humorous poem *M'Fingal*, which dealt with the opening scenes of the Revolution, Trumbull added in 1782 a quasiprophetic vision of the victories at Saratoga and Yorktown. By contrast, Freneau's poetry reflected the more intense emotions of the war. Passionate in his democratic Americanism, he displayed a lyric quality which Trumbull lacked. Only two magazines, both short-lived, were published: the *Pennsylvania Magazine*, which lasted hardly more than a year; and the *United States Magazine*, edited by Hugh Henry Brackenridge.[1]

Newspapers fared better, for both Whigs and Tories needed them for propaganda and the public demanded war news. Though there were somewhat fewer papers

[1] Alexander Cowie, *John Trumbull, Connecticut Wit* (Chapel Hill, 1929), chap. vii; Philip Freneau, *Poems* (F. L. Pattee, ed., Princeton, 1902-1907); L. N. Richardson, *A History of Early American Magazines, 1741-1789* (N. Y., 1931), chap. vii.

in 1778 than in 1775, in 1783 they had passed the pre-war figure. Moreover, some were now issued two or three times a week. In Massachusetts the only colonial journal still published in 1778 was the *Boston Gazette;* the pro-British *News-Letter* ended when the enemy withdrew from Boston. During the first year of the war, with the Whigs in control, New York newspapers had to be on that side or at least be neutral. After the destruction of Rivington's press in November, 1775, his *Gazetteer* was suspended. Gaine's *Mercury* showed cautious Whig leanings, while Holt's *Journal* was the patriot organ. When Howe came in, conditions were reversed. Holt took his *Journal* up state; Gaine sided with the Tory party; and in 1777 Rivington revived his *Gazetteer,* or *Royal Gazette,* as it was later named. This paper, the "lying *Gazette,*" as the patriots called it, was the most important Tory organ in the country, filling its columns with propaganda, abuse of Whig leaders and distorted war news. An arrangement by which the Loyalist journals appeared on different days of the week provided almost the equivalent of a daily newspaper. Meantime up-state Whigs had, besides John Holt's *Journal,* Samuel Loudon's *New-York Packet,* which he had transferred from New York to Fishkill.[1]

Philadelphia began the war with six newspapers, five English and one German. All but one were definitely Whig, and that one, James Humphreys's *Pennsylvania Ledger,* tried to be neutral. Denounced as a Tory, however, Humphreys was soon forced to quit. When General Howe took over, the Whig printers had to leave, three of their journals were suspended, and John Dunlap transferred his *Pennsylvania Packet* to Lancaster. Humphreys now revived his *Ledger,* and Benjamin Towne,

---

[1] Barck, *New York City,* chap. vii; Isaiah Thomas, *The History of Printing in America* (Am. Antiquarian Soc., *Archæologia Americana, Trans. and Colls.,* V-VI), *passim.*

a former Whig printer, also conducted a British organ. Other Tory papers were the *Royal Gazette* and the German *Pennsylvanische Staats-Courier*. When the British withdrew, the tables were again turned. The Whig printers came back and the Tory partisans had to flee, except Towne who again changed his spots and managed to stay in business. New Jersey, which had no prewar newspaper, possessed two before the conflict ended. To counteract Rivington's influence, the *New-Jersey Gazette* was founded in 1777. To this paper Governor Livingston, as "Hortensius," contributed vigorous Whig propaganda. The Maryland and Virginia press was less affected by the struggle. The *Maryland Gazette* at Annapolis and the *Journal* at Baltimore continued to appear and the chief change in Virginia was the removal of its newspapers from Williamsburg to Richmond. Of three prewar journals in Charleston the Loyalist printer of one departed, leaving the paper to his son. Of the two Whig editors, Peter Timothy published his *South-Carolina Gazette* until the British occupation when he was imprisoned and his sheet suspended.[1]

War-time journalism, Whig and Tory, dealt largely in propaganda. Rivington's *Royal Gazette* praised the proposals of the Carlisle peace commission of 1778 as highly magnanimous, while the Whig *Pennsylvania Packet* spoke of their final announcement as illustrating the "contemptible figure which the British king and ministry have cut in the present war." To Holt's *New-York Journal* the reception of the French envoy was a "noble sight," marking America's entry "among the powers of the earth . . . in robes of sovereignty"; but Rivington suggested that America had been "sold to the French King." After Major John André's execution Rivington's sheet denounced Washington as a "mur-

[1] Thomas, *History of Printing*, passim.

derer." More creditable was the comment of the Boston *Independent Chronicle*, which defended André's sentence but spoke of his courage and dignity in the face of death. The *Pennsylvania Packet* of November 14, 1778, contained savage lines about King George, one of which ran, "Go second Cain, true likeness of the first." [1]

Of patriotic songs the Revolution produced few that outlived the times. Perhaps the best known is Timothy Dwight's "Columbia":

> Columbia, Columbia, to glory arise
> The Queen of the world, and the child of the skies.

Military music was usually played with fife and drum. "Yankee Doodle," though not a native production, was, according to Lieutenant Anburey, "a favorite of favorites." One composer whose music proved popular in the camps was the Yankee singing master, William Billings. One of his songs began:

> Let tyrants shake their iron rod,
> And Slavery clank his galling chains;
> We fear them not, we trust in God;
> New England's God forever reigns. [2]

In spite of congressional disapproval of stage plays the theater, such as it was, also went to war. A few dramatic pieces were primarily for readers. One, entitled "The Fall of British Tyranny; or American Liberty Triumphant," was said to have been "lately planned at the Royal Theatrum Pandemonium at St. James'." British statesmen, Whig and Tory, were

[1] For war-time propaganda, see Philip Davidson, *Propaganda and the American Revolution* (Chapel Hill, 1941), chaps. xvii-xx; Frank Moore, ed., *Diary of the American Revolution* (N. Y., 1860), II, 78-82, 97-100, 457.

[2] J. C. Fitzpatrick, *The Spirit of the Revolution* (Boston, 1924), chap. x; Anburey, *Travels*, II, 31; Fannie L. G. Cole, "William Billings," Allen Johnson and Dumas Malone, eds., *Dictionary of American Biography* (N. Y., 1928-1937), II, 269-271.

dramatis personae, with American officers in a closing act. Two dramatic poems by Hugh H. Brackenridge, "The Battle of Bunker's Hill" and "The Death of General Montgomery," stressed the tragic element with an appeal to patriotism. In the former the British officers are not wholly odious and Howe is represented as appreciative of American gallantry. There was more bitterness in "The Death of General Montgomery," with Sir Guy Carleton exulting in the sufferings inflicted by his Indian allies. Interest in the stage owed something to British officers. They reopened New York's John Street Theatre and for a time played all the parts, but actresses were brought in later. The repertoire ranged from Shakespeare's "Richard II" to Sheridan's "School for Scandal." In Philadelphia, Howe's officers used the Southwark Theatre for theatricals, and the infection spread, as we have seen, to the American officers.[1]

In pictorial art Peale continued his labors, and his art collection was one of Philadelphia's show places. Francis Hopkinson made crayon portraits, and Pierre Eugène Du Simitière, a Swiss, portrayed Washington, Laurens, Steuben and Arnold. John Trumbull, after some service in the Continental army, went to London to work with Benjamin West, where his studies were interrupted by his arrest and imprisonment. But he was finally released and, after a short stay on the Continent, sailed home. He had, however, already done a likeness of Washington, and when the war ended he returned to his labors with West.[2]

American thinking about the arts and sciences tended to be markedly nationalistic, but in other respects long-time sectional prejudices lingered. John Adams reflected

---

[1] M. C. Tyler, *The Literary History of the American Revolution, 1763-1783* (2nd edn., N. Y., 1898-1900), II, 198-225; Barck, *New York City*, chap. ix. Details for this period are in G. C. D. Odell, *Annals of the New York Stage* (N. Y., 1927-1942), I.

[2] Adams, *Familiar Letters*, 215-217.

much New England opinion when in 1776 he maintained that "popular Principles and Maxims" were
"abhorrent to the inclinations of the Barons of the
South." Southerners were correspondingly suspicious
of New Englanders. Carter Braxton distrusted their
"purely democratical" institutions, and Edward Rutledge feared the "low Cunning" of the people and their
"levelling Principles . . . so captivating to the lower
class of Mankind." Washington was made commander
in chief partly to allay Southern fears that a victorious
Northern general might "give law to the Southern or
Western gentry." ¹

But the Northerners also had their mutual antagonisms. John Adams wondered whether "deceit or simple dulness" accounted for the "eccentric and retrograde
politics" of New York. A Connecticut colonel talked
of the "damn'd cowardly, rascally manner" of the Pennsylvanians. On the other hand, the young Philadelphian, Alexander Graydon, sympathized with General
Schuyler's treatment of certain New Englanders, as one
might deal with "a low and vexatious intruder."
Graydon thought better of the New Yorkers, who were
"sufficiently men of the world" to understand that "the
levelling principle" was "incompatible with good sol-
diership." Once, at Ticonderoga, Pennsylvanians came
to blows with New Englanders.²

Usually, however, the men from the different states
heartily joined in the common cause. Massachusetts
Adamses and Virginia Lees worked sympathetically together. Henry Lee, admiring Massachusetts institutions,
once expressed the hope to end his days there. John
Adams promised the British some "ugly knocks" if they

¹ Burnett, *Letters*, I, 127, 406, 420, 517.
² Adams, *Works*, IX, 407; Webb, *Correspondence and Journals*, I,
174-175; Alexander Graydon, *Memoirs of His Own Time* (J. S. Littell,
ed., Phila., 1846), 144-149; Thacher, *Military Journal*, 68-69.

attacked Charleston since the South Carolinians were "honest, sincere and brave." In Congress the members more directly responsible for administrative services, naval affairs and foreign relations found it easier to think in national terms and were stimulated by a sense of enhanced personal dignity. An article in a contemporary English journal said of the members generally: "From shopkeepers, tradesmen, and attorneys, they are become statesmen and legislators, and are employed in contriving a new system of government for an extensive empire, which they flatter themselves will become, and which indeed seems very likely to become, one of the greatest and most formidable that ever was in the world." The development of a more national outlook is perhaps most apparent in the army and the diplomatic service. Notwithstanding such episodes as the Conway Cabal, many of the ranking officers were prepared by their personal associations and their common trials for a loyalty transcending state boundaries. Horizons were widened also for some of the more enterprising business men who engaged in interstate enterprises.[1]

Americans abroad on public or private errands formed a small but sometimes influential element, distributed through such cities as Paris, Nantes, Brussels and Leyden. Even war-time residence in England was not considered necessarily unpatriotic. John Trumbull, the artist, and Benjamin Waterhouse, the future Harvard professor of medicine, are two cases in point. William Loughton Smith, later a South Carolina congressman, studied law in England during the war and, when his Americanism was questioned, replied that he had duly registered with the United States envoys in Paris "as a citizen of America." Probably residence in Europe helped some men

[1] B. J. Hendrick, *The Lees of Virginia* (Boston, 1935), 352; Adams, *Familiar Letters*, 292; Adams, *Works*, III, 384; Moore, *Diary*, I, 229.

to think of themselves as "citizens of America" rather than merely of particular states.[1]

Growing nationalism found expression on patriotic anniversaries. Formal observances of the Declaration of Independence began in 1776. Though men spoke in the plural of "Free and Independent States," toasts and resolutions also referred to "the freedom and independence of America." At Savannah the celebrators were told that "America" would become, "with the blessing of the Almighty, *great* among the nations of the earth." On the first anniversary in Philadelphia, Congress adjourned and a public celebration followed with music by Hessian prisoners. The next year Congress dined at the City Tavern with other dignitaries, civil and military. Of the thirteen toasts one was to "The happy era of the Independence of America." In 1779, when the anniversary fell on Sunday, Congress directed its chaplains to prepare appropriate sermons and, on the invitation of the French minister, members heard the *Te Deum* at the Catholic Church.[2]

The chief human symbol of a common Americanism was Washington. Even before he became commander in chief, he was mentioned as a leader under whom "several hundred thousand Americans . . . would face any danger." At Cambridge, Dr. Thacher was impressed by his "majestic" appearance, and a later observer declared there was "not a King in Europe but would look like a valet de chambre by his side." One Loyalist, noting his "tall and genteel appearance," thought him a "most surprising man, one of Nature's geniuses." Adverse opinions of Washington also existed. John Adams complained that some persons were in-

---

[1] H. R. Viets, "Benjamin Waterhouse," Johnson and Malone, *Dictionary of American Biography*, XIX, 529-532; W. L. Smith, "Journal, 1790-1791," Mass. Hist. Soc., *Proceeds.*, LI, 20-88.

[2] Moore, *Diary*, 269-284; *Pa. Packet*, July 6, 1778; Burnett, *Letters*, IV, 293-300.

clined to "idolise an image which their own hands have molten," and disliked the "superstitious veneration" of Washington. In the end, however, popular sentiment supported the commander in chief against his critics and, from 1778 on, his position in the public mind was assured.[1]

Foreign opinion may have helped to enhance American appreciation of Washington. The French Comte de Ségur said of him: "Simplicity, grandeur, dignity, calm, kindness, firmness were stamped upon his face and upon his countenance as well as his character." A sketch in the *London Chronicle,* reprinted in 1780 by an American newspaper, declared that "no man ever united in his own character a more perfect alliance of the virtues of the philosopher with the talents of a general." When Admiral D'Estaing in 1778 gave an entertainment on one of his ships in Boston Harbor, a picture of Washington was prominently displayed, and in 1779 copies of a full-length portrait of him by Peale were ordered by the Spanish agent, Juan de Miralles. The final victory naturally strengthened Washington's hold on the popular imagination. David Howell, a critical Rhode Islander, was deeply moved by the scene at Annapolis when Washington surrendered his commission, noting the "affectionate attachment" shown "to our illustrious Hero." Thus one result of the war was the embodiment of American unity in a truly heroic personality.[2]

National sentiment implies not only community of thought and feeling, but also awareness of what is distinctive. The differentiation of Americans from Eng-

---

[1] Margaret W. Willard, ed., *Letters on the American Revolution, 1774-1776* (Boston, 1925), 42, 228; Thacher, *Military Journal,* 30; Nicholas Cresswell, *Journal, 1774-1777* (N. Y., 1924), 251; Burnett, *Letters,* II, 263, 275.

[2] Gilbert Chinard, ed., *George Washington as the French Knew Him* (Princeton, 1940), 36; Moore, *Diary,* II, 101, 126, 302; Burnett, *Letters,* VII, 394-399.

lishmen was sharpened by Revolutionary propaganda and war-time animosities. After the French alliance a writer in the *Pennsylvania Packet* argued that this new association was safer than sympathetic relations with the mother country since the common inheritance of England and America would tend to perpetuate undesirable influences: the "pomp" of the Anglican Church, British class distinctions and the British political system "so perfect in theory, but so corrupt in practice." He thought there was danger also that republican simplicity and sound morals would be corrupted. Such contamination by America's connections with France was less likely because of natural barriers of language and religion. Good citizens should therefore keep alive anti-British feeling.[1]

American nationalism was, however, jealous even of France. There were misgivings about association with a "Popish" king and nation, and a Connecticut delegate queried whether it would not have been better to win without such aid. Henry Laurens was also troubled about "our delicate connection with France." The unsuccessful Franco-American operations of 1778 and later complications resulting from France's alliance with Spain emphasized the need of an independent course. Economic nationalism developed early, too. "Shall we," asked John Adams, "invite all Nations to come with their Luxuries, as well as Conveniences and Necessaries, or shall We think of confining our trade with them to our own Bottoms, which alone can lay a Foundation for great Wealth and naval Power?" Though foreign shipping was then essential, the concept of nationalist economics was already rooted in men's minds.[2]

If nationalism was developing, there was also some

---

[1] *Pa. Packet*, Aug. 1, 1778.
[2] Burnett, *Letters*, I, 174; III, 347, 391, 498; D. D. Wallace, *Henry Laurens* (N. Y., 1915), chap. xx.

international thinking. So far as Americans were influenced by European liberals, or sought their support, they thought of themselves as helping to realize the ideals of the Age of Enlightenment. The French king was toasted as "the magnanimous protector of the rights of mankind," and the hope was expressed that America's example might excite the oppressed everywhere to resist tyranny and secure their "natural and inalienable rights." America was not only taking her rightful place among the nations but introducing "a new era in the happiness of mankind." [1] Thus the long years of warfare brought intellectual as well as political adjustments. The next decade was to show how the new republican society would repair its losses, consolidate its gains and apply more effectively "the new mode of thinking."

[1] *Pa. Packet.* July 6, 14, 1778; John Rodgers, quoted in Humphrey, *Nationalism and Religion,* 99.

CHAPTER XIII

Republican Society

At the close of the war the United States numbered somewhat over three million souls. Phineas Bond, the British consul general, estimated the drain of population from the war at "perhaps little short of 100,000 men"; but no exact statistical evidence is available. Among the reasons for loss were deaths among soldiers and civilians, the large-scale exodus of Tories and probably some slackening of the birth rate due to the disturbance of normal family life. To some extent, however, these factors were offset by the considerable number of prisoners or deserters from the British and German troops who stayed on in the United States. Of the Germans there may have been as many as six or seven thousand.[1]

The Loyalists migrated chiefly to British North America. The most careful estimate is that for New York, where some thirty-five thousand may have departed, forming a much larger proportion of the population than in any other state. Nevertheless, even here the refugees were far outnumbered by the Tories who remained. Of this latter group, many were obscure persons, while others had been comparatively inactive. Some exiles returned after the war and, notwithstanding popular hostility and severe legislation, old animosities gradually softened.[2] Peter Van Schaack, the lawyer

---

[1] Phineas Bond, "Letters," Am. Hist. Assoc., *Ann. Rep. for 1896*, I, 648; Thomas Anburey, *Travels through the Interior Parts of America* (Boston, 1923), II, 179; E. C. Burnett, ed., *Letters of Members of the Continental Congress* (Wash., 1921-1936), II, 194; A. B. Faust, *The German Element in the United States* (Boston, 1909), I, 355-356.

[2] A. C. Flick, *Loyalism in New York during the American Revolution* (Columbia Univ., *Studies*, XIV, no. 1), chap. viii.

refugee, was restored to citizenship and readmitted to the bar, of which he continued to be a distinguished member. Before he left London he saw John Jay, and they met, wrote Jay, "with all the cordiality of old friends, who had long been absent, without the least retrospect to the cause of that absence." Richard Harison, another returned exile, became a delegate to the New York convention which ratified the Federal Constitution. William Seton, the first cashier of the Bank of New York, was another rehabilitated Tory.[1]

Philip Barton Key of Maryland, who had served in the British army, subsequently practised law in his native state and became successively member of the legislature and of Congress, receiving the half-pay of a British retired officer for more than twenty years after the war. One of the most successful Boston physicians in the seventeen-nineties was John Jeffries, a Harvard graduate who had served as a surgeon in the British army and practised in England before returning to his native city. Similarly, Samuel Curwen after an unhappy exile went back to his old Salem friends.

Practical considerations favored the rehabilitation of the Tories. In 1784 the New Haven town meeting voted to allow their return in the interest of business. President Ezra Stiles thought the Tories numerous enough there to count seriously in a local election. New York opponents of harsh legislation argued that it would keep out capital and in 1787 Jay reported that most of the Loyalists had been reinstated. Stephen Higginson of Massachusetts took a similar stand. Among influential Southerners, Jefferson favored reconciliation with open enemies, but not with those who "remained among us and strove to injure us by their

[1] H. C. Van Schaack, *Peter Van Schaack* (N. Y., 1842), 313, chaps. xix-xxi; E. W. Spaulding, *New York in the Critical Period* (D. R. Fox, ed., *N. Y. State Hist. Assoc. Ser.*, I), 129, 246-253.

treacheries." Charles Carroll, opposing the exclusion of Loyalists from legal practice, wished to end such "odious distinctions" and unite all citizens "in the pursuit of the common good." Forgetfulness of the past came most slowly in regions where savage fighting had occurred between Whigs and Tories. The South Carolina Tory, Love, a participant in a brutal massacre, was lynched after his discharge by a trial court. Aedanus Burke, the presiding judge, believed that Love's neighbors could forget injuries inflicted in "fair action," but not "wanton acts of barbarity." [1]

By 1789 most states had repealed legislation against the Loyalists conflicting with the peace treaty, though confiscated estates were not restored. Conservative Whigs were glad to have Tory support for strong government and for laws favorable to business. Of sixty conspicuous New York leaders during the "Critical Period," eleven were Loyalists, seven of whom advocated ratification of the Federal Constitution. Quite naturally John Jay and Alexander Hamilton favored conciliation. [2]

After the war the population of the country grew rapidly, partly through accessions from without. In spite of adverse legislation, slave importations during this period increased the number of Negroes by several thousand. More important was the resumption of immigration. Bond reported the arrival of over twenty-five thousand redemptioners and servants in Pennsyl-

---

[1] Oscar Zeichner, "The Rehabilitation of Loyalists in Connecticut." *New England Quar.*, XI, 308-330; Ezra Stiles, *Literary Diary* (F. B. Dexter, ed., N. Y., 1901), III, 70, 109-112; Thomas Jefferson, *Works* (P. L. Ford, ed., N. Y., 1904-1905), IV, 431-432; Kate M. Rowland, *Life and Correspondence of Charles Carroll of Carrollton* (N. Y., 1898), II, 67-70; J. D. Schoepf, *Travels in the Confederation, 1783-1784* (A. J. Morrison, ed., Phila., 1911), II, 204; Spaulding, *New York in the Critical Period*, chap. vi; Aedanus Burke to the Governor of South Carolina, *Am. Museum*, I (1787), 120-122.

[2] Spaulding, *New York in the Critical Period*, 132.

vania between 1783 and 1789, including Irish, Scots and Germans. Public opinion generally favored immigration. The young republic was conceived of as a land of freedom and economic opportunity for unfortunate Europeans. "It is our business," wrote John Adams, "to render our country an Asylum, worthy to receive all who may wish to fly to it." William Grayson of Virginia, hoping for speedy land sales and lower taxes, observed that "the want of inhabitants" was "perhaps our only calamity." Tench Coxe urged the outstanding advantages of Pennsylvania, which offered civil and religious liberty, land on easy terms, voting citizenship after two years' residence, and freedom from Old World restraints on trade and industry. Here too, he pointed out, newcomers would feel at home among neighbors speaking their own language, English, Dutch or German. On the other hand, both Bond and Lord Sheffield emphasized the difficulties that the foreign-born faced.[1]

Though law-abiding immigrants were welcomed, Congress, noting recent attempts to send convicts to America, urged the states to stop them. Franklin stressed the need of caution even in the case of other arrivals. He thought office seekers, military men and persons who relied on aristocratic connections were not needed. In the United States the stranger was asked not *"What is he?"* but *"What can he do?"* Industrious farm workers could, however, earn enough to buy land; the mechanic could practise his craft freely; servants or journeymen,

[1] Bond, "Letters," 581 ff., 643; Lord Sheffield, *Observations on the Commerce of the American States* (6th edn., London, 1784), 190 ff.; V. S. Clark, *History of Manufactures in the United States* (Carnegie Inst., Contribs. to Am. Econ. History; rev. edn., N. Y., 1929), I, 260; W. E. B. Du Bois, *The Suppression of the African Slave-Trade to the United States of America* (Harvard Hist. Studies, I), 50; Burnett, *Letters*, VIII, 141; Tench Coxe, *View of the United States of America* (Phila., 1794), 65-68, 101.

if "sober, industrious and frugal," might hope to become masters, heads of families and "respectable citizens." [1] Though immigration was much less than in later years, men were already thinking about the problem of assimilation. A German observer commented on the "promiscuous crowd of almost all nations in Europe," adding, "Such a mixture will require a long fermentation before it will contain the spirit, the feelings, and the imprint of a united people." A generation passed, however, before the newcomers materially affected institutional life. [2]

The postwar society lived within a governmental framework that contained elements both old and new. The local governments, which most nearly touched the ordinary citizen, were not radically altered. New England town meetings went on as before, and Virginia counties were administered much as in earlier days and largely by the same kind of people, though the royal governors no longer appointed the justices. Between these local communities and the extremely slight authority of the Confederation stood the states with their new constitutions. In Rhode Island and Connecticut the transition from colony to commonwealth proved simple. Royal collectors and admiralty courts had disappeared, but otherwise the form of government was little changed. A generation passed before these states replaced their colonial charters with constitutions of their own making. But in each of the former royal and proprietary provinces an old edifice was pulled down and a new one built, even though much of the same material was used. The process, begun in 1776, was nearly com-

---

[1] Burnett, *Letters*, VIII, 797; Benjamin Franklin, *Writings* (Albert Smyth, ed., N. Y., 1907), VIII, 603 ff.

[2] Max Farrand, "A Nation of Immigrants," *New Republic*, IX, 148 (Dec. 9, 1916); M. L. Hansen, *The Atlantic Migration, 1607-1860* (A. M. Schlesinger, ed., Cambridge, 1940), 53-58.

pleted with the adoption of the Massachusetts constitution of 1780.[1]

Naturally, the new governments were formed by supporters of the Revolution, but in their ranks were many who desired only a minimum of internal innovation. Between this conservative group and the more liberal elements compromises had to be effected. Some of the democratic leaders were, like Patrick Henry, "new men," but others, like the Virginia Lees and Edmund Randolph, belonged to the "first families." Henry, who called himself "a Democrat on the plan of our admired friend, J. Adams," complained of a "bias to Aristocracy" among the opulent.[2] Typical representatives of conservative views in the state conventions were Robert Carter Nicholas and Edmund Pendleton in Virginia, James Duane and John Jay in New York and Henry Laurens and John Rutledge in South Carolina.

This group included substantial landowners, well-to-do merchants and successful lawyers. One aggressive republican who gradually moved to the "right" was John Adams, chief architect of the Massachusetts constitution. To many of the Virginia gentry the first clause of the state bill of rights, drafted by George Mason, which declared all men "by nature equally free and independent," seemed to embody subversive doctrine, "the forerunner or pretext of civil convulsion." The conservatives were beaten on this issue as well as on the clause pledging the "free exercise of religion," but the constitution was not strictly democratic. Though it provided for annual elections, property qualifications remained and the method of apportionment still favored the tidewater planters as against the piedmont

---

[1] Allan Nevins, *The American States during and after the Revolution, 1775-1789* (N. Y., 1924), *passim*.

[2] W. W. Henry, *Patrick Henry* (N. Y., 1891), I, 411, 425.

and Valley farmers.[1] In the South the radicals were strongest in North Carolina, where they defeated the conservative tidewater planters, lawyers and merchants. All adult free men could vote for members of the lower house after one year's residence, but there were property qualifications for membership in the legislature.[2]

In Pennsylvania the radicals dominated the convention of 1776 through a combination of backcountry farmers with Philadelphia mechanics and small tradesmen. As a result, the new instrument reduced the representation of the conservative older counties and increased that of Philadelphia and the interior counties. The suffrage was somewhat broadened, no upper house was provided to check the popularly elected assembly, and the plural executive received no veto. Conservative opposition, combined with the need of a stronger executive, led to further constitutional changes in 1790, including provisions for a single executive with a veto on legislation, judicial service during good behavior and an upper house.[3]

The original constitutions of New York (1777) and Massachusetts (1780), being adopted after a longer war experience, were perhaps partly for that reason comparatively conservative. The presence of the British army in New York called for a strong executive there, and influential members of the convention represented the less democratic wing of the patriot party. Jay's "favorite maxim" was, according to his son, that "those who own the country ought to govern it." Except for city freemen previously admitted to the suffrage, the constitution provided that electors had to be either twenty-pound freeholders or renters of tenements worth forty shillings

[1] *Ibid.*, I, 425.

[2] G. J. McRee, *Life and Correspondence of James Iredell* (N. Y., 1857-1858), I, chap. ix.

[3] C. H. Lincoln, *The Revolutionary Movement in Pennsylvania, 1760-1776* (Univ. of Pa., *Ser. in History*, no. 1), 278-287; Nevins, *American States*, 197-200.

a year. Voters for governor and senators had to meet higher qualifications, and the governor was to serve for a three-year term. One liberal provision required the legislature to try the experiment of a secret ballot and another guaranteed religious liberty. The freehold qualification for voters did not prevent the yeoman farmers, led by Governor George Clinton, from dominating state politics during the next few years.[1]

The Massachusetts constitution has been called a merchants' and lawyers' instrument designed for "quarterdeck efficiency in government, and the protection of property against democratic pirates." In general, it mirrored the ideas of the commercial seaboard and a conservative reaction against Revolutionary radicalism, a point of view apparent in the manifesto, known as the "Essex Result," which advocated frank recognition of class interests in a bicameral legislature, with one house, chosen by the people, checked by an upper house. The popular chamber, though probably superior in "political honesty, probity, and a regard to the interest of the whole," would be liable to "crude and hasty determinations." The senate would give due influence to "gentlemen of education, fortune and leisure." Substantially, this doctrine was embodied in the constitution. Elections were based on property qualifications even higher than before the Revolution. Representation in the lower house was roughly in accordance with population, but in the senate, seats were allotted in proportion to taxes paid, thus favoring the wealthier Eastern counties. The property prerequisite for a senator was more than for a representative, and the governor, who had a veto, must have a freehold estate of at least a thousand pounds.[2]

[1] William Jay, *Life of John Jay* (N. Y., 1833), I, 70; Spaulding, *New York in the Critical Period*, chap. v.

[2] S. E. Morison, *Maritime History of Massachusetts, 1783-1860* (Boston, 1921), 28-29; text of "Essex Result" in Theophilus Parsons, *Memoir of Theophilus Parsons, Chief Justice of the Supreme Judicial Court of Massachusetts* (Boston, 1859), app. i.

Thus the early constitutions reflected various shades of opinion, from those favoring a comparatively advanced democracy to more conservative attitudes. It must be remembered, however, that property qualifications based on land were more easily met then by a preponderantly agricultural population than they would be now. From an eighteenth-century European standpoint the American states had gone far toward equalitarian democracy.

The social philosophy of these instruments definitely restricted the sphere of government. A relatively simple and rural society expected less of the state than is now thought necessary or desirable. The people retained the ultimate sovereignty and designated the government to act as their agent for limited purposes. They also shifted power from the executive to the legislature, which was, however, limited by a bill of rights. This document, unlike the English bill of rights of 1689, aimed to protect citizens against legislative as well as executive encroachments on their "natural rights." The legislature might not, for instance, dispense with jury trials or pass acts of attainder. The New Jersey constitution declared the right of trial by jury an irrepealable part of the law; and in the case of Holmes *v.* Walton in 1780 the state supreme court declared invalid a statute permitting a jury of fewer than twelve men.[1]

On the issue of hereditary privilege the basic laws were emphatic. Virginia declared that only public service could entitle any man to "separate emoluments or privileges from the community," but that such claims were not "descendible, neither ought the offices of magistrate, legislator, or judge to be hereditary." The Massachusetts instrument denounced as "absurd and un-

---

[1] Austin Scott, "Holmes vs. Walton: the New Jersey Precedent," *Am. Hist. Rev.*, IV, 456-469. For a different view, see L. B. Boudin, *Government by Judiciary* (N. Y., 1932), I, 531-555.

natural" the idea of "a man born a magistrate, law-giver, or judge." Finally, the Federal Constitution prohibited the grant of titles of nobility by state or federal authority. The exclusion of formal aristocracy was, of course, comparatively easy in a society in which hereditary titles were almost nonexistent. In 1775 Lord Fairfax was the only British peer permanently resident in any of the colonies; and the conspicuous colonial baronets, Sir John Johnson in New York and Sir William Pepperell in Maine, both became Loyalist exiles. Many persons, however, continued to believe that the "well-born" could best be trusted with civic responsibility.

As the state governments got under way, Americans differed widely as to how they should use their powers. Some wished the old order to be changed as little as possible, while others thought of the new governments as instruments of democratic social reconstruction. The Pennsylvania constitution limited imprisonment for debt and called for legislation regulating entail and humanizing the criminal law. The Massachusetts articles dealing with the arts and sciences indicate that the state was considered an appropriate agency for promoting culture. Meantime capitalists desired governmental coöperation in organizing economic resources and financing business enterprises. Recognizing the inadequacy of the state governments for such purposes, they favored a strengthened federal system to serve interstate interests.

Among those who advocated a species of social planning was Dr. Benjamin Rush. "The American war," he wrote in 1783, "is over but this is far from being the case with the American Revolution." His idea of a continuing revolution involved not merely matters of government and finance, but economic improvements, morals and manners. He was especially interested in civic education.[1] A more important champion of such reconstruction was Jefferson. Believing that only a truly democratic society could assure the success of political democracy, he wished to break up great estates by abolishing entail and primogeniture. Since slavery violated the principle of equal rights and preserved an undemocratic social tradition, he also favored gradual emancipation, while recognizing the complex problems which would follow. Similarly in education Jefferson sought equality of opportunity since genuine democracy required a widely diffused intelligence.[2]

John Adams, like Jefferson, condemned hereditary political privilege and disliked the hereditary membership of the Society of the Cincinnati. Like Jefferson also, he desired a "better system of education for the common people" to prevent "artificial inequalities" that were "prejudicial to society." Adams prided himself, however, on a realistic attitude, regarding social distinctions as stubborn facts to be frankly recognized. Had not America its "laborers, yeomen, gentlemen, esquires, honorable gentlemen, and excellent gentlemen"? There should be equality before the law, but differences of birth and wealth exerted "a natural and inevitable influence upon society." For a proper equilibrium between a "natural aristocracy" and the "commons" he looked to a bicameral legislature.[3]

Aside from constitutional provisions, it is hard to say how far the Revolution affected class distinctions. The confiscation of Loyalist estates and the abolition of primogeniture helped toward a wider distribution of landed property, and some large fortunes were broken

[1] Benjamin Rush, "Address to the People of the United States, *Am. Museum*, I, 8-11.
[2] Gilbert Chinard, *Thomas Jefferson* (Boston, 1929), 88-89, 119, 131, 507-509.
[3] John Adams, *Works* (C. F. Adams, ed., Boston, 1856), IV, 391-398; V, 488; IX, 546.

up in other ways. Meantime, however, "new men" who gained riches during the war acquired social prestige and political power, thus forming a new aristocracy beside the old or in place of it. Dr. J. D. Schoepf, a thoughtful observer of the American scene, remarked that without a nobility or gentry in the strict sense there were men whose exceptional ability or wealth caused them to "think and act precisely as do the nobility in other countries." In Virginia, Devereux Jarratt, in spite of his humble origin, regretted that the "high republican times" had caused "more *levelling* than ought to be, consistent with government." Nevertheless, there was some lessening of traditional deference to superior social status. The will of Thomson Mason, who died in 1785, advised his sons to avoid the tidewater aristocracy lest they "imbibe more exalted notions of their own importance." Jefferson, however, expected the "plebeian Interest" to prevail over "the old aristocratical interest." [1]

The biographer of Elbridge Gerry, whose memory went back to the last decade of the eighteenth century, noted the survival of the preëxisting attitudes in New England:

> Ancient habits could not at once be changed, and the forms of a society, which had been regulated by provincial imitation of English manners, continued to prevail. . . . The leaders of the Revolution rose upon the ruins of anti-republican prejudices . . . but they never attempted like the revolutionists of later times to confound all distinctions of society.

In Philadelphia, Noah Webster observed "the affectation of superiority in certain families"; and in New

---

[1] Schoepf, *Travels*, II, 205; Devereux Jarratt, *Life* (Balt., 1806), 14-15; Kate M. Rowland, *Life of George Mason, 1725-1792* (N. Y., 1892), II, 77; Stiles, *Diary*, III, 125.

York the aristocratic bias still exerted a marked influence on politics, though there was also talk of the "levelling" spirit and a lack of "due subordination." The "Republican Court" of 1789 preserved much of the older tradition in manners, but the prologue of Royall Tyler's "The Contrast," produced in New York in 1787, struck a more democratic note:

> Exult each patriot heart!—this night is shewn
> A piece, which we may fairly call our own;
> Where the proud titles of "My Lord! Your Grace!"
> To humble Mr. and plain Sir give place.[1]

Conservatives feared that social disintegration would follow the war-time interference with public order. The agrarian disturbances in New England culminating in Shays's Rebellion increased this sense of instability. Hostile critics abroad, making the most of such disorders, painted a gloomy picture of the United States drifting toward anarchy, and much was said of unruly frontier communities. Franklin and Jefferson insisted, however, that press reports were exaggerated and Jefferson noted the respect for life and property shown in the early stages of the Massachusetts uprising. A fair statement is that of Dr. David Ramsay: "To overset an established government unhinges many of those principles, which bind individuals to each other. A long time, and much prudence, will be necessary to reproduce a spirit of union and that reverence for government, without which society is a rope of sand."[2]

---

[1] J. T. Austin, *Life of Elbridge Gerry* (Boston, 1829), I, 131; Noah Webster, "General Description of the City of New-York," *Am. Mag.*, I (1787-1788), 226; Frank Monaghan, "The Results of the Revolution," A. C. Flick, ed., *History of the State of New York* (N. Y., 1933-1937), IV, 325; A. H. Quinn, ed., *Representative American Plays* (N. Y., 1917), 48.

[2] Franklin, *Writings*, IX, 489; Jefferson, *Works*, V, 238 ff.; David Ramsay, *The History of the American Revolution* (Phila., 1789), II, 323.

Generally speaking, the older private law survived the Revolution—the English common law, certain acts of Parliament and colonial statutes and judicial decisions— with some local variations. To quote the New York constitution: "such parts of the common law of England, and of the statute law of England and Great Britain, and of the acts of the Legislature of the colony of New York, as together did form the law of the said Colony" were to "be and continue the law of this State," subject to future legislation. About the extent to which this juristic inheritance needed adaptation to new conditions the early constitutions said little. A Virginia committee of which Jefferson, Pendleton and Wythe were members recommended some radical changes in the existing laws. According to Jefferson, the alterations would constitute "a system by which every fibre should be eradicated of antient or future aristocracy; and a foundation laid for a government truly republican." A principal result of these proposals was the repeal of primogeniture and entail.[1]

Jefferson also displayed a keen interest in penology and knew the European writings on this subject by Montesquieu and the Italian criminologist, Beccaria. His committee agreed to limit capital punishment to treason and murder, though this recommendation did not become law until 1796. In Pennsylvania the constitution directed the legislature to reform the colonial code so that punishments might be "less sanguinary, and in general more proportionate to the crimes." Franklin told an Italian jurist that no branch of law was more in need of reform. Rush not only opposed the death penalty for many crimes, but declared the time "not very distant, when the gallows, the pillory, the stocks, and the whipping post" would be regarded as barbarous. By 1786 Pennsylvania had reduced the

[1] Jefferson, *Works*, I, 77.

number of capital offenses and prohibited the more cruel forms of corporal punishment. The next decade brought further revision, the death penalty being eliminated except for murder in the first degree.[1]

In New York, where sixteen crimes were punishable by death for the first offense and severe flogging might be inflicted on women as well as men, the one substantial advance before 1790 was the constitutional provision securing the right of a defendant to counsel. This was nearly half a century before England established the principle. In New England some more or less academic discussion of penal reform took place. Yale seniors were set to debate whether American criminal law was not "too rigorous . . . for the present State of Society," and at the commencement of 1788 young Jeremiah Mason based his argument against capital punishment mainly on Beccaria. In general, the New England codes had been more humane than the British. An English visitor in Boston noted with surprise that forgery was not there a capital offense.[2]

Public interest was also being awakened to abuses in the management of prisons. As in England, such places were overcrowded and unsanitary, and the inmates were herded indiscriminately, with little or no regard to sex, age or degree of guilt. Early American reform efforts derived much inspiration from the work of John Howard, whose recently published *State of the Prisons*

[1] C. R. Lingley, *The Transition in Virginia from Colony to Commonwealth* (Columbia Univ., Studies, XXXVI, no. 2), 181-189; Chinard, *Jefferson*, 93-95; Jefferson, *Works*, II, 393 ff.; Franklin, *Writings*, IX, 1; Benjamin Rush, "An Enquiry into the Effects of Public Punishments upon Criminals, and upon Society," *Am. Museum*, II (1787), 142-154; Michael Kraus, "Eighteenth Century Humanitarianism," *Pa. Mag. of History and Biog.*, LX, 273 ff.; Nevins, *American States*, 454.

[2] *Ibid.*, 453; *The Constitution of the State of New York* (N. Y., 1777), Article XXXIV; G. B. Adams, *Constitutional History of England* (N. Y., 1934), 454; Stiles, *Diary*, III, 118, 328; Joseph Hadfield, *An Englishman in America, 1785* (D. S. Robertson, ed., Toronto, 1933), 185.

in England and Wales reached a third edition in 1784. With the formation at Philadelphia in 1787 of a society "for Alleviating the Miseries of Public Prisons" the influence of this "friend of mankind" was publicly acknowledged. Some of the worst penal abuses were presently remedied and in 1790 a law provided for other reforms. In New England, Isaiah Thomas published two articles commending the Philadelphia society; but its most significant influence appeared some years later in New York, where Thomas Eddy, Quaker migrant from Philadelphia, became the most effective advocate of prison reform.[1]

A special phase of penal reform pertained to the treatment of debtors. In 1785 they constituted half the inmates of Philadelphia prisons. Often dependent on charity even for the necessaries of life, they suffered, like other prisoners, from brutal keepers. Public attention began now to be drawn to these abuses. In 1786 Yale seniors argued the affirmative of the question: "Whether Imprisonment for Debt ought to be abolished in all civilized States." Here and there newspaper articles on the situation excited sympathy, and philanthropic men sought to ameliorate hardships. In 1783 the New York legislature voted to free insolvent persons from prison; but the bill was vetoed by the council of revision, and for nearly half a century the law remained with only minor changes. Partial remedies were all that public opinion would support. Meantime, the New York Society for the Relief of Distressed Debtors mitigated some cases of extreme need.[2]

[1] Kraus, "Eighteenth Century Humanitarianism," 272 ff.; Blake McKelvey, *American Prisons* (Univ. of Chicago, *Social Service Ser.*, 1936), 5-7; Nevins, *American States*, 458 ff.; L. N. Richardson, *A History of Early American Magazines, 1741-1789* (N. Y., 1931), 266.

[2] Nevins, *American States*, 456 ff.; Stiles, *Diary*, III, 209; Division of Archives and History, *The American Revolution in New York* (Albany, 1926), 236; S. I. Pomerantz, *New York, an American City, 1783-1803* (Columbia Univ., *Studies*, no. 442), 322 ff.

The most successful humanitarian effort of the Revolutionary era concerned slavery. Until 1783 the institution was not finally ended in any of the thirteen states. In that year, as we have seen, it became illegal in Massachusetts through judicial interpretation of its bill of rights. Three years earlier Pennsylvania had begun its program of gradual emancipation. The Quakers continued their efforts after the passage of this law and one of the last acts of that devoted Friend, Anthony Benezet, was a letter to Queen Charlotte on the slave trade. Revolutionary ideas of natural rights, as well as economic factors, contributed to the progress of abolitionism, which was also related to contemporary discussion in England. Granville Sharp, the outstanding British antislavery advocate, corresponded on this subject with Franklin, John Adams and Jay. Adams declared that Sharp "merited the respect and esteem of all men, amongst whom liberty and humanity are not disregarded." The Pennsylvania society "for Promoting the Abolition of Slavery and the Relief of Free Negroes unlawfully held in Bondage" elected Sharp an honorary member and corresponded with the English Society for the Abolition of the Slave Trade. The New York Society for Promoting the Manumission of Slaves, headed by Jay, had among its foreign associates Sharp, Lafayette and Brissot de Warville.[1]

The emancipation act of 1780 gradually reduced the number of slaves in Pennsylvania until by 1800 less than two thousand remained. During the postwar decade local reformers worked to improve the condition of Negroes generally and advance the antislavery cause in the country at large. In 1789 a society was formed for "the free instruction of orderly Blacks and People

---

[1] Adams, Works, VIII, 387; Anthony Benezet, "Letter on the Slave Trade," Am. Museum, I, 122-123; Michael Kraus, "Slavery Reform in the Eighteenth Century," Pa. Mag. of History and Biog., LX, 53-66.

of Color." In the other Middle Atlantic states, where slaves were more numerous, not even gradual emancipation was undertaken during this period. Nevertheless antislavery sentiment was growing. In New Jersey, where the Quakers were active, Governor William Livingston favored abolition and freed his own Negroes, and in 1786 the legislature prohibited further importations. In New York, which had more slaves than any other Northern state, Jay and his associates kept the issue alive. In 1777 he had proposed the constitutional prohibition of slavery, but the convention rejected it two to one. In 1784, when gradual emancipation was voted by both houses of the legislature, it was vetoed by the council of revision. Though some Negroes were freed because of army service or through the confiscation of Tory estates, and though voluntary manumission by owners was facilitated, New York in 1790 possessed more than twenty thousand slaves.[1]

In New England, which had few slaves, emancipation came more easily. In 1783 New Hampshire, like Massachusetts, excluded human bondage by judicial interpretation, and in 1784 Rhode Island and Connecticut passed gradual-emancipation acts. If the vested interest of New Englanders in domestic slavery was small, both Massachusetts and Rhode Island had been deeply involved in the oversea traffic. Though the importation of slaves into these states had been prohibited, their people could still sell Negroes elsewhere. By 1789, however, both these states and Connecticut had made this practice illegal. Nevertheless, some New Englanders continued in the business. In 1789 John Quincy Adams found "remnants" of it in Newport, and even a decade later John Brown of Providence did not see why Americans, as

[1] E. R. Turner, *The Negro in Pennsylvania* (Wash., 1911), chaps. vi, viii, xii; Theodore Sedgwick, *A Memoir of the Life of William Livingston* (N. Y., 1833), 398 ff.; Division of Archives and History, *American Revolution in New York*, 237.

well as Britons, should not engage in that "lucrative traffic." William Bentley's Salem diary noted violations of the law in that neighborhood and a tendency to connive at them. In the Federal Convention some New England delegates voted against prohibition of the slave trade before 1808; but their chief motive was probably to keep the Lower South in the Union and also to prevent more burdensome restraints on Congress's power to regulate commerce.[1]

White servitude seems not to have been much discussed and sales of white servants, for terms, were still held in American ports. Efforts were made, however, to protect such persons, notably by the German societies of Philadelphia, New York and Maryland, and in Pennsylvania also through the new office of "Register of German Passengers." Maryland reduced the period of maximum servitude to four years. Though in 1784 a New York newspaper article condemned "the traffic of White People, heretofore countenanced in this State," as contrary to Revolutionary principles, its protest proved ineffective.[2]

The status of women excited little attention except in relation to education. Dr. Rush was a promoter of two girls' schools in Philadelphia and set forth his liberal views for a wider public in *Thoughts upon Female Education* (1787). In Boston the selectmen approved a school for young ladies conducted by Caleb Bingham, a recent Dartmouth graduate who published, especially for his pupils, *The Young Ladys Accidence or a Short and Easy Introduction to English Grammar* (1785). Among the representative New Englanders of this period

[1] Du Bois, *Suppression of the Slave-Trade*, 73, 82, 229-232; J. Q. Adams, *Life in a New England Town* (Boston, 1903), 174; William Bentley, *Diary* (Salem, 1905-1914), I, 104 ff., 384-386.

[2] Samuel McKee, *Labor in Colonial New York, 1664-1776* (Columbia Univ., *Studies*, no. 410), 175-178; Erna Risch, "Immigrant Societies before 1820," *Pa. Mag. of History and Biog.*, LX, 15-33.

who taught girls either separately or in coeducational academies were Timothy Dwight, the Reverend Jedidiah Morse, author of the *American Geography*, and Noah Webster. Webster prepared a public lecture on the "Importance of Female Education in domestick Life, in Society, and in Government." [1]

Advocacy of female education was not, however, generally associated with "advanced" ideas on the status of the sex. Enos Hitchcock, a Providence clergyman who wrote on the training of girls and who rejected some traditional views of female inferiority, insisted on the subordinate position of the wife. There was, however, more emphasis on the mother's part in training sons for citizenship. A writer in the *Pennsylvania Gazette* in 1787 suggested that women had a peculiar interest in maintaining orderly republican institutions as against either monarchy or radical democracy. In monarchies they were considered primarily as "mothers for soldiers"; only under a free government could they "retain their rank as rational beings." Yale students went so far as to debate "Whether Women ought to be admitted into the Magistracy and Government of Empires and Republics." [2] Abigail Adams considered her American sisters superior to English society women, who seemed to abandon "the softness peculiarly characteristic of our sex for the masculine attire and manners of Amazonians." Jedidiah Morse, an orthodox New England pastor, thought the New England women he knew "genteel, easy and agreeable" as well as good household managers. One British visitor found the Boston ladies too reserved. [3]

[1] Mary S. Benson, *Women in Eighteenth-Century America* (Columbia Univ., *Studies*, no. 405), chap. v.

[2] *Ibid.;* Stiles, *Diary*, III, 167.

[3] Mrs. John Adams, *Letters* (C. F. Adams, ed., Boston, 1848), 175; J. T. Adams, *New England in the Republic* (Boston, 1926), 77-79; Bentley, *Diary*, I, 118; Hadfield, *Englishman in America*, 191; Jedidiah Morse, *The American Geography* (Elizabethtown, N. J., 1789), 148.

Other contemporary comments shed light on manners generally. Schoepf believed they were improving and that Philadelphians had profited by contact with the French. Noah Webster noted the prevailing "sociability and hospitality" of New York City with the passing of war-time animosities. The city was again the state capital and, between 1785 and 1790, also that of the Union. This had its advantages for the "best people," though sturdy patriots complained of extravagance in dress, the loss of republican simplicity and undue fraternizing with former Tories. At least one foreign observer found in Charleston "a finer mode of life" than in the Northern cities and "more evidence of courtesy . . . without punctiliousness." [1]

In most instances the leaders of colonial society formed the nucleus of the corresponding postwar group, reënforced by people who had gained prominence through public service or business enterprise. Some families had migrated from lesser communities to the larger centers. Boston attracted families from other Massachusetts towns and some New Englanders migrated to New York. Urban society retained much of its provincial flavor, and the innovations of fashion were not radical. When Washington was inaugurated, gentlemen dressed much as had their fathers—in cocked hats, wigs and queues, long coats and waistcoats, silk breeches with buckles, and long stockings. For women, English styles prevailed with some infusion of French modes. The most conspicuous change was the reappearance of the hoop skirt. [2]

In New England the relaxation of Puritan manners continued. Though dancing was no new thing in the

---

[1] Schoepf, *Travels*, I, 97 ff.; II, 164-167; Pomerantz, *New York*, 109-110, chap. ix; Noah Webster, "Description of New York in 1786," *N. Y. Directory for 1786*, xv.

[2] R. A. East, *Business Enterprise in the American Revolutionary Era* (Columbia Univ., *Studies*, no. 439), 230 ff.; W. B. Weeden, *Economic and Social History of New England* (Boston, 1890-1891), II, 858 ff.

towns, one is surprised to find Morse calling it "the principal and favorite amusement" in this region. The diary of John Quincy Adams, then a law student in Newburyport, gives a similar impression of gayeties there. Mrs. Adams's letters from abroad show her adjusting herself to European usage in such matters as theatrical and operatic entertainments. Stage dancing she saw at first with "disgust," but later "with pleasure" though not without misgivings. Opposition to the theater was weakening in Massachusetts, but the official ban was not finally removed until the next decade. Not all the foes of the drama lived in New England. When the Old American Company opened its New York season in 1785, seven hundred persons signed an unsuccessful appeal to the legislature to suppress the performances. In Philadelphia the Southwark Theatre reopened, though the opposition was strong enough to prevent formal repeal of the law against it until 1789.[1]

Organizations for social recreation remained much as in colonial days. Besides such older groups as the societies of St. George, St. Andrew and St. Patrick, there were more recent German societies. Brissot de Warville was pleased by the politeness and agreeable conversation of a Boston club. The Wednesday Evening Club there, visited by President Stiles in 1787, included clergymen, lawyers, physicians and merchants. He heard a lawyer tell of his travels and met Charles Bulfinch, then beginning his distinguished architectural career. In New York, convivial groups bore such names as Sub Rosa, Turtle and Black Friars. Among the craft organizations the Gold and Silver-Smith's Society and

[1] Morse, *American Geography*, 148; Mrs. Adams, *Letters*, 234; Justin Winsor, ed., *Memorial History of Boston, 1630-1880* (Boston, 1880-1881), IV, 359 ff.; Pomerantz, *New York*, 475; A. H. Quinn, *A History of the American Drama from the Beginning to the Civil War* (N. Y., 1923), 61-62.

the Society of Peruke Makers, Hair Dressers, etc. included social features.[1]

Masonry continued to flourish. The Massachusetts Grand Lodge of Scottish Rite Masons now took occasion to declare itself "free and independent in its government and official authority, of any other Grand Lodge, or Grand Master in the universe." Chancellor Robert R. Livingston headed the New York Grand Lodge of Free and Accepted Masons. President Stiles was told in 1784 that there were a hundred and eighty-seven organizations in the United States. He thought the fraternity would prosper unless it developed "sinister national & illiberal Views," in which case there might be a "storm." In 1787 the *American Museum* printed a defense of Masonry as helpful to good citizenship and a safeguard against exaggerated nationalism, which "often destroys in warlike republics, the love of general humanity." [2]

In brief, the young republic made some progress toward realizing the Revolutionary ideal of equality. State legislation had restricted the slave trade, and several Northern states had either ended human servitude or provided for gradual emancipation. The abolition of primogeniture and entail favored a wider distribution of landed property; hereditary privileges were constitutionally excluded; and some states had extended the suffrage. Yet the conservative classes were still strong. Though weakened by the emigration of Loyalists and the confiscation of Tory estates, they re-formed their lines with new accessions from the rising capitalist group. Class consciousness was too deeply rooted to be ignored except by doctrinaire reformers. The antislavery efforts

[1] J. P. Brissot de Warville, *New Travels in the United States* (London, 1792), 103; Stiles, *Diary*, III, 284; Pomerantz, *New York*, 468 ff.; *N. Y. Directory for 1786.*

[2] J. H. Tatsch, *Freemasonry in the Thirteen Colonies* (N. Y., 1929), chap. iv; Stiles, *Diary*, III, 105-106; anon., "The Influence of Free Masonry upon Society," *Am. Museum*, I, 469.

of Southern liberals failed save in the prohibition of Negro importations by the border states. Property qualifications, though sometimes reduced, were still general, and Jefferson's endeavors to equalize educational opportunities came to nil. In the eyes of advanced reformers certain features of the Federal Constitution, especially its protection of vested interests, seemed likely to interfere with the full realization of democratic ideals. John Quincy Adams considered regretfully that the adoption of the new system would be "a grand point gained in favour of the aristocratic party," and he added, "it is hard to give up a system which I have always been taught to cherish, and to confess that a free government is inconsistent with human nature." [1]

[1] Adams, *Life in a New England Town*, 46.

CHAPTER XIV

ECONOMIC RECOVERY AND ADVANCE

IF the so-called "Critical Period" had depressing aspects, it had also a record of important achievements—in economic recovery, in adjustment to new situations and in positive contributions to the building of a new order. The rural economy involved troublesome problems of reconstruction. The Southern tidewater campaigns of 1780 and 1781 had left their mark: houses burned, plantation products destroyed, slaves and livestock carried off. In the Lower South particularly, estates had been abandoned and titles confused by successive confiscations of property as control shifted from one party to the other. The planter also faced difficulties growing out of his earlier dependence on British merchants. What could he do about prewar debts and the system under which those debts had been incurred?

Pre-Revolutionary British claims against American debtors aggregated five million pounds, with more than four million charged against the inhabitants of the Southern states, those of Virginia owing much the largest amount. To get rid of this burden, the Virginia legislature in 1777 had passed a sequestration act permitting borrowers to defray their obligations to British creditors by paper-money payments to the state treasury. Many representative citizens followed this advantageous plan—when the act was repealed in 1780 sixty pounds of Virginia currency were worth only one pound sterling. With the coming of peace, however, the planters were confronted with the treaty agreement that the British should "meet with no lawful impediment to the recovery of the full value in sterling money of all *bona fide* debts heretofore contracted." Some influential politicians argued that the clause be disregarded. "If," it was said, "we are now to pay the debts due the British merchants, what have we been fighting for all this while?" One argument in defense of this position was the British failure to surrender the Western posts and to pay for slaves their armies had carried away. Nevertheless, George Mason and James Madison kept up the fight for an honest settlement, maintaining that the war had not been waged "to avoid our just debts, or cheat our creditors." Furthermore, it was important to meet existing obligations in order to secure future credits.[1]

American representatives abroad suggested compromise with British creditors. Insistence on immediate reimbursement, said Jefferson, would ruin both parties since the planters had not yet recovered from their war losses. One proposed compromise would have provided for gradual payment, with remission of the interest accruing during the war. Indeed, some British creditors were willing to accept such terms and thus avoid troublesome litigation. Nevertheless, during the Confederation period, the problem remained largely unsolved. In 1788 a Glasgow firm reported that of several "prominent Virginians" only three had offered to settle. It was natural, then, that such persons should oppose the provisions of the Constitution empowering the federal judiciary to hear suits brought by foreign creditors and requiring all judges to enforce treaties as "the supreme law of the land . . . anything in the constitution or laws of any state to the contrary notwithstanding." Debtors now had to face adverse judicial decisions or settlement out of court, with the payment of heavy obligations, often

---

[1] I. S. Harrell, *Loyalism in Virginia* (Durham, 1926), 26 ff., 80 ff.; W. W. Henry, *Patrick Henry* (N. Y., 1891), II, 187.

of long standing. Some hard-pressed borrowers found relief through migration to the West.[1]

In trying to avoid future dependence on British merchants the Virginia planters were asking whether wartime markets in Continental Europe could be retained and developed, thus breaking the mother country's monopoly. Immediate results proved disappointing, however, partly because of the strongly intrenched monopoly of the French farmers-general. In 1785 Jefferson declared that tobacco exports were going "almost entirely to England" to pay off the planters' debts. The same year Madison wrote, "Our trade was never more compleatly monopolized by G. B."[2] The people also felt at a disadvantage in relation to the Northern merchants, especially those of Baltimore and Philadelphia. Tobacco prices were low as compared with those prevailing in Philadelphia and imported goods cost more. Madison proposed a law for concentrating oversea commerce at Alexandria and Norfolk—"a Philadelphia or a Baltimore among ourselves"—but his suggestion was not adopted.[3]

The burden of indebtedness combined with the scarcity of hard money produced a strong inflationary movement. Though paper-money legislation finally failed of passage in Virginia and Maryland, the conservatives proved less successful in the Carolinas and Georgia, where extreme measures were adopted, including currency issues, stay laws, postponement of taxes and, in South Carolina, a law making land a legal tender. The peak of the South's difficulties was probably reached by

[1] Harrell, *Loyalism in Virginia*, 143-151, 176; Thomas Jefferson, *Works* (P. L. Ford, ed., N. Y., 1904-1905), V. 88-91, 309 ff.

[2] L. C. Gray, *History of Agriculture in the Southern United States to 1860* (Carnegie Inst., *Publs.*, no. 430), II, 599 ff.; Jefferson, *Works*, IV, 386, 470, 508; James Madison, *Writings* (Gaillard Hunt, ed., N. Y., 1900-1910), II, 147.

[3] *Ibid.*, II, 57, 65, 148; Gray, *Agriculture*, II, 597-599, 619-621.

1786, with some improvement during the next three years. Meantime permanent gains had been made through the elimination of quitrents and the abolition of entail and primogeniture.

In the matter of slavery Southern interests and opinions varied. In 1778 and 1783 Maryland and Virginia ended the slave trade, and in 1786 North Carolina imposed a prohibitory duty. Neither of the two southernmost states, however, went so far. Georgia continued the traffic without interruption, while South Carolina, which imported many Negroes after the war, contented itself with acts for a temporary suspension. The Philadelphia Convention reflected this divergence of Southern opinion. George Mason of Virginia called the "infernal traffic" a source of economic weakness. In the final balloting, Virginia voted against the compromise which prevented prohibition of the slave importations before 1808. South Carolina and Georgia, however, emphasizing their peculiar dependence on servile blacks, insisted on freedom of action. The South Carolina delegates were criticized at home for accepting any compromise, though C. C. Pinckney considered it unavoidable because of Northern "religious and political prejudices." [1]

Apart from idealistic considerations, the decadence of the plantation system favored the development of antislavery sentiment. Jefferson, regarding slavery as injurious also to the white owners, advocated gradual emancipation followed by colonization of the freedmen. The Marylanders, Charles Carroll and William Pinkney, expressed similar views. Such men were, however, in the minority. In 1786 Madison noted the scant courtesy with which antislavery petitions were treated and the unanimous rejection of a bill for "a general manu-

---

[1] Max Farrand, ed., *Records of the Federal Convention* (New Haven, 1911-1937), II, 364, 370-373, 416; III, 253-255.

mission." According to Jefferson, a few persons of "weight and worth of character" favored emancipation, while others, who approved it "in theory," lacked "the courage to divest their families of a property which however keeps their conscience inquiet." [1]

Plantation economy showed the continuing influence of prewar tendencies. Among contemporary observers, Phineas Bond observed that Maryland and Virginia lands, "greatly exhausted in the culture of tobacco," were being sown with grain. Meantime, however, new tobacco-growing areas appeared in the piedmont, the Lower South and Kentucky. Significant for the future was the modest advance in cotton culture. The number of bales exported rose from five in 1785 to nearly three hundred in 1788. Small as these figures seem, they encouraged proposals to stimulate production by bounties or protective duties. Rice and indigo were still the chief staples of South Carolina and, though rice exports were low after the war, they gradually increased. A similar recovery in indigo, however, proved only temporary.[2]

There was some discussion of the general position of farming in the social order. Jefferson thought the American commonwealths would be "virtuous" only as long as they were "chiefly agricultural." In crowded cities people would "become corrupt as in Europe." Washington after the war was much occupied with agricultural improvements. He corresponded with Arthur Young, the distinguished British authority whose *Annals of Agriculture* he read and admired, and Sir John Sinclair, later the first president of the British board of agriculture. Less conspicuous pioneers of scientific hus-

---

[1] Gray, *Agriculture*, II, 615-617; Jefferson, *Works*, IV, 49, 82-84, 447; J. R. Brackett, *Negro in Maryland* (Johns Hopkins Univ., *Studies*, extra vol. VI), 52-64, 148-155; Madison, *Writings*, II, 191 ff., 219.

[2] Gray, *Agriculture*, II, 605 ff., 679; Phineas Bond, "Letters," Am. Hist. Assoc., *Ann. Rep. for 1896*, I, 629.

bandry were John Alexander Binns, a Virginia farmer whose experiments promoted the use of gypsum as a fertilizer, and John Beale Bordley of Maryland, who in 1784 published a *Summary View of the Courses of Crops, in the Husbandry of England and Maryland.*[1]

Other persons were attracted by the trans-Alleghany country, whether as speculators or home makers, but this westward drain was offset by migration from the North and from Europe. A competent investigator believes that, in view of the shift of population from planters and slaves to white farmers, Southern society in this period more nearly resembled that of the Middle Atlantic states than at any other time before the Civil War.[2]

For the farmers of the Middle states the process of readjustment proved less difficult than for the Southerners. Despite talk of labor demoralized by army service, and the need to recover lost markets, there was soon a substantial improvement. Between 1786 and 1789 flour exports from Philadelphia more than doubled. Though rural New Yorkers shared in the postwar depression and complained of the scarcity of money, they probably suffered less than the city merchants. One source of anxiety in this period, as during the war, was the Hessian fly.[3] Suggestive of public interest in agricultural improvement was the formation in 1785 of the Philadelphia Society for Promoting Agriculture and the liberal space given to the subject in Carey's *American*

[1] Jefferson, *Works*, V, 374; P. L. Haworth, *George Washington: Farmer* (Indianapolis, 1915); George Washington, *Writings from the Original Manuscript Sources* (J. C. Fitzpatrick, ed., Wash., 1931-1940), XXVIII, 510 ff.

[2] Gray, *Agriculture*, II, 614.

[3] Bond, "Letters," 628-630; Tench Coxe, *View of the United States of America* (Phila., 1794), 64; E. W. Spaulding, *New York in the Critical Period* (D. R. Fox, ed., *N. Y. State Hist. Assoc. Ser.*, I), chap. i; P. W. Bidwell and J. I. Falconer, *History of Agriculture in the Northern United States, 1620-1860* (Carnegie Inst., *Publs.*, no. 358), 95.

Museum, which offered farmers premiums for superior products.[1]

As in the South, changes occurred in land tenure. Pennsylvania after making moderate compensation to the Penn family took over the ungranted proprietary lands and stopped quitrents. Though the lease-hold system was not abolished in New York until 1846, the payments were now to be made to the state and after 1786 might be commuted for a lump sum. At the close of the war only three manors survived. One of these had already been largely subdivided and the statutory abolition of entail and primogeniture (1782-1788) prepared the way for the future break-up of the Livingston and Van Rensselaer properties. The legislature also abolished certain feudal obligations already mostly obsolete, and the "Township Act" of 1788 eliminated the manor as a governmental unit. The status of tenants remained unsatisfactory, resulting in sporadic outbreaks during the next half-century that culminated in the antirent agitation of the eighteen-thirties and forties. In 1790, however, a visitor to the Van Rensselaer manor found over three thousand tenants with a rent roll of more than twelve thousand pounds in New York currency. The owner was represented as benevolent and popular, but determined to maintain his rights. In New York especially, the confiscation and sale of Tory estates brought a considerable redistribution of land ownership and undoubtedly had a certain leveling effect, partially offset, however, by new concentrations of property in the hands of speculative purchasers.[2]

[1] Articles by "Agricola," Cadwallader Ford, Joseph Greenleaf and Major Spooner in *Am. Museum,* I (1787), 37-41.

[2] W. R. Shepherd, *History of Proprietary Government in Pennsylvania* (Columbia Univ., *Studies,* VI), 86-93; Spaulding, *New York in the Critical Period,* chap. iii; Irving Mark, *Agrarian Conflicts in Colonial New York, 1711-1775* (Columbia Univ., *Studies,* no. 469), 206; H. B. Yoshpe, *The Disposition of Loyalist Estates* (N. Y., 1939); W. L. Smith, "Journal, 1790-1791," Mass. Hist. Soc., *Proceeds.,* LI, 54.

Contemporary accounts of rural New England differed. A young English traveler found that Rhode Island "peasants" were "miserably poor and in debt," but noted the charm of the Connecticut Valley with its "highly cultivated" lands. Agricultural improvement was being discussed in New England as well as elsewhere. In 1786 Metcalf Bowler of Providence published his *Agriculture and Practical Husbandry,* and four years later Samuel Deane, a Maine clergyman, brought out his *New England Farmer; or, Georgical Dictionary,* the first comprehensive work of its kind in the United States. Nevertheless, even so loyal a New Englander as Jedidiah Morse doubted whether there was much real advance in practical farming, for "common husbandmen" remained "in the old track of their forefathers." [1]

In other respects, too, the situation was unsatisfactory. The new Massachusetts constitution by favoring the mercantile interest through an undue representation of the maritime counties facilitated the repeal of debtor-relief legislation and the support of public credit by higher imposts and a hard-money policy. The agriculturist complained of deflation, lower prices for his products and more than his share of taxes. In January, 1782, a Worcester town meeting denounced the state liquor excise as an indirect and therefore disguised imposition "contrary to the genius of a free people" and declared spirituous beverages "absolutely necessary" for the refreshment of farm workers. Conservatives insisted that the husbandman's discontent was largely due to standards of living acquired in flush times which it was now hard to maintain. [2] Among still other rural

---

[1] Joseph Hadfield, *An Englishman in America, 1785* (D. S. Robertson, ed., Toronto, 1933), 175, 219; Jedidiah Morse, *The American Geography* (Elizabethtown, N. J., 1789), 182; James Warren, "Observations on Agriculture," *Am. Museum,* II (1787), 344 ff.

[2] R. V. Harlow, "Economic Conditions in Massachusetts during the American Revolution," Colon. Soc. of Mass., *Publs.,* XX, 183 ff.

grievances were excessive court expenses, harsh treatment of debtors, extortionate lawyers and scarcity of money. Continental veterans in the Connecticut Valley who had been paid in depreciated paper threatened to withhold their taxes. Joseph Hawley reported that citizens hitherto law-abiding were "on the point of turning to the Mobb," in which case sheriffs and their deputies would be "like Stubble before devouring fire." When the ringleader of a riot was arrested, his followers broke open the Springfield jail. Though order was restored, the situation remained critical and some malcontents declared that their present rulers were more expensive than "the Great men under George 3d." This was four years before the Shays uprising.[1]

The return of peace in 1783 led to an abnormal influx of British goods offered at low prices with liberal credits. Importers and their country customers bought more than they could afford and the merchants began to press their debtors. So commenced a new period of rural depression and smoldering resentment. The disorders proved most serious in Massachusetts, Rhode Island and New Hampshire, where demands for paper money and debtor-relief legislation became rife. The Shays revolt in Massachusetts started in 1786 with local meetings like those of 1782, chiefly in the inland counties. There were moderate demands for tax reform, but also such violent proposals as the "annihilation of the courts of common pleas and general sessions." Lawyers were denounced and jealousy of urban business was indicated by a proposal to remove the capital from Boston. On August 29 a mob seized the Northampton courthouse and prevented the judges from sitting. Similar disturbances occurred later in the western and central

---

[1] E. F. Brown, *Joseph Hawley, Colonial Radical* (N. Y., 1931), 184-189; E. F. Brown, ed., "Shays's Rebellion," *Am. Hist. Rev.*, XXXVI, 776-778.

counties and even farther east. State forces called to restore order were confronted by armed men, including Continental veterans; but serious fighting awaited the new year when the government, aided by contributions from well-to-do conservatives, was better prepared. The militia soon dispersed the poorly organized insurgents and order returned.[1]

Many who did not take up arms nevertheless sympathized with the rebels. President Stiles was told that more than two thirds of the Berkshire people did so. Similarly, Stephen Higginson believed the disaffection "much more deeply rooted, and extensive than was apprehended." He thought the radicals would not rest easy till they either controlled the government and "divided property with their betters," or were forced "to submit to their proper stations and mode of living." The government's first impulse after Shays's defeat was to take drastic action and several leaders were sentenced to death; but a reaction soon followed. The conservative governor was overwhelmingly defeated for reëlection and the membership of the legislature was radically changed. A new amnesty act was passed and the insurgent leaders were pardoned.[2]

In New Hampshire and Vermont also there were agrarian demonstrations with some rioting. The New Hampshire lawmakers were for a time besieged by a mob. Order was soon restored, however. The Rhode Island legislature, controlled by the radicals, enacted the desired paper-money and relief measures. In Connecticut, which was less disturbed, one worried observer reported some sympathizers there with "Shays and his

---

[1] Kenneth Colegrove, "New England Town Mandates," Colon. Soc. of Mass., *Publs.*, XXI, 428; J. T. Adams, *New England in the Republic* (Boston, 1926), chap. vi.

[2] *Ibid.*; Ezra Stiles, *Letters & Papers* (Isabel M. Calder, ed., New Haven, 1933), 73 ff.; Stephen Higginson, "Letters," Am. Hist. Assoc., *Ann. Rep. for 1896*, I, 743-760.

banditti." A few Massachusetts insurgents took refuge in New York, causing a certain amount of anxiety there for a time, though it soon passed.

To some conservative leaders the challenge of the radicals was perhaps not wholly unwelcome. Promoters of "big business" and a stronger national government used the Shays Rebellion to prove the need of a bulwark against subversive influences. In Massachusetts opinion shifted definitely in favor of the proposed federal convention. "A Citizen of Pennsylvania" emphasized the menace of a radicalism becoming more general and more formidable: "The ambition of the poor, and the avarice of the rich demagogue can never be restrained upon the narrow scale of a state government." Henry Lee reported to George Washington the prevailing dread of impending anarchy, and Jay was similarly disturbed. Washington himself was comparatively moderate. Deprecating the severity of the Massachusetts authorities, he recognized the danger "of entirely alienating the affections of a people from their government." Nevertheless, he too saw in the situation evidence of the need for a federal convention.[1] So it came about that many conservatives espoused the new Constitution, partly at least as a means of curbing the radicals, who in turn disliked its restraints on state legislation and feared that the commercial interests would dominate the government.

Another effect of the war was to foster interest in better communications. Washington was a leading promoter of public works, including improved highways. A less conspicuous advocate of good roads was the New

---

[1] R. A. East, "The Massachusetts Conservatives in the Critical Period," R. B. Morris, ed., *The Era of the American Revolution* (N. Y., 1939), 349-391; anon., "Address to the Freemen of the United States," *Am. Museum*, I, 429-432; E. C. Burnett, ed., *Letters of Members of the Continental Congress* (Wash., 1921-1936), VIII, 486; John Jay, *Correspondence and Public Papers* (H. P. Johnston, ed., N. Y., 1890-1893), III, 212; J. C. Fitzpatrick, *George Washington Himself* (Indianapolis, 1933), 455-457.

York engineer, Christopher Colles, who published his *Survey of the Roads of the United States of America* (1789), based on observations in New York and Pennsylvania. In 1785-1786 Virginia built a turnpike between Alexandria and the Shenandoah Valley, and Maryland authorized several from Baltimore westward. Pennsylvania also passed some road legislation.[1]

The best-known bridge to be built was the one across the Charles River between Boston and Charlestown. The master workman was Lemuel Cox, once imprisoned as a Loyalist. This structure, over fifteen hundred feet long, was opened in 1786 with elaborate festivities on the anniversary of Bunker Hill, and Cox was honored in a contemporary broadside as "our patriot Cox." Following the financial success of this enterprise two other long toll bridges were erected in this neighborhood, one across the Mystic from Boston to the North Shore and the other connecting Beverly with Salem. Progress elsewhere was slower. Philadelphia still had only a floating bridge across the Schuylkill, and New Jersey plans for toll bridges on the river crossings between New York and Philadelphia did not come to fruition until the next decade.[2]

Land travel continued to be difficult. An Englishman going by wagon from Albany to Boston spent four days on the way to Springfield, crossing the Connecticut in a flat-bottomed boat. It took three days more by the "great road" to reach Boston. In 1783 Jefferson, being misled about the ferries between Philadelphia and Baltimore, lost two days "braving all weather and plunging thro' thick and thin." His party arrived in Baltimore

[1] B. H. Meyer and others, *History of Transportation in the United States before 1860* (Carnegie Inst., *Publs.*, no. 215 C), 51; J. S. Davis, *Essays in the Earlier History of American Corporations* (*Harvard Econ. Studies*, XVI), II, 217-219.

[2] *Ibid.*, 204-213; Meyer and others, *Transportation*, 140.

on the fifth night from Philadelphia.[1] As the years passed, however, stage service was somewhat extended. A "flying machine" undertook to carry passengers the ninety-mile journey between New York and Philadelphia in a day. An important figure in this field was Levi Pease, a Massachusetts blacksmith who now began a line of stages from Boston to Hartford and later to New York. By 1786 the main mail route from New Hampshire to Georgia was served by stagecoaches, though postriders were employed on minor routes.[2]

Tavern accommodations varied, then as now. The bugs at one place, wrote a wayfarer in the South, "made a heartier dinner on me than I did on my bacon and eggs." In one stretch of twenty-six miles he found no tavern at all. An English traveler from Albany to Boston characterized the inns on the way as "indifferent," "tolerable" and "excellent." Brissot de Warville called the Pease tavern at Worcester "a charming house" offering "a good American dinner." According to Schoepf, the German hostelries in the Middle states provided warm stoves, good beer, sausages and sauerkraut.[3]

Since domestic trade was still carried largely by water, inland waterways were of the first importance. Jedidiah Morse waxed enthusiastic about the possibilities of improving them by means of canals so as to make the American states into "a cluster of large and fertile islands" in easy communication with one another. Interest in such projects produced more corporate charters

[1] Hadfield, *Englishman in America*, 172-180; Jefferson, *Works*, IV, 125-126.

[2] J. D. Schoepf, *Travels in the Confederation, 1783-1784* (A. J. Morrison, ed., Phila., 1911), I, 42; W. E. Rich, *The History of the United States Post Office to the Year 1829* (*Harvard Econ. Studies*, XXVII), chap. iv; O. W. Holmes, "Levi Pease, the Father of New England Stage-Coaching," *Journ. of Econ. and Business History*, III, 241-263.

[3] Smith, "Journal," 66-75; Hadfield, *Englishman in America*, 169 ff.; J. P. Brissot de Warville, *New Travels in the United States* (London, 1792), 123; Schoepf, *Travels*, II, 23.

and other legislative support than any comparable type of business enterprise, though the tangible results were disappointing.[1]

The improvement of the James and Potomac rivers had been discussed before the Revolution; and now, largely on George Washington's initiative, the subject was taken up by the two Chesapeake states, which presently granted identical charters to the Potomac Company. Washington was made president of the company and by May, 1785, over forty thousand pounds sterling of stock had been subscribed. Obstructions in the Potomac were to be removed as far as western Maryland and one or two locks built. Construction soon began and by 1789 boats descended from Cumberland to the Great Falls above Georgetown. But expert direction was lacking, further work was delayed, and the high hopes of the promoters were never realized. The James River Company, chartered the same year, was expected to clear navigation from the upper James to tidewater and dig a canal around the falls above Richmond. Progress proved slow, however, and, except in the immediate vicinity of Richmond, little was accomplished before the turn of the century.[2]

Two other projects, also unsuccessful, were the Susquehanna Canal from the lower Susquehanna to the Pennsylvania line, and one from the Chesapeake to the Delaware. In New York, too, there were ambitious but unrealized schemes. Christopher Colles in 1785 published his *Proposals for the Settlement of Western New York and for the Improvement of Inland Navigation between Albany and Oswego*, but the requisite capital

[1] Morse, *American Geography*, 36; Davis, *History of American Corporations*, II, 184.

[2] *Ibid.*, II, chap. iii; Corra Bacon-Foster, *Early Chapters in the Development of the Potomac Route to the West* (Wash., 1912); W. F. Dunaway, *James River and Kanawha Company* (N. Y., 1922), chaps. i-ii.

to carry out his program was not forthcoming. Somewhat later Elkanah Watson after visiting the Mohawk Valley interested Governor Clinton and General Schuyler in canal-building proposals. As a result, companies were formed to connect the Hudson with Lake Ontario and Lake Champlain, but these undertakings had to wait.[1]

In oversea navigation there was no marked improvement, though there was a tendency toward greater tonnage, especially in the East Indian and China trades, which needed more men and armament to cope with pirates. The *Massachusetts*, completed in 1789 and said to be the largest American vessel so far built, carried seventy-five officers and men with a possible armament of thirty-six guns. A little later came the *Grand Turk* of five hundred and sixty-four tons. Transatlantic voyages were still of uncertain length. In 1784 Bishop Thomas Coke spent forty-six days at sea between Bristol and New York, but in the same year Jefferson, sailing for France by way of an English port, reported a "remarkably short" voyage of "only 19 days from land to land." As in colonial times, British packets supplied a fairly regular passenger and mail service between Falmouth and New York, and there was a French line between New York and L'Orient.[2]

Largely through the efforts of Postmaster-General Ebenezer Hazard, improvements were introduced into the postal service: more stages over existing routes; new "cross-posts" from the "great post-road"; more frequent mails; and reduced postage. Letters went from New Hampshire to Georgia three times a week in summer and twice a week in winter. New interior routes were pro-

[1] Davis, *History of American Corporations*, II, 157 ff.
[2] W. B. Weeden, *Economic and Social History of New England* (Boston, 1890-1891), II, 822, 833; Thomas Coke, *Extracts of the Journals of Five Visits to America* (London, 1793), 7-13; Jefferson, *Works*, IV, 371; Rich, *United States Post Office*, 60.

vided in the Carolinas and Georgia, and an important extension was inaugurated from Philadelphia to Pittsburgh. Yet many towns near the coast had no post offices, and Pittsburgh had the only one beyond the Alleghanies. According to Hazard's successor, Samuel Osgood, there were eighty-nine offices in 1790. The highest postal revenue was at Philadelphia: $1530.73 for the quarter ending January 5, 1790. These small receipts resulted partly from the government's failure to enforce its monopoly of the mail service. Nor was the privacy of correspondence always respected. Jefferson and his Virginia friends protected themselves by using ciphers.[1]

Of slight immediate importance but of great future significance were the pioneer experiments in steam navigation. In 1784 James Rumsey showed Washington a model of a mechanism for propelling a boat upstream, which might prove "of the greatest possible utility in inland Navigation." With Washington's help Rumsey secured a monopoly for operating his invention in Maryland and Virginia waters. The use of steam was not then proposed; but in 1787 Rumsey exhibited a vessel propelled by water thrown out from the stern by a steam pump. After working on this device for several years and securing English and American patents, he died in England without attracting the necessary capital.[2]

About a year after Washington saw Rumsey's first model, he was visited by John Fitch. This Connecticut Yankee discussed his plans with Washington, secured monopoly rights from the Middle-state legislatures, and organized a company to promote his invention. By 1787 he had built a forty-five-foot boat with paddles

[1] *Ibid.*, chaps. iv-v; *American State Papers* (Wash., 1832-1861), *Post Office Department*, 9-12; J. B. McMaster, *History of the People of the United States* (N. Y., 1883-1913), I, 43; Jefferson, *Works*, IV, 434.
[2] George Washington, *Diaries, 1748-1799* (J. C. Fitzpatrick, ed., Boston, 1925), II, 282, 327.

worked by steam, which he exhibited to members of the Federal Convention. The next year Fitch constructed a larger vessel with a steam-driven paddle wheel, which moved twenty miles upstream in a little over three hours. Franklin mentioned this experiment to a French correspondent as important "philosophical news." By 1790 a third boat was making regularly scheduled trips on the Delaware and patents were secured from the American and French governments; but though Fitch went farther than Rumsey, he could not make his project commercially profitable.[1]

A fundamental problem confronting the American merchant was that of combining his new freedom from the British colonial system with the least possible loss of its advantages. As soon as peace was assured, British merchants turned their energies to recovering their old customers and for that purpose offered liberal credits. The consequent glutting of postwar markets embarrassed the mercantile community on both sides of the water and a severe depression followed. Stephen Higginson reported the export of so much cash that New England was "almost drained of Money," with trade "at a very low Ebb and still declining."[2]

The transition from war-time activities to normal conditions was further complicated by Great Britain's commercial policy. Though efforts to negotiate a commercial treaty failed, a few advantages previously enjoyed in the mother country's markets were in fact continued, including the exemption from "alien" duties on some raw materials shipped to British ports in British ships. Certain other American commodities were put on the same footing as imports from a British colony,

[1] *Ibid.*, II, 432; Ezra Stiles, *Literary Diary* (F. B. Dexter, ed., N. Y., 1901), III, 279; Benjamin Franklin, *Writings* (Albert Smyth, ed., N. Y., 1907), IX, 679.
[2] Higginson, "Letters," 719-725; *The Commerce of Rhode Island* (Mass. Hist. Soc., *Colls.*, LXIX-LXX), II, 166-176, 196.

and still others were admitted free. In general, however, it was assumed that the Americans, now outside the empire, must be treated like other foreigners. Furthermore, it was argued that, since British merchants would get most of the American trade in any case, the old commercial system should be maintained with no substantial concessions.[1]

The parliamentary duties on fish oil, blubber, whale fins and spermaceti eliminated an important market for the New Englanders, while their rum was kept from Newfoundland and Nova Scotia. Meantime, the shipping of the mother country was protected against competition by the exclusion of American vessels from the British West Indies. Furthermore, New England fish and lumber could not go to those islands, even in British ships. These measures, effectively enforced, would have had disastrous consequences for New England business. All persons interested in the fisheries—seamen, shipowners and other investors—would not only have lost a principal market for fish, but also the specie and bills of credit from this trade which had balanced an excess of imports over exports in the colonial account with Great Britain. So, wrote Higginson, the payment of American indebtedness must be indefinitely postponed and "despair and discontent" become general in the seaboard towns.[2] The old "bread colonies" also suffered from the closing of the West Indies to American shipping, though their foodstuffs could still be carried there in British ships.

To convince the British of the wisdom of a more liberal policy, it was pointed out that the Americans might otherwise turn to the French. Suggested concessions were the free admission of oil to Britain; the opening of

[1] E. R. Johnson and others, *History of the Domestic and Foreign Commerce of the United States* (Carnegie Inst., *Publs.*, no. 215 A), I, 129-131; Lord Sheffield, *Observations on the Commerce of the American States* (6th edn., London, 1784), 134 ff., 202 ff., 265.

[2] Higginson, "Letters," 719-725, 771.

the West Indian trade with the right to ship West Indian products to Britain; and the removal of restrictions on commerce with British North America.   In London John Adams did what he could and, meeting with no success, proposed retaliatory duties against imports carried in foreign or, specifically, British bottoms.   Something was done by the states.   New Hampshire charged foreign vessels a tax three times that required of American ships, and Pennsylvania imposed discriminating levies on the shipping of countries having no commercial treaty with the United States.   State action was obviously inadequate, however, and amendments to the Articles of Confederation permitting federal action were defeated.[1]

In view of the British restrictions attention was given to the possibility of developing markets in Continental Europe and its colonies.   During the war the French and Spaniards had relaxed their commercial regulations so that commerce with these countries had assumed large proportions. Now, however, France and Spain resumed, in the main, their prewar policies.   Though the French permitted a limited traffic with their West Indies, it was hampered by tariff duties.[2]

Meantime the commercial treaty of 1782 encouraged trade with Holland and the Dutch islands.   Americans sold Dutch traders tobacco and rice in exchange for various products from other Continental countries and the Far East: drygoods, hardware, French claret, Russia duck, tea and "Batavia arrack." Dutch firms maintained branches in the United States and were said to undersell the English.   Between 1785 and 1788 the shipping between Dutch and American ports greatly increased, the

[1] A. A. Giesecke, *American Commercial Legislation before 1789* (Univ. of Pa., *Publs.*, no. 23), 125 ff.

[2] Alexander Hamilton, *Industrial and Commercial Correspondence* (A. H. Cole, ed., *Business History Studies*, I), 165-180.

Americans exporting more than they imported. The Dutch also invested largely in American securities and, if more cautious about credits than the English, seem to have been fairly liberal. The volume of Dutch-American commerce is hard to estimate, however, since a ship's nationality was frequently disguised by various devices.[1] Efforts were also made to develop connections with the more northern European ports. Christopher Champlin of Newport had correspondents in Hamburg, Copenhagen, Göteborg and St. Petersburg. In 1783 Russian ships reached Baltimore with hemp and cordage, and a Salem ship made a pioneer voyage to St. Petersburg.[2]

The Mediterranean trade suffered, as in earlier years, from the Barbary pirates. The United States, no longer protected by the British navy, negotiated its own treaty with the emperor of Morocco in 1787, but could do nothing with Algiers and Tripoli. American ships were seized and their crews imprisoned. Protection was sometimes secured, however, by using forged passes, not readily distinguishable from those of European governments which had bought immunity.[3]

In spite of these efforts to increase trade with Continental Europe, the British retained a commanding lead. In 1789 more than seven eighths of the foreign tonnage in United States ports was registered as British. Of American exports, however, somewhat less than half went to Great Britain and her colonies. Most of the exports to the French and the Dutch went to their West Indian islands. Probably these destinations concealed some indirect trade with the British West Indies. Ameri-

---

[1] A. L. Kohlmeier, "The Commerce between the United States and the Netherlands," *Studies in American History Inscribed to James Albert Woodburn* (Indiana Univ., *Studies*, XII, nos. 66-68), 13-47.

[2] *Commerce of Rhode Island*, II, 213, 249 ff., 321, 361 ff.; Weeden, *Economic and Social History of New England*, II, 825.

[3] Bond, "Letters," 523.

can imports still came chiefly from the British Isles. During the Confederation the imports from Great Britain were more than double the exports to that country. In 1784 the ratio was nearly five to one.[1]

Notwithstanding legal prohibitions, American merchants partially recovered their prewar markets in the British West Indies, for the planters and officials oftentimes connived at irregular trading. Some illicit traffic was covered by "ingenious collusion" between partners in different countries, making it possible for a ship to pass as either British or American. In 1786 British regulations against foreign traders in the West Indies seem to have been largely evaded; but subsequent measures to prevent fraudulent use of British papers and American importations by way of the foreign islands proved somewhat more effective.[2]

Some enterprising merchants saw possibilities outside Europe and her colonies. Most significant in this respect was the beginning of the East Indian and China trades. Freed from the British colonial system and the monopoly of the East India Company, Americans could now compete with England and her European rivals. One group of Philadelphia and New York promoters, centering in Robert Morris, financed the *Empress of China* on her trip from New York to Canton in 1784. Her chief outward cargo was ginseng, valued by the Chinese for its medicinal qualities and exchangeable for tea and other Oriental goods. This profitable venture brought congratulations from Congress, and Major Samuel Shaw, its Yankee supercargo, became the first Ameri-

---

[1] Coxe, *View of the United States*, 412, 423; Timothy Pitkin, *A Statistical View of the Commerce of the United States* (Hartford, 1816), 30-31.

[2] L. J. Ragatz, *Fall of the Planter Class in the British Caribbean* (N. Y., 1928), chap. vi; Sheffield, *Observations*, app.; Bond, "Letters," 524, 530.

can consul at Canton.[1] Other voyages soon followed from Providence, Philadelphia, New York, Boston and other ports. In 1784 Elias Hasket Derby of Salem sent his *Grand Turk* to the Cape of Good Hope with rum, provisions and ginseng to be exchanged there for China tea and on a later occasion the ship went to Canton. In 1789 there were fifteen American vessels in China, including four of the Derby fleet. Other skippers sailed to British India and the Dutch East Indies. The British consul at Philadelphia was troubled by the frequent arrival of American ships which sold their rich Eastern cargoes more cheaply than did British ships.[2]

Interstate commercial rivalry was keen, leading individual states to discriminate against the goods and shipping of other members of the Confederation. Massachusetts resented Connecticut's failure to coöperate in retaliating against imports in British ships. Connecticut and New Jersey complained of New York's levying duties on their vessels in New York Harbor. By way of reprisal New London merchants boycotted New York, and New Jersey taxed the New York lighthouse on Sandy Hook. New Jersey emphasized its protest to Congress by refusing a congressional requisition. According to Nathaniel Gorham, "nothing but the restraining hand of Congress (weak as it is)" prevented New Jersey and Connecticut from "entering the lists very seriously with N— York," in which case "bloodshed would very quickly be the consiquence." Interstate business also suffered from scarcity of specie, conflicting money standards and depreciated paper.[3]

[1] K. S. Latourette, *The History of Early Relations between the United States and China* (Conn. Acad. of Arts and Sciences, *Trans.*, XXII), 10-14; K. W. Porter, ed., *The Jacksons and the Lees* (N. S. B. Gras, ed., *Harvard Studies in Business History*, III), I, 28-33.

[2] *Ibid.*; Bond, "Letters," 532-603, *passim*.

[3] Giesecke, *American Commercial Legislation*, 133-136; W. G. Brown, *Life of Oliver Ellsworth* (N. Y., 1905), 352; McMaster, *United States*, I, 404-406; Burnett, *Letters*, VIII, 318.

An important matter for New England was the recovery of the deep-sea fisheries. Fortunately this interest, strongly supported in the peace negotiations by John Adams, secured favorable terms. The Americans were conceded the right to fish on the Newfoundland Banks, in the Gulf of St. Lawrence "and at all other places in the sea where the inhabitants used at any time heretofore to fish." They might also dry or cure their catch on the unsettled shores of Nova Scotia and Labrador. New Englanders must further meet French competition, protected by Anglo-French treaties, and were hampered by discriminating duties favoring fish taken in French bottoms to the French West Indies. But, legally or illegally, Yankee skippers got fish into West Indian markets, even into the French islands. Though the annual tonnage employed in the codfishery between 1786 and 1790 averaged considerably less than between 1765 and 1775, conditions gradually grew better. By 1791 the tonnage exceeded the average for the last prewar decade. The whaling industry improved more slowly.[1]

Parallel with the general economic recovery that marked the later years of the Confederation there were forward steps in the organization and technique of business, due in large part to the growing strength of a vigorous group of men educated by the experience of the war and its aftermath. A primary concern of the mercantile community was a sufficient, stable and uniform currency. The supply of hard money had, as we have seen, been depleted to pay for postwar imports and by British trade regulations obstructing the flow of specie from the West Indies. As in colonial times, the coins were mainly of Spanish mintage and were variously rated in terms of

[1] Rufus King, "Letters," Mass. Hist. Soc., *Proceeds.*, XLIX, 83-85; Higginson, "Letters," 778-780; Hamilton, *Commercial and Industrial Correspondence*, 168-171; Pitkin, *Statistical View*, 38-46, 84-85.

pounds sterling and state currencies. Furthermore there were differences in their bullion content.

Under the Confederation, though money might be coined either by the states or by the Union, Congress had the exclusive right to regulate its value. Following war-time discussion of the subject by the Morrises and their recommendation of a decimal system, Jefferson came forward in 1784 with his "Notes on the Establishment of a Money Unit and of a Coinage for the United States," which proposed the familiar Spanish dollar as the unit of value. The next year Congress accepted the decimal system based upon the dollar. A contract was made for copper coinage, but the establishment of a mint had to wait until the Confederation gave place to the new Federal Union. Thus the Confederation initiated an essential reform.[1]

Closely associated with the coinage problem was the paper-money situation in the states. In some, new taxes permitted the partial retirement of bills and improved the credit of what remained; but the depression, as we have seen, brought fresh demands for inflation which reached their climax in 1785 and 1786. In contrast to the cheap-money victories in several commonwealths was the resistance by conservatives, notably in New England outside Rhode Island; in New York, where issues were so restricted as to prevent serious depreciation; and in the Chesapeake states, where inflationist sentiment, though formidable, was ultimately defeated. The popular agitation, however, proved sufficiently disturbing to indicate the need of federal control. So the Federal Convention, composed largely of merchants, lawyers and substantial landowners, readily agreed to place coinage and currency legislation under the exclusive jurisdiction of Congress. While this made the Constitution attractive

[1] H. W. Domett, comp., *A History of the Bank of New York* (N. Y., 1884), 20; Jefferson, *Works*, IV, 297-313.

to the mercantile and financial interests, it antagonized the agrarian and other debtor elements, which came dangerously near defeating ratification.[1]

The most important advance in business technique under the Confederation was in banking. For a time after the incorporation of the Bank of North America in 1780 subscriptions came in slowly, but an opportune remittance of specie by the French government enabled Congress to become the principal stockholder. Pennsylvania associates of Robert Morris, including his partner Thomas Willing, the bank's first president, formed the nucleus of the corporation; but there were numerous subscribers elsewhere. In 1786 a little more than half the shares were held in Philadelphia, slightly more than a quarter in other states, and some abroad, chiefly in Holland. To relieve doubts as to the validity of the federal incorporation, Pennsylvania granted the institution a state charter, and several states accorded it some kind of legal recognition. It was widely criticized, however, as an instrument of the money power and in 1786 Pennsylvania temporarily withdrew its charter.[2]

Though other banks were projected, only two were actually founded. In 1784 the Bank of New York was formed with a Revolutionary general at its head, Alexander Hamilton as a director and a former Loyalist as cashier. Though popular opposition prevented incorporation before 1791, the bank was able to carry on through the general depression, increasing its capital and paying dividends. The Massachusetts Bank of Boston, sponsored by Stephen Higginson and other important citizens, was chartered in 1784. Among its first directors and stockholders were leading business men in Boston,

---

[1] For a convenient summary of currency legislation, see Allan Nevins, *The American States during and after the Revolution* (N. Y., 1924), 517 ff.

[2] Davis, *History of American Corporations*, II, chap. ii.

Salem, Marblehead and Portsmouth with Robert Morris as a Philadelphia subscriber. Thus by 1789 there were successful banks in three business centers, promoted by influential groups with interstate connections and a practical interest in strong government. On such men Hamilton could rely to support his fiscal program.[1]

Activity in corporate organization was not confined to banking. Though only seven strictly business corporations had been authorized before 1781, in the next ten years thirty-three charters were issued to twenty-five companies. Small as these figures now seem, they mark the beginning of a rapidly rising curve. Among the business associations incorporated in the years 1781-1790 were fire-insurance undertakings in Philadelphia and New York; several Southern companies for improving inland navigation; toll-bridge companies; and three manufacturing concerns—one each in Connecticut, Massachusetts and New York. There was considerable criticism of corporations as such, due partly to traditional jealousy of monopolies and partly to the fear that they would lead to undue concentration of wealth. Even municipal charters and such mutual-benefit associations as a medical society or the New York Society of Tradesmen and Mechanics encountered opposition.[2]

Another significant development was the rise of a group of men dealing in negotiable paper—government securities or the notes of individuals and companies. Though not a wholly new phenomenon, this branch of business had expanded rapidly with the great volume of public securities put out to meet war-time needs. Besides paper currency, there were federal and state issues of interest-bearing certificates of indebtedness. During

[1] *Ibid.;* Domett, *Bank of New York,* chaps. i-iii; N. S. B. Gras, *The Massachusetts First National Bank of Boston (Harvard Studies in Business History,* IV), 18-30; East, *Business Enterprise,* chap. xiii.

[2] Davis, *History of American Corporations,* II, chaps. i, vi and *passim.*

the postwar depression an increasing number of persons had to sell government paper at low rates and this, too, aided the securities business, with New York City becoming the leading market. Stock quotations appeared in the press and before long the *Massachusetts Gazette* began publishing monthly quotations. In Philadelphia the new city charter provided for licensing brokers.[1]

Stockjobbing had an international phase since French and Dutch capitalists were interested in the American domestic and foreign debt. Jefferson advised certain Amsterdam bankers that such investments appeared to be safe despite some question about the domestic debt because of agitation to discriminate in favor of the original holders. Andrew Craigie told a London client that the American public debt offered "the best field in the world for speculation" though one in which "strangers" might "easily be lost." In 1788 Craigie was shipping abroad several hundred thousand dollars in American securities. The French writer, Brissot de Warville, came to this country to investigate the situation on behalf of Paris and Amsterdam bankers.[2] Apart from government securities, land still offered a favorite form of speculative activity. Westward expansion interested adventurous persons who bought land as they did stocks and bonds. That was true of Robert Morris, several other members of the Federal Convention and also some Europeans.[3]

As a field for capital investment manufactures lagged behind commerce and land. Progress toward economic independence was checked by the postwar renewal of British trade. In any case, some Americans were dubious about manufactures. Jefferson regarded "artificers" as

[1] *Ibid.*, I, 75-103.
[2] *Ibid.*, I, 185-189; Jefferson, *Works*, IV, 442-444.
[3] C. A. Beard, *An Economic Interpretation of the Constitution of the United States* (N. Y., 1913), chap. v.

"the instruments by which the liberties of a country are generally overturned," and Oliver Ellsworth believed his countrymen would "choose to be farmers, living independently on their freeholds, rather than to be manufacturers and work for a groat a day." Another doubter was Franklin, who thought large textile establishments had "generally failed" in the United States because unable to compete with imported goods of equal value.[1] Others felt differently, however. One argument urged for American manufactures was economy: citizens would be emancipated from "the madness of foreign finery" which "rages and destroys . . . threatening convulsions and dissolution to the political body." Among the societies formed to encourage home industry were the General Society of Mechanics and Tradesmen in New York and the Boston Association of Tradesmen and Manufacturers. The latter proposed an interstate campaign to free America from the humiliation of "lavishing her stores of wealth to promote the manufactures of Europe." [2]

Conspicuous advocates of protection were Mathew Carey, editor of the *American Museum,* and Tench Coxe, founder and first president of the influential Pennsylvania Society for the Encouragement of Manufactures and the Useful Arts. Coxe hoped for industrial development through technical improvements, through bounties and premiums and by attracting European skilled workers. He anticipated the use of steam-driven machinery, the increase of cotton production in the South and the utilizing of Pennsylvania's coal deposits. Public meetings in the interest of manufactures were held even in the South. A Charlestonian complained of

[1] Jefferson, *Works,* IV, 449; Brown, *Ellsworth,* 353; Franklin, *Writings,* VIII, 609.

[2] Samuel Rezneck, "The Rise and Early Development of Industrial Consciousness in the United States, 1760-1830," *Journ. of Econ. and Business History,* IV, 784 ff.

"infatuation" for foreign goods and hoped that "British cruelties and British manufactures" might be "equally despised by every American." Officeholders were urged to wear only American-made clothes and members of the Massachusetts legislature signed such an agreement among themselves.[1]

As we have seen, the states enacted some protective legislation, giving preference to local products or to American goods generally. Pennsylvania formally declared its intention to "protect" manufactures by duties on competing imports. This desire for more effective legislation worked in favor of the Federal Constitution; and when the new Congress met, protectionist petitions came in from Boston, New York, Philadelphia and Baltimore.[2]

As for actual accomplishments, the secretary of the Pennsylvania Society for the Encouragement of Manufactures reported that in four years flour milling had produced nearly a million bushels for export. He declared that the iron industry of Pennsylvania, New Jersey and Delaware annually turned out three hundred and fifty thousand tons of plate iron and nail cards and that nails were "becoming an article of export." These hopeful claims were partly supported by Consul Phineas Bond's reports, indicating that, in certain heavy products like anchors and forges (protected by transatlantic freight charges) and in steel making, native manufactures could compete with British wares.[3]

Though New England shipbuilding suffered through the temporary decline of the fisheries and the West Indian

[1] Coxe, *View of the United States*, chaps. iii-iv; anon., "Reflexions on the Policy of Britain with Regard to America," *Am. Museum*, II, 291-293.

[2] Giesecke, *American Commercial Legislation*, 133-134; Beard, *Economic Interpretation*, 40-49.

[3] W. Barton, "Remarks on the State of American Manufactures and Commerce," *Am. Museum*, VII (1790), 285 ff.; Bond, "Letters," 651 ff.

trade and from the loss of the English market for American-built ships, this slump was soon followed by a revival there and elsewhere. Distilling after a similar setback, attributed partly to the decline of the slave traffic, also somewhat recovered. In 1789 New England exported large quantities of rum to other states, and the Pennsylvania distilleries were growing rapidly. Bond reported substantial gains in New England textile manufactures. Over forty thousand yards of its linen were said to have been sold in Philadelphia, causing a reduction of imports from Ireland. Bond noted also that the Cabot cotton factory at Beverly imitated Manchester fabrics with considerable success. In 1788 Jeremiah Wadsworth and his associates, aided by temporary exemption from state taxes, set up a woolen factory at Hartford which a year later turned out over ten thousand yards of good cloth. This enterprise, however, soon had to be abandoned for lack of skilled workmen.[1]

Some progress occurred in the boot and shoe industry. New England exported shoes to other states and Higginson believed that in this industry it might become independent of Britain. According to Jedidiah Morse, the Lynn shops made a hundred and seventy thousand pairs annually. Similarly Bond spoke of Pennsylvania leather as "vastly improved." As to American paper, disparaged by Sheffield, Pennsylvania in 1789 possessed more than twenty-five mills with an output sufficient to prevent the importation "of any but the finer sort." One establishment boasted of five lately imported Irish workers. Sixty-three mills in the Delaware Valley were said to be making two hundred and fifty thousand dollars' worth of paper annually.[2]

[1] *Ibid.*, 630-638, 651; Weeden, *Economic and Social History of New England*, II, 856; Coxe, *View of the United States*, 76; Hamilton, *Industrial and Commercial Correspondence*, 3 ff., 65 ff.

[2] Morse, *American Geography*, 182; Bond, "Letters," 651 ff.; Higginson, "Letters," 730; Barton, "Remarks," 285 ff.

In competing with other popular forms of speculative investment industry was handicapped by a dearth of expert direction and skilled labor. Wadsworth's Hartford textile factory found few persons capable of making or operating the required machinery. As before the Revolution, American efforts to attract trained workmen from Europe and take advantage of new mechanical devices encountered obstacles abroad. British legislation against the emigration of skilled labor was now strengthened. In 1789 Samuel Slater, the textile expert, had to leave England in disguise. Parliamentary measures against the export of machinery were also stiffened. Nevertheless, Americans gradually learned to reproduce such equipment, either from skilled newcomers or by importing models. Coxe reported that his Pennsylvania society had "the movements and complete machinery" of Arkwright's water mill for cotton spinning.[1]

Thus the citizens of the infant republic were preparing for future industrial advance by informing themselves as to European developments and gaining experience through pioneer enterprises. The promoters of such undertakings desired government support through bounties, preferential duties and other concessions, hitherto provided by the states. They now looked for further aid from a stronger federal government, an expectation only partially realized in the tariff act of 1789.

[1] Hamilton, *Industrial and Commercial Correspondence*, 7-11; V. S. Clark, *History of Manufactures in the United States* (Carnegie Inst., Contribs. to Am. Econ. History; rev. edn., N. Y., 1929), I, 260; Coxe, *View of the United States*, 69; East, *Business Enterprise*, 310; Bond, "Letters," 581 ff.

CHAPTER XV

CULTURE IN THE NEW ORDER

THOUGH substantial progress had been made during the war toward religious liberty and equality, some forms of discrimination survived. Maryland had limited its constitutional guarantee of equality to Christians, and South Carolina had accorded toleration only to churches and individuals acknowledging one God, a future state of rewards and punishments and the duty of public worship, reserving the privilege of incorporation to groups professing the Protestant faith. Religious tests for office also remained. In the Carolinas and Georgia certain offices were confined to Protestants. Distrust of ecclesiastical influence is indicated in the constitutional exclusion of clergymen from the legislature, as in the Carolinas and Georgia, and by the Maryland rule limiting the landholdings of ecclesiastical corporations.[1]

After the war some restrictive features of the early constitutions were removed. Georgia legislators no longer had to be Protestants, and South Carolina ended the preferential status of Protestants, granting equal rights of religious profession and worship to "all mankind." Of prime importance was the action of Virginia, where, after the practical disestablishment of the Anglican Church, the precise status of religious societies had not been defined. Such men as Richard Henry Lee and Patrick Henry still believed that the state should, without discriminating in favor of any particular sect, assume

[1] Texts of constitutions in F. N. Thorpe, comp., *The Federal and State Constitutions* (59th Cong., 2 sess., *House Doc.*, no. 357). C. H. Moehlman, *American Constitutions and Religion* (Berne, Ind., 1938), includes most of the pertinent clauses.

some responsibility for the maintenance of the Christian religion. This point of view found expression in two important measures: the legal incorporation of the Episcopal Church, and the proposed "general assessment" bill which would have authorized a tax whose proceeds should be applied, at the option of the taxpayer, either to the denomination of his choice or to education.[1]

The former act, which guaranteed the property rights of that church, was, however, soon repealed, partly because it was thought to give the clergy too much power. The latter failed to pass. In Jefferson's absence abroad the chief spokesman against it was Madison, who, working with the Baptists, most of the Presbyterians and many liberal Episcopalians, advocated complete separation of church and state. Their success was followed in 1785-1786 by the passage of Jefferson's famous "Bill for Establishing Religious Freedom," with its preamble beginning: "Whereas Almighty God hath created the mind free . . . ." Coercion, it said, could only "beget habits of hypocrisy and meanness," whereas without it truth would prevail. No man, therefore, should be forced to attend or support any form of worship, or suffer discrimination of any kind because of his religious opinions. The statute concluded with a formal declaration that its repeal would violate "the natural rights of mankind."[2]

In New York the comparatively weak Anglican establishment was easily disposed of. The state constitution guaranteed liberty of "religious profession and worship . . . without discrimination or preference." Anti-

[1] For selected references for this and the following paragraphs, see E. B. Greene, *Religion and the State, the Making and Testing of an American Tradition* (N. Y., 1941), 86-88, 157. The fullest treatment (with documents) is in H. J. Eckenrode, *Separation of Church and State in Virginia* (Richmond, 1910).

[2] W. W. Hening, comp., *The Statutes-at-Large, Being a Collection of All the Laws of Virginia, 1619-1792* (Phila., 1823), XII, 84-86.

Catholic feeling found expression, however, in a clause requiring applicants for citizenship to renounce allegiance to foreign rulers "in all matters, ecclesiastical as well as civil"; but this provision became nugatory with the adoption of the Federal Constitution, which transferred control of naturalization to Congress. Though the other Middle states had no establishments to abolish, they retained religious qualifications for office. Pennsylvania legislators had to acknowledge the divine authority of the Old and New Testaments; in Delaware belief in the Trinity was required of state officials; and in New Jersey religious equality was promised only to Protestants. The second constitution of Pennsylvania, in 1790, was somewhat more liberal, opening public office to any believer in God and "a future state of rewards and punishments," thus including Jews and Deists. In 1792 Delaware forbade any religious test, but New Jersey failed to take similar action until much later.

In New England outside Rhode Island the colonial association of church and state continued. Even here, however, there was some progress. The Massachusetts constitution acknowledged every man's right to worship God "in the manner and season most agreeable to the Dictates of his own conscience," thus making possible the public worship of the Catholic Church. At the same time, however, Massachusetts asserted the duty of all men "publickly, and at stated seasons to worship the Supreme Being," and required legislation to enforce town provision for "public Protestant teachers of piety, religion, and Morality." Generally speaking, "public Protestant teachers" meant in practice Congregational ministers, though, as in colonial times, there were limited concessions to Quakers, Episcopalians and Baptists in the matter of church taxes. Religious tests for the governor, other principal officers and members of the legislature included not only public avowal of their belief in Christianity, but an express renunciation of all spiritual as well as political allegiance to any foreign ruler or prelate. Strictly interpreted, this clause excluded Catholics. Nevertheless the constitution declared solemnly that "no subordination of any one sect or denomination to another" should "ever be established by law." The Congregational establishments were also retained in New Hampshire and Connecticut. There were vigorous protests by the New England dissenters against these discriminatory provisions, but prosecutions for nonpayment of church taxes continued for many years. In Rhode Island, where religious liberty had always enjoyed wide scope, the legislature formally repealed the statute excluding Catholics from citizenship.

Under the Articles of Confederation religion was clearly not a federal matter and Congress expressly disclaimed such jurisdiction. The subject was, however, discussed in Congress and later in the Federal Convention. In the debate on the land ordinance of 1785 Madison objected successfully to a clause allotting one section in each township for the support of religion. Five states, however, voted for it. In the Northwest ordinance of 1787, Article I prohibited interference with anyone "on account of his mode of worship, or religious sentiments," and Article VI merely referred in general terms to religion as one object to be promoted through education.

Shortly afterward the Federal Convention adopted without serious opposition the prohibition of religious qualifications for "Office or public Trust under the United States." There were some objectors, however, in the state ratifying conventions. In Maryland Luther Martin declared that "in a Christian country, it would be at least decent to hold out some distinction between the professors of Christianity and downright infidelity or paganism." A member of the Massachusetts convention "shuddered at the idea that Roman Catholics, Papists and Pagans might thus be introduced into office," and a North Carolina critic complained of what he called "an invitation to Jews and Pagans of every kind to come among us." Among those who argued effectively against religious qualifications were clergymen. One Massachusetts Congregational minister called such tests "impious encroachments" upon the divine prerogative.[1]

A by-product of the debates on ratification was the enactment of a more general guarantee of religious liberty. Richard Henry Lee had argued that "the free exercise of religion" should be established "as a part of the national compact." Minority denominations also desired more protection and in doubtful states their support was important. As a result, the First Amendment included the familiar clause: "Congress shall make no law respecting the establishment of religion or prohibiting the free exercise thereof." Though neither this provision nor that prohibiting religious tests limited the action of state governments, they did embody liberal opinion in "the supreme law of the land."[2]

Political independence also stimulated the desire for ecclesiastical autonomy. This was especially necessary for the Anglican communicants, who had been dependent not only on the mother church but on the British state. Though in Anglican theory the continuity of the episcopate was essential, it appeared that Church of England prelates could not then legally consecrate bishops for

[1] E. F. Humphrey, *Nationalism and Religion in America, 1774-1789* (Boston, 1924), chap. xiv; James Madison, *Writings* (Gaillard Hunt, ed., N. Y., 1900-1910), II, 145; Max Farrand, ed., *The Records of the Federal Convention* (New Haven, 1911-1937), III, 227; Jonathan Elliot, ed., *The Debates in the Several State Conventions, of the Adoption of the Federal Constitution* (Wash., 1836), II, 148; IV, 199.

[2] E. H. Scott, ed., *The Federalist and Other Constitutional Papers* (Chicago, 1894), 871.

service in the independent United States. Fortunately, the Scotch branch of the Anglican communion had no such state connection, and the first American bishop, Samuel Seabury of Connecticut, was duly consecrated in 1784 by representatives of that church. Presently Parliament made similar action possible in the Church of England and bishops were accordingly consecrated for New York and Pennsylvania. Thus the Church of England in the colonies became in 1786 the "Protestant Episcopal Church in the United States of America." [1] The Dutch and German Reformed churches also instituted independent organizations.

The Methodists, not hitherto a distinct denomination, faced a different problem. John Wesley himself and some of his preachers, though still members of the Church of England, were not sympathetically regarded by their fellow churchmen. Furthermore, Wesley's followers in America realized that their difficulties could not be adequately dealt with at long range. Accordingly, in 1784 he chose Thomas Coke and Francis Asbury as superintendents in the United States, where they presently organized the Methodist Episcopal Church. On Wesley's death in 1791 it became wholly independent. By contrast, the Moravians continued for many years under the direction of authorities in Europe. A different position again was that of the Catholics, who remained necessarily subject to the Roman papacy. Instead, however, of their former dependence on the English vicar apostolic, they now received a special American organization headed by Father John Carroll of Maryland, who became first Superior of the American Mission and later Bishop. Other religious groups, including the Congregationalists, Presbyterians, Baptists and Luther-

[1] A. L. Cross, *The Anglican Episcopate and the American Colonies* (*Harvard Hist. Studies*, IX), chap. xii, app. xiv.

ans, being already self-governing, required no organic change.[1]

The churches also felt the impulse toward greater internal union. In the case of the Catholics, Bishop Carroll actively directed the clergy from Maryland to New England. The Episcopalians, beginning with three independent dioceses, soon set up a national organization governed by a general convention in which the bishops formed an upper house while clerical and lay representatives from each diocese comprised the lower house. The bishops themselves were chosen by diocesan conventions consisting of clerical and lay delegates. The Presbyterians likewise founded a federal organization with a general assembly of ministers and laymen chosen by the presbyteries. Somewhat later similar bodies were established by the Dutch and German Reformed churches. The American Methodists also organized a general conference for the United States. On the other hand, the Lutherans did not advance beyond regional associations, while the Congregationalists and Baptists held to the principle of loosely grouped, independent local churches.[2]

In the realm of religious thought and feeling certain developments stand out: first, an intellectual revolt against traditional orthodoxy; secondly, the effect of the Revolution in somewhat weakening accepted sanctions of personal conduct and profession; and, thirdly, the influence of emotional appeals on people who were dissatisfied with conventional forms and ready for what they considered a more vital personal religion adapted

---

[1] J. M. Buckley, *A History of Methodists in the United States* (Philip Schaff and others, eds., *The American Church History Series*, N. Y., 1893-1897, V), chaps. ix-x; J. T. Hamilton, *A History of the Church Known as the Moravian Church, or, The Unitas Fratrum* (Moravian Hist. Soc., *Trans.*, VI), chap. xxx; Peter Guilday, *The Life and Times of John Carroll* (N. Y., 1922), chaps. xiv, xix.

[2] Humphrey, *Nationalism and Religion*, chaps. vii-xi.

to the common man. These tendencies, already apparent in the colonies, were variously affected by the Revolution.

Radical opinion expressed itself both in headlong assaults on orthodox Christianity and in "peaceful penetration" within the churches. Ethan Allen's *Reason, the Only Oracle of Man* (1784), illustrates a crude form of frontal attack. Rejecting historic dogmas and declaring that "most of the human race" were "miserable Priest-ridden," he proposed to free them "from this ghostly Tyranny." An article in the *American Museum* spoke of Allen's "contemptible plagiarism of every hackneyed, worn out half-rotten dogma of the English deistical writers." Some New England ministers were deeply disturbed by this book, and when Allen died in 1789 President Stiles predicted future torments for this "profane and impious Deist." Even to own the book aroused suspicion of "infidel" sympathies.[1]

Stiles complained of increasing indifference to the religious attitudes of public men, observing even a tendency to regard Deists and indifferentists as "the most suitable persons for public office." He maintained, however, that Deism should be opposed only by "argument and truth." Stiles considered that Timothy Dwight's undiscriminating attack on heretical tendencies in his *Triumph of Infidelity* (1788) had "overshot the Mark, and hurt the Cause which he meant to defend." To Philip Mazzei, however, it seemed that his American friends combined tolerance with real respect for religion: atheism was unknown among them while skepticism was rare and usually not publicly avowed. Gibbon's *Decline and Fall of the Roman Empire* was read in New England and his unsympathetic treatment of Christianity noted. John

[1] Dana Doten, "Ethan Allen's 'Original Something,'" *New England Quar.*, XI, 362; anon., "On the Doctrine of Chance," *Am. Museum*, II (1787), 408-410; Ezra Stiles, *Literary Diary* (F. B. Dexter, ed., N. Y., 1901), III, 345; William Bentley, *Diary* (Salem, 1905-1914), I, 82.

Quincy Adams thought it "equally injurious to the author's character—as a philosopher and as an historian." [1] Popular discussion of Deism was not confined to New England. Noah Webster's *American Magazine* printed an anonymous article on discrepancies in the New Testament, followed by an anonymous reply. William Livingston and John Dickinson defended orthodoxy against "infidelity," and Livingston's *Thoughts on Deism* was frequently reprinted. Among the Southern gentry skepticism was common. Jefferson advised a young nephew to read the Bible as he read Livy or Tacitus, treating accounts of supernatural occurrences with reserve and relying on his own reason, "the only oracle given you by heaven." Deistic or rationalistic ideas were attributed to George Wythe in Virginia, Willie Jones in North Carolina and C. C. Pinckney in South Carolina. On the other hand, Patrick Henry was disturbed by "French infidelity" and Bishop William Meade noted the baneful influence of the alliance with "infidel France," nowhere more evident than in Virginia. While Henry valued Hampden-Sydney College as a bulwark of orthodoxy, Jefferson condemned the "religious phrensy" with which it inspired its students. [2]

More important probably than these external attacks on the Christian tradition were the latitudinarian tendencies within the churches, even among the clergy, as represented, for instance, by the Anglican, Provost William Smith of Philadelphia. A committee of which he

[1] J. W. Thornton, *The Pulpit of the American Revolution* (N. Y., 1860), 488-489; Stiles, *Diary*, III, 326; Filippo Mazzei, *Recherches historiques et politiques sur les États-Unis de l'Amèrique Septentrionale* (Paris, 1788), IV, 92; J. Q. Adams, *Life in a New England Town* (Boston, 1903), 112.

[2] *American Magazine*, I (1787-1788), 420-421, 491-492; H. M. Morais, *Deism in Eighteenth Century America* (Columbia Univ., *Studies*, no. 397), chap. iv; Thomas Jefferson, *Works* (P. L. Ford, ed., N. Y., 1904-1905), V, 324-326; VI, 23; W. W. Henry, *Patrick Henry* (N. Y., 1891), II, 198 ff.; William Meade, *Old Churches, Ministers and Families of Virginia* (Phila., 1857), I, 175.

was chairman proposed radical changes in the prayer book, including the omission of the Nicene and Athanasian creeds. In the end, however, the doctrinal statements of the English prayer book were retained with a few exceptions, chiefly those made necessary by the new political order.[1] Meanwhile in New England the revolt against Calvinism continued. After the Revolution the conflict between the "liberals" and the conservatives became more sharply defined, partly under the influence of English Unitarianism. In 1785 King's Chapel, the oldest Anglican church in Boston, was transformed under the leadership of young James Freeman into a Unitarian society. Another example of the drift from orthodoxy was William Bentley, pastor of a Congregational church in Salem, who declared that he had abandoned many of his "early prejudices," including the doctrine of the Trinity. Nevertheless he maintained his standing in the church. A young English visitor reported that the Bostonians, from being "perhaps the strictest Calvinists in the world," had gone to the opposite extreme, so that the "revolution of religion" had been "greater than that of politics."[2]

Aside from doctrinal issues, there were widespread complaints of apathy. In 1783 Schoepf noted the ruinous condition of Virginia churches and was told that religion had become "very faint." In New England, too, there was talk of lessened zeal. In 1790 a Connecticut preacher, describing local conditions, complained of the prevailing "profaneness, disregard of the Sabbath, neglect of family religion, unrighteousness, intemperance." The Reverend Jedidiah Morse thought a "more enlarged intercourse with mankind" had bred greater

---

[1] Stiles, *Diary*, II, 528; W. S. Perry, *History of the American Episcopal Church* (Boston, 1885), II, 101-118.

[2] Bentley, *Diary*, I, 98 and *passim*; Joseph Hadfield, *An Englishman in America, 1785* (D. S. Robertson, ed., Toronto, 1933), 184.

tolerance, a good thing if it did not "liberalize away all true religion." Dr. John Collins Warren of Boston, who spent his boyhood in a churchgoing household during this period, believed that in the community at large the characteristic "religious habits and opinions" of New England had weakened. Sabbath observance, however, was still strict enough to annoy foreign visitors.[1]

Generalizations about sexual morality are precarious, but European observers commonly took a favorable view of conditions. Brissot de Warville thought there was comparatively little prostitution even in the seaboard towns. For what there was he considered foreigners chiefly responsible. According to Schoepf, "Gallant adventures" were "little known and still less practised." He did not overlook, however, the numerous mulatto children born to "gentlemen" by slave mothers, or the evil influence on white children of "ignorant, careless, immoral" slaves. Though divorce legislation in New England had been comparatively liberal, the disuse after 1782 of the scarlet letter to mark persons found guilty of adultery suggests a more humane attitude. There was some discussion of the divorce question. Yale seniors debated, "Whether Christianity permits Divorces in any cases but Fornication or Adultery"; and in 1788 Benjamin Trumbull, the clerical historian of Connecticut, published *An Appeal to the Public with Respect to the Unlawfulness of Divorces.*[2]

While the older churches worked their fields with diminishing returns and suffered from the inroads of indifference or "infidelity," the so-called popular churches,

[1] J. D. Schoepf, *Travels in the Confederation, 1783-1784* (A. J. Morrison, ed., Phila., 1911), II, 62-63; Jedidiah Morse, *The American Geography* (Elizabethtown, N. J., 1789), 146-147; Edward Warren, *The Life of John Collins Warren* (Boston, 1860), I, 157.

[2] J. P. Brissot de Warville, *New Travels in the United States of America* (London, 1792), 202; Schoepf, *Travels,* I, 100-101; II, 92-93; Stiles, *Diary,* III, 201, 213; G. E. Howard, *A History of Matrimonial Institutions* (Chicago, 1904), II, chap. xii.

notably the Baptists, Methodists and "New Side" Presbyterians, vigorously cultivated neglected social groups.[1] As for the Baptists, the years between 1785 and 1789 were marked in Virginia by revivals which brought them several thousand new members. They had also to be reckoned with as a democratic force in politics. With increasing prosperity and the winning of some well-to-do converts came a certain change of outlook and more interest in ministerial education. Moreover, progress was made in reconciling differences between "Regular Baptists" and "Separates." Even in New England the Baptist churches gained rapidly, especially in the northern parts.[2]

Though the Methodists like the Baptists had been troubled by the war, they recovered quickly under capable leadership. Their revivals resembled those of the Baptists, but they developed a distinctive technique for consolidating their gains: classes for converts, an itinerant ministry, quarterly meetings, regional conferences with presiding elders and, over all, the general conference and the superintendents or bishops. In particular, Bishop Asbury proved himself a skillful leader and organizer. The Methodists won their greatest successes in the South. A Virginia revival, at its height while the Federal Convention was sitting, attracted attention throughout the country. According to one Baptist minister, the Methodist preachers in this region surpassed all others in "spreading their books and tenets among the people." Advancing into the Lower South and the Southwest, the Methodists reported in 1789 nearly seven thousand members in the North Carolina conference in-

---

[1] J. S. Bassett, "Development of the Popular Churches after the Revolution," Mass. Hist. Soc., Proceeds., XLVIII, 254-268.

[2] W. M. Gewehr, The Great Awakening in Virginia, 1740-1790 (Duke Univ., Publs., 1930), chaps. vii-xi; Isaac Backus, History of New England with Particular Reference to the Denomination of Christians Called Baptists (2nd edn., Newton, Mass., 1871), II, chap. xxiv.

cluding some from beyond the Alleghanies and over two thousand in Georgia. In 1787 they claimed for the country as a whole more than twenty-one thousand members, not counting four thousand Negroes.[1]

Another "popular" movement was that of the Universalists. Chiefly active in the North and particularly in New England, they were much less numerous than the Baptists and Methodists; but their doctrine of ultimate salvation for all men, presented by such preachers as John Murray and Elhanon Winchester, probably influenced many outside the fold. Smaller religious groups, mainly in New England and New York, were the Shaker followers of Ann Lee and a few disciples of Jemimah Wilkinson, the "Universal Friend."

The Catholics began a notable progress. For the first time they had an official head for the country as a whole. To the early congregations in Maryland and Pennsylvania were added parishes in states where the Mass had previously been forbidden by law. Formerly isolated members were formed into congregations and reënforced by immigration. Though the recognized Catholic population of the United States was estimated at about twenty-five thousand, chiefly in Maryland, Pennsylvania and New York City, the stage was set for a rapid advance.[2]

In the field of education clergymen occupied an important place, holding all but one of the college presidencies and a large proportion of the professorships. Perhaps equally significant was the interest of public men in education. In his *Defence of the Constitutions of the United States* (1787) John Adams insisted on instruction for "every class and rank of people, down to the

1 Gewehr, *Great Awakening*, chaps. vi-vii, esp. 168-173; Buckley, *Methodists*, 254, 258.
2 Guilday, *John Carroll*, 235.

lowest and the poorest." Community schools would "draw together the sons of the rich and the poor." [1] Similarly, Jefferson argued that, since the people were the "only safe depositories of political power," at least a modicum of education should be given free to all children for at least three years in publicly supported schools. The more capable boys should then be selected for free tuition in "grammar schools," and especially promising ones should proceed to college at public expense, though well-to-do parents might pay for the higher education of their sons without this sifting process. This proposal was as nearly democratic as could then and there be reasonably expected. Though Jefferson's plan was not adopted, he did not give up the fight. "Preach," he wrote to Wythe, "a crusade against ignorance . . . ." [2]

Benjamin Rush was another ardent advocate of free schools and even of federal support of education. He contended that politics and economics should be taught in a national university with special attention to agriculture and manufactures and that federal offices should be limited to men who had thus 'imbibed federal and republican ideas." Still another outstanding promoter of education was Noah Webster. Almost immediately after the war ended, he began publishing his *Grammatical Institute*, including a speller, a school reader and a grammar. The spelling book, which passed through many editions, appeared later as *The American Spelling Book*. He, too, advocated an American education emancipated from European traditions. In a new edition of his reader (1787) he included American pieces and in his preface urged the importance to youth of "the writ-

[1] John Adams, *Works* (C. F. Adams, ed., Boston, 1856), IV, 199; VI, 168, 425.
[2] Jefferson, *Works*, IV, 60-65; V, 154.

ings that marked the Revolution," which were "not inferior in any respect to the orations of Cicero and Demosthenes." [1]

Postwar educational legislation in New England tended to follow colonial precedents. The Massachusetts school law of 1789, for instance, was largely a codification of existing arrangements, including the public support of elementary and grammar schools. Enforcement of these latter provisions, however, still depended on community sentiment and the efficiency of local officials. Jedidiah Morse admitted that grand juries were lax in presenting cases of neglect. One result of the division of towns into school districts was to shorten school terms. On the other hand, legislative charters encouraged private schools, though generally without state appropriations. Some academies, however, were helped in other ways, as when Phillips Academy at Andover was partially exempted from taxation. [2]

The Middle states tended to continue their *laissez-faire* attitude toward education. No general school legislation was adopted in New Jersey or Delaware, and little in Pennsylvania, though some aid was given to particular institutions, including the new colleges at Lancaster and Carlisle. In 1786 Pennsylvania also granted certain unappropriated lands to provide money for public schools. New York did somewhat better, thanks largely to the efforts of Governor George Clinton and his political associate, Ezra L'Hommedieu. In 1782 Clinton urged on the legislature "the peculiar duty of the government of a free state" to support education, pointing

---

[1] Benjamin Rush, "Address to the People of the United States," *Am. Museum*, I (1787), 10; A. O. Hansen, *Liberalism and Education* (N. Y., 1926), esp. chaps. iii, vi; Noah Webster, *A Grammatical Institute of the English Language* (4th edn., Hartford, 1787), pt. iii, preface.

[2] G. H. Martin, *Evolution of the Massachusetts School System* (N. Y., 1894), 74-86; Morse, *American Geography*, 165; *Acts and Resolves of Massachusetts for 1786-87* (Boston, 1893), 509.

out that the war had produced "a chasm in education, extremely injurious to the rising generation." Acts of 1784 and 1787 established a "University of the State of New York" with a board of regents charged with general responsibility for education. The regents presently resolved that elementary instruction "ought not to be left to the discretion of private men, but be promoted by public authority." Otherwise, however, not much was accomplished. Though in 1786 certain lands were set apart for an educational fund, no general school law was passed for many years.[1]

Maryland, Virginia and South Carolina took no steps whatever toward a public educational system, while North Carolina did nothing more than to authorize in 1789 the setting up of a state university. The institution did not open until 1795. More than any other Southern commonwealth, Georgia, under the leadership of Lyman Hall and Abraham Baldwin, both native New Englanders and Yale graduates, showed a serious interest in educational planning. Following an appeal from Governor Hall, the legislature granted twenty thousand acres for "a college or Seminary of learning." A later act "for the more full and complete Establishment of a public School of Learning" was passed in 1785 to inaugurate something like the New York plan of a central educational authority, in which all public schools were to be "parts and members of the University." Baldwin was chosen president of this institution, and discussed with Ezra Stiles his ambitious hopes for a university to "comprehend the whole of the *Res Literaria*."

---

[1] Mathew Carey and John Bioren, *Laws of the Commonwealth of Pennsylvania, 1700-1802* (Phila., 1803), chap. mccxiii; Division of Archives and History, *The American Revolution in New York* (Albany, 1926), 245; *Laws of the State of New York* (N. Y., 1792), I; F. P. Graves, "History of the State Education Department," A. C. Flick, ed., *History of the State of New York* (N. Y., 1933-1937), IX, 3-8.

One academy had then been opened and two others authorized, but the college had to wait.[1]

Though state responsibility for education was being more widely recognized, tangible achievements still stemmed largely from individual initiative. Colleges and academies, old and new, generally relied upon private gifts and tuition fees, with the state contributing mainly by issuing charters and making such special concessions as exemption from taxes, land grants or the authorizing of lotteries. Among the substantial patrons of higher education were the public-spirited men in Pennsylvania who founded a Presbyterian college at Carlisle, named for John Dickinson, one of its chief benefactors. Franklin, who helped to secure gifts for this institution, also became the largest single contributor to Franklin College, established at Lancaster under the auspices of the German Reformed and Lutheran churches. British donations were still sought and received. In 1785 the English liberal, Thomas Brand Hollis, observed the Fourth of July, a day "ever to be celebrated," by sending books to the Harvard library. Through Franklin's influence the Quaker physician, Dr. John C. Lettsom, gave books to Dickinson College. President John Wheelock also raised funds for Dartmouth from British sources.[2]

In secondary education the new academies were especially significant. In 1786 Stiles reported that "Academy-making" was proceeding rapidly. He listed thirteen in Connecticut, all but two of which had been

[1] Walter Clark, ed., *State Records of North Carolina* (Winston, 1895-1906), XXV, 21-24; A. D. Chandler, comp., *The Colonial Records of the State of Georgia* (Atlanta, 1904-1910), XIX, pt. ii, 300, 363; Stiles, *Diary*, II, 165-166.

[2] C. J. Stillé, *Life and Times of John Dickinson, 1732-1808* (Pa. Hist. Soc., *Memoirs*, XIII), 325-327; Benjamin Franklin, *Writings* (Albert Smyth, ed., N. Y., 1907), I, 209-210; IX, 15, 371; S. E. Morison, *Three Centuries of Harvard* (Cambridge, 1936), 167.

set up after 1780, but he admitted that some of these schools were meagerly equipped.[1] Of the few New York academies founded after the war, two were promoted by Dutch Reformed clergymen: Erasmus Hall at Flatbush, which still exists, and a school at Schenectady which became the starting point of Union College. Pennsylvania had its Presbyterian, Episcopal, Quaker and Moravian schools, some new and some revived after wartime suspension.[2]

There are comments on Virginia academies by James Madison in answer to Jefferson's inquiry about suitable schools for his nephews. Madison spoke well of the "very flourishing" school kept by an Episcopal clergyman and also of the Hampden-Sydney Presbyterian academy. He complained, however, that private schools suffered from frequent changes of masters and methods. Some Southern boys still went abroad. Charles Carroll of Carrollton continued a family tradition by sending his son to a Jesuit school in Liège and later a daughter abroad to a convent school. South Carolina youths were said to return from English schools "little more improved & much more dissipated than they went."[3]

Of the colleges Yale stood first in enrollment, with two hundred and seventy students in the academic year 1783-1784.[4] The annual average of Harvard's graduates during the ten years following the war was somewhat smaller than in the prewar decades.[5] Outside New

[1] Stiles, *Diary*, III, 247-248.

[2] G. F. Miller, *The Academy System of the State of New York* (Albany, 1922), 18; E. T. Corwin and others, *A History of the Reformed Church, Dutch, the Reformed Church, German, and the Moravian Church in the United States* (Schaff and others, *American Church History Series*, VIII), 191.

[3] Madison, *Writings*, II, 139, 221, 239; Kate M. Rowland, *Life and Correspondence of Charles Carroll of Carrollton* (N. Y., 1898), II, 101, 106; Timothy Ford, "Diary, 1785-1786," *S. C. Hist. and Geneal. Mag.*, XIII, 192.

[4] Stiles, *Diary*, III, 114.

[5] Morison, *Three Centuries of Harvard*, 151-152.

England the colleges fared less well. Queen's College did not reopen for several years. Columbia had fewer than forty students in 1787. New Jersey College at Princeton survived but also with diminished numbers. At Philadelphia the division between the old college and the new state university continued until 1791. William and Mary, another war casualty, had in the first year of peace about a hundred students. By 1789, however, the aggregate attendance at all the older institutions of higher learning was probably not far from the prewar figure.

Changes in the curriculum were comparatively few. Harvard appointed its first salaried teacher of French. Though Silas Deane's plan of a French professorship at Yale was not carried out, President Stiles was sufficiently interested in the subject, at the age of fifty-six, to read Racine's plays with a private tutor. At Columbia one professor was named to teach German along with geography, but the first modern-language chair was that held by Charles Bellini at William and Mary. Though a certain amount of science was taught, no college teacher in this field was quite the equal of John Winthrop, who died during the war. Some scientific instruction in chemistry and natural history was offered by medical professors. Harvard's President Joseph Willard contributed to the publications of the American Academy. At Yale, scientific lectures were given by young Josiah Meigs, later a professor there and subsequently president of the University of Georgia. The college also appropriated money for the purchase of physical apparatus in England. Yale and Princeton classes in politics used Montesquieu's *Spirit of the Laws,* and President Madison chose Adam Smith's *Wealth of Nations* as a William and Mary textbook. Yale disputations dealt with such political issues as the free navigation of the

Mississippi and the eligibility of "Infidels and Libertines" for public office.[1]

In Maryland, which had no college before the Revolution, four new institutions had been founded by 1791: Washington College at Chestertown, St. John's at Annapolis, Cokesbury near Baltimore, and Georgetown in what is now the District of Columbia. St. John's grew out of the old King William School at Annapolis, and was associated with Washington College in a somewhat shadowy "University of Maryland." Cokesbury, established primarily to train Methodist preachers, was soon abandoned.[2] In the neighboring state of Virginia, Hampden-Sydney Academy now became Hampden-Sydney College, its ardent Calvinism in marked contrast with the mild Anglicanism of William and Mary.

The colleges did not lack critics. Francis Hopkinson wrote a satire on "Modern Learning Exemplified by a Specimen of a Collegiate Examination." Harrison Gray Otis, the future senator, assured a Harvard classmate that he would be glad to get away from "the sophisticated Jargon of a superstitious Synod of pension'd Bigots." At Yale there was talk of undue clerical control. Certain observers, however, were more friendly. Jefferson, after some reforms for which he was largely responsible, declared optimistically that in most subjects needed by young Americans they could do as well at William and Mary as in Europe. John Quincy Adams, a graduate of Harvard in 1787 after a previous period of study at Leyden, wrote many years later, "My short discipline of fifteen months at Harvard University was

---

[1] *Ibid.*, 82, 164-171; Stiles, *Diary*, III, 127, 130, 135, 142, 155, 167, 258, 346; P. A. Bruce, *History of the University of Virginia, 1819-1919* (N. Y., 1920-1922), I, 51-55; Brander Matthews and others, eds., *A History of Columbia University, 1754-1904* (N. Y., 1904), 64, 76.

[2] B. C. Steiner, *History of Education in Maryland* (Wash., 1894), chap. iii, 229-245, 273.

the introduction to all the prosperity that has ever befallen me." [1]

Legal education was still chiefly acquired through apprenticeship. Among the abler practitioner-teachers were the future Massachusetts chief justice, Theophilus Parsons, who guided Rufus King and John Quincy Adams; Egbert Benson of New York, in whose office Chancellor James Kent studied; and Peter Van Schaack, the rehabilitated Loyalist. In Litchfield, Connecticut, Tapping Reeve gave unusually systematic instruction in what came to be known as the Litchfield Law School. At William and Mary, George Wythe served as professor of "Law and Police."

Few leaders of the colonial bar continued in practice. Some were Loyalist exiles while others were too busy with politics. Conspicuous among the older lawyer-politicians still active was Patrick Henry, who was regarded as a highly successful criminal lawyer—too successful, according to one of his contemporaries. [2] Most leaders in the profession were younger men who had begun their careers shortly before or during the war: Ellsworth and Parsons in New England, Hamilton and Burr in New York, Wilson and the younger Ingersoll in Pennsylvania, Martin in Maryland, John Marshall and Spencer Roane in Virginia, and Iredell in North Carolina. Ellsworth, Wilson and Iredell were soon to become justices of the United States Supreme Court, while Parsons and Roane became distinguished state judges.

Agrarians and debtors commonly regarded lawyers as largely responsible for their troubles. John Quincy

---

[1] G. E. Hastings, *Life and Works of Francis Hopkinson* (Chicago, 1926), 418; Morison, *Three Centuries of Harvard*, 175, 179; Stiles, *Diary*, III, 59, 121; Adams, *Life in a New England Town*, 7; Bruce, *University of Virginia*, I, 54.

[2] W. L. Smith, "Journal, 1790-1791," Mass. Hist. Soc., *Proceeds.*, LI, 68.

Adams while a law student found the "popular odium" attached to the profession so great that "the most innocent and irreproachable life cannot guard a lawyer against the hatred of his fellow-citizens." Edmund Randolph reported that the Virginia bar was overstocked, with more than ordinary ability required to earn a livelihood. The profession was charged with exploiting legal technicalities. Abraham Clark, a New Jersey signer of the Declaration, who tried to simplify legal procedure, was quoted as saying that his system, "Clark's Practice-Law," would, if adopted, "tear off the ruffles from the lawyers' wrists." [1]

Most of the outstanding lawyers, especially in the North, favored the new Federal Constitution. Among the notable exceptions, however, were Patrick Henry, Luther Martin and Alexander Hamilton's New York colleagues at the Philadelphia Convention. Popular resentment of the stand taken by the Federalist lawyers was expressed in a New York manifesto condemning the Constitution as "monarchical, aristocratical, oligarchical, tyranical, diabolical," produced by a convention of whom "one half were lawyers!" [2]

Medical training was still handicapped by popular prejudice. The "Medical Institution" at Harvard, founded in 1782, was slow in getting under way, and in 1784 the Harvard professors were refused clinical facilities in the Boston almshouse. Inability to get material for dissection by legitimate methods led to graverobbing. In New York public protests culminated in the "Doctors' Riot" in 1788 when militia were called out. Three persons were killed and others injured, including John Jay who had tried to pacify the rioters.

[1] Adams, *Life in a New England Town*, 57, 58, 73; Frances N. Mason, ed., *John Norton and Sons* (Richmond, 1937), 495; Theodore Sedgwick, *A Memoir of the Life of William Livingston* (N. Y., 1833), 434 n.

[2] *Daily Advertiser* (N. Y.), March 4, 1789.

Jefferson believed that medical students still needed to go abroad. The Pennsylvania Hospital continued to be the most efficient institution of its kind in the country. Manasseh Cutler praised the pains taken with patients, "the spacious and clean apartments" and the general good order. He saw twenty or thirty students make the rounds with Dr. Rush, noting his comments on significant cases. But even here conditions were bad enough. Insane patients, some of whom were "nearly or quite naked," were kept in cells ten feet square, partly underground.[1]

Among the professional leaders were John and Samuel Bard in New York—the latter, Washington's personal physician—Edward Holyoke and John Warren in Boston, and Benjamin Rush, now probably the most able and vigorous, if not always the soundest, of the Philadelphia group. In New York the prewar medical society was reorganized, and at Philadelphia Dr. John Morgan founded a "College of Physicians" whose members were expected to advance the healing art. Massachusetts formed a medical society, and in 1788 the one in New Haven issued a volume of *Cases and Observations.*[2] Medical essays were also published by the American Philosophical Society and the American Academy of Arts and Sciences. But professional differentiation came slowly. The New York directory for 1786 listed, along with doctors and surgeons, such combinations as surgeon and dentist, surgeon barber, surgeon and apothecary, and physician and apothecary. In dentistry John Green-

---

[1] Morison, *Three Centuries of Harvard,* 171; Matthews and others, *Columbia University,* 332; D. M. Schneider and H. E. Barnes, "Care of the Needy, the Sick and Homeless Children," Flick, *History of the State of New York,* VIII, 312; S. I. Pomerantz, *New York, an American City, 1783-1803* (Columbia Univ., *Studies,* no. 442), 350, 401; W. P. and Julia P. Cutler, *Life, Journals, and Correspondence of Rev. Manasseh Cutler* (Cincinnati, 1888), I, 279-280.

[2] "Constitution of the College of Physicians of Philadelphia," *Am. Museum,* II, 405-407; Stiles, *Diary,* III, 328.

wood of New York did something to improve American practice. His most distinguished patient was George Washington.

Of scientific progress in the new nation Franklin took a hopeful view. The first volume of the American Academy of Arts and Sciences asserted the stimulating effect of political freedom upon the diffusion of knowledge, engaging the mind in "noble and generous pursuits." Even "civil wars and commotions," said Dr. Benjamin Waterhouse, were likely to foster intellectual advance. Another optimist was Noah Webster. "The minds of the people," he wrote, "are in a ferment, and consequently disposed to receive improvements." [1] The learned societies at Philadelphia and Boston were now joined by the Connecticut Academy of Arts and Sciences, organized in 1786. An ambitious project was that of Quesnay de Beaurepaire for an Academy of Sciences at Richmond on the French model, with branches in other cities and distinguished foreign intellectuals as nonresident associates. A building was erected and studies were planned, but Jefferson kept aloof and the enterprise failed. Another undertaking of scholarly significance was the Philological Society, founded by Noah Webster in 1788 for "ascertaining and improving the American tongue." [2]

Among native imprints in science, geographical works and travel books bulked large, including Jedidiah Morse's *Geography Made Easy* (1784), followed by his *American Geography* (1789); John Filson's *Kentucky* (1784); Thomas Hutchins's *Narrative and Topograph-*

---

[1] American Academy of Arts and Sciences, *Memoirs*, I (1785), preface, pt. iii; Benjamin Waterhouse, *A Synopsis of a Course of Lectures, on the Theory and Practice of Medicine* (Boston, 1786); Emily E. F. Ford and Emily E. F. Skeel, eds., *Notes on the Life of Noah Webster* (N. Y., 1912), II, 456.

[2] Stiles, *Diary*, III, 262 and *passim*; Bruce, *University of Virginia*, I, 55 ff.; H. R. Warfel, *Noah Webster, Schoolmaster to America* (N. Y., 1936), 185-187.

ical Description of Louisiana and West Florida (1784) ; and Christopher Colles's *Survey of the Roads of the United States* (1789). American interest in Buffon continued. Though Jefferson rejected his theories of animal degeneration in the New World, he considered him "the best informed of any Naturalist who has ever written." Madison owned numerous volumes of Buffon's works and the two Virginians discussed the French master's theory of "central heat." American contributions in botany included Humphrey Marshall's description of trees and shrubs in *Arbustrum Americanum, the American Grove* (1785), and Manasseh Cutler's creditable studies of New England flora. Popular interest is suggested by articles in the *Massachusetts Magazine* (1789-1790) on "American Natural History." Samuel Latham Mitchill published magazine essays on geology; and there were other articles on paleontology. John Morgan was said to own a large collection of fossils from the Ohio country.[1]

Some Americans followed European studies in physics and chemistry. Sir William Nicholson's standard British manual of "natural philosophy" (1781) was reprinted at Philadelphia in 1788. Lavoisier's epochmaking work in chemistry won him election as foreign associate of the Philosophical Society, though he was probably best known in the United States through a manual by his early disciple, Fourcroix, which Professor Aaron Dexter used in his Harvard teaching. Jefferson thought chemistry "among the most useful of sciences, and big with future discoveries for the utility and safety of the human race." Madison, who was also interested, asked Jefferson about an inexpensive set of chemical apparatus. Though no significant contributions were made by Americans, Charles Vancouver in 1785 pub-

[1] Jefferson, *Works*, III, 431; IV, 209; Madison, *Writings*, II, 28-30; Schoepf, *Travels*, I, 266-270.

lished at Philadelphia *A Compendium of Chemical, Experimental and Natural Philosophy*. Sir William Herschel's astronomical work was also known and extracts from his writings appeared in the *American Museum*. Stiles's diary frequently mentioned him.[1]

One intellectual interest stimulated by political independence concerned the "American language." Should the speech and writing of the new nation conform to English standards? On this subject opinions differed. Franklin thought the British should encourage emigration to the United States because this would increase the number of people who would read English authors. Otherwise the foreign elements in the population might "drown and stifle the English." He cared little for an "American language" and, though he favored phonetic spelling, was something of a purist in other respects. Another conservative was President John Witherspoon who, though a staunch Whig, disliked departures from English usage.[2]

The most vigorous advocate of linguistic emancipation was Noah Webster, whose *Spelling Book* gradually displaced Dilworth's English textbook. Webster prefaced his work with a strenuous assertion of nationalism, which appeared also in his *Grammar* and *Reader*. For America to adopt the maxims of the Old World would be to "plant the seeds of decay in a vigorous constitution." Arguing in his *Dissertations on the English Language* (1789) for an "American tongue," he insisted that national honor required "a system of our own, in language as well as government." Dissimilarities in

[1] Brissot de Warville, *New Travels*, 107-110; Thomas Jefferson, *Writings* (H. A. Washington, ed., Wash., 1853-1854), II, 431; Stiles, *Diary*, III, 226, 261, 398, 415; William Herschel, "An Account of Three Volcanos in the Moon," *Am. Museum*, II, 488; Benjamin West, "A Short Account of the Planet Herschel," *ibid.*, III (1788), 265.

[2] Franklin, *Writings*, IX, 263-264; X, 75-77; "Druid" papers in M. M. Mathews, ed., *The Beginnings of American English* (Chicago, 1931), chap. ii.

situation and experience would gradually produce a language "as different from the future language of England, as the modern Dutch, Danish, and Swedish are from the German."[1]

Webster desired not only divergence from British English, but also uniformity of American usage, "demolishing those odious distinctions of provincial dialects." After presenting his views in various parts of the Union he believed that such uniformity could be achieved. His textbooks exerted a certain influence in this direction, though his New England standards did not go unchallenged. Webster felt his optimism was justified by existing conditions. Were there, he asked, in the United States a hundred words, other than those of purely local application, which were not "universally intelligible"? There might indeed be difficulties in maintaining this degree of uniformity because of non-English immigration, but education would overcome this obstacle.[2]

One reason for Webster's hopeful attitude was his estimate of the intelligence and literacy of the average rural dweller, whom he considered far superior to the "illiterate peasantry of England." Most of them, he thought, read newspapers and, besides the Bible "found in all families," other substantial books. Even if he overstated the case for the country as a whole, he was doubtless right in believing rural Americans better off in this respect than their English contemporaries. If literacy is defined in a broader sense, many eighteenth-century political leaders compare favorably with their successors in the next century. This was certainly true of such men as John Adams, Jay, Hamilton, Franklin

[1] Webster, *Grammatical Institute* (1783 edn.), introduction, and his *Dissertations on the English Language* (Boston, 1789), 20-23.

[2] Webster, *Grammatical Institute*, introduction, and his *Dissertations*, 288-290.

and his Philadelphia friends, and Jefferson's circle of Virginia intimates. George Wythe could guide Jefferson's nephew in the classics, reading with him "Aeschylus and Horace, one day, and Herodotus and Cicero's orations, the next." In Philadelphia, Schoepf found people of all classes using the Library Company's collection. But Franklin, while stating there were more readers than before the Revolution, believed there was less demand for serious works.[1]

Journalism after the war showed some advance over earlier years. The number of newspapers almost doubled between 1783 and 1790, reaching a total of about ninety, though some were short-lived. Besides six Boston papers, Massachusetts had seven more in other towns. Up-state New York had six and there were several in inland Pennsylvania, including one at Pittsburgh. Weekly issues continued to be the rule, though by 1785 Philadelphia, Charleston and New York had dailies. For the most part they were still limited to four pages. Nor had the contents changed much: shipping notices, scanty news items from other states and from Europe, legislative proceedings, public announcements, political communications, some literary articles, and advertisements.

The Philadelphia press was probably the strongest in the country. Besides those that survived the war two new papers made their appearance: Francis Bailey's *Freeman's Journal* (1781) and Mathew Carey's *Pennsylvania Herald* (1785). Bailey's contributors included both Federalists and anti-Federalists. The *Herald* enjoyed a special reputation for its legislative reports. During the Pennsylvania debates on the Federal Constitution its young editor, Alexander J. Dallas, printed the fullest accounts; but Federalist opposition apparently

---

[1] *Ibid.*, 289; "The Taliaferro Family," *William and Mary College Quar.*, XX, 213; Schoepf, *Travels*, I, 86; Franklin, *Writings*, IX, 488.

forced their discontinuance and later that of the newspaper itself. Partisan postmasters were also accused of detaining opposition newspapers. The author of the "Centinel" letters against ratification, complaining that an important manifesto of his party had been suppressed, alleged a conspiracy "to muzzle or demolish every newspaper that allowed free discussion." There was doubtless some justification for such charges.[1]

In New York most papers were under Federalist influence, with Thomas Greenleaf's *New-York Journal* as the principal organ of the anti-Federalists.[2] In New England, Benjamin Russell's *Massachusetts Centinel and the Republican* (later the *Columbian Centinel*) supported ratification of the Constitution while Benjamin Edes's *Boston Gazette,* the old radical mouthpiece, took the opposite side. Russell was the outstanding Boston journalist. The *Centinel's* reports of the Massachusetts ratifying convention of 1788 have been described as "probably the first systematic attempt at reporting for any Boston paper." [3] Baltimore, with its rapidly growing population, had two important papers: the *Maryland Gazette* and the *Maryland Journal,* of Federalist leanings but politically fair.[4] In Virginia, Williamsburg was replaced as a journalistic center by Richmond, which now possessed three newspapers. Farther South, Charleston also maintained three journals.

As earlier, magazines found the going difficult. New York had Noah Webster's short-lived *American Maga-*

[1] J. B. McMaster and F. D. Stone, eds., *Pennsylvania and the Federal Constitution, 1787-1788* (Phila., 1888), 15, 212, 664-668; C. H. Lincoln, "Francis Bailey," Allen Johnson and Dumas Malone, eds., *Dictionary of American Biography* (N. Y., 1928-1937), I, 494-495.

[2] E. W. Spaulding, *New York in the Critical Period* (D. R. Fox, ed., N. Y. State Hist. Assoc. Ser., I), 38-40, 259-261.

[3] Justin Winsor, ed., *Memorial History of Boston, 1630-1880* (Boston, 1880-1881), III, 617 ff.

[4] B. C. Steiner, "Maryland's Adoption of the Constitution," *Am. Hist. Rev.,* V, 26.

zine (1787-1788), a vehicle for his political and educational theories. Between 1783 and 1786 the *Boston Magazine* presented a little original matter, including essays by the historian Jeremy Belknap, but gave most of its space to reproductions from British publications. In 1789 Isaiah Thomas founded the *Massachusetts Magazine*, which lasted till 1796—longer than any predecessor. Besides miscellaneous reprints from British and American sources, it published some original prose and poetry and appealed to the popular taste by illustrations and sentimental fiction. Another New England venture, associated with the "Hartford Wits," was the *New Haven Gazette and the Connecticut Magazine* (1786-1789), which from the standpoint of literary history proved more significant than the Boston periodicals. Its contributors included Timothy Dwight, John Trumbull, Joel Barlow and David Humphreys. Edited by Josiah Meigs, it was the literary organ of New England conservatism. Its chief effusion was a collaboration: "The Anarchiad, a Poem on the Restoration of Chaos and Substantial Night." "Anarch" was presented, in the manner of Milton's Satan, as the personification of the subversive spirit. At first apparently triumphant, he was finally overcome by the defenders of order.[1]

Outstanding among Philadelphia publishers was Mathew Carey, a young Irish radical who arrived there in 1784 and served for a time as chief editor of the *Columbian Magazine*. He soon left it, however, to found the *American Museum*, an important repository of material relating to the Revolution and the American scene. During the constitutional debate of 1787-1788 Carey, though himself a Federal sympathizer, printed

---

[1] L. N. Richardson, *A History of Early American Magazines, 1741-1789* (N. Y., 1931), chaps. viii-xi; V. L. Parrington, ed., *The Connecticut Wits* (N. Y., 1926), 429-473.

communications on both sides. Notwithstanding his special interest in economics and politics he devoted a third of the space in his first number to "Select Poetry." By 1789 the subscription list, ranging from New England to the Lower South, numbered nearly seventeen hundred, among whom were Washington, Jefferson and Madison. Rush used the *Columbian Magazine* to advocate his reforms, while Jeremy Belknap contributed to it his "American Plutarch, or a Biographical Account of the Heroic and Virtuous Men . . . of the United States." A poetry section was entitled "The Columbian Parnassiad." [1]

Despite the effects of the war the lending libraries quickly resumed their former importance. The Redwood Library at Newport had lost more than half its books, while all the institutional libraries of New York had parted with either the whole or a considerable part of their collections. Five years after the British evacuation, however, the New York Society's Library was revived and by 1790 it had greatly increased its prewar strength. Another institution which survived the war, the Charleston Library Society, now published a catalogue. Though Boston had no institution similar to those in New York, Philadelphia and Charleston, Harvard, which by 1790 owned about thirteen thousand volumes, possessed the largest college collection, and probably the largest of any kind, in the country. Among the smaller towns, Wethersfield, Connecticut, formed its Union Library Society in 1783, and a Massachusetts town, named for Benjamin Franklin, received through his good offices books selected by Richard Price as "most proper to inculcate Principles of sound Religion and just Government." [2]

[1] Richardson, *Early American Magazines*, 314-333; *American Museum*, I and II, *passim*, esp. I, 69-94.

[2] Stiles, *Diary*, III, 162-163; Frank Monaghan, "The Results of the Revolution," Flick, *History of the State of New York*, IV, 349-350;

American copyright legislation now had its inception, thanks largely to the efforts of Noah Webster who, as a writer of textbooks intended for interstate circulation, had a personal stake in the matter. Such statutes were secured in all the original thirteen states; and in 1790 Congress enacted the first general copyright law.[1]

Of the prewar booksellers, James Rivington and Hugh Gaine remained after the British evacuation of New York, though Rivington soon failed. Some of the Philadelphia bookmen also survived the war, but Robert Bell, the ablest of them, died in 1784. Perhaps the most interesting personality in the book trade was Isaiah Thomas, who had his headquarters at Worcester with branches elsewhere, including one in Baltimore. Besides distributing his own publications and continuing to conduct his newspaper, he imported many English works.[2]

The public was still reading books mainly by British authors. Fanny Burney's *Evelina* (1778), which scored a brilliant success in England during the war, quickly interested Americans. Gibbon's *Decline and Fall* (1776-1788) was read, and the poets, Burns and Cowper, were just rising above the American horizon. Burns's *Poems Chiefly in the Scottish Dialect* (1783) and Cowper's *Task* (1785) were both soon reprinted in the United States. Sheridan's *School for Scandal*, first played in London in 1777, was published in America shortly after the war. Continued interest in earlier English fiction led to the printing of Richardson's novels and two of Fielding's. The years from 1786 to 1789 also saw four issues of *Robinson Crusoe*. Among British

A. B. Keep, *History of the New York Society Library* (N. Y., 1908), 212; Schoepf, *Travels*, I, 86; Franklin, *Writings*, IX, 300; S. W. Adams and H. R. Stiles, *The History of Ancient Wethersfield* (N. Y., 1904), I, 657.

[1] Ford and Skeel, *Noah Webster*, I, chaps. iii-iv.

[2] Isaiah Thomas, *The History of Printing in America* (Am. Antiquarian Soc., *Archæologia Americana. Trans. and Colls.*, V-VI), I, lxxv ff.

juveniles Thomas reprinted *Goody Two Shoes* and *The House That Jack Built*. Curiously enough, one of Thomas's most successful ventures was his reprinting of a standard British spelling book—this in spite of the increasing popularity of Webster's speller, which he also issued.[1]

Among books of American authorship those dealing with politics have best stood the test of time. *The Federalist* by Hamilton, Madison and Jay, which appeared first in the newspapers and then promptly in book form, has become a classic. The controversial essays of anti-Federalist writers are less familiar, though some still deserve study. The most ambitious exposition of political theory was John Adams's *Defence of the Constitutions of the United States*, the first volume of which was printed in time to influence members of the Federal Convention.[2]

Among the "Hartford Wits" John Trumbull owes his fame chiefly to his earlier writings, but his associates —Timothy Dwight, Joel Barlow, Lemuel Hopkins and David Humphreys—published their work mainly after the war. "Well-born" by New England standards, they believed in the republican idea and in a grandiose future for their country, but, as shown in the *Anarchiad*, they wished to defend the existing social order against radicalism. In other poems the writers emphasized the note of patriotism. Dwight's *Conquest of Canaan* (1785), an epic with a Biblical theme, contains allusions to the Revolutionary War, and his *Greenfield Hill*, published in 1794 but composed earlier, pictures New England rural scenes and glorifies America,

[1] J. B. McMaster, *History of the People of the United States* (N. Y., 1883-1913), I, 74-79; Charles Evans, comp., *American Bibliography* (Chicago, 1903-1934), VII, nos. 20303, 20991; Annie R. Marble, *From 'Prentice to Patron* (N. Y., 1935), chap. ix.

[2] Charles Warren, *The Making of the Constitution* (Boston, 1928), 155-157.

by heaven design'd
th' example bright, to renovate mankind.

Barlow's *Vision of Columbus* (1787) was similarly "designed to exhibit the importance of this country in every point of view as the noblest and most elevated part of the earth," the "last and greatest theatre for the improvement of mankind."

Notwithstanding the native themes of these and other contemporary poets, their writings were not distinctively American in language or style. "Every poet," wrote Humphreys, "who aspires to celebrity strives to approach the perfection of Pope." Outside New England also, most men of literary pretentions were conservatives, among them Francis Hopkinson who continued to produce light essays in prose and verse. A notable exception was Philip Freneau. The fighting democracy of his Revolutionary poems was to reappear later; but for the present he was drawing inspiration from his experience as a sea captain for such spirited lyrics as "Verses Made at Sea in a Heavy Gale" and "The Hurricane." During this period Freneau's verses were twice published in book form.[1]

Nearly all the plays produced in the United States were still of British authorship, but there were two notable exceptions. In 1787 Royall Tyler, a young Harvard graduate who had fought in the Revolution, saw his play "The Contrast" presented at the John Street Theatre. In it he contrasted American simplicity and honesty, embodied in the hero and heroine, with Old World sophistication. "I have learned," said the hero, "that probity, virtue, honour, though they should

---

[1] F. L. Pattee, *The First Century of American Literature* (N. Y., 1935), 62, and his *Poems of Philip Freneau* (Princeton, 1902-1907), I, 293; II, 250; Parrington, *Connecticut Wits*, 220; S. M. Tucker, "The Beginnings of Verse," W. P. Trent and others, eds., *The Cambridge History of American Literature* (N. Y., 1917-1921), I, 169.

not have received the polish of Europe, will secure to an honest American the good graces of his fair country-woman, and, I hope, the applause of The Public." The same idea was expressed in the humorous Yankee character of Jonathan, and in these lines of the prologue:

Why should our thoughts to distant countries roam
When each refinement may be found at home.

"The Contrast" was also performed in Philadelphia and Baltimore. Another American play seen in New York in 1789 was William Dunlap's "The Father, or American Shandyism." [1] The output of historical works was slight. Popular interest in military history is indicated by the reprinting in America, soon after its publication in London, of Sir Henry Clinton's *Narrative*, defending his record against the charges of Cornwallis. Another controversial piece, Joseph Galloway's criticism of Howe, was published in Philadelphia in 1787 as a *Short History of the War in America under the Command of Sir William Howe*. In 1789 appeared the comprehensive accounts of the war by William Gordon and David Ramsay. Though both works relied unduly upon the British *Annual Register*, Gordon's treatise is useful on a few matters falling within his personal experience, and Ramsay's *History of the American Revolution*, in spite of obvious defects, contains some original observations. George R. Minot's *History of the Insurrection* (1788) was a scholarly conservative's account of the Shays Rebellion. Jeremy Belknap's *History of New Hampshire* (1784-1792) was also an excellent work of its kind.

As for the fine arts, a writer in the *American Museum* in 1787, eager to "explode the European creed" of America's inferiority in culture, noted the distinguished

[1] A. H. Quinn, ed., *Representative American Plays* (N. Y., 1917), 45-77.

English careers of the American-born West and Copley and the more recent work of John Trumbull and Gilbert Stuart. Besides Charles Willson Peale, still painting American subjects, there were two other creditable artists: Ralph Earle, a New England pupil of West, and Robert Pine, an Englishman who spent his last years in Philadelphia and is best known for his portraits of the Washington family at Mt. Vernon. Trumbull, after further study abroad, was already becoming the outstanding figure in depicting the Revolution and its leaders. His first war scenes were the "Battle of Bunker's Hill," with the death of Warren, and the "Death of General Montgomery in the Attack on Quebec." On seeing the Bunker Hill picture in London Abigail Adams wrote, "My whole frame contracted, my blood shivered, and I felt a faintness at my heart. He [Trumbull] is the first painter who has undertaken to immortalize by his pencil those great actions, that gave rise to our nation." Before 1789 Trumbull had begun his notable small canvass of the signers of the Declaration of Independence and, besides, painted three other episodes: the "Surrender of Cornwallis," the "Death of General Mercer" and the "Capture of the Hessians at Trenton." [1]

In architecture the so-called colonial style still prevailed in the better houses. A well-known example and one of the best of its kind was the Providence home of the wealthy merchant, John Brown. Other contemporary work in this mode was that of Samuel McIntire in Salem and eastern Massachusetts. Meanwhile, Jefferson's influence in favor of classical forms commenced to be felt. He gave Virginia the designs of the Maison Carré to serve as the model for the state capitol, begun in 1785. Jefferson also encouraged Charles Bulfinch, who after travel abroad returned to Boston and by 1789

---

[1] Anon., "Thoughts on American Genius," *Am. Museum*, I, 206-209; Mrs. John Adams, *Letters* (C. F. Adams, ed., Boston, 1848), 277.

was receiving commissions for churches and other buildings. Bulfinch is said to have been influenced by the Adam brothers, then the leading "classical architects" in England.[1]

All in all, life in the "Critical Period" was far from dark, whether from an economic standpoint or from that of cultural progress. The conflict with Britain had brought its setbacks and left difficult problems in its train, but the war-time experience and the freedom it had won contained seeds of new life.

[1] Fiske Kimball, *Domestic Architecture of the American Colonies and the Early Republic* (N. Y., 1922), 145 ff., and his *Thomas Jefferson, Architect* (Boston, 1916), *passim*.

CHAPTER XVI

HORIZONS WEST AND EAST

THOUGH British recognition of American sovereignty beyond the Alleghanies offered new opportunities to home seekers, much of the westward movement was still into untenanted areas on the eastern side of the mountains. Suggestive in this connection is the removal of Southern state capitals from tidewater locations to the inland towns of Richmond, Raleigh, Columbia and Augusta. Similar shifts in the North, though not actually made, were discussed. Beyond the mountains the problem of colonization was far from simple. Within the treaty limits of the United States there were British posts throughout the Great Lakes region and as a result thirteen years passed before it was really open to American occupation. South of the Ohio, the Gulf Coast was in Spanish hands, including the mouth of the Mississippi. Even north of the thirty-first parallel Spain refused to accept the boundaries set by the Anglo-American peace treaty and continued to keep a governor at Natchez. Another complication in the Gulf region was the presence of British traders in the Floridas.

The Western Indians, generally allied with the British during the war, had resented the surrender of their country to the Americans. Nevertheless some cessions of Indian land were secured by peaceful means. Except for a few reservations in New York, the native title had by 1790 been extinguished in that state and in western Pennsylvania. By the treaty of Fort Stanwix in 1784 the Iroquois yielded also their claims farther west, and the next year four Western bands did the same for the greater part of the present state of Ohio. Other tribes, however, remained hostile and there were almost continuous border disturbances. In the Southwest the Kentuckians also were menaced by Indian incursions and the Tennessee pioneers suffered severely at the hands of the Cherokee and the Creek, partly because of white encroachments on the red men's lands. Though United States commissioners negotiated a treaty with the Cherokee, it was practically nullified because a considerable part of the land then reserved to the savages had already been occupied by Tennessee frontiersmen; and so the warfare went on. The only area beyond the Alleghanies in which white colonization made much progress was in the valleys of the Ohio and its two great tributaries, the Cumberland and the Tennessee.[1]

The situation proved disappointing also to Americans interested in Western trade. In the Northwest the British not only continued to hold their posts, but largely succeeded in preventing their rivals from dealing with the adjacent Indians.[2] In the South, American traders carried peltry overland on pack horses to the Atlantic Seaboard; but there, too, British traders operated from bases within Spanish jurisdiction. Notwithstanding all such difficulties, however, the rising capitalists of the East were strongly attracted toward the new country. Leading merchants, planters and politicians invested either in that section or in the "wild lands" of Maine and western New York. Some became actual settlers, while others acted as absentee owners, holding land for future sale or lease. Nathaniel Gorham, a Massachusetts merchant-politician and delegate to the Federal Con-

[1] A. P. Whitaker, *The Spanish-American Frontier: 1783-1795* (Boston, 1927), chaps. i-vi; S. C. Williams, *History of the Lost State of Franklin* (rev. edn., N. Y., 1933), 259-261.

[2] W. E. Stevens, *The Northwest Fur Trade, 1763-1800* (Univ. of Ill., *Studies*, XIV, no. 3), chaps. iii-iv.

vention, was one of the principals in the Phelps-Gorham purchase of lands in western New York. Another merchant-politician, Elbridge Gerry, owned shares in the Ohio Company, among whose chief promoters were Generals Rufus Putnam and Samuel H. Parsons and the Reverend Manasseh Cutler. Other members of the Federal Convention interested in Western lands were George Washington, George Mason, Robert Morris and James Wilson. North Carolina politicians also were conspicuous land speculators, and a New Jersey group headed by John Cleve Symmes promoted a settlement centering about Cincinnati. Though there were conflicts of interest between promoters and settlers, no sharp line existed between them. The Allens in Vermont, Putnam and Parsons in the Northwest and many of the Kentucky and Tennessee leaders acted in both capacities.[1]

The frontier attracted lawless as well as law-abiding elements. The former were publicized by unsympathetic critics and blamed for needless conflicts with the Indians. General Josiah Harmar, who commanded United States forces on the Ohio, referred to the squatters there as "banditti" whose conduct was "a disgrace to human nature"—a description which hardly applied to all men whom the army removed for lack of proper land titles. Among the better settlers were war veterans who had bought tracts with army scrip. In 1783 one such group, whom Washington considered peculiarly fitted for frontier life, planned a settlement north of the Ohio. War experience sometimes determined the choice of locations, as when Yankees who had engaged in border fighting in western New York later settled there. Unfortu-

[1] C. A. Beard, *An Economic Interpretation of the Constitution* (N. Y., 1913), chap. v; T. P. Abernethy, *Western Lands and the American Revolution* (N. Y., 1937), chaps. xxi ff.; R. A. East, *Business Enterprise in the American Revolutionary Era* (Columbia Univ., *Studies,* no. 439), 318 ff.

nately, a great deal of the army scrip was sold to speculators.[1]

Since migration proceeded northward and southward
as well as westward, all the older sections participated.
Connecticut folk were active in colonizing Vermont and
western New York. Pennsylvanians and Jerseymen
went to the upper Ohio and sometimes to Kentucky.
Most of the Kentucky and Tennessee pioneers, however,
hailed from Maryland, Virginia and North Carolina.
Still other Southerners moved to sparsely populated
areas in Georgia. The motives for change varied with
the individual. Restless and adventurous persons
wanted to avoid the social patterns of a settled community. A New Jersey migrant willing to stop in a
region that was partly occupied found others eager to
go farther: "It seems as if people were mad to git afloat
on the Ohio." One man, complaining of too many
neighbors though the nearest was seven miles off, said
his hunting was spoiled and he hated to pay taxes.
Probably, however, most persons were prompted chiefly
by the desire to establish permanent homes. Thus a
Virginia planter planned to sell his property to buy land
in Kentucky in order to "give each of his children a
sufficient portion." Soil exhaustion in the tobacco
country sent some younger sons of planter families to
Kentucky. Vermont attracted followers of Shays and
other Bay Staters escaping from burdensome taxation.[2]

The profit motive in pioneering is illustrated by the

[1] George Washington, *Writings from the Original Manuscript Sources*
(J. C. Fitzpatrick, ed., Wash., 1931-1940), XXVII, 16-18; Justin
Winsor, *The Westward Movement* (Boston, 1897), 270.

[2] Israel Shreve, "Journal from Jersey to the Monongahala, August 11,
1788," *Pa. Mag. of History and Biog.*, LII, 203; J. D. Schoepf, *Travels
in the Confederation, 1783-1784* (A. J. Morrison, ed., Phila., 1911),
I, 236, 261; T. D. Clark, *A History of Kentucky* (Carl Wittke, ed.,
Prentice-Hall History Series, 1937), 107; Fairfax Harrison, *Landmarks
of Old Prince William* (Richmond, 1924), I, 334; I. B. Wilbur, *Ira
Allen* (Boston, 1928), chap. xi.

case of Hugh White who in 1784 moved with four adult sons from Connecticut to the New York frontier. Having bought land there and advertised his holdings widely, he excited a wave of migration from his home state. William Cooper, the founder of Cooperstown, went from New Jersey to Otsego County, New York, where after preliminary exploration he purchased a large tract, of which forty thousand acres were quickly sold to prospective settlers. He then set up a store and saw the newcomers through a food shortage. Landowner, judge, politician and friend of education, Cooper was long the leading personality of this region. Among the Virginia settlers in Kentucky were many comparatively well-to-do persons: army officers, planters and professional men. Some planters prepared the way by sending out an advance guard of overseers and slaves. "The country," wrote a contemporary, "began to be chequered with genteel men," whose presence influenced "the backwoods people who constituted the first emigrants." [1]

Travel to the West continued to be difficult and often proved dangerous. One route to the Ohio was by pack horse and wagon from Philadelphia to Pittsburgh and thence by boat down the Ohio. From the Chesapeake country the Ohio Valley could be reached partly by river boats, but the most common way was through Cumberland Gap and the Wilderness Road to Kentucky. Migrants from Philadelphia generally arrived at Pittsburgh only after a long, rough journey. A New Jersey party took twenty-five days to get to its destination in western Pennsylvania. One traveler from Pittsburgh to Lexington went down the Ohio in a boat which had a fireplace in one cabin and two other cabins par-

[1] Lois K. Mathews, *Expansion of New England* (Boston, 1909), chap. vi; F. W. Halsey, *Old New York Frontier* (N. Y., 1901), 339, 357 ff.; Gilbert Imlay, *A Topographical Description of the Western Territory of North America* (3rd edn., London, 1797), 153; Clark, *History of Kentucky*, 91.

titioned with blankets. Among the various river craft were flat boats with partially covered decks, keel boats and more primitive vessels. Virginians going by land through Cumberland Gap encountered still other difficulties. One trip from near Richmond to Harrodsburg, Kentucky, began the last week of May and ended early in July with the party in fear of Indian attack. Soon after this journey the Kentuckians suffered a disastrous defeat in a battle with the savages at Blue Licks.[1]

The matter of land titles still caused trouble. State preëmption laws sometimes gave preference to actual settlers, but in the Southwest there was generally no orderly method. Virginia and North Carolina granted immense tracts without public surveys, the result being that overlapping claims led to endless litigation in which the ordinary frontiersman found himself at a serious disadvantage in competing with the well-to-do. Another difficulty was the engrossment of land by speculative purchasers. Ira Allen declared that a large proportion of the Vermont settlers had bought defective titles.[2]

Land grants were at first made only by the states, but the situation changed as state cessions to the Union rendered possible a federal system in the Northwest. In 1785 Congress authorized comprehensive surveys and the forming of rectangular townships six miles square, which soon afterward were laid out in what is now eastern Ohio. Certain tracts were not included: the Connecticut Reserve in northern Ohio, Virginia bounty lands along the river, and vested rights in the old French villages; but valid titles elsewhere in the Northwest now

[1] Mary Dewees, "Journal from Philadelphia to Kentucky, 1787-1788," *Pa. Mag. of History and Biog.*, XXVIII, 182 ff.; Shreve, "Journal," 193 ff.; C. H. Ambler, *History of Transportation in the Ohio Valley* (Glendale, Calif., 1932) ; Thomas Speed, *The Wilderness Road* (Filson Club, *Publs.*, no. 2), 19-20, 57-63.

[2] L. C. Gray, *History of Agriculture in the Southern United States to 1860* (Carnegie Inst., *Publs.*, no. 430), II, 622-629; Wilbur, *Ira Allen*, I, 489.

had to be secured from federal authorities. Congress, eager to make the public lands a source of revenue, sold three important tracts to groups of promoters. On one of these, the Ohio Company, consisting of New Englanders, founded Marietta in 1788. Another, farther down the Ohio, was colonized by John Cleve Symmes and his New Jersey associates. The third, or Scioto purchase, went to a group of speculators headed by the New Yorker, William Duer. The settlers about Marietta and Cincinnati, unlike those south of the Ohio, enjoyed protection by federal troops.

Meantime many New Englanders were trekking into Maine and Vermont and into northern, central and western New York. The population of Maine, estimated in 1777 at about a sixth that of Massachusetts proper, rose to nearly a quarter in 1790, and two new counties had been created. Vermont's total, reckoned at approximately thirty thousand in 1784, increased to around eighty-five thousand in 1790, a number exceeding that of three of the original thirteen states.[1] One group of the westward-moving throng halted in the Hudson Valley, where Nantucketers and Rhode Islanders founded Hudson, soon a flourishing port for deep-sea whalers. To the north a small settlement at Troy was rapidly built up by New Englanders. Especially important was the Yankee migration to central and western New York, including the upper Susquehanna Valley, the "Finger Lake" region and the Genesee country bordering on Lake Ontario. So far, New England settlers in the Northwest Territory were few, but the movement inaugurated by the Marietta pioneers assumed larger proportions during the next quarter-century. The total

[1] E. B. Greene and Virginia D. Harrington, comps., *American Population before the Federal Census of 1790* (N. Y., 1932), 30, 46, 86-88; Wilbur, *Ira Allen*, I, 416, 444; II, 4.

of New England migrants northward and westward may well have exceeded a hundred thousand.[1]

New York, with its large unexploited areas, sent comparatively few settlers out of the state. More departed from New Jersey. One transplanted Jerseyman reported that his neighbors in western Pennsylvania were "most all from Jersey." Others from that state went to the Symmes tract and to Kentucky. In 1790 over sixty thousand persons lived in the four trans-Alleghany counties of Pennsylvania. Pennsylvanians also migrated to West Virginia and Kentucky. To take care of her people in the upper Ohio Valley, Virginia organized three new counties between 1784 and 1789. Kentucky was growing rapidly and in 1790 a "rough census" indicated over seventy thousand inhabitants, including over twelve thousand slaves. Though Tennessee developed more slowly, its population in 1790 was estimated at 35,691.[2]

A considerable part of the American people were in motion. The exodus of so many—perhaps a quarter of a million in all—from settled areas to "wild lands" affected the communities they left behind. Newspapers in the old states noted the departure of emigrants and the sale of farms to provide funds for acquiring new homes. Slow communications did not prevent Easterners from keeping in touch with Western relatives and friends. From Kentucky, Mrs. James Wilkinson reported to her Philadelphia father her difficulties of

---

[1] Mathews, *Expansion of New England*, chap. vi; Ezra Stiles, *Literary Diary* (F. B. Dexter, ed., N. Y., 1901), III, 240; W. L. Smith, "Journal, 1790-1791," Mass. Hist. Soc., *Proceeds.*, LI, 55 ff.; Halsey, *Old New York Frontier*, 339-340; A. W. Lauber, "The Valleys of the Susquehanna and the Delaware," A. C. Flick, ed., *History of the State of New York* (N. Y., 1933-1937), V, chap. iv; P. D. Evans, "The Frontier Pushed Westward," *ibid.*, chap. vi.

[2] Shreve, "Journal," 202; W. F. Dunaway, *A History of Pennsylvania* (Carl Wittke, ed., *Prentice-Hall History Series*, 1935), 234; C. H. Ambler, *A History of West Virginia* (same ser., 1933), 174; Greene and Harrington, *American Population*, 191, 194.

adjustment to frontier conditions and the gradual progress in social amenities. Readers of the *Massachusetts Spy* learned of social affairs in Marietta, including a ball at which the ladies were "as well accomplished in the manners of polite circles . . . as any in the old states." Carey's *American Museum* printed many Western items: Indian troubles on the Ohio, a "nest of pirates" at Muscle Shoals on the Tennessee, the "State of Franklin" and the Mississippi question.[1]

Eastern opinions of the westward movement differed. New England promoters like Oliver Phelps, Nathaniel Gorham and the leaders of the Ohio Company naturally encouraged emigration. David Howell of Rhode Island suggested that the West would not only provide a federal revenue, but strengthen republican institutions. "When the states on the eastern shores . . . shall have become populous, rich and luxurious, and ready to yield their liberties into the hands of a tyrant," he said, "the gods of the mountains will save us." In the Federal Convention Roger Sherman of Connecticut urged fair treatment of the West, reminding his colleagues that their children and grandchildren might well be citizens of the newer communities.[2]

George Mason also opposed "degrading discriminations" and James Madison said the new commonwealths should be treated as "equals and as brethren." To Washington, westward migration seemed as inevitable as "the influx of the tides," though he favored first an orderly extinction of Indian titles, solid settlements ad-

---

[1] Mathews, *Expansion of New England*, chap. vi; B. W. Bond, *Civilization of the Old Northwest* (N. Y., 1934), 32; Ann B. Wilkinson, "Letters from Kentucky, 1788-1789" (T. R. Hay, ed.), *Pa. Mag. of History and Biog.*, LVI, 33 ff.; "Chronicle," *Am. Museum*, II (1787), 1 ff. (The "Chronicle" appears with separate pagination at end of volume.)

[2] A. B. Hulbert, *Ohio in the Time of the Confederation* (Marietta, 1918), 69 ff.; Max Farrand, ed., *The Records of the Federal Convention* (New Haven, 1911-1937), III, 3, 454.

joining the older states, and internal improvements directing commerce to the East rather than southward through Spanish territory. Other Easterners, however, feared the effects of the "vast drain" of population. Rufus King deemed every migrant to the trans-Alleghany region a "total loss" to the Union. Elbridge Gerry wished to limit the representation of new states lest they "oppress commerce and drain our wealth into the Western Country." Gouverneur Morris similarly predicted the Westerners would "ruin the Atlantic interest." [1]

Settlers in western New York and the Northwest were much less troubled by the Indians than the pioneers of Kentucky and Tennessee, where raids on exposed "stations" still occurred. A typical station was an inclosure, consisting of one-story or two-story log cabins or block houses, with connecting stockades, where occupants of outlying farms could, if threatened, take refuge. In such places as Lexington and Louisville conditions of living were more normal, but elsewhere field workers had to carry arms, and the loss of life was heavy. Kentucky and Tennessee, though within the jurisdiction of adjoining Eastern states, could not count on their protection against Indian raiders. The Westerners also faced the problem of maintaining order among themselves. By 1783 Kentucky possessed county courts and a superior court of its own from which, however, appeals had to be taken to Richmond. Meanwhile Tennesseans complained that North Carolina failed to provide them with sufficient agencies for the administration of justice. [2]

In 1790 the postmaster-general listed only one regu-

[1] *Ibid.*, I, 372-373, 446, 533-534, 578; II, 2-3; Washington, *Writings*, XXVII, 133 ff., 471 ff.; Rufus King, "Letters," Mass. Hist. Soc., *Proceeds.*, XLIX, 87-89.

[2] T. P. Abernethy, *From Frontier to Plantation in Tennessee* (Chapel Hill, 1932), 13, 158; Clark, *History of Kentucky*, 92, 115; Williams, *Lost State of Franklin*, 63.

lar route across the mountains, that from Philadelphia
to Pittsburgh, and at first this mail went only once a
fortnight. No post office existed in Kentucky or Tennessee, in New York west of Albany or in Vermont. In
such areas letters must be intrusted to occasional travelers.
There was also the problem of marketing products and
obtaining supplies. In 1789 a visitor in Vermont reported famine conditions and in that year the New York
frontier was likewise suffering, largely because of poor
communications. In Tennessee the first real road between Nashville and the Holston Valley settlements was
opened in 1788. Peltry was carried to the East on pack
horses. Much of this trade went through the Shenandoah Valley to Baltimore and Philadelphia. Kentucky
had similar difficulties, though James Wilkinson's voyage
down the Mississippi with tobacco and provisions indicated possibilities of trade with New Orleans. Such exchanges were handicapped, however, not only by Spanish regulations but by the need of taking return cargoes
upstream.[1]

Under such circumstances separatist movements developed. Their promoters were usually content with
self-government within the Union, but in a few instances the leaders talked of independence, or carried
on negotiations with British or Spanish agents. This
rebellious spirit lifted its head even in New England,
where in 1786 a Maine convention complained of insufficient representation in the Massachusetts legislature,
unfair taxation and the heavy cost of judicial proceedings; but thirty years passed before Maine became a

---

[1] *American State Papers* (Wash., 1832-1861), *Post Office Department*,
9-12; W. E. Rich, *The History of the United States Post Office to the
Year 1829* (*Harvard Econ. Studies*, XXVII), chaps. iv-v; Wilbur,
Ira Allen, I, 523 ff.; Halsey, *Old New York Frontier*, pt. viii, chap. iv;
Williams, *Lost State of Franklin*, chap. xxxii; Abernethy, *Frontier to
Plantation*, 149 ff.

separate state.[1] The statehood movement in Vermont, which had gone on through the war, continued until even New Yorkers were willing to end the long and futile controversy. Even so, Vermont did not enter the Union until 1791. Meantime some Vermont leaders had been intriguing with the British.

Kindred movements sprang up in western Pennsylvania and western North Carolina. In 1782 the Pennsylvania legislature took the separatists seriously enough to impose the death penalty. At the same time, however, they sent a Presbyterian minister to reason with the malcontents. Another plan, advocated by Colonel Arthur Campbell, proposed a new state extending from West Virginia to northern Alabama. Among the reasons given for such projects were the burdensome taxation by the seaboard legislatures and the pioneers' desire to exert greater control over land policies.[2]

North Carolina's cession of her Western lands, though soon withdrawn, brought to a head another separatist movement. Believing themselves now free to set up a state government, the eastern Tennessee settlers in 1784 held a convention, appealed to Congress, organized a temporary association and in a later convention voted to form the "State of Franklin." After a precarious existence of about four years the new "state" collapsed because of opposition in North Carolina and violent differences among the Westerners themselves as well as Indian troubles. The result was that the Tennesseans remained under North Carolina until the territory was ceded to the United States in 1790.[3]

The most formidable secessionist movement developed

[1] Edward Stanwood, "The Separation of Maine from Massachusetts," Mass. Hist. Soc., *Proceeds.*, ser. 3, I, 125-164.

[2] F. J. Turner, "Western State-Making in the American Revolutionary Era," *Am. Hist. Rev.*, I, 86-87, 256 ff.; Abernethy, *Western Lands and the American Revolution*, 291.

[3] Williams, *Lost State of Franklin*.

in Kentucky, then a part of Virginia. The people objected to the determination of civil and military questions at Richmond and furthermore feared that their need for a free outlet down the Mississippi to the Gulf lacked support in Congress. Though the Virginia leaders generally sympathized with the Kentuckians on this latter issue, not all of them regarded the matter as urgent. The Westerners were especially disturbed when certain members of the Confederation seemed ready to give way on the Mississippi question, for a time at least, in order to secure Spanish markets for Eastern merchants. Some settlers also objected to "a set of Nabobs in Virginia" getting an undue share of Kentucky lands. In 1784 the people petitioned Congress for separate statehood, a proposal requiring Virginia's consent, but nothing was done and the agitation in Kentucky continued through a series of conventions. Finally, in 1786, the Virginia legislature agreed on certain conditions. Further action was delayed, however, and in the meantime certain Kentucky leaders engaged in treasonable intrigues with the Spanish authorities in New Orleans. Fortunately this "Spanish Conspiracy" collapsed and, when the new Federal Constitution was ratified, Kentucky's admission to the Union was assured.[1]

Though probably few frontier leaders seriously expected to place themselves under Spanish control, some of them went very far in that direction. In order to secure commercial privileges for himself, James Wilkinson not only assured the governor at New Orleans that he could transfer his allegiance to the king of Spain "without loss of conscience or of honor," but he actu-

---

[1] Turner, "Western State-Making," 261-262; E. C. Burnett, ed., *Letters of Members of the Continental Congress* (Wash., 1921-1936), VII, 446-451; Abernethy, *Western Lands and the American Revolution*, 302-309; Whitaker, *Spanish-American Frontier*, chaps. v-viii; W. R. Shepherd, "Wilkinson and the Beginnings of the Spanish Conspiracy," *Am. Hist. Rev.*, IX, 490 ff., 748 ff.

ally did so. Similarly George Morgan, another promoter of Western colonization, intended to become a Spanish subject provided his proposed settlement of New Madrid, on the west bank of the Mississippi, obtained religious liberty and certain other privileges.[1]

The best safeguard against separatist tendencies was Congress's decision to confer eventual statehood on Western colonies in the areas ceded by the states. This principle, formulated during the war and reaffirmed in Jefferson's draft ordinance for the Western territories and in the congressional ordinance of 1784, was embodied in the Northwest ordinance of 1787. Within little more than a decade after the peace, three inland states were added to the Union, with six seats in the Senate and several in the House of Representatives. Furthermore, their political outlook was to some extent shared by representatives of the newly settled communities in the older states. Even Eastern speculators in trans-Alleghany lands had some understanding of frontier problems, and the federal government, now the largest owner of Western lands, was interested in developing them as a source of revenue.

As a stabler society emerged here and there from primitive conditions, the type of Western settlers tended to change. Representatives of the Virginia gentry who moved to Kentucky with their slaves organized a plantation life similar to that of their old homes. To a considerable extent Western politicians belonged to this class. In the words of a recent student, "political office, even on the frontier, was rarely sought by any but the natural leaders of society." George Nicholas, Kentucky's first attorney-general, was the son of a well-known Virginia lawyer and Revolutionary leader and his mother

---

[1] Shepherd, "Wilkinson and Beginnings of Spanish Conspiracy," 496-497; Max Savelle, *George Morgan, Colony Builder* (N. Y., 1932), 204 ff.

belonged to one of the "first families." Other families which played important rôles on both sides of the mountains were the Marshalls and Breckenridges.[1]

At some points urban life was emerging. In 1783 Pittsburgh was the principal settlement on the upper Ohio, though as late as 1790 it numbered less than four hundred people, largely engaged in "catering" to westbound travelers. The New Englanders possessed a genuine community life at Marietta almost immediately and, though Cincinnati had few inhabitants in 1789, it too was regularly laid out as a town. Nashville, with its courthouse, public square, jail and pillory, was the earliest urban center in Tennessee. In Kentucky, Lexington soon forged to the front as the principal market town and the meeting place of the first state legislature. Gilbert Imlay, a contemporary observer, described Kentucky's progress "from dirty stations or forts and smoky huts" to "fertile fields, blushing orchards, pleasant gardens . . . neat and commodious houses, rising villages and trading towns." Kentucky was beginning to export tobacco and to breed better cattle. By 1789 it possessed a commercial distillery and had devised a process for improving whisky which was presently to establish the reputation of "Kentucky Bourbon." Linen was manufactured from Kentucky flax, some of which went to Eastern markets, and a Kentucky Manufacturing Company was organized for textiles.[2]

In sparsely settled areas it was hard to maintain churches, though this proved less true of the New England migrants. Congregational churches were quickly

---

[1] Abernethy, *Frontier to Plantation*, 149.
[2] Schoepf, *Travels*, I, 241-246; Bond, *Civilization of the Old Northwest*, chap. ii; W. R. Jillson, *Pioneer Kentucky* (Frankfort, 1934), 90; Imlay, *Topographical Description of the Western Territory*, 152-153; Abernethy, *Frontier to Plantation*, 195; Clark, *History of Kentucky*, 239; U. B. Phillips, *Life and Labor in the Old South* (Boston, 1929), 84.

planted in western New York as well as at Marietta. In the Southwest fewer immigrants came from compact communities with strongly established religious traditions. Episcopalian influence was comparatively weak and the three major groups were the Presbyterians, Baptists and Methodists.[1] The Presbyterians, who early formed a congregation at Cincinnati, soon had a few ministers in Kentucky. One of them, David Rice, sat in the convention which framed the first state constitution. By 1788 the Kentucky churches had organized the Transylvania presbytery. In Tennessee another Princeton graduate, Samuel Doak, established a presbytery with twenty churches. He too was politically influential.[2] The Virginia migrants to Kentucky included a considerable number of Baptists. By 1785 they had formed eighteen churches. A frontier revival increased the membership and soon there were three Baptist associations, besides one in "Franklin." Meanwhile the Methodists sent preachers all the way from the upper Ohio to Tennessee, and Bishop Asbury himself traveled widely through the West, where the denomination also maintained "circuit riders" and "local preachers."[3]

Though there were comparatively few Catholics in Kentucky, Bardstown had a resident priest by 1787 and built its first Catholic church in 1790. Many pioneers, however, remained aloof from any faith, whether because of hostility to traditional theology, preoccupation

[1] Williston Walker, *A History of the Congregational Churches in the United States* (Philip Schaff and others, eds., *The American Church History Series*, N. Y., 1893-1897, III), 309-311; Mathews, *Expansion of New England*, chaps. vi-vii; Bond, *Civilization of the Old Northwest*, chap. xv; Isaac Backus, *History of New England, with Particular Reference to the Denomination of Christians Called Baptists* (2nd edn., Newton, Mass., 1871), II, chap. xxiv.

[2] Williams, *Lost State of Franklin*, 94, 270.

[3] *Ibid.*, 268 ff.; W. W. Sweet, ed., *Religion on the American Frontier, 1783-1850* (N. Y. and Chicago, 1931-1939), I, 21 ff.; II, 8 ff.; Francis Asbury, *Journal, 1771-1815* (N. Y., 1821), I, 399 ff.; II, *passim*.

with practical problems or remoteness from religious services. Some of the Kentucky "gentry" had been affected by Virginia liberalism of the Jeffersonian type and others were "infidels" of a less intellectual sort. By contrast, church members were commonly "fundamentalists."

The frontier attracted a certain number of educated persons. Humphrey Marshall, a pioneer settler, became the earliest formal historian of Kentucky, and Isaac Shelby, its first governor, had a fair schooling and serious intellectual interests. Among the "Franklin" leaders one was a Princeton graduate, another had studied at Liberty Hall and a third at a Presbyterian academy in North Carolina. A list of one hundred and thirteen petitioners from eastern Tennessee to the North Carolina legislature included only two who had to use marks for their signatures.[1]

Local provisions for education varied. Vermont on the northern frontier named a legislative committee in 1789 to prepare plans for a college, and two years later the University of Vermont was established at Burlington, with Ira Allen as one of its chief promoters. In western Pennsylvania, Thaddeus Dod, a young Presbyterian minister, opened in 1782 what has been called "the first classical school west of the Alleghanies." Seven years later he was made principal of an academy which eventually became Washington College. In 1787 the legislature granted five thousand dollars to endow an academy at Pittsburgh.[2]

Nor was education wholly neglected in the Southwest. John Filson, author of the well-known *Discovery, Settlement, and Early State of Kentucke,* was one of the

---

[1] Williams, *Lost State of Franklin,* 299, 317, 320; Abernethy, *Frontier to Plantation,* 10.

[2] Wilbur, *Ira Allen,* I, 533-534; Mathew Carey and John Bioren, comps., *Laws of the Commonwealth of Pennsylvania, 1700-1802* (Phila., 1803), III, 184, 209.

pioneer schoolmasters in Kentucky. In 1787 two academies were advertised in Lexington, which also had a Society for the Improvement of Knowledge. Kentucky's chief educational institution was the Transylvania Seminary, which was incorporated and financially aided by the state of Virginia. Opened at Lexington in 1789, it offered at first only elementary instruction. Both in Kentucky and Tennessee, education owed much to Presbyterian ministers. One of their early schools was Martin's Academy in eastern Tennessee (1783). Another was Davidson Academy at Nashville.[1]

Western journalism began with the *Pittsburgh Gazette,* founded by John Scull and Joseph Hall in 1786. To its first issue Hugh H. Brackenridge, then a local lawyer, contributed an idealized picture of the infant community. The second newspaper was the *Kentucke Gazette* at Lexington. In his opening announcement (1787) the editor, John Bradford, promised to deal not only with Western topics but with world affairs and "all the Republic of letters." Bradford also issued the *Kentucke Almanac* (1788) and *Kentucke Miscellany,* the first book printed in the district.[2]

Even beyond the Mississippi a new day was beginning to dawn. In 1783 the young Connecticut Yankee, John Ledyard, published the *Journal* of his voyage with Captain James Cook along the shores of the Pacific Northwest. He discussed with Robert Morris the possibilities of the fur trade in this far country and Jefferson listened sympathetically to Ledyard's suggestion of an overland expedition to the Pacific. Ledyard died shortly after-

[1] Clark, *History of Kentucky,* chap. xiii; W. W. Hening, comp., *The Statutes-at-Large, Being a Collection of All the Laws of Virginia, 1619-1792* (Phila., 1823), XI, 282; XII, 642; Abernethy, *Frontier to Plantation,* 197; Williams, *Lost State of Franklin,* 317.

[2] J. C. Andrews, *Pittsburgh's Post-Gazette* (Boston, 1936), chaps. i-ii; C. M. Newlin, *The Life and Writings of Hugh Henry Brackenridge* (Princeton, 1932), 71 ff.; W. R. Jillson, *The First Printing in Kentucky* (Louisville, 1936), 19-20.

ward, but already Eastern merchants were thinking of the North Pacific Coast as a source of supply for the China trade. In 1787 a Boston group sent Captains John Kendrick and Robert Gray, commanding the *Columbia* and the *Lady Washington,* to that region. Arriving there the following year, they collected furs which were shipped to China, thus beginning a rapidly growing commerce and bringing the Oregon country within the horizon of the Atlantic ports.[1]

As interest in the unfolding West developed, national feeling in the country as a whole seemed to gain ground. The common experience of having fought for independence was an important factor. When Franklin returned to Philadelphia in 1786, he noted the general rejoicing on the anniversary of the day when he and his associates had "hazarded Lives and Fortunes." In New York that year the city and state governments, Congress and the Society of the Cincinnati joined in commemorating the occasion, with bells ringing and the thunder of cannon. At a dinner given by the Cincinnati one of the customary thirteen toasts was: "May the powers of Congress be adequate to preserve the General Union." Two years later in far-off Kentucky the celebration reflected patriotism not unmixed with doubts. One toast was: "The Western World—perpetual union, on principles of equality, or amicable separation"; but the last word was more hopeful: "The Commonwealth of Kentucke, the fourteenth luminary in the American Constellation, may she reflect upon the original States the wisdom she has borrowed from them." [2]

The happy outcome of the war confirmed Washington's unique position as national hero. When Lafayette

[1] Thomas Jefferson, *Works* (P. L. Ford, ed., N. Y., 1904-1905), V, 183; K. S. Latourette, *The History of Early Relations between the United States and China* (Conn. Acad. of Arts and Sciences, *Trans.,* XXII), 30 ff.

[2] Benjamin Franklin, *Writings* (Albert Smyth, ed., N. Y., 1907), IX, 523; Burnett, *Letters,* VIII, 401, 799, *n.* 4.

visited Boston in 1784, the toast to Washington was
accompanied by the display of his portrait crowned with
laurels and supported by the French and American en-
signs. Morse and Webster included sketches of him in
their textbooks, and poems were written in his honor.
Congress ordered for the permanent capital an equestrian
statue by "the best artist in Europe." His portrait hung
in the New York City Hall and Noah Webster declared
that his likeness was "destined to grace the walls of every
Council chamber in the new world." The most notable
contribution to the commemoration of Washington in
art was the work of the French sculptor, Jean Antoine
Houdon.[1]

The terms "nation" and "national" were often on
people's lips. Tom Paine declared in his last "Crisis"
paper, "Our citizenship in the United States is our national character. Our citizenship in any particular state
is only our local distinction. . . . Our great title is
AMERICANS." Similarly, Washington wrote to William
Gordon, "We are known by no other character among
Nations than as the United States. Massachusetts or
Virginia is no better defined, nor any more thought of
by Foreign Powers than the County of Worcester in
Massachusetts is by Virginia, or Gloucester in Virginia
is by Massachusetts." Jefferson, though an ardent Virginian, agreed that in all external matters Americans
must be "one nation only, firmly hooped together."[2]

While particularism was still strong, Americanism did,
as we have seen, express itself in many ways—in literature, in Webster's zeal for a unified American speech, in

---

[1] J. B. McMaster, *History of the People of the United States* (N. Y.,
1883-1913), I, 217; Jedidiah Morse, *The American Geography* (Elizabethtown, N. J., 1789), 127-139; Burnett, *Letters*, VII, 260-266;
Noah Webster, "Description of New York in 1786," *N. Y. Directory
for 1786*, p. v. See also Dixon Wecter, *The Hero in America* (N. Y.,
1941), chap. vi.

[2] Thomas Paine, *Writings* (Daniel Conway, ed., N. Y., 1894-1896),
I. 375; Washington, *Writings*, XXVII, 50; Jefferson, *Works*, V, 78.

his interest and that of Rush in a national program for education. Business also was thinking more nationally. A writer in the *American Museum* for 1787 advocated extreme economic nationalism: the "working up" of all "native commodities to the last degree of manufacture"; curtailing foreign imports; a maximum use of American shipping; and limiting officeholding to natives "with very few exceptions." Differences of origin were recognized as obstacles to unity; but Morse struck an optimistic note in his *American Geography*, predicting that "the language, manners, customs, political and religious sentiments of the mixed mass" would be so assimilated that such distinctions would be lost in the "general and honorable name of *Americans*." [1]

Patriotism did not exclude a reasonable degree of international outlook. Some Americans, at least, understood that their country could not wholly detach itself from the transatlantic world. Washington, no sentimentalist, called himself "a citizen of the great republic of humanity at large." He looked for a time "not very remote" when "free and liberal commerce" would "pretty generally succeed to the devastation and horrors of war." In a similar spirit Paine believed Americans should "exhibit on the theatre of the Universe a character hitherto unknown," having "as it were, a new creation intrusted to our hands." In spite of Jefferson's theoretical preference for a rural society standing "with respect to Europe precisely on the footing of China," he admitted that his countrymen, having "a decided taste for navigation and commerce," must continue to deal with Europe. [2] In fact, both Jefferson and Adams were largely occupied abroad with efforts to improve trade relations. Across the Atlantic men like Turgot and

---

[1] Anon., "Causes of Country's Growing Rich," *Am. Museum*, I, 13; Morse, *American Geography*, 68.

[2] Paine, *Writings*, I, 371; Jefferson, *Works*, IV, 469.

Richard Price hoped the Old World might profit by the new republic's example.   Americans, said the Italian Mazzei, had contributed important values to humanity: the realization of natural rights in institutions notwithstanding such inconsistencies as slavery; service to the cause of peace; and the hope of human perfectibility through human intelligence.[1]

Many United States citizens were traveling abroad. "I hardly know," wrote Abigail Adams from London, "how to think myself out of my own country, I see so many Americans about me."   Paris also had a considerable American society, in which the wealthy William Bingham and his wife were conspicuous.   To be sure, Jefferson and the Adamses were generally critical of European society.   Jefferson considered the French superior to the "rich, proud, hectoring, swearing, squibbling carnivorous animals" across the Channel, but he did not want his compatriots to adopt French manners. A visit to France, he told James Monroe, would "make you adore your own country."   Mrs. Adams, who regarded both France and England as "old corrupted countries," thought Americans should be grateful for their "happier land, a land of liberty and virtue, comparatively speaking."   Back at Braintree after his European service, John Adams missed the bookshops and his literary acquaintances in London, but "in all other respects" believed himself better off.   Notwithstanding Franklin's more cosmopolitan outlook and his liking for the French, he advised an English mother to educate her children in America, where manners were "simple and pure."[2]

Though American devotees of fashion were sometimes

---

[1] Filippo Mazzei, *Recherches historiques et politiques sur les États-Unis de l'Amèrique Septentrionale* (Paris, 1788), IV, 237 ff.

[2] Mrs. John Adams, *Letters* (C. F. Adams, ed., Boston, 1848), 173, 260-265; Jefferson, *Works*, IV, 424-426; John Adams, *Works* (C. F. Adams, ed., Boston, 1856), IX, 558; Franklin, *Writings*, IX, 90.

ridiculed for aping European manners, this affectation, as in the case of Charleston, might go along with "inveterate enmity" toward Britain.[1] Similarly in literature flaming patriotism might be expressed in characteristic eighteenth-century English. If magazines printed more American material than before, they still relied largely on British sources, while on the stage the plays and actors were generally British. The next decade was to show that even party alignments might be complicated by European developments.

By the time the Confederation gave way to the "more perfect union" of the new Constitution, Americans had gone far in their detachment from Old World dominance. Independent politically, they had progressed in economic self-sufficiency and had done something to apply republican ideals to social reconstruction. A further pull away from Europe resulted from the westward movement and the new problems and vistas that it opened. Yet the ocean which separated the people from their ancestral homes remained an area where their interests and those of Europe inevitably met, in conflict or in mutually profitable exchanges. Even on the frontier, men had to take account of British and Spanish policies, while on the seaboard, escape from the Old World was still less possible. Americans needed foreign markets and looked abroad as well for much that seemed essential to comfortable living. English social conventions influenced the "best people" and scientific advance depended largely on the flow of ideas from Europe. In spite of political independence and the westward extension of their horizon the most respected citizens of the young republic still lived in an Atlantic, rather than a strictly American, world.

Something of this dualism of European tradition and

[1] Timothy Ford, "Diary, 1785-1786" (J. W. Barnwell, ed.), S. C. Hist. and Geneal. Mag., XIII, 192 ff.

ideas based on American experience appeared in the Constitution of 1787 as that document was rounded out by the first ten amendments. The distribution of functions among legislative, executive and judicial branches of the government was not a native invention, but followed roughly the British system as interpreted by its French admirer, Montesquieu. The independence of the judicary, a cardinal maxim of British policy since the Revolution of 1688, figured importantly in the American Constitution, though the precise method of securing it differed somewhat. The idea of a bicameral legislature formed another part of the European inheritance, while the provisions for the protection of parliamentary privilege likewise stemmed from British precedent. So also did the bill of rights and related clauses of the original Constitution, which reasserted doctrines familiar to seventeenth-century Englishmen: security for personal liberty through jury trial, due process of law and the writ of habeas corpus; the prohibition of excessive bail or cruel and unusual punishments; and the right to petition for relief of grievances.

Though much of the governmental fabric rested on Old World principles and practices, the total result was quite unlike anything to be found in Europe. There had been earlier federations of a sort, from those of ancient Greece to the unions of Swiss cantons and Dutch provinces; but the American Union, with its skillful division of powers between national and state authorities, was unique. Though elective monarchies were not unknown, nothing in Europe resembled the American president intrusted with large powers but chosen for a limited term. Partly because of the requirements of the federal system Congress, unlike Parliament, was not given unlimited sovereignty. Whereas the English bill of rights was directed only against abuse of royal authority, the corresponding American provisions aimed to protect the individual against usurpations by the legislative branch. Among other distinctive products of native experience in the Constitution was the prohibition of religious tests, of any "establishment of religion" and of any interference with its free exercise.

In the field of literature a work of art, say a play of Shakespeare, may have borrowed freely from earlier writers and yet be accepted as essentially a new creation. If the same principle be applied to politics, Gladstone's much criticized characterization of the Constitution as the most wonderful work ever struck off at a given time by the brain and purpose of man is not so unreasonable as it has been made to appear.

The new Constitution reflected in many of its provisions the social conditions of the time in which it was written. So far as it dealt with economic matters, it was undeniably influenced by vigorous capitalist groups, formed in part during the war and matured during the years of peace. Interested in promoting internal improvements, the exploitation of Western lands, industrial projects, the organization of investment capital through banks and the merchandising of public securities, the "big business" of that day wanted a strong central authority for protection and active assistance. In particular, these groups now secured federal regulation of interstate and foreign commerce, together with safeguards against excessive paper-money issues and measures impairing contract obligations. Distrust of the moneyed interests undoubtedly prompted much of the rural opposition to the Constitution.

Yet the conflict over the adoption of the Constitution may easily be misunderstood if considered simply as an alignment between capitalist promoters and democratic agrarians, between conservatives and radicals. If the new system represented a retreat from the equalitarian aspirations of 1776, particularism and the defense of local interests did not always imply strictly democratic principles. On the other hand, the makers and champions of the Constitution were, by and large, the men of wider experience and consequently broader horizons. For some this larger experience had come through legislative and administrative service in the Confederation; for others, through association in the army or in business enterprises with persons from different parts of the Union. Similarly, the more important men who served the Confederation abroad—Franklin, Adams, Jay and Jefferson—all shared, though in differing degrees, a national point of view.

Important too as a factor making possible the "more perfect union" was the gradual development, from pre-Revolutionary years through war-time and postwar experiences, of ideas and emotions associated with what may be called Americanism. It was a state of mind shared by men of divergent local interests and traditions. It was therefore a powerful unifying influence, preparing the way for a genuinely national outlook. There is no need here to discuss the nationalist and states rights' theories as to the nature of the Constitution. On that issue, now more academic than practical, men differed then as well as in later years. It is perhaps safest to conclude with Madison that the Philadelphia plan was, "in strictness, neither a national nor a federal Constitution, but a composition of both." [1]

[1] Alexander Hamilton and others, *The Federalist* (H. C. Lodge, ed., N. Y., 1907), 239.

CHAPTER XVII

CRITICAL ESSAY ON AUTHORITIES

PHYSICAL SURVIVALS

THE "march of progress" has destroyed many objects characteristic of the Revolutionary Generation, but what remain are better guarded than they once were. Charleston retains much of its eighteenth-century aspect. Among its notable structures are the Brewton-Pringle mansion (1765) and St. Michael's Church, completed four years earlier. In Boston, within easy walking distance of the common, are the "Old State House" (1713), Faneuil Hall (1742, rebuilt after a fire in 1762), the Old South Meeting House (1729) and King's Chapel (1749), all associated with important events of the Revolutionary era. Philadelphia has preserved its impressive civic center, with public buildings begun shortly before the war and completed soon after it: Independence Hall, Congress Hall and City Hall. In lower New York the old city has almost disappeared, but there are two significant exceptions: Fraunces Tavern (1719), memorable for its Long Room where Washington dined in 1783 with his fellow officers; and St. Paul's Chapel, built in 1764. In what was then the rural area of upper Manhattan the most interesting survival is the country house of Roger Morris (1765). Contemporary structures elsewhere in Greater New York are indicated in A. E. Peterson's *Landmarks of New York* (N. Y., 1927). Among the smaller provincial capitals, Annapolis has some fine Georgian houses built in the seventeen-sixties and seventeen-seventies. Of interest also in this connection are Newport, R. I., Portsmouth, N. H., and the "North Shore" ports of Massachusetts.

Our knowledge of the physical scene has been enlarged through reconstructions. The most impressive example is the restoration of colonial Williamsburg by John D. Rockefeller, jr. The restored area includes the Governor's Palace, the Capitol, Raleigh Tavern, the jail, many private dwellings and the original grounds of William and Mary College. Another type of reconstruction, undertaken by the National Park Commission, is the Jockey Hollow camp near Morristown, illustrating living conditions in the Continental army. In the Museum of the City of New York may be found miniature reproductions of eighteenth-century scenes.

For domestic interiors and furnishings special wings of the New York Metropolitan Art Museum and the Boston Museum of Fine Arts and similar exhibits elsewhere are important. For the Metropolitan, see the *Handbook of the American Wing* by R. T. H. Halsey and C. O. Cornelius (5th edn., N. Y., 1932). The Powel room in this museum was taken from a Philadelphia residence known to members of the Continental Congress. Paintings of the period are on display in many art galleries and historical museums in the seaboard states. David Rittenhouse's orrery may be seen at the University of Pennsylvania. A convenient guide to these and similar remains is the *Handbook of American Museums* (Wash., 1932) published by the American Association of Museums.

The following publications offer interesting pictorial material: R. H. Gabriel, ed., *The Pageant of America* (15 vols., New Haven, 1925-1929); L. V. Lockwood, *Colonial Furniture in America* (new edn., 2 vols., N. Y., 1921); and Elizabeth McClellan, *Historic Dress in America* (Phila., 1904). See also the works on architecture listed later. A useful cartographic manual is C. O. Paullin, *Atlas of the Historical Geography of the United States* (J. K. Wright, ed., Carnegie Inst., *Publs.*, no. 401, 1932).

BIBLIOGRAPHICAL AIDS

The last three volumes of Justin Winsor's monumental *Narrative and Critical History of America* (8 vols., Boston, 1884-1889) are still valuable. For scholarly articles, see A. P. C. Griffin, comp., *Bibliography of American Historical*

Societies (Am. Hist. Assoc., *Ann. Rep. for 1905,* II), and the annual *Writings on American History,* now published by the American Historical Association (a cumulative index is in preparation). Also helpful are the bibliographical publications and manuscript guides issued by the Library of Congress, the public libraries of Boston and New York and certain universities and historical societies. *A Guide to the Principal Sources for Early American History in the City of New York* by E. B. Greene and R. B. Morris (N. Y., 1929) describes materials, printed and manuscript, for various phases of social history. E. G. Swem's *Virginia Historical Index* (2 vols., Roanoke, 1934-1936) provides a key to material in seven Virginia publications. The Massachusetts Historical Society has facilitated the use of its monumental *Collections* and *Proceedings* by publishing general indexes and a *Handbook of the Publications and Photostats, 1792-1933* (Boston, 1934).

GENERAL NARRATIVES

A good general account embracing the whole of this period is Edward Channing, *A History of the United States* (6 vols., N. Y., 1905-1925), III. A. B. Hart, ed., *The American Nation: a History* (28 vols., N. Y., 1904-1918), devotes volumes viii-x to the Revolutionary era. C. H. Van Tyne's projected *History of the Founding of the American Republic* was unfortunately interrupted by his death, with two volumes published: *The Causes of the War of Independence* and *The War of Independence* (Boston, 1922-1929), which carry the story to 1778, including some material on social history. Books presenting differing points of view are S. G. Fisher, *The Struggle for American Independence* (2 vols., Phila., 1908); Henry Belcher, *The First American Civil War* (2 vols., London, 1911); G. O. Trevelyan, *The American Revolution* (new edn., 4 vols., N. Y., 1926-1929), esp. vol. i; and W. E. H. Lecky, *American Revolution* (arranged and edited by J. A. Woodburn from Lecky's *History of England in the Eighteenth Century;* N. Y., 1898). Belcher is a partisan on the Loyalist side,

Trevelyan writes from the standpoint of an English Whig sympathizer with the Revolution and Lecky from that of a fair-minded conservative. To the books on the colonial background listed in the preceding volume of this series should be added T. J. Wertenbaker, *The Founding of American Civilization, the Middle Colonies* (N. Y., 1938), and *The Old South, the Founding of American Civilization* (N. Y., 1942) ; and L. H. Gipson, *The British Empire before the American Revolution* (I-V, Caldwell, Idaho, and N. Y., 1936-1942, in progress).

GENERAL DOCUMENTARY SERIES

Peter Force, comp., *American Archives* (ser. 4, 6 vols., and ser. 5, 3 vols.; Wash., 1837-1853), is merely a fragment of a larger project covering the colonial and Revolutionary periods, but for the years 1774-1776 it is indispensable. It reprints official and unofficial records throwing light on both social and political conditions. Other material collected for this series is in the Manuscript Division of the Library of Congress. More useful for the student of social history than the formal proceedings in the *Journals of the Continental Congress* (W. C. Ford and others, eds., Wash., 1904-1937) is E. C. Burnett, ed., *Letters of Members of the Continental Congress, 1774-1789* (8 vols., Wash., 1921-1936).

PERSONAL MATERIAL

COLLECTED WORKS: Until recently the best edition of Washington's *Writings* was that of W. C. Ford (14 vols., N. Y., 1889). Unless otherwise indicated, however, references in this volume are to the most recent and extensive compilation: George Washington, *Writings from the Original Manuscript Sources* (J. C. Fitzpatrick, ed., 33 vols., Wash., 1931-1941). Fitzpatrick also edited George Washington, *Diaries, 1748-1799* (4 vols., Boston, 1925). The writings of Mr. and Mrs. John Adams are to be found in the following collections edited by C. F. Adams: John

Adams, *Works* (10 vols., Boston, 1856); John and Abigail Adams, *Familiar Letters during the Revolution* (Boston, 1875); and Mrs. Adams, *Letters* (4th edn., Boston, 1848). See also John Adams, Samuel Adams and James Warren, *Warren-Adams Letters* (Mass. Hist. Soc., *Colls.*, LXXII-LXXIII, 1917-1925). A standard edition of Franklin's works is Benjamin Franklin, *Writings* (Albert Smyth, ed., 10 vols., N. Y., 1907). As for Thomas Jefferson, the references in this volume, unless otherwise indicated, are to his *Works* (P. L. Ford, ed., 12 vols., N. Y., 1904-1905; originally issued in 10 vols., 1892-1899, as *Writings*). Other editions are those of H. A. Washington (9 vols., Wash., 1853-1854) and A. A. Lipscomb (20 vols., Wash., 1903). James Madison, *Writings* (Gaillard Hunt, ed., 9 vols., N. Y., 1900-1910), is the most satisfactory compilation.

DIARIES: The following are especially useful for social and cultural history: Ezra Stiles, *Literary Diary* (F. B. Dexter, ed., 3 vols., N. Y., 1901), and same author, *Extracts from Itineraries and Other Miscellanies with a Selection from His Correspondence* (same ed., New Haven, 1916); William Bentley, *Diary* (4 vols., Salem, 1905-1914), I, the record of a liberal New England minister; Christopher Marshall, *Extracts from the Diary Kept in Philadelphia and Lancaster, during the American Revolution, 1774-1781* (William Duane, ed., Albany, 1877); John Rowe, *Letters and Diary* (Annie R. Cunningham, ed., Boston, 1903); the diaries of Landon Carter in *William and Mary College Quarterly*, ser. 1, XIII-XVIII, XX-XXI, *passim;* and J. Q. Adams, *Life in a New England Town* (Boston, 1903; also in Mass. Hist. Soc., *Proceeds.*, ser. 2, XVI), a youthful diary. For a useful list of such materials, see Harriet M. Forbes, comp., *New England Diaries, 1602-1800* (Topsfield, Mass., 1923).

AUTOBIOGRAPHIES: Especially suggestive for social attitudes are Devereux Jarratt, *Life Written by Himself* (Balt., 1806), showing the outlook of a humbly born Virginian who became an Anglican clergyman, and Alexander Graydon, *Memoirs of His Own Time* (J. S. Littell, ed., Phila.,

1846). The fragmentary autobiographies of John Adams and Jefferson are in their collected works.

TRAVEL ACCOUNTS

The following are among the more important by native Americans: Josiah Quincy, "Journal," Mass. Hist. Soc., *Proceeds.*, XLIX; and W. L. Smith, "Journal," *ibid.*, LI (a Southerner's notes of travel from New England to South Carolina, 1790-1791). Accounts by Britons include Andrew Burnaby, *Travels through the Middle Settlements in North-America, in the Years 1759 and 1760* (London, 1775); Lord Adam Gordon, "Journal of an Officer's Travels in America and the West Indies, 1764-1765," N. D. Mereness, ed., *Travels in the American Colonies* (N. Y., 1916); Francis Asbury, *Journal, 1771-1815* (3 vols., N. Y., 1821); Hugh Finlay, *Journal* (Brooklyn, 1867), recording the observations of a surveyor of the post roads in 1773 and 1774; [Janet Schaw], *Journal of a Lady of Quality . . . 1774 to 1776* (Evangeline W. and C. M. Andrews, ed., New Haven, 1921); Thomas Anburey, *Travels through the Interior Parts of America* (2 vols., London, 1789; edn. cited, Boston, 1923), by a young officer taken prisoner with Burgoyne's army; Nicholas Cresswell's *Journal* (N. Y., 1924) for the years 1774-1777; Joseph Hadfield's diary, published as *An Englishman in America, 1785* (D. S. Robertson, ed., Toronto, 1933); and J. F. D. Smyth, *Tour in the United States of America* (London, 1784).

French travelers are listed in Frank Monaghan, comp., *French Travellers in the United States, 1765-1932* (N. Y., 1933). Works translated into English include Claude Blanchard, *Journal* (William Duane, tr., Thomas Balch, ed., Albany, 1876); Marquis de Chastellux, *Travels in North-America* (2 vols., London, 1787); and J. P. Brissot de Warville, *New Travels in the United States of America* (London, 1792). An anonymous "Journal of a French Traveller in the Colonies, 1765," appears in *Am. Hist. Rev.*, XXVI, 726-747, and XXVII, 70-89. Among other foreign works of travel or description are Francisco Miranda, *Diary . . . Tour of the United States, 1783-1784* (W. S. Robertson, ed., N. Y., 1928), and A. J. Morrison, ed., *Travels in the Confederation, 1783-1784* (2 vols., Phila., 1911), a translation from the journal of the German army surgeon, J. D. Schoepf. Some results of personal observation are recorded in Filippo Mazzei, *Recherches historiques et politiques sur les États-Unis de l'Amèrique Septentrionale* (4 vols., Paris, 1788).

NEWSPAPERS, MAGAZINES AND ALMANACS

For accounts of eighteenth-century newspapers, see Isaiah Thomas, *The History of Printing in America* (rev. edn., 2 vols., Am. Antiquarian Soc., *Archæologia Americana, Trans. and Colls.*, V-VI, Albany, 1874), written by a Revolutionary journalist; and F. L. Mott, *American Journalism, a History of Newspapers in the United States through 250 Years, 1690 to 1940* (N. Y., 1941). The most comprehensive list is C. S. Brigham, ed., *Bibliography of American Newspapers* (to 1820), in alphabetical order by states, in successive volumes of the American Antiquarian Society's *Proceedings*, n.s., XXIII-XXXVII (1913-1928). The most detailed description of early American periodicals is L. N. Richardson, *A History of Early American Magazines, 1741-1789* (N. Y., 1931), which should be supplemented by F. L. Mott, *A History of American Magazines, 1741-1850* (N. Y., 1930). There is no comprehensive treatment of almanacs. Besides the guides listed in J. T. Adams, *Provincial Society* (*A History of American Life*, III), 345, see N. W. Lovely, "Notes on New England Almanacs," *New England Quar.*, VIII, 264-277; Sam Briggs, *The Essays, Humor and Poems of Nathaniel Ames, Father and Son . . . from Their Almanacks* (Cleveland, 1891); and C. N. Greenough, "New England Almanacs, 1766-1775, and the American Revolution," Am. Antiquarian Soc., *Proceeds.*, n.s., XLV, 288-316. The American Antiquarian Society, located at Worcester, Massachusetts, possesses an extensive collection of almanacs.

BIOGRAPHIES

The best guide to the literature on the men and women of the Revolutionary Generation is Allen Johnson and Dumas Malone, eds., *Dictionary of American Biography* (20 vols. and index vol., N. Y., 1928-1937), which the present writer has used to an extent not adequately indicated by the footnote citations.   Most of the volumes in J. T. Morse, jr., ed., *American Statesmen* (rev. edn., Boston, 1899), have been superseded for this period, but among the exceptions are M. C. Tyler, *Patrick Henry* (III), and George Pellew, *John Jay* (IX).   Of biographies especially useful for social and intellectual history, the following deserve mention: J. C. Fitzpatrick, *George Washington Himself* (Indianapolis, 1933), based on exceptional familiarity with Washington's writings, though not always fair to his contemporaries; Carl Van Doren, *Benjamin Franklin* (N. Y., 1938); Gilbert Chinard, *Thomas Jefferson, the Apostle of Americanism* (Boston, 1929), and his *Honest John Adams* (Boston, 1933); J. C. Miller, *Samuel Adams, Pioneer in Propaganda* (Boston, 1936), which does not wholly supplant the filio-pietistic life by Adams's great-grandson, W. V. Wells (3 vols., Boston, 1865); Esther Forbes, *Paul Revere and the World He Lived In* (Boston, 1942); G. C. Groce, *William Samuel Johnson* (N. Y., 1937); W. G. Sumner, *Financier and Finances of the Revolution* (2 vols., N. Y., 1891); E. P. Oberholtzer, *Robert Morris, Patriot and Financier* (N. Y., 1903); Helen Hill, *George Mason, Constitutionalist* (Cambridge, 1938); Kate M. Rowland, *Life and Correspondence of Charles Carroll of Carrollton* (2 vols., N. Y., 1898); Ellen S. Smith, *Charles Carroll of Carrollton* (Cambridge, 1942); W. W. Henry, *Patrick Henry* (3 vols., N. Y., 1891); G. J. McRee, *Life and Correspondence of James Iredell* (2 vols., N. Y., 1857-1858); and D. D. Wallace, *Henry Laurens* (N. Y., 1915).   See also lives of the following colonial governors: John Wentworth, by L. S. Mayo (Cambridge, 1921); Thomas Hutchinson, by J. K. Hosmer (Boston, 1896); and Robert Eden, by B. C. Steiner (Balt., 1898).   Other biographies are noted in connection with special topics.

STATE AND LOCAL HISTORY AND RECORDS

THE STATES: Local history helps to guard the social historian against facile generalization. Two excellent cooperative histories of states are A. B. Hart, ed., *The Commonwealth History of Massachusetts* (5 vols., N. Y., 1928-1930), and A. C. Flick, ed., *History of the State of New York* (10 vols., N. Y., 1933-1937). All the New England states receive attention in J. T. Adams, *Revolutionary New England* (Boston, 1923), and his *New England in the Republic* (Boston, 1926); and in W. B. Weeden, *Economic and Social History of New England* (2 vols., Boston, 1890-1891).

The following are good studies of particular commonwealths: R. F. Upton, *Revolutionary New Hampshire* (Hanover, 1936); C. L. Becker, *The History of Political Parties in the Province of New York, 1760-1766* (Univ. of Wis., *History Ser.*, II, no. 1, 1909); N. Y. Division of Archives and History, *The American Revolution in New York* (Albany, 1926); Leonard Lundin, *Cockpit of the Revolution* (*Princeton History of New Jersey*, II; Princeton, 1940); C. H. Lincoln, *The Revolutionary Movement in Pennsylvania, 1760-1776* (Univ. of Pa., *Ser. in History*, no. 1, 1901); C. A. Barker, *The Background of the Revolution in Maryland* (*Yale Hist. Publs. Miscellany*, XXXVIII, 1940); C. R. Lingley, *The Transition in Virginia from Colony to Commonwealth* (Columbia Univ., *Studies*, XXXVI, no. 2, 1910); H. J. Eckenrode, *The Revolution in Virginia* (Boston, 1916); Edward McCrady, *History of South Carolina under the Royal Government, 1719-1776* (N. Y., 1899), and his *History of South Carolina in the Revolution* (2 vols., N. Y., 1901-1902). Among important contemporary histories are Thomas Hutchinson, *History of the Colony [and Province] of Massachusetts Bay* (3 vols., London, 1765-1828; now available in an excellent edition by L. S. Mayo, Cambridge, Mass., 1936); Jeremy Belknap, *The History of New Hampshire* (3 vols., Phila. and Boston, 1784-1792), which carries the narrative through this period with a summary of conditions at its close; William Smith, *History of the Late Province of New York* (2 vols., N. Y. Hist. Soc., *Colls.*, IV-V, 1829-1830), which stops at 1762 but has a survey of society on the eve of the Revolution; and David Ramsay, *History of the Revolution of South Carolina* (2 vols., Trenton, 1785).

STATE RECORDS AND HISTORICAL SOCIETY PUBLICATIONS: These include a great mass of material relating to the Revolutionary Generation. Outstanding are the historical societies of Massachusetts (including the Massachusetts Historical Society, the American Antiquarian Society and the Colonial Society of Massachusetts), Connecticut, New York, New Jersey, Pennsylvania, Maryland and Virginia. Among the public records listed in earlier volumes of the *History of American Life*, several continue through, or into, the Revolutionary period, including W. W. Hening, comp., *The Statutes-at-Large, Being a Collection of All the Laws of Virginia, 1619-1792* (13 vols., Phila. and N. Y., 1823); *Acts and Resolves of the Province of Massachusetts Bay* (17 vols., Boston, 1869-1910); W. H. Browne, ed., *Archives of Maryland* (41 vols., Balt., 1883-1922); and W. L. Saunders, ed., *Colonial Records of North Carolina, 1662-1776* (10 vols., Raleigh, 1886-1890), continued as *State Records* (16 vols., Winston and Goldsboro, 1895-1905) edited by Walter Clark. Among the more important legislative records are H. R. McIlwaine and J. P. Kennedy, eds., *Journals of the House of Burgesses of Virginia, 1727-1776* (8 vols., Richmond, 1905-1910), and its continuation in the *Journals of the House of Delegates, 1776-1790* (4 vols., Richmond, 1828).

LOCAL HISTORIES AND RECORDS: The chief historical studies of the larger towns are J. T. Scharf and Thompson Westcott, *History of Philadelphia* (3 vols., Phila., 1884); Carl and Jessica Bridenbaugh, *Rebels and Gentlemen, Philadelphia in the Age of Franklin* (N. Y., 1942), which gives a rounded picture of the city's life in the period 1740-1775; I. N. P. Stokes's monumental *Iconography of Manhattan Island* (6 vols., N. Y., 1915-1928), with maps, views and a "Chronology" which includes extracts from the sources;

Justin Winsor, ed., *Memorial History of Boston, 1630-1880* (4 vols., Boston, 1880-1881); and Gertrude S. Kimball, *Providence in Colonial Times* (Boston, 1912). Much imperfectly exploited material for social history exists in municipal publications, notably the Boston town records, printed by the Record Commissioners of that city in their *Reports* (Boston, 1876-1908) and including some records of other towns now annexed to the city; the *Minutes* of the Common Council of the City of New York, 1675-1776 (8 vols., N. Y., 1905), continued in the *Minutes, 1784-1831* (19 vols., N. Y., 1917); and the Philadelphia *Minutes* of the Common Council (Phila., 1847). There are numerous accounts of New England country towns, the ablest probably being C. F. Adams's history of Quincy (Braintree) in his *Three Episodes of Massachusetts History*, II (Boston, 1892). Informative for social conditions in western Massachusetts is H. C. Parsons, *A Puritan Outpost* (N. Y., 1937), a history of Northfield. For rural New York, see H. B. Dawson, *Westchester County, New York, during the American Revolution* (Morrisania, N. Y., 1886), and Otto Hufeland, *Westchester County during the American Revolution* (N. Y., 1926). A first-rate piece of Virginia local history is Fairfax Harrison, *Landmarks of Old Prince William* (2 vols., Richmond, 1924).

THE IMPERIAL SETTING

Excellent general surveys are C. M. Andrews, "The Government of the Empire," J. H. Rose and others, eds., *The Cambridge History of the British Empire* (8 vols., N. Y., 1929-1940), I, and his *The Colonial Background of the American Revolution* (New Haven, 1924). Special aspects are treated in L. W. Labaree, *Royal Government in America* (*Yale Hist. Publs. Studies*, VI, 1930); G. L. Beer, *British Colonial Policy, 1754-1765* (N. Y., 1907); *Essays in Colonial History Presented to Charles McLean Andrews by His Students* (New Haven, 1931); and R. B. Morris, ed., *The Era of the American Revolution* (N. Y., 1939). For the correspondence of important royal officials, see Cadwallader Colden, *Letter Books* (N. Y. Hist. Soc., *Colls.*, IX-X, 1877-1878) ; his *Letters and Papers* (*ibid.*, L-LVI, 1918-1923) ; and Thomas Gage, *Correspondence with the Secretaries of State, 1763-1775* (C. E. Carter, ed., 2 vols., New Haven, 1931-1933).

AGRICULTURE AND RURAL LIFE

There is a comprehensive *Bibliography of the History of Agriculture in the United States* (Wash., 1930) by E. E. Edwards.   Authoritative works are P. W. Bidwell and J. I. Falconer, *History of Agriculture in the Northern United States, 1620-1860* (Carnegie Inst., *Publs.*, no. 358, 1925), and L. C. Gray, *History of Agriculture in the Southern United States to 1860* (2 vols., *ibid.*, no. 430, 1933). Other useful books on the plantation system are U. B. Phillips, *American Negro Slavery* (N. Y., 1928), and his *Life and Labor in the Old South* (Boston, 1929) ; and A. O. Craven, *Soil Exhaustion as a Factor in the Agricultural History of Virginia and Maryland, 1606-1860* (Univ. of Ill., *Studies*, XIII, no. 1, 1926).   U. B. Phillips, ed., *Plantation and Frontier* (J. R. Commons and others, eds., *A Documentary History of American Industrial Society*, Cleveland, 1909-1911, I-II), is the best collection of sources. The diaries of Landon Carter (already mentioned) and P. V. Fithian's *Journal and Letters, 1767-1774* (J. R. Williams. ed., Princeton, 1900), illustrate life on two plantations. The latter's account of his Virginia experiences has been reëdited with additional material by H. D. Farish under the title *Journal and Letters of Philip Vickers Fithian, 1773-1774: a Plantation Tutor of the Old Dominion* (H. D. Farish, ed., *Williamsburg Restoration Historical Studies*, III, Richmond, 1943).   A recent study of landlord-tenant relations in the North is Irving Mark, *Agrarian Conflicts in Colonial New York, 1771-1775* (Columbia Univ., *Studies*, no. 469, 1940).   For contemporary discussion, see the following: Jared Eliot, *Essays upon Field-Husbandry in New-England* (Boston, 1760; now conveniently available in an edition by H. J. Carman and R. G. Tugwell, Columbia Univ., *Studies in the History of American Agriculture,* no. 1, 1934); *American Husbandry* (published anonymously, London, 1775, and recently edited by H. J. Carman, *ibid.,* no. 6, 1939); and Samuel Deane, *The New-England Farmer; or, Georgical Dictionary* (Worcester, 1790; 2nd edn., 1797).

BUSINESS

GENERAL WORKS: Many phases of business are covered, with extensive bibliographies, in E. R. Johnson and others, *History of the Domestic and Foreign Commerce of the United States* (Carnegie Inst., *Publs.,* no. 215 A, 1915); A. M. Schlesinger, *The Colonial Merchants and the American Revolution, 1763-1776* (Columbia Univ., *Studies,* LXXVIII, 1918); and R. A. East, *Business Enterprise in the American Revolutionary Era* (*ibid.,* no. 439, 1938). An important contemporary survey of American trade is Lord Sheffield, *Observations on the Commerce of the American States* (6th edn., London, 1784), much of it dealing with pre-Revolutionary conditions. Among the studies that treat particular areas are Virginia D. Harrington, *The New York Merchant on the Eve of the Revolution* (Columbia Univ., *Studies,* no. 404, 1935); C. C. Crittenden, *The Commerce of North Carolina, 1763-1789* (*Yale Hist. Publs. Miscellany,* XXIX, 1936); and Leila Sellers, *Charleston Business on the Eve of the American Revolution* (Chapel Hill, 1934). David Macpherson, *Annals of Commerce* (4 vols., London, 1805), is valuable for statistics.

COMMUNICATIONS: Seymour Dunbar, *A History of Travel in America* (4 vols., Indianapolis, 1915), and Alice M. Earle's interesting *Stage-Coach and Tavern Days* (N. Y., 1900) leave something to be desired. Among the local studies are C. P. Gould, *Money and Transportation in Maryland, 1720-1765* (Johns Hopkins Univ., *Studies,* XXXIII, no. 1, 1915), and W. J. Lane, *From Indian Trail to Iron Horse. Travel and Transportation in New Jersey, 1620-1860* (*Princeton History of New Jersey,* I; Princeton, 1939). For postal service, see William Smith, *The His-*

tory of the Post Office in British North America, 1639-1870 (Cambridge, England, 1920); W. E. Rich, *The History of the United States Post Office to the Year 1829* (*Harvard Econ. Studies,* XXVII, 1924); R. L. Butler, *Doctor Franklin, Postmaster General* (N. Y., 1928); and the contemporary account in Finlay's *Journal* (already cited).

BUSINESS CORRESPONDENCE AND ORGANIZATION: Among the compilations that shed light on business conditions in various places are in Massachusetts: A. E. Brown, ed., *John Hancock, His Book* (Boston, 1898); Rowe, *Letters and Diary* (already mentioned); and K. W. Porter, ed., *The Jacksons and the Lees* (2 vols., N. S. B. Gras, ed., *Harvard Studies in Business History,* III, 1937); in Rhode Island: *The Commerce of Rhode Island* (Mass. Hist. Soc., *Colls.,* LXIX-LXX, 1914-1915); in New York: John Watts, *Letter Book* (N. Y. Hist. Soc., *Colls.,* LXI, 1928); and in Virginia: Frances N. Mason, ed., *John Norton & Sons, Merchants of London and Virginia, Being the Papers from Their Counting House for the Years 1750 to 1795* (Richmond, 1937). Information regarding business organization appears in J. S. Davis, *Essays in the Earlier History of American Corporations* (2 vols., *Harvard Econ. Studies,* XVI, 1917); C. M. Andrews, "Boston Merchants and the Non-Importation Movement," Colon. Soc. of Mass., *Publs.,* XIX, 159-259; and New York Chamber of Commerce, *Colonial Records, 1768-1784* (J. A. Stevens, ed., N. Y., 1867).

SPECIAL BRANCHES OF TRADE: For commerce with the West Indies, see H. C. Bell, "The West Indian Trade before the American Revolution," *Am. Hist. Rev.,* XXII, 272-287, and Agnes Whitson, "The Outlook of the Continental Colonies on the British West Indies, 1760-1775," *Polit. Sci. Quar.,* XLV, 56-86; and for the African slave trade, consult Phillips, *American Negro Slavery* (already mentioned), and W. E. B. Du Bois, *The Suppression of the African Slave-Trade to the United States of America* (*Harvard Hist. Studies,* I, 1896). Important sources are in Elizabeth Donnan, ed., *Documents Illustrative of the History of the Slave Trade to America* (4 vols., Carnegie Inst., *Publs.,* no. 409,

1930-1935). Informative works on the fisheries include Raymond McFarland, *A History of the New England Fisheries* (Univ. of Pa., *Publs. in Political Economy and Public Law*, no. 24, 1911); Alexander Starbuck, *History of the American Whale Fishery from Its Earliest Inception to the Year 1876* (Waltham, Mass., 1878); and W. S. Tower, *History of the Whale Fishery* (Phila., 1911).

MANUFACTURES

The best general introduction is V. S. Clark's *History of Manufactures in the United States* (Carnegie Inst., *Contribs. to Am. Econ. History*, rev. edn., 3 vols., N. Y., 1929), I, which should be supplemented by studies of particular industries, notably A. H. Cole, *The American Wool Manufacture* (2 vols., Cambridge, 1926); A. C. Bining, *British Regulation of the Colonial Iron Industry* (Phila., 1933), and his *Pennsylvania Iron Manufacture in the Eighteenth Century* (Pa. Hist. Comn., *Publs.*, IV, 1938); C. S. Boyer, *Early Forges and Furnaces in New Jersey* (Phila., 1931); Kathleen Bruce, *The Virginia Iron Manufacture in the Slave Era* (N. Y., 1931); and Blanche E. Hazard, *The Organization of the Boot and Shoe Industry in Massachusetts before 1875* (*Harvard Econ. Studies*, XXIII, 1921). Two books deal with a variety of skilled crafts: G. F. Dow, *The Arts & Crafts in New England, 1704-1775, Gleanings from Boston Newspapers* (Topsfield, Mass., 1927), and R. S. Gottesman, *The Arts and Crafts: Advertisements from New York Newspapers, 1726-1776* (N. Y., 1938).

LABOR SYSTEMS

Besides the works on plantation agriculture and the slave trade listed earlier, an important collection of sources is Helen T. Catterall, ed., *Judicial Cases Concerning Slavery and the Negro* (5 vols., Carnegie Inst., *Publs.*, no. 374, 1926-1937), I-III. The best studies of white servitude are C. A. Herrick, *White Servitude in Pennsylvania* (Phila., 1926), and E. I. McCormac, *White Servitude in Maryland*,

1634-1820 (Johns Hopkins Univ., *Studies*, XXII, nos. 3-4, 1904). Samuel McKee, *Labor in Colonial New York, 1664-1776* (Columbia Univ., *Studies*, no. 410, 1935), deals with both servile and free labor. See also M. W. Jernegan, *Laboring and Dependent Classes in Colonial America, 1607-1783* (Univ. of Chicago, *Social Service Monographs*, no. 17, 1931).

POPULATION AND IMMIGRATION

Contemporary population estimates are assembled in *American Population before the Federal Census of 1790* (N. Y., 1932), compiled by E. B. Greene and Virginia D. Harrington. On a different plan is Stella H. Sutherland, *Population Distribution in Colonial America* (N. Y., 1936). The best analysis of immigrant elements is the "Report" of the Committee on Linguistic and National Stocks in the Population of the United States, printed in Am. Hist. Assoc., *Ann. Rep. for 1931*, I, with important annexes by M. L. Hansen and H. F. Barker. Most books in this field must be read with due allowance for ancestral loyalties. Among the more valuable are S. C. Johnson, *A History of Emigration from the United Kingdom to North America, 1763-1912* (London School of Econs. and Polit. Sci., *Monograph Ser.*, no. 34, 1913); A. B. Faust, *The German Element in the United States* (2 vols., Boston, 1909); A. H. Hirsch, *The Huguenots of Colonial South Carolina* (Durham, 1928); G. F. Donovan, *The Pre-Revolutionary Irish in Massachusetts, 1620-1775* (Menasha, Wis., 1932); A. L. Lebeson, *Jewish Pioneers in America* (N. Y., 1931); and L. M. Friedman, *Early American Jews* (Cambridge, 1934).

THE FAMILY AND THE STATUS OF WOMEN

The best treatment of early American marriage law is in G. E. Howard, *A History of Matrimonial Institutions* (3 vols., Chicago, 1904), II-III. A. W. Calhoun, *A Social History of the American Family* (3 vols., Cleveland, 1917-

1919), is fuller but less scholarly. Three useful books on the status and activities of women are Mary S. Benson, *Women in Eighteenth-Century America* (Columbia Univ., *Studies*, no. 405, 1935); Elizabeth A. Dexter, *Colonial Women of Affairs* (rev. edn., Boston, 1931); and Julia C. Spruill, *Women's Life and Work in the Southern Colonies* (Chapel Hill, 1938).

THE PROFESSIONS

THE LAW: Valuable for an understanding of the status of the legal profession are Charles Warren, *History of the American Bar* (Boston, 1911); Emory Washburn, *Sketches of the Judicial History of Massachusetts from 1630 to the Revolution in 1775* (Boston, 1840); E. A. Jones, *American Members of the Inns of Court* (London, 1924); and P. M. Hamlin, *Legal Education in Colonial New York* (N. Y., 1939). For representative practitioners, see William Tudor, *The Life of James Otis* (Boston, 1823); E. F. Brown, *Joseph Hawley, Colonial Radical* (N. Y., 1931); L. H. Gipson, *Jared Ingersoll* (*Yale Hist. Publs. Miscellany*, VIII, 1920); G. C. Groce, *W. S. Johnson* (N. Y., 1937); Theodore Sedgwick, *A Memoir of the Life of William Livingston* (N. Y., 1833); H. C. Van Schaack, *Peter Van Schaack* (N. Y., 1842); E. P. Alexander, *A Revolutionary Conservative, James Duane of New York* (D. R. Fox, ed., *N. Y. State Hist. Assoc. Ser.*, no. 6, 1938); and W. B. Reed, *Life and Correspondence of Joseph Reed* (2 vols., Phila., 1847).

MEDICINE: F. H. Garrison, *Introduction to the History of Medicine* (rev. edn., Phila., 1929), chap. xi, gives a good summary of early American medicine with a bibliography. A convenient general manual is F. R. Packard, *History of Medicine in the United States* (rev. edn., 2 vols., N. Y., 1931). Among useful local studies are Stephen Wickes, *History of Medicine in New Jersey, and of Its Medical Men. from the Settlement of the Province to A.D. 1800* (Newark, 1879), and H. R. Viets, *A Brief History of Medicine in Massachusetts* (Boston, 1930). Individual physicians are dealt with in N. G. Goodman, *Benjamin Rush, Physician and Citizen* (Phila., 1934); Edward Warren, *John Warren* (Boston, 1874); and J. E. Gibson, *Dr. Bodo Otto and the Medical Background of the American Revolution* (Springfield, Ill., 1937). For medical education, see Joseph Carson, *A History of the Medical Department of the University of Pennsylvania* (Phila., 1869); T. F. Harrington, *The Harvard Medical School* (3 vols., N. Y., 1905); and S. F. Batchelder, *Bits of Harvard History* (Cambridge, 1924), chap. v.

RELIGION, THE CHURCHES AND THE CLERGY

W. W. Sweet, *Religion in Colonial America* (N. Y., 1942), is a general treatment. A useful manual, with bibliography and excerpts from sources for the years 1774-1789, is E. F. Humphrey, *Nationalism and Religion in America* (Boston, 1924). See also P. G. Mode, ed., *Source Book and Bibliographical Guide for American Church History* (Menasha, Wis., 1921). Works dealing with particular religious groups are numerous. Valuable for the Anglicans are W. S. Perry, *History of the American Episcopal Church* (2 vols., Boston, 1885), and A. L. Cross, *The Anglican Episcopate and the American Colonies* (*Harvard Hist. Studies*, IX, 1902). Important sources are in W. S. Perry, comp., *Historical Collections Relating to the American Colonial Church* (5 vols., Hartford, 1870-1878); W. S. Perry and F. L. Hawks, comps., *A Documentary History of the Protestant Episcopal Church in the United States* (2 vols., 1863-1864); and Herbert and Carol Schneider, eds., *Samuel Johnson, President of King's College; His Career and Writings* (4 vols., N. Y., 1929). Among the studies of Congregationalism are Williston Walker, *A History of the Congregational Churches in the United States* (Philip Schaff and others, eds., *The American Church History Series*, 13 vols., N. Y., 1893-1897, III); Alice M. Baldwin, *The New England Clergy and the American Revolution* (Duke Univ., Publs., 1928); J. C. Meyer, *Church and State in Massachusetts, 1740-1833* (Cleveland, 1930); J. W.

Thornton, ed., *The Pulpit of the American Revolution* (N. Y., 1860); Alden Bradford, *Memoir of the Life and Writings of Rev. Jonathan Mayhew* (Boston, 1838); and Mary L. Gambrell, *Ministerial Training in Eighteenth-Century New England* (Columbia Univ., *Studies*, no. 428, 1937). For the Presbyterians, see C. A. Briggs, *American Presbyterianism, Its Origin and Early History* (N. Y., 1885), and V. L. Collins, *President Witherspoon* (2 vols., Princeton, 1925).

The development of other denominations is treated by the following authors in the *American Church History Series* (already cited): A. H. Newman (Baptists); H. E. Jacobs (Lutherans); J. M. Buckley (Methodists); E. T. Corwin (Dutch Reformed); J. H. Dubbs (German Reformed); A. C. and R. H. Thomas (Society of Friends); and J. T. Hamilton (Moravians; more fully in his *A History of the Church Known as the Moravian Church, or, the Unitas Fratrum,* in Moravian Hist. Soc., *Trans.,* VI, 1900). An important contemporary history of the Baptists is Isaac Backus, *History of New England, with Particular Reference to the Denomination of Christians Called Baptists* (2nd edn., 2 vols., Newton, Mass., 1871). For the Quakers, see also Isaac Sharpless, *The Quakers in the Revolution* (same author, *A History of Quaker Government in Pennsylvania,* Phila., 1898-1899, II). W. M. Gewehr, *The Great Awakening in Virginia, 1740-1790* (Duke Univ., *Publs.,* 1930), is useful for popular religious movements in the South.

Leading authorities for the Catholic Church are J. G. Shea, *Life and Times of the Most Rev. John Carroll* (same author, *History of the Catholic Church in the United States,* 4 vols., N. Y., 1886-1889, II), and Peter Guilday, *The Life and Times of John Carroll* (N. Y., 1922). These should be supplemented by Sister Mary Augustina (Ray), *American Opinion of Roman Catholicism in the Eighteenth Century* (Columbia Univ., *Studies,* no. 416, 1936), and A. J. Riley, *Catholicism in New England to 1788* (Catholic Univ. of America, *Studies,* XXIV, 1936). For religious "liberalism" or "radicalism," see H. M. Morais, *Deism in Eighteenth Century America* (Columbia Univ., *Studies,* no.

397, 1934), and, for the European background, Leslie Stephen, *History of English Thought in the Eighteenth Century* (3rd edn., 2 vols., N. Y., 1902), I, and Preserved Smith, *A History of Modern Culture* (2 vols., N. Y., 1930-1934), II.

EDUCATION

COMMON SCHOOLS: Important for both elementary and secondary education are the *Circulars of Information* of the U. S. Bureau of Education and the *Contributions to Education* of Teachers College of Columbia University. Further material appears in Jernegan, *Laboring and Dependent Classes in Colonial America* (already cited), and in two monographs by R. F. Seybolt: *Source Studies in American Colonial Education: the Private School* (Univ. of Ill., Bur. of Educational Research, *Bull.*, no. 28, 1925), and *The Evening School in Colonial America* (*ibid.*, no. 24, 1925). Two recent works by Thomas Woody, *Early Quaker Education in Pennsylvania* (Teachers College, Columbia Univ., *Contribs.*, no. 105, 1920) and *Quaker Education in New Jersey* (Phila., 1923), include the later years of the eighteenth century. For secondary education, E. E. Brown, *The Making of Our Middle Schools* (rev. edn., N. Y., 1914), provides the best introduction.

HIGHER EDUCATION: The following are histories of the principal eighteenth-century colleges: Josiah Quincy, *History of Harvard University* (2 vols., Cambridge, 1840); S. E. Morison, *Three Centuries of Harvard, 1636-1936* (Cambridge, 1936); H. B. Adams, *The College of William and Mary* (U. S. Bur. of Educ., *Circular of Information*, no. 1, 1887); F. B. Dexter, *Biographical Sketches of Yale College with Annals of the College History, 1701-1792* (4 vols., N. Y., 1885-1904); John Maclean, *History of the College of New Jersey* (2 vols., Phila., 1877); N. F. Moore, *An Historical Sketch of King's College* (N. Y., 1846); Brander Matthews and others, eds., *A History of Columbia University, 1754-1904* (N. Y., 1904); T. H. Montgomery, *A History of the University of Pennsylvania, from Its Foundation to A.D. 1770* (Phila., 1900); E. P. Cheyney, *History of the University of Pennsylvania, 1740-1940* (Phila., 1940); R. A. Guild, *History of Brown University, with Illustrative Documents* (Providence, 1867); L. B. Richardson, *History of Dartmouth College* (2 vols., Hanover, 1932); and W. S. Demarest, *History of Rutgers College, 1766-1924* (New Brunswick, N. J., 1924).

POSTWAR EDUCATIONAL DISCUSSION: A. O. Hansen, *Liberalism and Education in the Eighteenth Century* (N. Y., 1926), is the best single work. For the life and writings of Noah Webster, see Emily E. F. Ford and Emily E. F. Skeel, eds., *Notes on the Life of Noah Webster* (2 vols., N. Y., 1912), and H. R. Warfel, *Noah Webster, Schoolmaster to America* (N. Y., 1936).

READING MATTER AND SPEECH

PRINTING AND THE BOOK TRADE: Useful for this subject are Hellmut Lehmann-Haupt, ed., *The Book in America* (N. Y., 1939), esp. pt. i by L. C. Wroth; J. T. Winterich, *Early American Books & Printing* (Boston, 1935); L. C. Wroth, *The Colonial Printer* (rev. edn., Portland, Me., 1938); Thomas, *History of Printing* (cited earlier); and Charles Evans, comp., *American Bibliography; a Chronological Dictionary of All Books, Pamphlets, and Periodical Publications Printed in the United States of America from the Genesis of Printing in 1639 Down to and Including the Year 1820* (new edn., 12 vols., N. Y., 1941-1942), of which vols. iii-viii cover this period. A good account of a colonial library is A. B. Keep, *History of the New York Society Library* (N. Y., 1908).

LITERATURE: The standard work is still M. C. Tyler, *The Literary History of the American Revolution, 1763-1783* (2nd edn., 2 vols., N. Y., 1898-1900). Consult also W. P. Trent and others, eds., *The Cambridge History of American Literature* (4 vols., N. Y., 1917-1921), I; and, for provocative discussion, V. L. Parrington, *The Colonial Mind* (same author, *Main Currents in American Thought*, N. Y., 1927-1930, I). Books dealing with particular writers include V. L. Parrington, ed., *The Connecticut Wits* (N. Y., 1926) ; C. B. Todd, *Life and Letters of Joel Barlow* (N. Y., 1886) ; Alexander Cowie, *John Trumbull, Connecticut Wit* (Chapel Hill, 1936) ; C. M. Newlin, *The Life and Writings of Hugh Henry Brackenridge* (Princeton 1932) ; Philip Freneau, *Poems* (F. L. Pattee, ed., 3 vols., Princeton, 1902-1907) ; and G. E. Hastings, *Life and Works of Francis Hopkinson* (Chicago, 1926). A useful brief selection of prose and poetry is F. C. Prescott and J. H. Nelson, eds., *Prose and Poetry of the Revolution* (N. Y., 1925). A convenient guide to political writings is R. G. Adams, *Political Ideas of the American Revolution* (Durham, 1922). For periodical publications, see the earlier heading, "Newspapers, Magazines and Almanacs."

SPEECH: H. L. Mencken, *The American Language* (4th rev. edn., N. Y., 1936), and G. P. Krapp, *The English Language in America* (2 vols., N. Y., 1925), deal briefly with this period. A more detailed treatment is M. M. Mathews, ed., *The Beginnings of American English* (Chicago, 1931).

INTERNATIONAL ASPECTS OF CULTURE: Of particular value in this connection are H. M. Jones, *America and French Culture, 1750-1848* (Chapel Hill, 1927), and Bernard Faÿ, *L'Esprit Révolutionnaire en France et aux États-Unis* (Paris, 1925). The latter appears in English translation by Ramon Guthrie as *The Revolutionary Spirit in France and the United States* (N. Y., 1927).

SCIENCE

Preserved Smith, *History of Modern Culture* (earlier cited), II, chaps. i-iv, is useful for the European background. For developments in America, see E. G. Conklin and others, *The Early History of Science and Learning in America* (Am. Philosophical Soc., *Proceeds.*, LXXXVI, no. 1, 1942) ; F. E. Brasch, "The Royal Society of London and Its Influence upon Scientific Thought in the American Colonies," *Scientific Mo.*, XXXIII, 336-355, 448-469; Michael Kraus, "Scientific Relations between Europe and America in the Eighteenth Century," *ibid.*, LV, 259-272; Helen D. Behnke, "Colonial Theories Concerning the Cause of Disease," *Medical Life*, XLI, 59-74; and W. M. and Mabel S. C. Smallwood, *Natural History and the American Mind* (*Columbia Studies in American Culture*, no. 8, 1941). Among the principal original sources are the *Transactions* of the American Philosophical Society (Phila., from 1769) and the *Memoirs* of the American Academy of Arts and Sciences (Boston, from 1785). Important for particular men are William Darlington, *Memorials of John Bartram and Humphrey Marshall* (Phila., 1849); J. E. Smith, ed., *A Selection of the Correspondence of Linnæus, and Other Naturalists* (2 vols., London, 1821); and I. B. Cohen, ed., *Benjamin Franklin's Experiments* (Cambridge, 1941).

THE ARTS

THE THEATER: The standard work is G. O. Seilhamer, *History of the American Theatre* (3 vols., Phila., 1888-1891). G. C. D. Odell, *Annals of the New York Stage* (13 vols., N. Y., 1927-1942), I, gives many details; and Eola Willis, *The Charleston Stage in the Eighteenth Century, with Social Settings of the Time* (Columbia, S. C., 1924), reproduces contemporary material. F. R. Dulles, *America Learns to Play* (N. Y., 1940), deals with the theater as well as other forms of amusement. For playwriting, see A. H. Quinn, *A History of the American Drama, from the Beginning to the Civil War* (N. Y., 1923), and his edition of *Representative American Plays* (N. Y., 1917).

MUSIC: J. T. Howard, *Our American Music* (N. Y., 1931), includes the colonial period. For special aspects, see O. G. Sonneck, *Early Concert Life in America, 1731-1800* (Leipzig, 1907); W. O. Gould, *History of Church Music in America* (Boston, 1853); and Raymond Walters, *The Bethlehem Bach Choir* (Bethlehem, Pa., 1923).

PAINTING: F. W. Bayley and C. E. Goodspeed have published a revised edition of William Dunlap's important *Rise and Progress of the Arts of Design in the United States* (2 vols., Boston, 1934). Other studies are J. H. Morgan,

Early American Painters (N. Y., 1921); Cuthbert Lee, *Early American Portrait Painters* (New Haven, 1930); Alan Burroughs, *Limners and Likenesses* (*Harvard-Radcliffe Fine Arts Series*, 1936); and F. W. Bayley, *The Life and Works of John Singleton Copley* (Boston, 1915). See also John Singleton Copley and Henry Pelham, *Letters & Papers, 1739-1776* (Mass. Hist. Soc., *Colls.*, LXXI, 1914). G. C. Groce has prepared for the Historical Records Survey a preliminary inventory of *Early American Portrait Artists* (Newark, N. J., 1940).

ARCHITECTURE: H. D. Eberlein, *The Architecture of Colonial America* (Boston, 1921), and Fiske Kimball, *Domestic Architecture of the American Colonies and the Early Republic* (N. Y., 1922), provide general surveys. Works of a more local character, cited in Adams, *Provincial Society*, 346, are also useful for this later period. A special study of considerable value is D. J. Baum and others, eds., *Great Georgian Houses of America* (2 vols., N. Y., 1933-1937).

INLAND AMERICA

THE OLD WEST: For westward and northward movements in and from New England, see Lois K. Mathews, *The Expansion of New England* (Boston, 1909), and D. R. Fox, *Yankees and Yorkers* (N. Y., 1940). F. W. Halsey, *Old New York Frontier* (N. Y., 1901), and Ruth L. Higgins, *Expansion in New York, with Especial Reference to the Eighteenth Century* (Ohio State Univ., *Contribs.*, no. 14, 1931), deal with eighteenth-century western settlements in New York. For inland Pennsylvania, consult Lincoln's *Revolutionary Movement in Pennsylvania* (cited earlier), and for the Connecticut settlement in the Wyoming Valley, J. P. Boyd, ed., *The Susquehannah Company Papers* (4 vols., *Sheldon Reynolds Memorial Publs.*; Wilkes-Barre, 1930-1933). Studies of the Southern backcountry include C. H. Ambler, *Sectionalism in Virginia from 1776 to 1861* (Chicago, 1910); Harrison's *Landmarks of Old Prince William* (already mentioned); J. S. Bassett, "The Regulators of North Carolina," Am. Hist. Assoc., *Ann. Rep. for 1894,*

141-212; W. A. Schaper, "Sectionalism and Representation in South Carolina," *ibid.*, *1900*, I, 245-460; and R. L. Meriwether, *The Expansion of South Carolina, 1729-1765* (Kingsport, Tenn., 1940). A useful older book is Alexander Gregg, *History of the Old Cheraws* (N. Y., 1867).

THE NEW FRONTIERS: Conditions on the Northern frontier receive study in M. B. Jones, *Vermont in the Making, 1750-1777* (Cambridge, 1939); C. M. Thompson, *Independent Vermont* (Boston, 1942); I. B. Wilbur, *Ira Allen—Founder of Vermont* (2 vols., Boston, 1928); and John Pell, *Ethan Allen* (Boston, 1929). Of the older books on the trans-Alleghany country the two most important are Francis Parkman, *The Conspiracy of Pontiac and the Indian War after the Conquest of Canada* (several editions, Boston, from 1851 on); and Justin Winsor, *The Westward Movement* (Boston, 1897), less readable and not fully documented, but a storehouse of information. For a discriminating critique by F. J. Turner of Theodore Roosevelt's *Winning of the West* (4 vols., N. Y., 1889-1896), see *Am. Hist. Rev.*, II, 171-176. On British policy, colonial promotion and land speculation, C. W. Alvord, *The Mississippi Valley in British Politics* (2 vols., Cleveland, 1917), is the outstanding work. T. P. Abernethy, *Western Lands and the American Revolution* (N. Y., 1937), is chiefly concerned with the Southwest. For Indian relations, see the valuable contemporary work of the Indian trader, James Adair, *The History of the American Indians* (London, 1775; S. C. Williams, ed., Johnson City, Tenn., 1930); W. E. Stevens, *The Northwest Fur Trade, 1763-1800* (Univ. of Ill., *Studies*, XIV, no. 3, 1928); Arthur Pound, *Johnson of the Mohawks* (N. Y., 1930); and A. T. Volwiler, *George Croghan and the Westward Movement* (Cleveland, 1926). Important collections of sources for Western history are Gage, *Correspondence* (already cited); Sir William Johnson, *Papers* (James Sullivan and others, eds., 9 vols., Albany, 1921-1939); and several volumes of the *Collections* of the Illinois State Historical Library, edited by C. W. Alvord and C. E. Carter. A. B. Hulbert, *Historic Highways of America* (16 vols., Cleveland, 1902-1905), and C. H. Ambler, *A History of Transportation in the Ohio Valley* (Glendale, Calif., 1932), deal with routes of travel.

TRANS-ALLEGHANY SETTLEMENTS: Original records relating to the upper Ohio Valley from 1774 to 1781 were edited first by R. G. Thwaites and Louise P. Kellogg jointly and later by Miss Kellogg (Madison, 1905-1917), as follows: *Documentary History of Dunmore's War, 1774; Revolution on the Upper Ohio; Frontier Defence on the Upper Ohio; Frontier Advance on the Upper Ohio;* and *Frontier Retreat on the Upper Ohio.* The course of settlement is described in S. J. and Elizabeth H. Buck, *The Planting of Civilization in Western Pennsylvania* (*Western Pennsylvania Series;* Pittsburgh, 1939); C. H. Ambler, *A History of West Virginia* (Carl Wittke, ed., *Prentice-Hall History Series;* N. Y., 1933); A. S. Withers, *Chronicles of Border Warfare* (R. G. Thwaites, ed., Cincinnati, 1895); and P. V. Fithian, *Journal, 1775-76* (R. G. Albion and Leonidas Dodson, eds., Princeton, 1934). For the Southwest, see Archibald Henderson, *The Conquest of the Old Southwest* (N. Y., 1920); R. G. Thwaites, *Daniel Boone* (N. Y., 1902); J. A. James, *Life of George Rogers Clark* (Chicago, 1928), which should be supplemented by the volumes of Clark papers James edited in the *Collections* of the Illinois State Historical Library; T. D. Clark, *A History of Kentucky* (Carl Wittke, ed., *Prentice-Hall History Series;* N. Y., 1937), chaps. i-vi; and T. P. Abernethy, *From Frontier to Plantation in Tennessee* (Chapel Hill, 1932). C. W. Alvord, *The Illinois Country, 1673-1818* (C. W. Alvord, ed., *The Centennial History of Illinois,* I, Springfield, 1920), chaps. xii-xviii, gives an excellent view of conditions in the Northwest. For later developments, see the heading, "The West in the Early Republic."

SOCIAL ASPECTS OF THE REVOLUTIONARY MOVEMENT

American society at the end of the colonial era is considered in James Schouler, *Americans of 1776* (N. Y., 1906); Michael Kraus, *Intercolonial Aspects of American Culture on the Eve of the Revolution* (Columbia Univ., *Studies,* no. 302, 1928); and C. L. Becker's excellent *The Eve of the Revolution* (Allen Johnson, ed., *The Chronicles of America Series,* 50 vols., New Haven, 1918-1921, XI). Particular aspects—economic, social, intellectual, religious, political and personal—are dealt with in many of the works earlier mentioned. On the spread of revolutionary feeling, Richard Frothingham, *The Rise of the Republic of the United States* (Boston, 1872), is still useful. The mechanics of Whig and Tory organization and propaganda are most fully described, with extensive bibliography, in Philip Davidson, *Propaganda and the American Revolution* (Chapel Hill, 1941). O. M. Dickerson, ed., *Boston under Military Rule, 1768-1769, as Revealed in a Journal of the Times* (Boston, 1936), reprints one of the most interesting series of Whig newspaper propaganda. Whig and Tory pamphlets are listed and discussed in Adams, *Political Ideas of the American Revolution* (earlier cited). See also H. L. Calkin, "Pamphlets and Public Opinion during the American Revolution," *Pa. Mag. of History and Biog.,* LXIV, 22-42.

Helpful for understanding the course of the Loyalists are Lorenzo Sabine, *Biographical Sketches of Loyalists of the American Revolution* (rev. edn., 2 vols., Boston, 1864), a pioneer American effort to present the Loyalist position; C. H. Van Tyne, *The Loyalists in the American Revolution* (N. Y., 1902); and D. P. Coke, *The Royal Commission on the Losses and Services of American Loyalists, 1783 to 1785* (H. E. Egerton, ed., Oxford, 1915). Local studies include A. C. Flick, *Loyalism in New York during the American Revolution* (Columbia Univ., *Studies,* XIV, no. 1, 1901), one of the best; E. A. Jones, *The Loyalists of Massachusetts* (London, 1930), and his *New Jersey Loyalists* (Newark, 1927); I. S. Harrell, *Loyalism in Virginia* (Durham, 1926); and W. H. Siebert's numerous studies of Tories in different localities, of which the most extensive is *Loyalists in East Florida, 1774 to 1785* (2 vols., Fla. State Hist. Soc., *Publs.,* no. 9, 1929). Biographies of individuals include Gipson's able life of *Jared Ingersoll* (cited earlier); E. E.

Beardsley, *Life and Correspondence of the Right Reverend Samuel Seabury* (Boston, 1881); and E. H. Baldwin, "Joseph Galloway," *Pa. Mag. of History and Biog.*, XXVI, 161-191, 289-321, 417-442. Among Loyalist personal records are Samuel Curwen, *Journal and Letters, 1775-1784* (G. A. Ward, ed., N. Y., 1842); Thomas Hutchinson, *Diary and Letters* (P. O. Hutchinson, ed., 2 vols., Boston, 1884-1886); Jonathan Boucher, *Reminiscences of an American Loyalist, 1738-1789* (Jonathan Bouchier, ed., Boston, 1925), and Boucher's letters in *Maryland Mag. of History*, VII-IX; James Murray, *Letters* (Nina M. Tiffany, ed., Boston, 1901); and Ann Hulton, *Letters of a Loyalist Lady* (Cambridge, 1927).

SOLDIER AND CIVILIAN, 1775-1783

MILITARY OPERATIONS: From a present-day standpoint no adequate military history of the Revolution has yet appeared. The best study of a limited period is Allen French, *The First Year of the American Revolution* (Boston, 1934). The following are useful earlier works of a general scope: Charles Stedman, *History of the Origin, Progress, and Termination of the American War* (2 vols., London, 1794), by a British officer; H. B. Carrington, *Battles of the American Revolution* (N. Y., 1876); J. W. Fortescue, *A History of the British Army* (13 vols., London, 1899-1930), III, useful in spite of its British partisanship; and J. B. Lossing, *Pictorial Field Book of the American Revolution* (rev. edn., 2 vols., N. Y., 1855). Of treasonable movements the most recent account is Carl Van Doren, *Secret History of the American Revolution* (N. Y., 1941). For naval warfare G. W. Allen, *A Naval History of the American Revolution* (2 vols., Boston, 1913), and C. O. Paullin, *The Navy of the Revolution* (Cleveland, 1906), are good. For privateering, see the last paragraph of this section.

MILITARY ADMINISTRATION AND SOLDIER LIFE: L. C. Hatch, *The Administration of the Revolutionary Army* (*Harvard Hist. Studies*, X, 1904), should be supplemented for New England by French's *First Year of the American*

Revolution and, for a comparative view, by E. E. Curtis, *The Organization of the British Army in the American Revolution* (*Yale Hist. Publs. Miscellany,* XIX, 1926). For army life, see C. K. Bolton, *The Private Soldier under Washington* (N. Y., 1902), and J. C. Fitzpatrick, *The Spirit of the Revolution* (Boston, 1924). Dr. James Thacher's *Military Journal during the American Revolutionary War* (Boston, 1823) is an interesting personal record.

POLITICAL AGENCIES: The fundamental sources for Congress are the *Journals of the Continental Congress* and Burnett's *Letters* (both cited earlier). Burnett's prefaces to the successive volumes have been expanded into his work, *The Continental Congress* (N. Y., 1941). J. F. Jameson, *Essays in the Constitutional History of the United States in the Formative Period, 1775-1789* (Boston, 1889), and J. B. Sanders, *Evolution of Executive Departments of the Continental Congress* (Chapel Hill, 1935), are also important. A recent discussion of economic and social issues in the formation of the Confederation is Merrill Jensen, *The Articles of Confederation* (Madison, 1940). For war-time fiscal policies, see Sumner, *Financier and Finances of the Revolution,* and Oberholtzer, *Robert Morris, Patriot and Financier* (both cited earlier); C. J. Bullock, *The Finances of the United States from 1775 to 1789* (Univ. of Wis., Econs., Polit. Sci., and History Ser., I, no. 2, 1895); and biographies of the war governors, notably *Jonathan Trumbull* (Boston, 1919) by a descendant of the same name; *George Clinton* (N. Y., 1938) by E. W. Spaulding; and *William Livingston* by Sedgwick (cited earlier).

WAR-TIME BUSINESS: Besides a good brief discussion in Channing's *History of the United States,* III, 388-408, East's *Business Enterprise in the American Revolutionary Era* (mentioned earlier) contains a detailed study and is an excellent guide to the sources. Special studies of war-time commerce are J. F. Jameson, "St. Eustatius in the American Revolution," *Am. Hist. Rev.,* VIII, 683-708, and Friedrich Edler, *The Dutch Republic and the American Revolution* (Johns Hopkins Univ., *Studies,* XXIX, no. 2, 1911). For privateering, see, in addition to the naval histories already mentioned, G. W. Allen, *Massachusetts Privateers of the Revolution* (Mass. Hist. Soc., *Colls.*, LXVII, 1927). There is as yet no adequate study of profiteering or enemy trade. For war-time land speculation, see Abernethy, *Western Lands and the American Revolution* (cited in an earlier connection).

POSTWAR SOCIETY

GENERAL ACCOUNTS: Aside from the authorities already listed, certain works dealing specifically with the postwar years are worth noting. Outstanding is J. B. McMaster's pioneer *History of the People of the United States* (8 vols., N. Y., 1883-1913), I. Much has been done in this field since it was published. A suggestive brief survey of conditions is J. F. Jameson, *The American Revolution Considered as a Social Movement* (Princeton, 1922). For a fuller account, see Allan Nevins, *The American States during and after the Revolution* (N. Y., 1924), which contains extensive bibliographical notes.

POLITICAL RECONSTRUCTION AND SOCIAL PHILOSOPHY: Useful monographs are S. B. Harding, *The Contest over the Ratification of the Federal Constitution in the State of Massachusetts* (*Harvard Hist. Studies*, II, 1896); F. G. Bates, *Rhode Island and the Formation of the Union* (Columbia Univ., *Studies*, X, no. 2, 1898); E. W. Spaulding, *New York in the Critical Period* (D. R. Fox, ed., *N. Y. State Hist. Assoc. Ser.*, I, 1932); J. P. Selsam, *The Pennsylvania Constitution of 1776* (Phila., 1936); Lingley's *Transition in Virginia from Colony to Commonwealth* (cited before); and L. I. Trenholme, *Ratification of the Federal Constitution in North Carolina* (N. Y., 1932). For reconstruction in a city, see S. I. Pomerantz, *New York, an American City, 1783-1803* (Columbia Univ., *Studies*, no. 442, 1938). The postwar constitutions may be found in *The Federal and State Constitutions, Colonial Charters, and Other Organic Laws of the States, Territories, and Colonies Now or Heretofore Forming the United States of America*

(7 vols., 59th Cong., 2 sess., *House Doc.*, no. 357, 1909), edited by F. N. Thorpe. Since the debates on the Federal Constitution involved social as well as political issues, the following documentary collections are essential: Max Farrand, ed., *Records of the Federal Convention* (4 vols., New Haven, 1911-1937), with important supplementary matter; Jonathan Elliot, ed., *The Debates in the Several State Conventions, on the Adoption of the Federal Constitution with the Journal of the Federal Convention* (4 vols., Wash., 1836); J. B. McMaster and F. D. Stone, eds., *Pennsylvania and the Federal Constitution, 1787-1788* (Phila., 1888); [Hamilton, Jay and Madison], *The Federalist* (N. Y., 1788 and later edns.); P. L. Ford, ed., *Essays on the Constitution of the United States, Published 1787-88* (Brooklyn, 1892), and his *Pamphlets on the Constitution of the United States, Published during Its Discussion by the People, 1787-88* (Brooklyn, 1888). The social philosophy of the Constitution makers and its relation to economic interests are vigorously discussed in C. A. Beard, *An Economic Interpretation of the Constitution* (N. Y., 1913).

ECONOMIC AND SOCIAL CONDITIONS: Important collections of correspondence are the "Letters" of Phineas Bond (the British consul) and Stephen Higginson in Am. Hist. Assoc., *Ann. Rep. for 1896,* I, 513-659, 704-841, and the *Belknap Papers* (Mass. Hist. Soc., *Colls.,* XLII-XLIII, LIV, 1877-1891). Useful, if not infallible, is Jedidiah Morse's pioneer *American Geography* (Elizabethtown, N. J., 1789). A contemporary work dealing with the outstanding instance of agrarian discontent is G. R. Minot, *The History of the Insurrections in Massachusetts, in the Year 1786, and the Rebellion Consequent Thereon* (Worcester, 1788), reflecting a conservative outlook. Adams's *New England in the Republic* (cited before), W. A. Dyer, "Embattled Farmers," *New England Quar.,* IV, 460-481, and Brown's *Joseph Hawley* (cited earlier) offer more sympathetic accounts of the uprising.

Contrasting views of American trade are presented in Lord Sheffield's *Commerce of the American States* (mentioned before) and Tench Coxe's *View of the United States of*

America (Phila., 1794). See also "Observations of London Merchants on American Trade, 1783," *Am Hist. Rev.*, XVIII, 769-780, and a contemporary Continental European view, *ibid.*, XVI, 567-578. A useful compilation is Timothy Pitkin, *A Statistical View of the Commerce of the United States of America* (2nd edn., N. Y., 1817; 3rd edn., New Haven, 1835). The following deal with special topics: S. E. Morison, *The Maritime History of Massachusetts, 1783-1860* (Boston, 1921); K. S. Latourette, *The History of Early Relations between the United States and China, 1784-1884* (Conn. Acad. of Arts and Sciences, *Trans.*, XXII, 1917); R. E. Peabody, *Merchant Venturers of Old Salem* (Boston, 1912); and Major Samuel Shaw, *Journals* (Josiah Quincy, ed., Boston, 1847), recording a pioneer voyage to China.

For an understanding of business promotion Davis's *Essays in the Earlier History of American Corporations* and East's *Business Enterprise in the American Revolutionary Era* (both cited earlier) are of special importance. Two internal-improvement projects are described in Corra Bacon-Foster, *Early Chapters in the Development of the Potomac Route to the West* (Wash., 1912), and W. F. Dunaway, *History of the James River and Kanawha Company* (N. Y., 1922). For postal developments, consult particularly Walter Lowrie and others, eds., *American State Papers: Documents, Legislative and Executive* (38 vols., Wash., 1832-1861), *Post Office Department, 1789-1833*. For banking projects, consult Lawrence Lewis, *A History of the Bank of North America* (Phila., 1882); B. A. Konkle, *Thomas Willing and the First American Financial System* (Phila., 1937); H. W. Domett, comp., *A History of the Bank of New York, 1784-1884* (N. Y., 1884); Allan Nevins, *History of the Bank of New York and Trust Company* (N. Y., 1934); and N. S. B. Gras, *The Massachusetts First National Bank of Boston, 1784-1934* (*Harvard Studies in Business History*, IV, 1937). For industrial promotion, see Alexander Hamilton, *Industrial and Commercial Correspondence* (A. H. Cole, ed., *Business Hist. Studies*, I, 1928), and Samuel Rezneck, "The Rise and Early De-

velopment of Industrial Consciousness in the United States,"
Journ. of Economic and Business History, IV, 784-811.

THE WEST IN THE EARLY REPUBLIC

In addition to works listed under the caption, "Inland
America," see A. P. Whitaker, *The Spanish-American Fron-
tier: 1783-1795* (Boston, 1927), and Gilbert Imlay, *A
Topographical Description of the Western Territory of
North America* (3rd edn., London, 1797), by an early Ken-
tucky settler.   For separatist movements, consult F. J.
Turner, "Western State-Making in the American Revolu-
tionary Era, II," *Am. Hist. Rev.,* I, 251-269, and the fol-
lowing special studies: W. R. Shepherd, "Wilkinson and the
Beginnings of the Spanish Conspiracy," *ibid.,* IX, 490-506;
J. R. Jacobs, *Tarnished Warrior: Major General Wilkinson*
(N. Y., 1938); S. C. Williams, *History of the Lost State
of Franklin* (rev. edn., N. Y., 1933); and J. P. Boyd,
"Attempts to Form New States in New York and Pennsyl-
vania," N. Y. Hist. Assoc., *Quar. Journ.,* XII, 256-270.
On beginnings in the Northwest, see W. P. and Julia P.
Cutler, *Life, Journals and Correspondence of Rev. Manasseh
Cutler* (2 vols., Cincinnati, 1888); W. H. Smith, *The St.
Clair Papers.   The Life and Public Services of Arthur
St. Clair* (2 vols., Cincinnati, 1882); A. B. Hulbert, *Ohio
in the Time of the Confederation* (Marietta, 1918); and
B. W. Bond, *Civilization of the Old Northwest* (N. Y.,
1934).   Sources for the religious history of the West may
be found in W. W. Sweet, ed., *Religion on the American
Frontier, 1783-1850* (3 vols., N. Y. and Chicago, 1931-
1939).

INDEX

457

John Adams

*Defender of the constitutional rights of King George's American subjects;
then scholarly advocate of a free, well-ordered Republic*

A Charleston Mansion: The Miles Brewton House

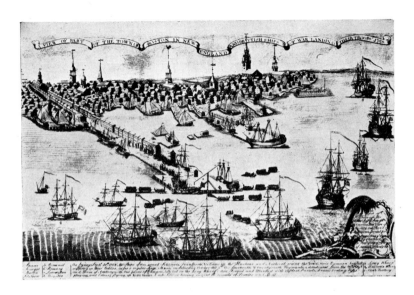

Paul Revere's Boston, 1768

Revolutionary Towns

Bernard Ratzen's New York, 1766

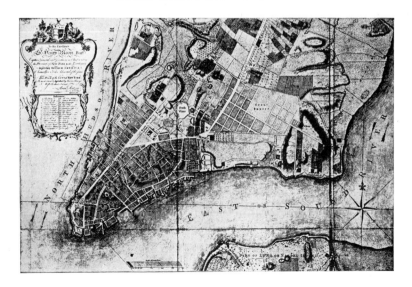

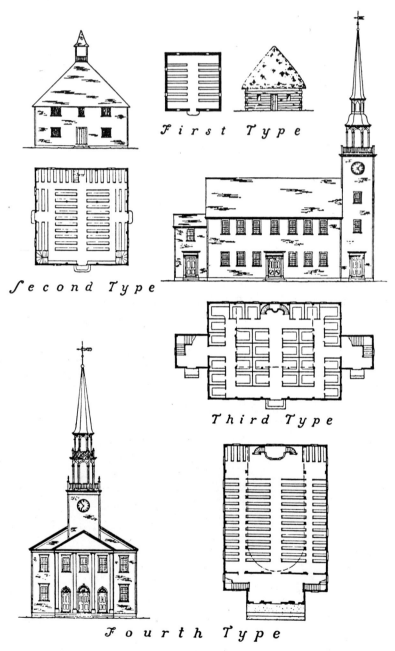

First Type

Second Type

Third Type

Fourth Type

The Development of the New England Meetinghouse

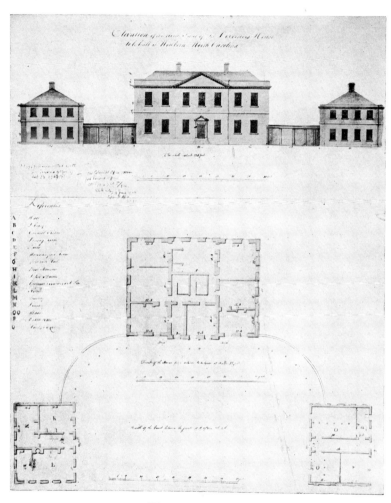

Tryon's Palace

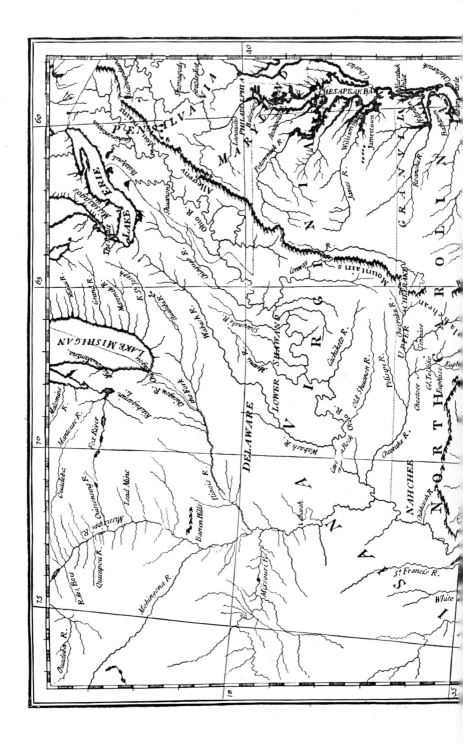

Jos. Chadwick del.

A Westerly View of the Colledges in Cambridge New England

A. Harvard Hall   B. Stoughton   C. Massachusett   D. Hollis   E. Holden Chapel

S. Harris sculp.

Pohick Church

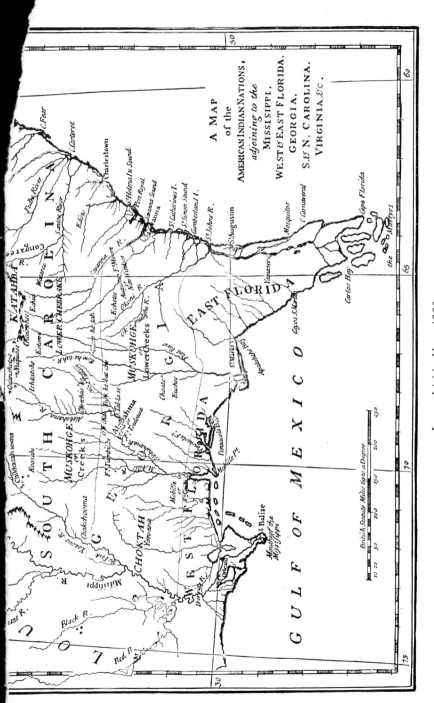

James Adair's Map, 1775

The West

EDES & GILL'S
NORTH-AMERICAN
ALMANACK
For the Year of our Lord
1769.

Being the First after BISSEXTILE or LEAP-YEAR.
Calculated for the Meridian of BOSTON, N.E. Latt. 42° 25' North.

CONTAINING,

An Extract from the History of *Publius Clodius Britano Americanus*;
Judgment of the Weather ; Sun and Moon's Rising & Sitting ;
Time of High Water ; Public Roads, with the best Stages or
Houses to put up at ; Eclipses ; Courts in *Maſſachuſetts-Bay*,
New-Hampſhire, *Connecticut*, and *Rhode-Iſland* ; Feaſts & Faſts
of the Church of England, &c. &c. *To which is added*,
The CHARTER of the Province of the *Maſſachuſetts-Bay*.

THERE will be Five ECLIPSES this Year in the following
Order, *viz.* — The Firſt of the SUN, *January* 7th invisible.
—The Second of the SUN, *June* 4th, invisible.—The Third of
the MOON, *June* 19, visible and Total. Beginning, 1h. 45m. 25ſ.
Middle, 3h. 30m. 57ſ. End, 5h. 17m. 28ſ. Duration, 3h. 32m. 3ſ.
Digits eclipsed, 11 19.—The Fourth of the SUN, *November* 28th,
invisible.—The Fifth and laſt of the MOON, *December* 13th, vi-
ſible. Beginning, 0h. 18m. 8ſ. Middle, 1h. 41m. 15ſ. End,
3h. 3m. 10ſ. Duration, 2h. 47m. 2ſ. Digits eclipsed, 8 56.

The FRONTISPIECE repreſents

*Two Female Figures. The principal, richly decorated, is ſeated on
a Throne with an Imperial Diadem on her Head, and a Spear
in her left Hand. The other Figure exhibits a Virgin with a
Civic Crown, in the utmoſt Agonies of Diſtreſs and Horror. The
Cap of Liberty falling from the Spear of one, and tottering to
fall from the other. The Label of one, is* Collidimur *; of the other,*
Frangimur. *Two Ships are repreſented to View in a Tempeſt in
the Inſtant of daſhing to Pieces againſt one another, and ſinking
between the Rocks of* Sylla *and* Caribdis. *In the Interim are
ſeen two Arch-Angels, flying as " on the Wings of the Wind."
The Label of the one is, " Shall not the Lord of all the Earth do
" Right." The other is, " The Fool" only " hath ſaid in his
" Heart there is no God." Above all, in a Glory, is inſcribed
theſe Words, " The Lord GOD Omnipotent reigneth, let the
" Earth rejoice !"*

BOSTON : Printed and Sold by EDES & GILL, in Queen-Street.
[Price *Four Shillings* per Dozen, and *Six Pence* ſingle.]

J. Yeates

COMMON SENSE;

ADDRESSED TO THE

INHABITANTS

OF

AMERICA,

On the following interesting

SUBJECTS.

I. Of the Origin and Design of Government in general, with concise Remarks on the English Constitution.

II. Of Monarchy and Hereditary Succession.

III Thoughts on the present State of American Affairs.

IV. Of the present Ability of America, with some miscellaneous Reflections.

Man knows no Master save creating HEAVEN,
Or those whom choice and common good ordain.

THOMSON.

PHILADELPHIA;

Printed, and Sold, by R. BELL, in Third-Street.

MDCCLXXVI.

A Revolutionary Privateer

I am

your affectionate father

Wil Livingston

Baden Town 19 Jany 1784

A War Governor
William Livingston of New Jersey

Robert Morris
Painted by Gilbert Stuart

An Ironmaster's Home
The John Jacob Faesch House, Dover, New Jersey

A Tory Printer

James Rivington and his newspaper

A Woman Patriot

Mrs. Catharine Van Rensselaer Schuyler

John Beale Bordley, Agricultural Reformer

An American Artist Shows His Work
Young William Dunlap and His Parents

NOTES on the ſtate of VIRGINIA;

written in the year 1781, ſomewhat corrected and enlarged in the winter of 1782, for the uſe of a Foreigner of diſtinction, in anſwer to certain queries propoſed by him reſpecting

MDCCLXXXII.

The Title Page of Thomas Jefferson's
NOTES ON VIRGINIA

William Cooper
A Developer of Western New York